INSIDER DEALING:
Law and Regulation

Gil Brazier, LLB, MPhil (Vict),
Solicitor of the Supreme Court

Cavendish
Publishing
Limited

First published in Great Britain 1996 by Cavendish Publishing Limited, The Glass House, Wharton Street, London WC1X 9PX.

Telephone: 0171-278 8000 Facsimile: 0171-278 8080

British Library Cataloguing in Publication Data
Brazier, Gil
Insider Dealing
I. Title
344.206926

ISBN 1-874241-02-3

Printed and bound in Great Britain by
Biddles Ltd, Guildford and King's Lynn

For Marjorie, Norah and Ross,
and for Helen and Duncan who might not have approved
of this exercise.

'Do not suppose that I have come to abolish the Law ... I did not come to abolish but to complete ... If any man ... sets aside even the least of the Law's demands, and teaches others to do the same, he will have the lowest place in the kingdom of Heaven, whereas anyone who keeps the Law, and teaches others so, will stand high in the kingdom of Heaven. I tell you, unless you show yourselves far better men than ... the doctors of the law, you can never enter the kingdom of Heaven'.

[from *The Sermon on the Mount*; Matthew 5, 17–20]

PREFACE

In writing this book, I must thank my family for their indulgence and my publishers for their patience and good humour (particularly Kate Nicol and Karen Smith, my editors). I would like to thank John Powell and Eva Lomnicka for their help and support. I would also thank Julian Richardson, David Linton, Cheryl Holder, Valerie Giles, Hugh Hamilton and Caroline Richards for encouragement at various stages.

Regulatory law is usually based upon primary or secondary legislation (such as the Financial Services Act 1986, the Criminal Justice Act 1993 or the Public Offers of Securities Regulations 1995), the enactment of which (or part of which) may well have been prompted by the need for EC co-ordination. Its development is essentially then 'driven' by those regulating the City who may be directed or checked by the government. Those 'regulators' include (in no particular order of precedence) the Bank of England, the Securities and Investments Board, the Securities and Futures Authority, the Takeover Panel or one of the various 'markets' (such as the London Stock Exchange which is of particular significance in the fight against insider dealing: see 'Insider dealers under notice' and 'SE sleuths on the trial of big insider dealing rings' by Robert Miller and Jon Ashworth, *The Times*, 9 September 1996) on or pursuant to which securities, commodities or derivatives and the like are traded. The concerns of those regulators are fuelled by the activities of those they regulate together with any public or press reaction to what is or is not done. Very often, political considerations and pressures are relevant.

The result of this 'witches' brew' is that matters rarely stand still for long. I have tried to state things as they stand at 30 June 1996 (although it has been possible to include mention of certain subsequent developments), but I must add a cautionary note. Before acting in reliance on any material or statements which follow, readers should ensure that the position has not changed (perhaps by taking appropriate professional advice) and should always, if at all possible, refer directly to up-to-date primary sources.

Gil Brazier
The Law Society Library,
113 Chancery Lane, London WC2

CONTENTS

Contents

TABLE OF CASES

TABLE OF STATUTES

TABLE OF STATUTORY INSTRUMENTS

CHAPTER 1

THE SECURITIES INDUSTRY
IN THE UNITED KINGDOM

INTRODUCTION

Some initial thoughts on insider dealing

The basic purpose of this book is to set out and explain the present law **1-01** and practice governing the commission of the criminal offence of insider dealing (together with certain other securities 'market' offences) in the UK. Since 1987, it is said that approximately 104 cases of insider dealing have been investigated by the Surveillance or Insider Dealing Unit of the London Stock Exchange and subsequently reported to the relevant government department (which, for these purposes, remains the Department of Trade and Industry). Of that number, only 33 cases have been the subject of a criminal prosecution and around half that number have resulted in conviction of the defendants charged. Those figures are not particularly impressive given that insider dealing is regarded by many 'in the know' as being a fairly regular occurrence. Unfortunately, where unusual or even just coincidental share transactions have occurred and probable insider dealing has been identified by the London Stock Exchange, it has not always been possible to bring to book the people thought to be 'behind' what has taken place. Often, those instigating such share transactions have hidden their identities behind nominee companies situated well outside the UK and the jurisdiction of its courts. The result has often been that only those directly involved in 'fronting' the insider dealing (usually just 'small fry') have been caught.

A recent example of a case involving basic insider dealing resulted **1-02** in the conviction of two chartered accountants who were found guilty of insider dealing on the London Stock Exchange.[1] The two persuaded others to buy shares in a company (Aaronson Brothers, a UK building products supplier) when they knew its share price would rise because of an imminent and hostile takeover bid. The shares in question were subsequently sold for a total profit of £4,500. Each was found guilty of counselling or procuring others to deal in securities contrary to the

---

1 *R v Morrisey & Staines* (1994) unreported but referred to on p 24 of *The Times* Business News, 18 January 1994.

Company Securities (Insider Dealing) Act 1985[2] and fined £1,500. They could have been sent to prison. In sentencing the two defendants, Judge David Selwood is reported as commenting that 'This offence goes to the heart of the way in which the Stock Exchange in this country, and in London in particular, is organised ... This was a deliberate flouting of the law, which was passed to protect the market ...'.

1-03   The offence of insider dealing will be dealt with in detail in later chapters of this book. The purpose of this first chapter is to explain how the 'market' referred to by the judge in the case mentioned in para 1-02 above came about and how its present regulation developed. As an introduction to that material, it is relevant first to set out some background information on the development in the UK of the registered company and the way in which trading in its securities has developed over the years which ultimately has led to the various incarnations of the Stock Exchange in London. The chapter will then discuss the devolution of securities law in the UK and the way in which regulation of the securities industry has developed.

THE HISTORICAL DEVELOPMENT OF
THE 'REGISTERED COMPANY'

The modern commercial 'company'

1-04   Normally, where insider dealing may be an issue, some buying or selling[3] has occurred or may occur in relation to securities issued (or securities which relate to securities issued) by a modern commercial company. Such a 'company' will be a company formed and registered under the Companies Act 1985. At the moment, there are a number of ways in which 'modern' companies may be constituted.

1-05   Perhaps the most common kind of company encountered in modern practice is the limited liability company. Section 1(1) of the Companies Act 1985 provides that: 'Any two or more persons associated for a lawful purpose may, by subscribing their names to a memorandum of association and otherwise complying with the requirements of this Act

---

2   The Company Securities (Insider Dealing) Act 1985.

3   'Dealing' in investments or in securities has been defined quite widely by relevant legislation. See for instance paras 12, 28(1)(d) and 28(2) of Schedule 1 to the Financial Services Act 1986 in relation to 'dealing in investments'. See also s 55 of the Criminal Justice Act 1993 in relation to 'dealing in securities'. Essentially, subject to those provisions and the definitions they contain, 'dealing' can encompass any acquisition or disposal of the securities in question. In simple terms, they are being bought or sold.

in respect of registration, form an incorporated company, with or without limited liability.' Such companies will usually be 'companies limited by shares'. That is to say, they will be companies having the liability of their members limited by the memorandum of association to the amount (if any) unpaid on the shares held by them.[4]

Registered companies can, however, be 'companies limited by guarantee' where the liability of the members is limited by the memorandum to such amount as the members may respectively thereby undertake to contribute to the assets of the company in the event of its being wound up.[5] Companies can also be 'unlimited companies' where the liability of the members is unlimited.[6] With effect from 22 December 1980, it has not been possible to form a company limited by guarantee with a share capital.[7]

1-06

Registered companies can be 'public companies' or 'private companies'. A 'public company' is defined[8] as a company limited by shares (or limited by guarantee and having a share capital) being a company the memorandum of association of which states that it is to be a public company and in relation to which the provisions of the Companies Act 1985 (or the former Companies Acts)[9] as to the registration (or re-registration) of a company as a public company have been complied with on or after 22 December 1980. A 'private company' is defined as a company that is not a public company.

1-07

---

4   A 'company limited by shares' is defined as such by s 1(2)(a) of the Companies Act 1985 (hereafter 'CA 1985'). For these purposes, s 735(1)(a) CA 1985 provides that a 'company' means a company formed and registered under that Act or an 'existing company'. An 'existing company' is defined by s 735(1)(b) as meaning a company formed and registered under the former Companies Acts but does not include a company registered under the Joint Stock Companies Acts, the Companies Act 1862 or the Companies (Consolidation) Act 1908 in Ireland. See Note 9 below for further reference to these expressions.

5   A 'company limited by guarantee' is defined as such by s 1(2)(b) CA 1985.

6   An 'unlimited company' is defined as such by s 1(2)(c) CA 1985.

7   By virtue of s 1(4) CA 1985.

8   'Public company' and 'private company' are defined as such by s 1(3) CA 1985.

9   The 'Companies Acts' are defined by s 744 CA 1985 as meaning the Companies Act 1985, the Company Securities (Insider Dealing) Act 1985 and the Companies Consolidation (Consequential Provisions) Act 1985. The 'former Companies Acts' are defined by s 735(1)(c) CA 1985 as meaning the Joint Stock Companies Acts, the Companies Act 1862, the Companies (Consolidation) Act 1908, the Companies Act 1929 and the Companies Acts 1948 to 1983. The 'Joint Stock Companies Acts' are defined by s 735(3) CA 1985 as meaning the Joint Stock Companies Act 1856, the Joint Stock Companies Act 1857, the Joint Stock Banking Companies Act 1857 and the Act to enable Joint Stock Banking Companies to be formed on the principle of limited liability, or any one or more of those Acts (as the case may require), but does not include the Joint Stock Companies Act 1844.

Historical developments

1-08   As a commercial vehicle, the modern registered company has, however, taken some little time to reach its present state. The following paragraphs contain a brief summary of its likely development from earlier modes of trading.

Medieval guilds

1-09   The medieval guild is thought to have been one of the very earliest forms of business association. Their development was closely linked to the acquisition and enforcement of trade monopolies.

1-10   It was a basic premise of the early common law that an individual did not acquire a legal monopoly over a particular trade in a particular place, thereby entitling him to prevent others from trading similarly, merely by having a *de facto* monopoly; perhaps by being the only one so trading at a particular time. The only advantage he might have obtained from being first in line was goodwill.[10] However, it seems that it was sometimes possible for a monopoly to be acquired by prescription, particularly in the case of a mill, if it could be demonstrated that local residents had used that mill to grind their corn since time immemorial.

1-11   The other main way of acquiring a monopoly was by grant from the Crown. Most of the guilds and livery companies (which were, effectively, trade associations) were created in this way. The guilds sought to preserve a monopoly of trade in a particular area by regulating the activities of their members. The main object of the charters which were granted by the Crown was to confer on guilds the right for their members to associate and for a governing body to be established. Usually, the charters also provided that no one could follow the trade in the area (or city) in question unless he was a member of that guild. This imposed regulation and presumably also a measure of discipline on the members of the guild.[11] At best, however, the monopoly which the guild and its members sought to create, and then preserve, was usually no more than a partial monopoly. It was usually the case that individual

---

10   This was so held in 1410 in *Case of Gloucester School* (1410) YB Hil 11 Hen IV, 47, pl 21 in which two schoolmasters brought an action against another teacher who had recently set up a rival school in the same town. This forced them to reduce their own fees in order to compete with him. It was however held that they had no cause of action against him because they had no exclusive right to provide education and it was lawful for any qualified schoolmaster to teach children.

11   This may, in fact, be one of the best early examples in the law of England and Wales of the concept of 'self-regulation' applying to persons carrying on a particular trade or business under the auspices of a 'governing' body. It is doubtful, however, whether those regulating investment business today would much enjoy any monopolistic comparisons with medieval guilds.

traders still managed to carry on business to some extent at least and some flourished.

Early partnerships

As the Middle Ages progressed, some individual traders found it convenient to join together in what seems now to have been an early form of partnership. They would normally each introduce capital to provide funding for the arrangement and would each hope to share in any resulting profits. As now, such 'partnerships' were thought to have had no separate legal existence or personality apart from that of the individual partners themselves. No corporation was created by the arrangement itself. Generally speaking, as now, the traders (as partners) would be liable for any debts which arose and their liability was unlimited. Essentially, such a partnership was a convenient form of trading arrangement between individual traders. The property and debts of the partnership were regarded as the property and debts of the partners and such arrangements would normally cease on the death of any one partner.

1-12

In theoretical terms, the modern 'company' is said to represent a kind of fusion between the separate legal concepts of partnership and of incorporation.[12] A corporation is a separate legal 'person' capable, for instance, of contracting in its own name and of owning land and other property. Corporations are also separate and distinct from their shareholders. At common law, those 'members' are not liable for the debts of the corporation in question. Also, in granting charters of incorporation, the Crown had no power to incorporate persons so as to make them liable for the debts of the corporation.[13] As indicated in para 1-12 above, a partnership in English law was not regarded as a corporation, being merely the 'aggregate' trading arrangement of the individual partners. However, the expression 'company' was regarded as being capable of including a partnership, hence the 'fusion' referred to above. But how did 'companies', as such, come about?

1-13

Royal charters

At common law, the Crown is thought to have exercised its right to grant charters of incorporation from the 14th century onwards. Mostly, those recipient companies were livery companies; guilds or trade

1-14

---

12   For a fuller explanation see, for example, Charlesworth & Cain's *Company Law* (11th edn) at p 5.

13   *Per* Lindley LJ in *Elve v Boyton* [1891] 1 Ch 501 at p 507 (CA).

associations having the privilege of being a corporation. From the time of Elizabeth I,[14] however, the Crown is thought to have encouraged the creation of commercial corporations in this way, usually through the grant of exclusive rights to conduct a particular trade overseas. Such a right was conferred, upon the incorporation of a merchant trading company, by virtue of the royal prerogative to license overseas trade. Without such a royal 'licence', it seemed that no subject could lawfully trade overseas. This was to the benefit of the Crown in that it was thereby able to control trade in the areas in question. Companies such as the East India Company (trading in Asia), the Levant Company (trading in and around the Mediterranean) and the South Sea Company thus came about.

Monopolies

1-15   However, towards the end of the reign of Elizabeth I, the whole question of monopolies was under attack. The matter was raised as a grievance at the Parliaments of 1597 and 1601. Although a constitutional issue, it was initially left to the courts and the common law to sort out. In 1602, it was decided that monopolies were generally invalid as they tended to operate in restraint of trade, causing increased prices and reduced quality.[15] That decision did not, however, strike at the guilds or trade associations which were said to be directed at regulating rather than restricting trade. It was, however, followed by the creation of many 'trading' companies such as the pinmakers (in 1605) and the brickmakers (in 1614).

1-16   James I, however, apparently for the good political reason that he was having problems with greedy ministers, embodied the 1602 decision in an Act of Parliament which declared monopolies for the sole buying, selling, making or using of any thing within the realm to be void with certain exceptions.[16] Those exceptions included charters granted to 'corporations, companies or fellowships of any art, trade, occupation or mystery'. That exception was used as a means of avoiding the 1602 decision. Instead of patents or monopolies being granted to individuals, a company was formed which could take advantage of what would effectively amount to a private monopoly. Examples of these companies

---

14 Elizabeth I, the last Tudor monarch, acceded to the throne on 17 November 1558. Her successor, James I, the first Stuart monarch, acceded to the throne on 24 March 1603.

15 The case was *Case of Monopolies, Darcy v Allen* (1602) 11 Co Rep 84, Moore KB 671, Noy 173. This involved an action on the case brought for the infringement of a patent granting the plaintiff the sole right to import foreign playing cards. The court declared the patent to be void and gave judgment for the defendant.

16 This was the famous Statute of Monopolies 1623, 21 Jac 1, c 3.

included the Yarmouth saltmakers (formed in 1636). The era of the monopolistic trading company, however, ended later in the 17th century when the merchant companies also came under attack. In fact, it was decided by the courts that the Crown could not grant the right to enforce a trading monopoly by forfeiture.[17]

'Regulated companies'

The earliest trading companies were 'regulated companies'. They were companies in which each member traded with his own stock on his own account, albeit subject to the constitution of the company. Most were overseas trading companies such as the Baltic and the Levant companies and the traders were subject to the discipline of the governing bodies of those companies although, in effect, they were fairly loose associations of the traders in question.   **1-17**

'Joint stock companies'

Towards the end of the 17th century, a different type of company emerged. This was the 'joint stock company'. Such companies, which included the East India Company, traded as separate legal persons with assets or stock contributed by their members. Each member contributed to the merchandise to be sold at the end of the particular trading venture and each would share proportionately in any profits resulting at that time. Initially, these companies could only be created by Royal Charter or by a special Act of Parliament but, in spite of these technical difficulties, companies such as the East India Company were successful in raising quite substantial amounts of money to finance their trading ventures.[18]   **1-18**

Incorporated companies were seen as possessing certain distinct advantages over other trading 'vehicles'. They were capable of existing in perpetuity and did not automatically wind-up on the death of a member. The property of the company was under the control of the board of governors or directors of the company. The company could contract in its own name and, generally speaking, individual members were not liable for its debts. However, as time went on, the need to obtain a Royal Charter or to have special legislation enacted proved to   **1-19**

---

17   The relevant cases were *Horne v Ivy* (1670) 1 Sid 441 (which concerned the Canary Island Company) and *Nightingale v Bridges* (1690) 1 Show KB 135 (which concerned the Royal African Company).
18   For instance, the East India Company, which was formed to trade with the Indies, is reckoned to have raised around £1,500,000 by public subscription for its trading voyages in 1617.

be too cumbersome. Although some initiative was shown in acquiring the charters of moribund companies,[19] generally speaking, there was a decline in the number of companies formed for the purpose of foreign trade.

'Deed of settlement' companies

1-20   However, there seemed to be no similar decline as to the number of domestic companies being formed. Some were established with a permanent share capital and shares which could be transferred freely. Many such companies were formed without the benefit of special Acts of Parliament through an arrangement which took the form of a deed of settlement containing provisions including those governing the relationship of the members (*inter se*) and also providing for the transfer of their shares. In many ways, the provisions of such a deed of settlement were similar to the constitution of an incorporated company. In terms of conceptual law, however, such 'companies' were probably no more than partnerships with the liability of the members remaining unlimited. However, they fell out of favour with the legislature largely due to the activities of fraudulent promoters and unscrupulous share dealers.

The South Sea Bubble

1-21   At the end of the 17th century, the practice grew of lending money to the government in return for the payment of interest. In fact, the Bank of England was formed in 1694 when the government incorporated a number of its creditors. In 1719, the Bank of England was out-bid by the South Sea Company which offered £7.5 million to acquire the whole of the national debt. The South Sea Company considered that such an arrangement would enable it to raise large sums of money to continue its trading activities in the South Seas which were supported by the government.

1-22   In 1720, the Bubble Act 1719[20] was passed which prohibited unincorporated trading companies from acting or presuming to act as corporations. It also prohibited the use of charters other than for the purpose or purposes for which they had originally been granted. The rationale for this legislation was the intention to benefit the South Sea Company (and to encourage further investment in its stock) but also to

---

19   For instance, a banking company acquired the charter of the Sword Blade Company which had been incorporated in 1690 to manufacture hollow sword blades.

20   The Bubble Act 1719 (6 Geo 1, c 18).

clamp down on the activities of unincorporated trading companies and their promoters. Other companies which were trading in the same areas as the South Sea Company were prosecuted. Unfortunately, this led to widespread panic and the value of stock in the South Sea Company fell rapidly.[21] The Bubble Act 1719 had the effect of suppressing unincorporated companies without providing any real alternative.

Private subscription

The intended and the actual effect of the Bubble Act 1719 made it hard for companies to raise money by public subscription for many years. Instead, such capital came to be provided by wealthy private investors. At the same time, from around 1760, a limited number of companies were incorporated by special Act of Parliament to finance the construction of railways and also for canal excavation. Unincorporated companies also continued to be formed by deeds of settlement under which members agreed to take shares and to abide by the applicable regulations. The management of the company would be entrusted to directors (or sometimes to so-called 'governors') and the regulations, as mentioned in para 1-20, would usually provide for the transfer of shares. As before, these associations were treated as partnerships and the members were liable for debts. The Bubble Act 1719 was repealed in 1825 by the Bubble Companies etc Act 1825.

1-23

The coming of limited liability

By means of the Bubble Companies etc Act 1825, in grants of future charters, the Crown was empowered to provide that members of the corporation in question should be personally liable for the debts of that corporation to the extent provided for in the charter. This is thought to represent the beginnings of the notion of 'limited liability'. By virtue of the Chartered Companies Act 1837,[22] the Crown was further empowered to grant letters patent. That is to say, the Crown was able to grant the advantages of incorporation to a body of persons associating together for trading purposes but without having to grant a charter. The persons in question had to register a deed of partnership dividing-up the relevant trading capital into shares and also providing for their transfer. The Act imposed certain other requirements which had to be satisfied. Once that was the case, limited liability was available. The association of

1-24

---

21 The value of stock in the South Sea Company fell in six months from 1,000% to 125%. The company was however rescued by government intervention and remained in existence until 1807.

22 The Chartered Companies Act 1837 (7 Will.4 & 1 Vict c 73).

persons did not, however, become a body corporate. They merely had the advantage of limited liability which would not otherwise have been the case.

The coming of the registered company

1-25   In 1841, a committee was set up to consider the whole area of company law reform. Chaired by WE Gladstone, its recommendations led to the Joint Stock Companies Act 1844.[23] That Act provided for the incorporation of companies by registration without the need for a special Act of Parliament or for the obtaining of a Royal Charter. As is now the case, certain documents setting out details of the constitution and organisation of the company and also its membership had to be registered (at that stage, with the Registrar of Joint Stock Companies) and were then open to public inspection. The effect of registration was, however, curious.

1-26   In effect, the companies in question were obviously still regarded as partnerships because their members remained liable for any debts as they would have remained liable for the debts of a partnership. The Joint Stock Companies Act 1844 did not provide for all the usual consequences of incorporation (such as limited liability for members) to follow on from the fact of registration although a company so registered could hold property and sue in its own name. The Act did, however, provide that a balance sheet should be presented at the annual general meeting of the company, that an auditor should be appointed to report on the balance sheet and that the audited balance sheet should be filed with the Registrar. It also made it compulsory for partnerships with more than 25 members to register as companies.

1-27   Limited liability for registered companies was not introduced by legislation until the Limited Liability Act 1855,[24] which limited the liability of a shareholder to the amount (if any) unpaid on his shares despite warnings that this would encourage fraud and other dubious conduct by potential promoters and directors of companies. However, 75% of the share capital of the company had to be subscribed for and the company could not continue in business if it lost the same proportion of its capital. The Joint Stock Companies Act 1856[25] tended to simplify company formation and registration. It substituted two basic documents (the memorandum of association and the articles of association) for the deed of settlement which was no longer required. Seven signatures were

---

23   The Joint Stock Companies Act 1844 (7 & 8 Vict c 110).
24   The Limited Liability Act 1855 (18 & 19 Vict c 133).
25   The Joint Stock Companies Act 1856 (19 & 20 Vict c 47).

necessary for the memorandum. A company could register its own articles or adopt a model set which was annexed to the Act. Once registered, a certificate of incorporation was issued to the company which could then commence business.

The Companies Act 1862[26] repealed and consolidated the previous legislation relating to companies. It established liability for members to be limited by guarantee and, generally speaking, prohibited any alteration of the objects clause of a memorandum of association. The model set of articles attached to the Act was called Table A. This Act remained the principal source of 'company' legislation until the Companies (Consolidation) Act 1908.[27] The Companies Act 1867[28] contained a power enabling reductions of share capital to be made. The Directors' Liability Act 1890[29] introduced the concept of the directors being liable to compensate persons who were induced to subscribe for shares on the basis of false statements made in a share prospectus. Following on from that, the Companies Act 1900[30] set out the first legislative requirements for the contents of a share prospectus, provided for the compulsory audit of the accounts of a company and also contained provisions relating to the registration of charges. The Companies Act 1907[31] made a distinction between private and public companies, private companies being companies prohibited from inviting the public to subscribe for their shares or debentures. As such, they were relieved from the need to make their balance sheets public whereas public companies were obliged to submit their balance sheets to the Registrar of Companies.

1-28

Subsequent landmark legislation

The Companies (Consolidation) Act 1908[32] consolidated the Companies Act 1862 and all intervening company legislation. The next landmark was the Companies Act 1929[33] which was, again, a consolidating Act. It also introduced some new material such as provisions relating to the redeemable preference share, minority protection rights and certain

1-29

---

26 The Companies Act 1862 (25 & 26 Vict c 89) was the first of the so-called 'Companies Acts' which have, periodically, consolidated and restated company and related areas of law in one 'bumper' Act of Parliament.
27 The Companies (Consolidation) Act 1908 (8 Edw 7, c 69).
28 The Companies Act 1867 (30 & 31 Vict c 131).
29 The Directors' Liability Act 1890 (53 & 54 Vict c 64).
30 The Companies Act 1900 (63 & 64 Vict c 48).
31 The Companies Act 1907 (7 Edw 7, c 50).
32 The Companies (Consolidation) Act 1908 (8 Edw 7, c 69).
33 The Companies Act 1929 (19 & 20 Geo 5, c 23).

accounting provisions relating to holding companies and to subsidiary companies.

1-30   The Companies Act 1948[34] was, again, a consolidating Act coming into operation on 1 July 1948. It adopted many of the recommendations of the Cohen Committee on company law amendment,[35] particularly those relating to company accounts. For the first time, the auditor of a private or public company was required to have a professional qualification. Also, provision was made for greater disclosure in the accounts of companies and for group accounts. The Act introduced the concept of the 'exempt private company' which did not need to make public its balance sheet and profit and loss account. Generally speaking, 'exempt private companies' were small 'family' companies as opposed to private companies which were simply subsidiaries of public companies.

1-31   The Companies Act 1948 remained the principal Act of Parliament dealing with company legislation until the Companies Act 1985[36] consolidated the law and all intervening current legislation relating to company law. There were, of course, intervening Acts of Parliament relating to company and commercial law, many of which introduced important changes .

1-32   The Companies Act 1967[37] implemented some of the recommendations of the Jenkins Committee on company law reform[38] and amended the Companies Act 1948 in a number of respects. For instance, it abolished the status of exempt private company. There were also important new provisions relating to company accounts. The accounts of a subsidiary company had to disclose the name of its ultimate holding company. Accounts had to give details of the emoluments of directors and the salaries of employees earning over £10,000 per annum. The turnover for the year had also to be stated. There were provisions relating to the directors' report and the principal activities of the company and its subsidiaries over the year in question had to be stated.

1-33   The Companies Act 1967 also contained provisions penalising dealing by directors (and their spouses or children) in certain options to buy or sell securities of the company (or associated companies) quoted on a stock exchange and also for securing the disclosure of certain

---

34 The Companies Act 1948 (11 & 12 Geo 6, c 38). For some historical and background material, see 'The Marconi Affair' by Mark Lewis, (1989) L Ex 554–555.

35 See the Cohen Report (1945 Cmnd 6659).

36 The Companies Act 1985 (1985 c 6).

37 The Companies Act 1967 (1967 c 81).

38 See the Jenkins Report (1962 Cmnd 1749).

material facts concerning directors. There were provisions for securing disclosure of the beneficial ownership by a person of 10% or more of unrestricted voting rights relating to the company. Importantly, Part III of the Companies Act 1967 gave the then Department of Trade wide powers to compel companies to produce books and company papers for inspection. In 1996, the Department of Trade and Industry is still the main government department dealing with the investigation and prosecution of insider dealing although the Treasury is charged with responsibility for matters of 'policy'.

The Companies Act 1976[39] enacted the Companies (No 2) Bill 1976 which included a number of the provisions set out in the Companies Bill 1973. It amended various accounting provisions, including the law relating to the filing of company accounts and the keeping of accounting records. It provided for the disqualification of persons taking part in the management of companies if they were persistently in default in complying with the requirements of company law relating to the delivery of documents to the Registrar of Companies. It contained new provisions relating to the qualifications, appointment, resignation and powers of auditors. It also required that a statement should be made of the first directors and secretary of the company, together with the intended situation of its registered office, and should be delivered to the Registrar of Companies on application being made for registration of the company.   **1-34**

The Companies Act 1980[40] amended certain aspects of company law. It introduced changes relating to the classification and registration of companies. New definitions were introduced for public and private companies. Provision was made for the registration and re-registration of companies and new requirements were set out for the issue, payment and maintenance of capital. New pre-emption rights were given to shareholders and provision was made for the variation of certain classes of shares. Restrictions were also placed on the distribution of profits and assets and, most important for the purposes of this book, insider dealing finally became a criminal offence for the first time.   **1-35**

The Companies Act 1981[41] included provisions relating to company accounts, thereby implementing a European Community Directive. It reduced the amount of information required to be filed with the Registrar of Companies by small and medium-sized companies. The arrangements for the approval of company names were simplified. Companies were permitted to purchase their own shares and   **1-36**

---

39   The Companies Act 1976 (1976 c 69).
40   The Companies Act 1980 (1980 c 22).
41   The Companies Act 1981 (1981 c 62).

management buy-outs were facilitated. Also, restrictions on the use of share premium accounts were relaxed but the law relating to the disclosure of interests in shares was strengthened. The powers of investigation and enquiry of inspectors appointed by the Department of Trade and Industry were strengthened and further restrictions were imposed on the activities of fraudulent directors.

1-37   In 1985, most of the legislation governing company law (which, generally speaking, meant the Companies Acts 1948–1983) was consolidated in the Companies Act 1985 and in three short yet important 'satellite' Acts of Parliament. Those Acts were the Business Names Act 1985,[42] the Company Securities (Insider Dealing) Act 1985[43] and the Companies Consolidation (Consequential Provisions) Act 1985.[44] The Companies Act 1989,[45] which followed, made amendments to the above and to other intervening legislation, such as the Financial Services Act 1986.[46]

The continued non-codification of company law

1-38   It should be noted that no attempt has been made to codify company law by reducing to one written source all the primary and secondary legislation and relevant common law on the subject. Generally speaking, the various 'bumper' Companies Acts (such as the Companies Act 1948 and the Companies Act 1985) have simply consolidated provisions previously set out in several other Acts. Consequently, a significant part of company and commercial law is still to be found in decided cases.

THE DEVELOPMENT OF SECURITIES TRADING

The early stages

1-39   The beginnings and some of the development of the modern commercial 'company' are set out above.[47] Historically speaking, trading in the shares of companies continued in the 17th century but became more organised with the Stock Exchange itself being incorporated in the reign

---

42 The Business Names Act 1985 (1985 c 7).

43 The Company Securities (Insider Dealing) Act 1985 (1985 c 8).

44 The Companies Consolidation (Consequential Provisions) Act 1985 (1985 c 9).

45 The Companies Act 1989 (1989 c 40).

46 The Financial Services Act 1986 (1986 c 60).

47 See, for instance, in paras 1-17 to 1-20 above.

of William III.[48] Share transfers became more prevalent with regard to joint stock companies where members did not trade on their own account as private individuals but, instead, contributed to the assets of the company forming its joint stock. Generally speaking, shares in joint stock companies were freely transferable and trading in them is thought to have started in some earnest where merchants sought to protect themselves (by 'hedging') against the risks inherent in the provision of funds for foreign trading ventures. For instance, trading ventures to the Arctic Circle led to the establishment of the Muscovy Company and to India and the East Indies led to the establishment of the East India Company.

Trading ventures

The Muscovy Company came about as a result of the attempt by Sebastian Cabot to find a north-east trade route to the Far East in 1553. Apparently, some 250 merchants each subscribed £27 to fund the project. Fund raising by the East India Company was more successful and it is thought to have been the first company to raise equity capital on a large scale (apparently some £1,600,000 over a period of 20 years or so). There were also instances, in the late 16th and early 17th centuries, of capital being raised in this way to provide funds for domestic ventures. For instance, the Earl of Bedford devised a project which involved drainage of the Fens in order to provide more agricultural land as well as fresh water for London. A company called 'The Government and Company of the New River brought from Chadwell and Amwell to London' was founded in 1609 and became, effectively, the first water company in Britain.

1-40

Share trading in London

Before the end of the 17th century, there was an organised stock and share market in London and newspapers carried stock exchange news. In particular, a paper entitled 'The Course of the Exchange and Other Things' set out prices for commodities and some shares and is considered to have been the main predecessor of the Official Daily List of the Stock Exchange. By the end of the 17th century, daily trading in shares had increased substantially.[49] Indeed, matters had developed to such an extent that there were even early instances of what we might

1-41

---

48 William III, House of Stuart, acceded to the throne on 28 December 1694. His successor, Anne, acceded on 8 March 1702.

49 Some commentators have noted that, by the end of the 17th century (in particular, by 1695), it was estimated that some 140 joint stock companies had been incorporated with an overall market capitalisation of approximately £4,500,000.

now regard as market manipulation and insider dealing. A Parliamentary Commission, which reported in 1696, said that: '... the pernicious art of stockjobbing hath, of late, so perverted the end design of Companies and Corporations, erected for the introducing or carrying on of manufactures, to the private profit of the first projectors, that the privileges granted to them have commonly been made no other use of but to sell again, with advantage, to innocent men'.[50] Accordingly, in 1697, the government brought in legislation designed to 'restrain the number and ill-practices of brokers and stock-jobbers'.[51]

Early regulation of share traders

1-42   The main result of that Act of 1697 was that stock brokers and stock jobbers had to hold a licence, granted by the Lord Mayor of London and the Court of Aldermen,[52] before they could carry on their business as such. The licences were limited to 100 and also entitled the licensee to wear a specially struck silver medal embossed with the Royal Arms. A potential broker had first to take an oath that he would 'truly and faithfully execute and perform the office and employment of a broker between party and party, without fraud or collusion'.[53] Such brokers were not allowed to deal on their own account[54] but only on behalf of their clients and anyone who tried to operate as a broker without a licence was liable, if caught, to spend a period of time in the City pillory. Whether this was a more effective deterrent than the present sanctions for carrying on unauthorised investment business is strongly arguable.

---

50 From the Report of the Parliamentary Commission of 1697 on stockjobbing.

51 However, by 1720, the Act of 1697 (which was designed to regulate brokers and jobbers) had lapsed by common consent.

52 Which apparently cost only £2.

53 However, there seems to be little evidence of any determined prior investigation being carried out into the 'fitness and properness' of a potential oath-taking licensee. This is perhaps consistent with the way the 'oath' is thought to have developed as part of the English common law. Known as 'wager of law', it became a more civilised alternative to the various forms of 'ordeal' as the means of settling a dispute. One of the parties would swear as to the truth of his case. He would do so perhaps not 'on the Bible' (although the 'oath' does seem to have become more prevalent with Christianity) but in similar fashion. There would then be no further investigation of the facts in dispute. His oath would be accepted as the end of the matter. It would be treated as precluding judgment. Wager of law was not formally abolished until 1833.

54 It is interesting that, in early February 1994, the US Securities and Exchange Commission was reported to be investigating personal share dealing by managers at 30 mutual fund companies, the US equivalent of the unit trust. Official suspicion seems not to have changed much over the years. Officials of the SEC commented that the enquiry could even lead to legislation banning personal share-dealing by fund managers. They were going to investigate the 1993 personal dealing records of all portfolio managers at the mutual fund companies in question in relation to companies in respect of which they also served as directors.

The early development of the Stock Exchange

Generally speaking, the position set out in paras 1-41 and 1-42 above continued for a number of years[55] until around 1720 when the South Sea Bubble burst.[56] Notwithstanding more recent commercial scandals,[57] the collapse of the South Sea Company remains one of the most infamous episodes in British commercial history. It was not until the next century that the 'stock market' got back into shape when many joint stock companies were formed to finance and manage projects both in the UK and abroad.

1-43

In 1824, there were some 156 companies quoted on the Stock Exchange. Over the course of the next year, prospectuses for 624 companies were issued with capital requirements of £372 million. The largest group was formed by general investment companies. Canals and railways were next, followed by mining and then insurance companies. This development was not restricted to the City of London. Provincial stock exchanges also came to be established. By the middle of 1845, regional stock exchanges had been formed in 12 towns with five surviving the trading slump of 1845 to become permanent institutions.

1-44

In the early days of the Stock Exchange,[58] the brokers and jobbers had plied their trade in coffee houses near Threadneedle Street and Cornhill in the City of London. Much of this trade was conducted in two coffee houses in particular. They were called 'Garraway's' and 'Jonathan's' and were situated near Change Alley. Unfortunately, they were damaged by fires around 1748 and brokers started to trade in 'New Jonathan's' which was rebuilt in Threadneedle Street. An entrance fee was charged to discourage undesirables and the brokers and jobbers are said to have soon started to call this establishment 'the Stock Exchange'.

1-45

This continued until 1801, when 'New Jonathan's' was shut down. It reopened a month later as the 'Stock Subscription Room'. It was no longer an informal 'club'. Members had to be elected. They risked a fine if found guilty of 'disorderly conduct'. The premises occupied by the 'Stock Subscription Room' were, however, found to be too small and, in the same year of 1801, the foundation stone for a new building was laid in Capel Court. Those premises lasted into the present century when the decision was taken to build what is the Stock Exchange tower building. In 1812, members had also drawn up a new set of rules governing how

1-46

---

55 Bridging the Houses of Stuart and Hanover. Queen Anne acceded to the throne and reigned from 8 March 1702 until 1714. George I, the first Hanoverian monarch, acceded to the throne and reigned from 1 August 1714 until 1727.

56 See paras 1-21 to 1-24 (above) for a summary of the South Sea Bubble and its consequences.

57 Such as the events leading up to the death of Robert Maxwell, also the collapse of the Bank of Credit and Commerce International (BCCI) and the problems of Barings.

58 Which had been incorporated in the reign of William III.

they could operate. They could not, for instance, be involved in any other business and failures had to be made public[59] immediately so there could be a fair distribution of assets to creditors. Thus were sown the seeds of self-regulation. Along with the banking, insurance and commercial communities operating within what became known as 'the Square Mile', the brokers and jobbers whose activities led to the development of the Stock Exchange contributed much to the position of 'the City' as it is today.

The City of London

1-47   In practical and administrative terms, the City is run by the Corporation of the City of London. Its officers, the City elders or aldermen, are not elected democratically by those who live and work in the area. Instead, they are chosen mainly by the various and old-established Livery companies.

1-48   A major criticism of the City over the years, for which more than a little justification can be found, has been its apparent opposition to change. This has caused it to be subjected to many practical and political pressures. In regulatory terms, those actively involved in the securities industry in the City were usually members of the Stock Exchange or one of the other trading exchanges operating within the Square Mile. Over more recent years, since the basic prohibition contained in s 3 of the Financial Services Act 1986[60] against carrying on unauthorised investment business was brought into force,[61] such persons needed to obtain membership of The Securities Association (or TSA) or the Association of Futures Brokers and Dealers (the AFBD), which bodies subsequently merged to form the present Securities and Futures Authority (the SFA).[62] It will be appreciated that there has therefore been more than just a measure of securities regulation[63] for the City to contend with.

---

59 By being 'chalked-up' above the clock.

60 The Financial Services Act 1986 (1986 c 60)(hereafter 'FSA1986').

61 With effect from 29 April 1988.

62 The merger took place in 1991.

63 Being regulation established under the aegis of the FSA 1986, and termed 'self-regulation', involving self-regulating organisations formed to regulate particular sectors of the financial services industry.

Practical and political pressures

Practical pressures have of course included weathering each and every   1-49
economic crisis which has affected the country over the years. There
have been other problems as well. An example of a local threat which
may yet remove significant business from within the Square Mile is the
challenge of the 'Docklands' development to the pre-eminent position of
the City. In the early 1980s, attempts were made to build what amounted
to a second 'City' on reclaimed land a few miles to the east. Although
that plan did not meet with the immediate success that was hoped,[64] it
did have the effect of encouraging the City to relax its planning
restrictions with the result that the late 1980s saw a considerable amount
of redevelopment throughout the City and other sites close by.[65]
Unfortunately, at least some of this redeveloped property became ready
for occupation when the recession of the late 1980s was at its worst and
lay unoccupied despite the best efforts of landlords, which have
included premium and rent reductions to encourage the occupancy of
both new and existing tenants.

There have also been many political pressures on the City. As its   1-50
main perceived *raison d'être* has always been the making of money, it has
largely been regarded as the preserve of the well-off and thus a target for
the political 'left'. Indeed, in recent times, in the context of the City and
the rich, a Labour Chancellor of the Exchequer[66] is generally believed to
have talked about squeezing and squeezing 'until the pips squeak'.
There is, however, a curious 'political' paradox in the relationship
between Westminster and the Square Mile. There has, of course, been a
Conservative government in power throughout the 1980s and, unlike
the Labour Party, Conservative governments have traditionally been
thought to look favourably upon the City. However, it is the
Conservative Party which has presided over large scale reform of the
City including, in particular, the occurrence of 'Big Bang' in 1986 along

---

64 Which led to the collapse of Olympia & York in 1992. There were a number of
reasons, both financial and logistical. An important logistical problem was the time it
took to get out to the Docklands development for most daily Home Counties
commuters to and from the City of London. Not surprisingly, many old-established
firms were loath to move from their old haunts. There was though a steady influx of
national newspapers into the area. In 1996 the infrastructure problems may well have
been solved. Only time will tell whether this will be enough.

65 An apparently successful example being the 'Broadgate' development just to the
north of Liverpool Street railway station. This more commercial approach to
proposed development within the City is believed to have continued in an attempt
to encourage the various large securities houses, brought about by mergers and
link-ups, to base their head offices within its environs as opposed to the Docklands
development.

66 Alleged to have been Denis (now Lord) Healey but, recently, he has seemed to
distance himself from the comment.

with the Financial Services Act 1986. That Act followed many enquiries into the City instigated by Labour politicians[67] and the subsequent deliberations of the Gower committee in 1982 and 1984. Over recent years, the Labour Party[68] seems largely to have made its peace with the City or, at least, to have reached a *modus operandi* for reacting to 'City' issues. Along with the internal reforms instigated by Tony Blair, it is this accommodation which has led to allegations that it was 'formerly' a socialist party. Some might indeed view this in a cynical vote-gathering sense although perhaps it would be fairer to regard it simply as an acknowledgement of the continued importance of the City as a financial centre.

The recent evolution of securities trading

1-51   One of the most important areas of change in securities trading over the last 15 years or so has been the growth of dealing in respect of foreign securities. In 1979, UK exchange control restrictions were abolished and this enabled investors to buy and sell foreign securities without having to pay the expensive dollar premium. Unfortunately, most of this business was transacted by foreign firms as few members of the Stock Exchange were in a position, with either the expertise or inclination, to deal in foreign securities.

1-52   What this trend represented was just one constituent part of the growth of an international equities market, with shares being offered for initial subscription and then subsequently being traded on a worldwide basis. The economic theory behind the international equity offers which were made by many major companies across a number of national markets was that the more international the spread of shareholders in a company, the less likely its share price would be subject to purely national crises such as a stock market crash causing price volatility.

1-53   However, not only did members of the Stock Exchange in London lose business to foreign firms, it seemed that London (as an international securities market) was losing out to New York. Part of the reason for that was simple economics of scale, namely the volume of trading on the New York equities market. Other reasons included the way dealers in London charged fixed minimum commissions and had either to be stock brokers or stock jobbers.[69] A further reason was the stamp duty charge

---

67 For instance, the commissions of enquiry chaired by Lord Radcliffe and by Lord Wilson.

68 Through the work of credible politicians such as the late John Smith (when Leader of the Party), Dr Marjorie Mowlem (who, for some time, was its spokesperson on City affairs) Alistair Darling, and now Mike O'Brien (the most recent incumbent).

69 See paras 1-64 to 1-66 (below).

on share transactions. Whatever was the 'real' reason, London seemed at that time to be losing out.

London, however, became an important centre for the issue and subsequent trading of Eurobonds. Essentially, a Eurobond is a fixed interest debenture issued by a large company. As such, the relevant instrument will be denominated in a chosen currency and will be repayable usually over a long period. In simple terms, Eurobonds are an additional mechanism enabling companies to borrow money. The subsequent trading of such bonds was a natural development and was linked to the growth of currency trading, through what became known as the 'Euromarkets', which followed a widespread relaxation of exchange controls. Currency trading led to a pool of finance becoming available and bond issues, which enabled companies to borrow from that pool, resulted. Some years on, Eurobonds are now a relatively sophisticated means of raising money (for the issuing company) and of investing money (for those in a position to subscribe). It should, however, be noted that Eurobonds, *per se*, have nothing necessarily to do with the European Community and are perhaps more likely to be denominated in US dollars or German marks than in Euros.[70]   **1-54**

London also became a centre for the issue and subsequent trading of commercial paper. The issue of commercial paper by companies was another way for them to raise finance more cheaply than through bank borrowing. As with Eurobonds, secondary trading of the instruments so issued also developed where initial subscribers wished to redeem their investment before its stated maturity. Also, commercial paper itself has become quite sophisticated. For instance, as with certain 'equity-convertible' Eurobonds, some commercial paper may confer the right of conversion into an equity holding on its maturity.   **1-55**

Coupled with the development of sophisticated securities markets, trading innovative products and instruments, was another development over the years. This was the rise and rise of the institutional investor at the expense of the private investor. 'Institutional' investors are investment managers, pension fund managers and companies engaging in increased own-account treasury activities. The effect of the increased involvement in securities trading of such persons was that larger tranches of shares in individual companies changed hands in particular deals and it was said to have became less profitable for securities firms to do business with, and for, private individuals.   **1-56**

It also became harder for smaller firms of stock jobbers to stay in business. That was because, in simple terms, they could not afford to   **1-57**

---

70 Formerly the European Currency Unit: the infamous 'ECU'.

make a market in all of the shares listed on the Official List of the Stock Exchange in London. They needed more capital backing to be able to do this but, for many years, the maximum holding which a non-member of the Stock Exchange could have in a member firm was restricted. The restriction was, however, relaxed from 10% to just below 30% in 1982[71] and even that restriction was abolished in March 1986. The effect of these relaxations was that many clearing banks, merchant banks and foreign banks acquired firms of brokers and jobbers. In the mid to late 1980s, the expression 'securities house' became commonplace in the UK.

1-58   The thinking behind all of this was that, as markets developed worldwide, only those firms which could compete across the entire range of securities and related investment services were likely to flourish and increase in profitability. Only such firms would be attractive to the large institutional investor because all of its business could be dealt with 'in-house'. As mentioned in para 1-57 above, as this process of expansion continued, private investors lost out. It is thought that they were charged more commission than before and it therefore became more expensive for them to deal. The excuse usually given by the City was that it was said to be more costly for large securities houses to move small tranches of shares for private individuals than it was for them to move large tranches for institutional investors. Not surprisingly, there is little firm statistical evidence one way or the other.

1-59   The 'big is beautiful'[72] trend was, however, bucked to some extent, by the growth in the UK of a number of 'niche' firms offering 'execution-only' services. These may well have been based on the so-called 'discount brokers' in the United States of America who merely provide mainly private investors with a dealing only service without investment management or any related advice.

Early legislative regulation

1-60   The best known example of legislation relating to the securities industry in the UK prior to the Financial Services Act 1986 was the Prevention of Fraud (Investments) Act 1958.[73] That Act repealed and consolidated relevant provisions, *inter alia*, of the Prevention of Fraud (Investments) Act 1939[74] and also of the Companies Act 1947.[75] It was aimed at

---

71 To be precise, a holding of up to 29.9% became allowable.

72 Although not necessarily profitable. For some further background reading, see 'Inter-Market Volatility Linkages: the London Stock Exchange and London International Financial Futures Exchange', published by the SIB in June 1992 and 'Regulation of the United Kingdom Equity Markets', two papers published by the SIB on 21 June 1995.

73 The Prevention of Fraud (Investments) Act 1958 (6 & 7 Eliz 2, c 45).

74 The Prevention of Fraud (Investments) Act 1939 (2 & 3 Geo 6, c 16).

75 The Companies Act 1947 (10 & 11 Geo 6, c 47).

preventing 'share hawking', the private offer of securities in companies which had filed neither a prospectus nor a statement in lieu of a prospectus and, also, fraud in connection with dealings in securities. The expression 'securities' was defined[76] as including shares, stock, debentures, debenture stock, bonds and rights or interests (whether described as units or otherwise) in any securities.

The basic effect of the Prevention of Fraud (Investments) Act 1958,[77] was that 'dealing in securities' was prohibited except in the case of persons licensed for that purpose by the Department of Trade or persons not requiring such a licence. No licence was required by a member of any recognised stock exchange (such as the London Stock Exchange) or recognised association of dealers in securities, by the Bank of England, by any statutory or municipal corporation or any exempted dealer or by any person acting in the capacity of manager or trustee of a unit trust scheme authorised by the Department of Trade.[78] Contravention of that basic prohibition, set out in s 1 of the Act, was a criminal offence punishable by imprisonment for up to two years or by the imposition of a fine[79] or by both.   **1-61**

Section 14 of the Prevention of Fraud (Investments) Act 1958 provided that a person, from outside those set out in para 1-61 above, could commit an offence if he distributed (or caused to be distributed) a circular which (to his knowledge) invited persons to acquire, dispose of, subscribe for or underwrite securities. However, no offence would be committed if the circular amounted to a prospectus which complied with the requirements of the Companies Act 1948. Alternatively, in relation to a corporation incorporated in Great Britain which was not a registered company, no offence would be committed if the circular amounted to a document containing the information required by s 417 of the Companies Act 1948. A circular could be in the form of a newspaper, journal, magazine or other periodical publication. However, no offence was committed if a circular was distributed by or on behalf of a corporation to certain persons in connection with a *bona fide* invitation to enter into an underwriting agreement. Those persons were holders of securities, creditors or employees of the corporation in question or its subsidiary or, additionally, a person whose business involved the acquisition and disposal or the holding of securities.   **1-62**

Section 13 of the Prevention of Fraud (Investments) Act 1958[80] provided that any person who, by any statement, promise or forecast   **1-63**

---

76   See s 26 of the Prevention of Fraud (Investments) Act 1958.
77   See s 1 of the Prevention of Fraud (Investments) Act 1958.
78   See s 2 of the Prevention of Fraud (Investments) Act 1958.
79   Of £500.
80   Which was the legislative precursor of s 47(1) of the Financial Services Act 1986. Section 13 was amended by virtue of s 21 of the Protection of Depositors Act 1963.

which he knew to be misleading, false or deceptive, or by any dishonest concealment of material facts or by the reckless making (dishonestly or otherwise) of any statement, promise or forecast which was misleading, false or deceptive, induced or attempted to induce another person to enter into (or offer to enter into) any agreement for acquiring, disposing of, subscribing for or underwriting securities, was guilty of a criminal offence. On conviction, the person in question could be sent to prison for up to seven years. Section 13, set out above, is clearly the forerunner of s 47(1) of the Financial Services Act 1986.

Market developments

1-64   Historically, trading on the Stock Exchange had developed on the basis of a split between members who bought and sold and generally made a market in shares and securities (who were known as 'jobbers') and dealers who acted as middlemen or agents for outside investors (who were known as 'brokers'). Generally, when a broker received instructions from a client, usually to buy or sell securities, he would bring that business to a jobber. It was the jobber who would acquire or dispose of the securities in question on behalf of the broker and he would do so on the basis of a fixed-minimum commission. He was obliged to quote firm buy and sell prices and made his living (his 'turn') through the price 'spread' which was the difference between the buy and sell price of the securities in question.[80a]

1-65   The existence of fixed-minimum commissions was regarded by many[81] as preventing competition between dealers and of thereby pushing up the cost to investors of 'dealing on the Stock Exchange'. Perhaps unnecessarily, this led the Office of Fair Trading to bring an action against the Stock Exchange before the Restrictive Practices Court.

80a This came to be described frequently as a 'quote-driver' system to contrast it with attempts that are being made (in 1995–1996) by the London Stock Exchange to introduce electronic 'order-matching' securities frauding. Based on US-style securities trading regimes, such a system would narrow or even eliminate the spread between the buy and sell price for shares. Its potential introduction has, however, been eventful (and seems to have led to the removal from office by the Stock Exchange of its Chief Executive, Michael Lawrence, but see 'MPs to demand OFT inquiry into Exchange' by Robert Miller, *The Times*, 29 February 1996) and is the subject of further consultations by the Stock Exchange and by the Securities and Investments Board as this book is being finalised for publication. 'Order matching' is favoured by many foreign investment houses, who see the quote-driver system of SEAQ (see para 1-71) as being inefficient. See 'Stock Exchange clears way for trading reforms' by Patricia Tehan and Robert Miller, *The Times*, 31 May 1996. See also para 1-75, below and comments on Sequence VI. Overall see the framework proposals published by the Exchange ('Introduction of the Electronic Order Book – The Proposal') on 3 October 1996. Subject to further consultations, it is hoped that this new system will be in place by the summer of 1997.

81 Including, it would seem, the Conservative government, led by Mrs Thatcher.

The Council of the Stock Exchange would have preferred the alternative of a public enquiry to investigate the problems inherent in the system but, effectively, the government went to law. This was a strange decision and one which may well have precluded a thorough investigation.[82] Fixed commissions perpetuated the distinction between brokers and jobbers which was termed 'single capacity'. Essentially, that meant that brokers could only be brokers and jobbers could only be jobbers. At that time, it was said that no other major exchange maintained the same distinction between its trading members. In other countries, 'securities houses' acted as both brokers and jobbers. That is to say, they were able to carry on business as 'one-stop' securities businesses. The case brought by the Office of Fair Trading was eventually settled. The Secretary of State for Trade and Industry[83] offered to drop the matter in return for the abolition by the Stock Exchange of fixed-minimum commissions. Although this was a relatively simple change, it became known as the so-called 'Big Bang'.

The expression 'Big Bang' came, however, to encompass many other changes to the way the City in general, and the Stock Exchange in particular, went about its daily business. Commentators knew that the abolition of minimum commissions would force many traders (particularly smaller firms of jobbers) out of business. The Council of the Stock Exchange had hoped to continue with the single capacity system described in paras 1-64 and 1-65 above. However, those of its members who were jobbers did not believe that the system could continue after minimum commissions had been abolished. They could not then be sure that brokers were bringing all their business to them as jobbers and were not seeking to do deals direct. In response, the jobbers decided that they wanted to deal direct with customers which they could not do under single capacity. Dual capacity thus came about with firms acting both as brokers and market makers. **1-66**

On 4 June 1985, members of the Stock Exchange were faced with two further matters. They had first to decide whether persons who were not members of the Stock Exchange could be permitted to own the entirety of a member firm.[84] They decided that this was an acceptable change and the necessary resolution was passed with the required majority. **1-67**

---

82   And this was a point well made on a number of occasions by Sir Nicholas Goodison, the then Chairman of the Stock Exchange.

83   Who was then Cecil (now Lord) Parkinson. And see J Lynton Jones, 'Big Bang and the Stock Exchange' (1986) 7(3) Co Law 99–103. For more recent comment see 'Taking Stock of a City Institution' by Anthony Newburger, *The Times*, 10 January 1996.

84   Instead of up to 29.9%.

1-68   The second matter considered was whether the constitution should be amended to move ownership of the Stock Exchange from individual members to member firms. Proposals were also formulated whereby members would be able to sell their shares in the Exchange to newcomers. This second resolution was narrowly defeated and, for a time, it was feared that potential new members might go elsewhere with the result that London might lose new business. The Stock Exchange sought to prevent that occurrence in March 1986 by creating a new class of corporate membership. Corporate members would each own one share in the Exchange, which could be acquired from the Council, which would give them the right to participate in all the trading activities carried on pursuant to the Exchange. They would also be able to make use of its settlement and other back-up facilities. Also, no such corporate member would need to have an individual member of the Stock Exchange on its board of directors or employed as one of its staff. The Exchange did, however, retain the right to discipline individual employees.

1-69   A further development came in November 1986 when the Stock Exchange merged with the International Securities Regulatory Organisation (or ISRO) to form 'The International Stock Exchange of the UK and Northern Ireland'. ISRO came about when certain securities houses trading international securities did not wish to become part of the reformed Exchange and formed their own body. There was then a measure of competition between the Exchange and ISRO, to say the least. In the final analysis, however, ISRO accepted the view[85] that a united securities market was the only way of producing a powerful competitor for international business. The merger therefore went ahead.

1-70   A further act in this brief review of market developments came with the stock market crash of October 1987. This occurred shortly after 'Big Bang' and was triggered by a massive drop in equity values on Wall Street. The immediate effect of that blow to market confidence was softened in the UK by serious storms which took place just before the intervening weekend. That is why the crash was not really felt in London until the so-called 'Black Monday' of 19 October 1987. By the end of the following day, the Financial Times 100-Share Index had lost more than 20% of its overall value. The crash affected other financial centres. The Stock Exchange in Hong Kong was closed for a week. Share prices fell in Sydney and also in Tokyo. In fact, the effect on prices lasted for many months and it was not until the end of 1988 that most shares had demonstrated a recovery of some sort.

---

85   Of Sir Nicholas Goodison, the then Chairman of the Stock Exchange.

The info-tech applications of SEAQ, SEATS and now Sequence

The improved communications and computer technology available to   1-71
the securities industry during the 1980s also played its part. Perhaps the
best known 'working' example in the UK was the automated quotations
system which replaced floor trading on the Stock Exchange. Its full name
was the 'Stock Exchange Automated Quotations System', or 'SEAQ'. It
was based upon the American 'National Association of Securities
Dealers Automated Quotations System' or 'NASDAQ', which is a quote-
driven electronic securities exchange run by the National Association of
Securities Dealers. SEAQ replaced the old arrangements on 27 October
1986.

Essentially, the system has been operated by market makers, who   1-72
have been the dominant traders on the Stock Exchange, inputting the
prices at which they are prepared to buy and/or sell the shares in respect
of which they make a market. SEAQ is a quote-driven competitive
market maker trading system. Each security has a number of registered
market makers who are required to quote firm bids and offers for the
security on the SEAQ quotation display system in a stated size at least as
large as the minimum quote size attributable to the security under the
rules of the exchange. Market makers can change a price in response to
altered circumstances. However, once so entered, a market maker is
committed to deal with a broker acting on behalf of a customer at the
quoted price for trades at or below the quoted size, which will relate to a
number of shares. He is also obliged to deal with other market makers at
the quoted price but only up to the normal market size for the equity in
question. In either scenario, the quoted price may be open to negotiation
by potential buyers or sellers. It will though displayed to the market
through a screen-based information service.[86]

The SEAQ system has covered more than 3,500 securities, divided   1-73
into three main groupings termed alpha, beta and gamma stocks. Alpha
stocks were traded most frequently and market makers who dealt in
such stocks were obliged to input the trade into the system immediately.
From there, the details were passed to the SEAQ service on Topic. Not
all trades in beta securities were entered through the system and not all

---

86 Formerly through the SEAQ service on Topic which was an electronic share
information service operated by the Stock Exchange and available by subscription
at varying levels of sophistication. Topic was, however, scheduled to be 'switched
off' by January 1995, leaving the Exchange to concentrate more on its regulatory
role. Market rivals Reuters, ICV, Telekom and Automated Data Processing were
reported as competing to replace Topic on the basis of share price and company
data provided by the Exchange.

market makers made a market in beta stocks. Only indicative quotes, as opposed to binding prices, were provided for gamma stocks.

1-74   At present, where shares are listed on the FT-SE 100, they are likely to have many interested market makers and to be 'liquid' stocks. Companies outside the FT-SE 100 will have far fewer interested market makers. Any market in their shares will not be as liquid. If such a company has a strong regional identity, it is possible that a market maker in that locality will make a market in those stocks. Where no, or only one, market maker is concerned with a particular security, the competing market maker system cannot apply. The London Stock Exchange has also provided an alternative trading system called the 'Stock Exchange Alternative Trading Service', or 'SEATS'. This covered approximately 136 listed and Unlisted Securities Market[87] stocks which were largely illiquid and had no, or only one, interested market maker. Any order by a member firm was displayed alongside any available quote from a market maker. On 19 June 1995, a new market for small-company shares was launched by the Stock Exchange. Called the Alternative Investment Market (or 'AIM'), it has replaced the Unlisted Securities Market and also the 'Rule 4.2' trading facility on the Stock Exchange for smaller companies and rarely-traded shares. This was because the Exchange decided, following consultation, to have only two markets. However, this desire for simplification has not been entirely successful. Not all affected companies wanted their shares listed on the AIM. Some broking houses recently brought companies to the market. There have also been some problems with companies brought to the market. To enable such shares to be traded, Ofex was launched by a market participant in October 1995. Not being an 'exchange', it has been described as an unregulated, off-exchange trading facility for shares in unquoted companies. It is not regulated by the Stock Exchange, so deals are said to be done 'off-exchange' and its purpose is to match potential buyers and sellers of shares. Another 'market' newcomer is Tradepoint Financial Networks, which provides a neutral, order-driven electronic securities trading system. Launched in September 1995, and recognised as an investment exchange by the Securities and Investments Board, it provides for the instant publication of trading prices and volumes and also anonymity for potential parties. Bargains are struck when buy and sell orders match.[88] Further competition for the Stock Exchange has

---

87   The so-called Unlisted Securities Market (or USM) was a market for the trading of shares which had not been admitted to the Official List.

88   Trade Point Financial Networks was itself listed on the AIM in April 1996. For recent comment, see 'Big Bang II' by Kirstie Hamilton, *The Sunday Times*, 20 August 1995. A consequence of the above is that the Stock Exchange amended rule 4.18 of the Listing Rules to enable member firms to make good use of the facilities of competing exchanges such as Tradepoint. Previously, rule 4.18 prevented member firms from quoting better prices elsewhere than those they were quoting through SEAQ.

come from US and other banks locating their investment banking operations in London but dealing on 'exchanges' in other European countries. It may also come from the European Association of Securities Dealers Automated Quotation system (or 'EASDAQ') which is expected towards the end of 1996. It will target young international companies.

The 'system' itself continues to be monitored by the Surveillance   **1-75**
Unit maintained by the Exchange which watches for unusual price movements or for transactions which may be indicative of insider dealing or, even, of market manipulation.[89] It is also worth mentioning that the Stock Exchange has been introducing a new electronic trading and information system, called 'Sequence'. Aimed at providing a single integrated system, there have been a number of 'stages' to Sequence. Sequence IV was, for instance, said to deliver a service for SEATS and the AIM. Sequence VI went 'live' in August 1996 with the aim of providing full electronic trading and the capacity to facilitate order-matching.

TAURUS and Crest

During the last few years, a costly attempt was made to establish and to   **1-76**
develop an electronic paperless settlement system to replace Talisman, the current system of Stock Exchange trading. Called the 'Transfer and Automated Registration of Uncertificated Stock', or 'TAURUS', it was intended to cut dealing costs by replacing the existing paper-based system of share registration and transfer with a fully automated electronic system. Share certificates and stock transfer forms would disappear with shares being held instead in computer-based accounts with statements being sent to shareholders recording their transactions.

However, practical tests were run in January 1993 which uncovered   **1-77**
fundamental flaws in the proposed system. A review concluded that it would almost double the existing costs to redesign the relevant software. By then, it is understood that the proposed system had already run up development costs of around £100 million. It could not be expected to become fully operational until the Autumn of 1995. Accordingly, on Thursday 11 March 1993, the Council of the Stock Exchange was told that TAURUS could not be salvaged in its present form. Peter Rawlins, the Chief Executive of the Stock Exchange, resigned and it is thought that many other jobs were lost as a result of the collapse of the project.

The Bank of England set up a working party on securities settlement   **1-78**
to decide whether anything could be salvaged from the work already

---

89   The work of that Unit is described in more detail in Chapter 8.

done on TAURUS. Possible solutions at that stage included a two-tier system of settlement for private and for institutional investors. TAURUS was originally aimed at institutional investors but was extended to private investors. That extension is thought to have caused many problems for the development of the system. Another was the sheer size and complexity of London as a financial centre. The Royal Bank of Scotland announced that it was going to lead an initiative to discover a rapid and cost-effective replacement for TAURUS. Other institutions called for a basic electronic settlement system to be established for institutional investors providing for a rolling settlement system with payments being made 10 days after transactions were effected. Settlement would be faster as and when share certificates no longer needed to move between institutional investors. The elimination of share certificates was the long-term objective although their immobilisation, in the short term, was more feasible. A further idea suggested at that stage was the establishment by the Bank of England of a clearing house to settle, within a few days, the institutional transactions that account for most of the value of trades effected through the Stock Exchange. Such a clearing house could incorporate the institutional net settlement system or a central nominee shareholder.

1-79   Following the abortive TAURUS project, a new paperless settlement system called 'Crest' was developed to replace the traditional account system of settlement and to dispense with the need for certificate-based dealing. It is thought that Crest will cost between £20 and £30 million as opposed to the much larger figure postulated for TAURUS. Computer-based, it has been designed to minimise risk in the settlement system by cutting the amount of time and paper involved in completing securities transactions. Presently being tested, under the supervision of the Bank of England, the system was expected to 'go live' on 15 July 1996 with the first settlement expected to take place on 19 August 1996.[90] Once up and running, it is expected that most active investors will trade shares either through the medium of a nominee account operated by their broker (who will hold shares on their behalf) or by becoming a sponsored member of Crest (in which case, transactions will be routed through a

---

90   See the Transfer of Functions (Financial Services) Order 1992 (SI 1992/1315), s 207 CA 1989 and the Uncertified Securities Regulations 1995 (SI 1992/3272). There has been much Press comment on Crest and its likely effects. See, for instance, 'Will small investors get fair shares under Crest?' by Marianne Curphey, *The Times*, 17 February 1996; 'Countdown to paperless trading with Crest' by Caroline Merrall, *The Times*, 27 April 1996; and 'All change for the on-screen route to faster transactions' by Sharon Colback, *The Sunday Times*, 3 March 1996. After one or two final problems, the system as a whole was 'approved' by the SIB on 11 July 1996 with Crest Co Ltd, the operating company, becoming a Recognised Investment Exchange. It 'went live' as expected on 15 July 1996. See also SI 1996/1322.

broker but without share certificates changing hands). The intention is then to cut down further the time within which securities transactions must be completed, which is likely to be the final nail in the coffin of paper retention in share transactions.

Rolling settlement

For many years, securities transactions were conducted on the basis of two and three week account periods where investors traded throughout an account period before settling during a single day a week later. One of the risks, however, in delaying settlement is that one of the parties to a transaction may suffer financial difficulties and be unable to complete. To forestall this, the London Stock Exchange moved to a system of 10-day rolling settlement (called 'T + 10') in July 1994. A year later, five-day rolling settlement was introduced ('T + 5') under which all deals must be settled within five days. The intention, following the successful launch of Crest is to move to a 'T + 3' system which may not, in all circumstances, give investors sufficient time to send/receive cheques and/or share certificates through the post. This seems likely to push many towards the use of nominee accounts which brokers are likely to make a cheaper mode of dealing to encourage paperless transactions. The move to shorter rolling settlement, however, is seen by many as representing the best way of reducing market risk and of bringing London into line with other markets worldwide which operate, or are contemplating the introduction of, T + 3, or even T + 2, settlement.

1-80

Share dealing and the 'information super-highway'

The final development which must be mentioned involves the Internet. In September 1995, following a contractual dispute, the Stock Exchange was reported as having reached agreement with Electronic Share Information and Sharelink for the provision of real-time share prices and related information enabling this to be accessed over the Internet. It was also reported as having reached agreement with Infotrade (a subsidiary of Mitsubishi) to provide similar information to its so-called Personal Finance Network. Ultimately, the aim of companies such as those mentioned seems to be to enable private investors to use the Internet to deal in shares. However, initially the Stock Exchange has been concerned about the security implications of the Internet and the possibility that persons might be able to 'hack' into confidential client information and this may well hold-up such developments. For the moment, it seems that investors using such information services will only be able to deal in the usual way via a separate arrangement with a broker or perhaps by using a private (non-Internet) computer-link with

1-81

the firm in question. In time, though, dealing may well become feasible via the Internet.[90a]

THE DEVOLUTION OF SECURITIES LAW

'Securities'

1-82   The expression /securities',/ in this context, is used in the wide sense of meaning any shares, debentures or other instruments which may be issued by a company and either listed[91] or offered to others for purchase or subscription. The aim of this section is to explain briefly the recent devolution of securities law in the UK.

UK legislation

1-83   In 1985, most of the legislation governing company law[92] was consolidated in the Companies Act 1985 and in three short 'satellite' Acts. Those Acts were the Business Names Act 1985, the Company Securities (Insider Dealing) Act 1985 and the Companies Consolidation (Consequential Provisions) Act 1985. The Companies Act 1989, which followed, made amendments to the above and to other legislation, such as the Financial Services Act 1986, and added certain new provisions. The law governing the public issue of securities and of prospectuses required a company to issue a prospectus if it wished the public to buy its shares. Further provisions then applied controlling the contents, issue, publication and subsequent registration of that prospectus. This was not significantly changed by the process of consolidation, referred to above.

European Community law

1-84   European Community law then reared its ugly head. In 1984, the Stock Exchange (Listing) Regulations 1984,[93] which came into full operation on 1 January 1985, adopted and gave effect as part of UK law to three

---

90a As for the future of the London Stock Exchange, its July 1996 'medium term' business plan outlined a cost cutting exercise which will involve a reduction in its workforce. There is also the intention to expand its trading areas to include emerging markets, EC and non-EC securities. It was however received with less than enthusiasm. See 'Exchange on the road to nowhere', *The Times* (Pennington column), 2 July 1996.

91 For instance, on the Official List of the Stock Exchange in London.

92 Which is to say, the Companies Acts 1948–1983.

93 SI 1984/716.

European Community Directives. Those Directives were the Admissions Directive,[94] the Listing Particulars Directive[95] and also the Interim Reports Directive.[96] They were designed to impose and provide for a minimum and equivalent standard of investor protection and for greater interpenetration of national securities markets in the European Community. They were underpinned by the fact that, on the Continent, the listing of securities is regarded as a process separate to and distinct from any offer which is made of them, whether for subscription or for purchase. The distinction between offers for sale of unlisted securities which were not to be the subject of an application for listing on the Stock Exchange and issues of securities which were intended to be admitted to the Official List of the London Stock Exchange was given statutory form in the Financial Services Act 1986.

The Financial Services Act 1986

The Financial Services Act 1986 repealed the Stock Exchange (Listing)   **1-85**
Regulations 1984. Parts IV and V of the Financial Services Act 1986 were intended to provide the framework for the regulation of both listed and unlisted securities in the UK, thus removing 'securities' law from the ambit of the Companies Act 1985. The thinking was that the regulation of listing and related matters would be overseen by the London Stock Exchange whilst the Secretary of State[97] would be responsible for unlisted securities. The two regimes would be distinct. However, Part V of the Financial Services Act 1986[98] never came into force. Initially the 'prospectus' provisions of the Companies Act 1985 continued to apply to offers of unlisted securities. Part IV of the Financial Services Act 1986[99] has, however, been in force for some time now.

The Treasury consulted further on these matters during the spring   **1-86**
and summer of 1994. Given the problems they identified in ensuring

---

94 79/279/EEC. The full name of this Directive is Council Directive (EEC) 79/279 of 5 March 1979 co-ordinating the conditions for the admission of securities to official stock-exchange listing.

95 80/390/EEC. The full name of this Directive is Council Directive (EEC) 80/390 of 17 March 1980 co-ordinating the requirements for the drawing up, scrutiny and distribution of the listing particulars to be published for the admission of securities to official stock-exchange listing.

96 82/121/EEC. The full name of this Directive is Council Directive (EEC) 82/121 of 15 February 1982 on information to be published on a regular basis by companies the shares of which have been admitted to official stock-exchange listing.

97 Now a Treasury Minister.

98 Which would have dealt, if implemented, with offers of unlisted securities.

99 Which deals with the official listing of securities.

nce with the Public Offers Directive,[100] it was decided that the Offers of Securities Regulations 1995 would be made instead under the European Communities Act 1972.[101] Part V of the Financial Services Act 1986 was never implemented. At the time of writing, it is thought that this might all come to pass by the end of 1994.

THE REGULATION OF THE SECURITIES INDUSTRY

Investor protection

1-87　The Financial Services Act 1986 is concerned with investor protection. Before that Act, the UK lacked any comprehensive regulation of the financial services industry as it affected investors. Instead, there was a combination of piecemeal statutory intervention[102] with a measure of industry self-regulation.[103] There was no central agency with overall control of the investment and securities sector.[104] In the early 1980s, however, rapidly developing investment markets, the desired harmonisation of the relevant laws of European Community member states and a number of scandals in the investment sector led to calls for a comprehensive review of the law on investor protection.

Professor Gower

1-88　Such a review, of the law relating to investor protection was carried out by Professor LCB Gower, who recommended a widescale overhaul of the regulatory regime.[105] Although he initially favoured the creation of a central agency, his considered recommendations were essentially for a comprehensive system of regulation designed to enhance investor protection within a statutory framework based as far as possible on self-regulation but subject to a measure of 'governmental' surveillance and intervention.

---

100 89/298/EEC. Sometimes called the Prospectus Directive, the full name of which is Council Directive (EEC) 89/298 of 17 April 1989 co-ordinating the requirements for the drawing-up, scrutiny and distribution of the prospectus to be published when transferable securities are offered to the public.

101 The European Communities Act 1972 (c 68). See paras 2-42 to 2-48, above. Further, see SI 1995/1537 which came into force on 19 July 1995.

102 The main example being the Prevention of Fraud (Investments) Act 1958 and its system of 'licensed dealers'.

103 For instance, by the Stock Exchange of its members.

104 In contrast to the Securities and Exchange Commission in the USA.

105 See 'Review of Investor Protection', a discussion document (1982), *Review of Investor Protection Report*, Part I, Cmnd 9125 (1984); 'Review of Investor Protection Report', Part II (1985).

The Financial Services Act 1986

The recommendations made by Professor Gower were, in essence, accepted[106] and the Conservative government published the Financial Services Bill in December 1985. Although it was the subject of intensive lobbying by 'interested' parties,[107] the Bill emerged largely intact and led to the Financial Services Act 1986 which received the Royal Assent on 7 November 1986. The so-called 'Big Bang', when, generally speaking, minimum commissions on transactions by Stock Exchange member firms were abolished and the single capacity dealing system[108] was abandoned, had taken place on 27 October 1986.

1-89

The regulatory system

The pivotal role of the Securities and Investments Board will be explained and examined in Chapter 2. Postulant regulatory bodies resulting from the basic structure of the Financial Services Act 1986 prepared rulebooks with a view to obtaining recognition from the Securities and Investments Board and the five so-called 'self-regulating organisations' which applied received recognition early in 1988. A date known as 'P' Day, and was in fact 27 February 1988, was chosen as the deadline by which all investment businesses had to apply for authorisation. A subsequent date which was known as 'A' Day, which was in fact 29 April 1988, was chosen as the date when s 3 of the Financial Services Act 1986 was to come into force, prohibiting the carrying on of investment business in the UK without due authorisation.

1-90

---

106 But see *Financial Systems in the UK*, a new framework for investor protection, Cmnd 9432 (1985) and also 'Regulation of Investment Business – The New Framework' published by the SIB in December 1985.

107 For instance, what is now Schedule 1 to the FSA was heavily amended as the Financial Services Bill passed through the parliamentary stages. See, for instance, House of Commons Official Report (6th Series), 31 October 1986, at columns 600–615.

108 Which divided members of the Stock Exchange into market makers or brokers.

CHAPTER 2

THE REGULATION OF SECURITIES BUSINESSES IN THE UNITED KINGDOM

INTRODUCTION

The ambit of the Financial Services Act 1986

The Financial Services Act 1986[1] is comprised of 10 Parts together, **2-01** initially, with 17 supplemental Schedules. For the purposes of this book, some of those Parts and Schedules are more important than the others.

Part I is entitled 'Regulation of Investment Business'[2] and includes **2-02** the basic prohibition in s 3 against engaging in unauthorised investment business[3] together with the criminal sanctions for breach of that provision which are set out in s 4.[4] It also contains other important matters, including s 47 (which deals with misleading statements and practices),[5] s 56 (which deals with unsolicited calls),[6] s 57 (which places certain restrictions on advertising relating to investments or investment agreements) and ss 75 and 76 (which relate to collective investment schemes).

---

1   The Financial Services Act 1986 (1986 c 60)(hereafter 'FSA 1986').

2   Comprising ss 1 to 128C. And see Eva Lomnicka, 'The new regulatory regime for investment business'(1988/89) 37 *King's Counsel* 7–10.

3   Section 3 FSA 1986 (which is entitled 'Persons entitled to carry on investment business') provides that:

     'No person shall carry on, or purport to carry on, investment business in the United Kingdom unless he is an authorised person under Chapter III or an exempted person under Chapter IV of this Part of this Act'.

4   Section 4 of the FSA 1986 (which is entitled 'Offences') provides in subsection (1) that 'Any person who carries on, or purports to carry on, investment business in contravention of section 3 above shall be guilty of an offence and liable –

     (a)   on conviction on indictment, to imprisonment for a term not exceeding two years or to a fine or to both;

     (b)   on summary conviction, to imprisonment for a term not exceeding six months or to a fine not exceeding the statutory maximum or to both'.

     Section 4(2) does, however, provide a defence because 'In proceedings brought against any person for an offence under this section it shall be a defence for him to prove that he took all reasonable precautions and exercised all due diligence to avoid the commission of the offence'.

5   See Chapter 10 for discussion of the offences contained in s 47 FSA 1986.

6   In conjunction with the Common Unsolicited Calls Regulations (Release 101 from the Securities and Investments Board).

2-03   Part IV is entitled 'Official Listing of Securities'[7] and deals with the listing of securities, generally speaking on the Official List of the Stock Exchange in London. It provides the statutory framework for the Stock Exchange 'Yellow Book' which contains the Listing Rules.[8]

2-04   It was intended that Part V, entitled 'Offers of Unlisted Securities'[9] would provide the statutory basis for offers of unlisted securities. Until it became effective, the 'prospectus' provisions of the Companies Act 1985[10] were to remain in force. Part V was, however, repealed.[11] Such public offers are now subject to the Offers of Securities Regulations.[12]

2-05   Of the supplemental Schedules, Schedule I (which is entitled 'Investments and Investment Business') is the most important in practice. It contains detailed categories of 'investments' subject to the Financial Services Act 1986. On the basis of those investments, it goes on to specify the 'investment activities' regulated by that Act and also those investment-related activities[13] which are excluded from its ambit.

The basic prohibition

2-06   Section 3 of the Financial Services Act 1986 provides that no person shall carry on or purport to carry on investment business in the UK unless he is an authorised person[14] or an exempted person.[15] That prohibition, which in practice usually requires persons to obtain authorisation before commencing any investment business in the UK, came into force on 29 April 1988. Breach of s 3 can amount to a criminal offence[16] and, additionally, can also render relevant contracts unenforceable.[17]

---

7   Comprising ss 142–57 (inclusive).

8   See paragraphs 2-49 to 2-65, below, further. See also, comments in paragraphs 1-43 to 1-46, 1-64 to 1-70, and 1-82 to 1-86, above for some relevant historical material.

9   Which comprised ss 158–171 (inclusive).

10   1985 c 6. See Part III ('Capital Issues') and Schedule 3 ('Mandatory Contents of Prospectus') CA 1985.

11   Part V FSA 1986 was repealed with effect from 19 June 1995. See art 2 of SI 1995/1538.

12   See paragraphs 2-65 to 2-72, below, further.

13   Termed 'Excluded Activities'.

14   Under Chapter III ('Authorised Persons') of Part I (the 'Regulation of Investment Business') of the Financial Services Act 1986.

15   Under Chapter IV ('Exempted Persons') of Part I FSA 1986.

16   By virtue of s 4 ('Offences') FSA 1986.

17   By virtue of s 5 ('Agreements made by or through unauthorised persons') FSA 1986.

THE REGULATORY HIERARCHY

The Financial Services Act 1986

With some exceptions, the Financial Services Act 1986[18] provides the statutory framework for the present regulation of the financial services and securities industry in the UK. Generally speaking, implementation of the various provisions of that Act took place over a period of time by means of commencement orders in the form of statutory instruments made by the Secretary of State.[19]

2-07

The Secretary of State

The Financial Services Act 1986 contains many powers and functions exercisable by the 'Secretary of State'. A regulatory body called the Securities and Investments Board was established under that Act to which the Secretary of State delegated many of those powers and functions. The Secretary of State has also promulgated much secondary legislation under the Financial Services Act 1986, in the form of statutory instruments. Until 6 June 1992, the relevant Secretary of State was the Secretary of State for Trade and Industry. Generally speaking, it is now a Treasury Minister following a transfer of functions (including that of responsibility for financial services) from the Department of Trade and Industry to the Treasury.[20]

2-08

The Securities and Investments Board

As primary delegatee of the Secretary of State, the Securities and Investments Board is colloquially known as the chief UK investment industry 'watchdog'. The SIB may directly authorise persons to conduct investment business in the UK if such persons make application to it.[21] It may also 'recognise' various bodies (such as self-regulating organisations)

2-09

---

18 The FSA 1986 has suffered EC-driven incursions. Recently, see the Financial Services Act 1986 (Investment Services) (Extension of Scope Act) Order 1995 (SI 1995/3271) giving effect to Council Directive of 10 May 1993 on investment services in the securities field (93/22/EEC). And see the SIB Discussion Paper 'Implementation Services Directive and Capital Adequacy Directive (July 1994).

19 See paragraph 2-08 below.

20 By virtue of the Transfer of Functions (Financial Services) Order 1992 (SI 1992/1315).

21 See ss 25–30 (inclusive) FSA 1986. See also 'An Introduction to SIB' (published by the SIB on 19 June 1996).

enabling them to admit persons to membership thereby authorising those persons to conduct investment business in the UK.[22]

The self-regulating organisations

2-10   The SIB presently recognises five self-regulating organisations.[23] They are as follows:

- the Securities and Futures Authority (known as the SFA), which regulates mainstream stockbroking and securities business and also authorises most investment firms doing corporate finance and related business;

- the Investment Management Regulatory Organisation (known as IMRO), which regulates investment management;

- the Life Assurance and Unit Trust Regulatory Organisation (known as LAUTRO), which has regulated the promotion of life assurance and related products;

- the Financial Intermediaries, Managers and Brokers Regulatory Association (known as FIMBRA), which has regulated the activities of independent intermediaries;

- the Personal Investment Authority (known as the PIA), which regulates those investment firms having direct contact with the general public.

2-11   The SFA is the main 'FSA' regulator of the securities industry and regulates the investment business conducted by most securities industry professionals in the City of London.[24] It is capable of regulating stock broking, market making and the related activities of sophisticated financial intermediaries. It makes clear that those activities undertaken within corporate finance business, which amount to investment business, also fall within its regulatory scope. Although the SFA can regulate investment management, this is unusual in practice and firms are normally expected to seek membership of IMRO if they want to

---

22 See ss 7–14 (inclusive) FSA 1986 with regard to persons authorised through membership of self-regulating organisations. See ss 15–21 (inclusive) of the FSA 1986 with regard to persons authorised by recognised professional bodies, and see SIB Guidance Releases 3/95 and 4/95 of September 1995 in relation to 'Standards of Regulation' for SROs and RPBs. The Chairman of the SIB has said recently that the guiding principles were 'delegation downwards but accountability upwards'. See 'Tailor the rules to reward the good and punish the bad' by Sir Andrew Large, *The Times*, 24 August 1996.

23 Of these, LAUTRO and FIMBRA are in the process of being wound-up. Initially, they were expected to cease to be recognised from October 1994 but this was delayed. See 'Relocation of Recognition of FIMBRA and LAUTRO as Self-Regulating Organisations', a report to SIB by Lord Oliver and Dame Margaret Booth (June 1994) and also SIB Guidance Release No 3/95 (published on 14 September 1995).

24 Please refer to Chapter 9 at paragraph 9–55 *et seq*, below, for a fuller treatment of the role and significance of the SFA. Its predecessor SROs were the AFBD and TSA.

engage in investment management where such management is to be undertaken within and will be the principal activity of the firm.

The PIA is the 'newest' of the self-regulating organisations. Receiving recognition from the SIB in 1994,[25] its regulatory scope encompasses the areas of investment business previously regulated by FIMBRA and LAUTRO and also some of the scope of IMRO. Essentially, the PIA regulates those investment firms having direct contact with the general public. It represents a successor body to FIMBRA and LAUTRO. At a number of stages during 1993–1994, it seemed unlikely that the PIA would receive enough industry support to make it viable. However, it was ultimately supported by the banks and life offices and therefore proceeded to the recognition stage for the purposes of s 10 of the Financial Services Act 1986.

2-12

The obligations of authorised persons

Persons may become authorised for the purposes of the Financial Services Act 1986 in a number of ways. A number are authorised directly by the SIB.[26] Many more become members of SROs[27] or are certified[28] for these purposes[29] by one of the professional bodies 'recognised' for the purposes of the Financial Services Act 1986. These

2-13

---

25 The PIA received formal recognition from the SIB on 18 July 1994.

26 Section 25 FSA 1986 provides that 'A person holding an authorisation granted by the Secretary of State ... is an authorised person'. Under s 114(1) and (4) of that Act, the Secretary of State has power to transfer certain functions (which the Act otherwise stipulates to be exercisable by the Secretary of State) to a 'designated agency'. By means of a number of delegation orders (including the Financial Services Act 1986 (Delegation) Order 1987 (SI 1987/942), most of those functions (including the power to grant authorisations pursuant to s 27 of the Act) were transferred to the Securities and Investments Board. Under s 27 of the Act, persons have been able to apply to the SIB to be authorised and regulated by the SIB rather than by one of the SROs. In its role as a regulator, the relevant SIB internal division dealing with authorisations and subsequent monitoring came to be known informally as 'SIBRO'. That notwithstanding, the SIB has always been widely seen as a reluctant regulator. This was confirmed in the review document 'Financial Services Regulation – Making the Two Tier System Work' by Andrew Large, SIB Chairman, which was published in May 1993 (see, for instance, paragraphs 8.2, 8.11 and 8.13 of that document). This basic reluctance is thought to have continued despite the needs for 'passport' regulation of EC investment business.

27 Section 7(1) FSA 1986 provides that '... a member of a recognised self-regulating organisation is an authorised person by virtue of his membership of that organisation'.

28 Section 15(1) FSA 1986 provides that 'A person holding a certificate issued ... by a recognised professional body is an authorised person'. Such certificates may be issued by a recognised professional body to an individual, a body corporate, a partnership or to an unincorporated association.

29 Essentially, as authorised persons. And see SIB Guidance Release No 4/95 (published on 14 September 1995), further.

include the Institute of Chartered Accountants of England and Wales[30] and also The Law Society,[31] which are both Recognised Professional Bodies by virtue of ss 17 and 18 of that Act.[32]

2-14   Authorised persons are subject to the rules of their regulator which govern the conduct of investment business and related matters. Most mainstream investment businesses are members of SROs.

2-15   In their dealings with customers, it was envisaged that SRO members would essentially be subject to a 'three-tier' rulebook structure:[33] this would comprises the 10 Statements of Principle (promulgated by the SIB)[34] as the first tier; the 40 Core Conduct of Business Rules (also promulgated by the SIB)[35] together with certain designated rules made by the SIB pursuant to s 63A of the Financial

---

30   Known as the 'ICAEW'.

31   Which regulates the conduct and business of solicitors.

32   Section 17(1) FSA 1986 provides that a professional body may apply (to the SIB) for an order declaring it to be a recognised professional body for the purposes of that Act. Section 18(1) goes on to provide that, on an application being duly made (which would include the provision of all necessary information), the SIB may make an order declaring the applicant to be a recognised professional body. Schedule 3 to the FSA 1986 sets out certain requirements for recognition of a professional body, including the need for conduct of business rules which afford an adequate level of protection for investors. A recognition order may be made if it appears from the information furnished that the requirements of Schedule 3 and also of s 18(3) are satisfied as regards the body. Section 18(3) provides that the body must have rules which impose limits on the kinds of investment business which may be carried on by persons certified by it. The circumstances in which they may carry on such business must also be specified.

33   The history of the 'three-tier' structure may be traced through a number of consultative and other documents issued by the SIB. The first tranche of rules was made by the SIB on 7 October 1987. In November 1988, the SIB published, on a consultative basis, proposals ('Conduct of Business Rules: A New Approach') for a major review of the conduct of business rules. In March 1989, the SIB published a paper ('A Wider Role for SIB's Principles of Conduct: the Next Stage of the New Approach') on how it saw the next stage of the new approach to rulebooks. In June 1989, the SIB Board discussed proposals for a 'New Settlement involving principles and core rules'. In August 1989, the SIB published a discussion paper ('Regulation of the Conduct of Investment Business: a Proposal') which included proposals for the two upper tiers of principles and designated or 'core' rules. In March 1990, the SIB published the final text of the 10 principles which came into effect in April 1990. In January 1991, the SIB published the final version of its 'Principles and Core Rules for Conduct of Investment Business'.

34   The 10 principles came into effect in April 1990. The Statements of Principle were published by the SIB on 15 March 1990.

35   The final version of the SIB core rules, the Core Conduct of Business Rules, was published on 30 January 1991.

Services Act 1986,[36] which would thus be applicable to members of SROs, which together would constitute the second tier. These were to be supplemented by additional 'third tier' material promulgated by the SRO in question as being of particular relevance to the investment business of its members.[37] In 1994, however, the Core Conduct of Business Rules were dedesignated by the SIB so as not to apply directly to members of SROs. Designated status was also removed from certain provisions relating to client money and financial supervision.[37a]

Authorised persons are also required by their regulator to maintain financial resources sufficient to enable them to carry on the investment business for which they are authorised. They also have to notify the regulator on the occurrence of certain specified events, including the departure of key executive officers and the like.

2-16

Recognised investment exchanges

Generally speaking, an investment exchange provides facilities whereby investments may be bought and sold. It enables such transactions to be completed and settled. In providing such facilities, it will also supervise what is done by and between those persons it allows to use them. As will be seen,[38] such a role involves exchanges based in the UK in

2-17

---

36 Such as the Financial Services (Client Money) Regulations 1991 (see SIB Rules Releases 104 (published on 6 November 1991), 116 (18 June 1992), 134 (23 March 1994), 137 (which contains the current text, reissued as amended on 29 April 1994) as updated by 143 (4 August 1994); and see also 165 (27 June 1996)) and the Common Unsolicited Calls Regulations 1991 (see SIB Rules Release No 101 (published on 27 June 1991)).

37 In August 1991, IMRO was the first SRO to publish its new rulebook, incorporating principles, core rules and third tier material. The core rules promulgated by the SIB were 'designated' in respect of IMRO in November 1991. See the Core Conduct of Business Rules Commencement (IMRO) Order 1991 (SIB Rules Release No 105, published on 28 November 1991). The SFA published its new rulebook in December 1991 and the core rules were 'designated' in respect of the SFA in April 1992. See the Core Conduct of Business Rules Commencement (SFA) Order 1992 (SIB) Rules Release No 111, published on 25 March 1992). The PIA published its rulebook which came into force with effect from 18 July 1994.

37a For background material, see 'Dedesignation of the Core Conduct of Business Rules, the Client Money Regulations and the Financial Supervision Rules' (a SIB Consultative Paper published in August 1994). See, then, the Financial Services (Dedesignation) Rules and Regulations 1994 (SIB Rules Release No 149, published on 24 November 1994). The dedesignation specified in that instrument came into operation on 17 November 1994 and the Core Conduct of Business Rules Commencement (IMRO) Order1991 and the Core Conduct of Business Rules Commencement (SFA) Order 1992 were revoked. See also paragraphs 9-60 to 9-63, below, in relation to the SFA.

38 From paragraph 2-26 below.

carrying on investment business.[39] However, if an exchange becomes a recognised investment exchange,[40] it will be regarded as an exempted person for the purposes of the Financial Services Act 1986 and will not need to obtain authorisation.[41] It should, however, be noted that there is nothing in the Financial Services Act 1986 requiring an exchange to become 'recognised'. It could, as an alternative, obtain authorisation through membership of the Securities and Futures Authority[42] or from the SIB. In practice, however, the usual course of action has involved exchanges seeking to become recognised investment exchanges.

2-18   To obtain 'recognition', any body corporate or unincorporated association may apply to the SIB[43] for an order declaring it to be a recognised investment exchange for the purposes of the Financial Services Act 1986. Before making such an order, it must appear to the SIB that certain requirements are satisfied by the applicant exchange.[44] For instance, it must have financial resources sufficient for the proper performance of its functions.[45] Its rules and practices must ensure that business conducted by means of its facilities is done so in an orderly manner and so as to ensure proper protection for investors.[46] It must limit potential dealings on the exchange to investments in which there is a proper market.[47] Where relevant, it must require those issuing investments to be dealt in on the exchange to enable persons dealing in those investments to obtain proper information for determining their

---

39   The relevant investment activity is that of 'arranging deals in investments' for the purposes of paragraph 13 in Part II of Schedule 1 FSA 1986. A person will be 'arranging deals' for those purposes if he makes, offers or agrees to make 'arrangements with a view to a person who participates in the arrangements buying, selling, subscribing for or underwriting investments'. An investment exchange will be making such arrangements with a view to its members participating by using its facilities and buying and/or selling shares etc. As such members will have to pay the exchange for the privilege of being members, the exchange will be carrying on the investment activity by way of business. For these purposes, s 1(2) FSA 1986 provides that 'investment business' means 'the business of engaging in one or more of the activities which fall within the paragraphs in Part II of Schedule 1'. Section 3, of course, provides that 'No person shall carry on, or purport to carry on, investment business in the UK unless he is an authorised person under Chapter III or an exempted person under Chapter IV of this Part of this Act'.

40   For the purposes of Chapter IV in Part I FSA 1986.

41   Section 36(1) FSA 1986 provides that 'A recognised investment exchange is an exempted person as respects anything done in its capacity as such which constitutes investment business'. And see the Financial Services Act 1986 (EEA Regulated Markets) (Exemption) Order 1995 (SI 1995/3273).

42   Which at the moment would be the relevant self-regulating organisation.

43   Pursuant to s 37(1) FSA 1986.

44   These are contained in Schedule 4 FSA 1986.

45   By virtue of paragraph 1 of Schedule 4 FSA 1986.

46   By virtue of paragraph 2(1) of Schedule 4 FSA 1986.

47   By virtue of paragraph 2(2)(a) of Schedule 4 FSA 1986.

current value.[48] It must have in place arrangements for ensuring the performance of transactions effected pursuant to its facilities[49] and must either have or secure the provision on its behalf of satisfactory arrangements for recording transactions effected pursuant to the exchange.[50] The exchange must have adequate arrangements and resources for the effective monitoring and enforcement of compliance with its rules and with any clearing arrangements made by it.[51] It must also be able and willing to promote and maintain high standards of integrity and fair dealing in the carrying on of investment business.[52] Once recognised, a recognised investment exchange must of course continue to satisfy the SIB with regard to the requirements referred to above.

There are, at present, seven recognised investment exchanges.[53] Of these, Tradepoint,[53a] the London Stock Exchange,[54] the London International Financial Futures and Options Exchange[55] and the London Securities and Derivatives Exchange Limited[56] currently trade equities or equity derivatives. The best known 'RIE' remains, probably, the London Stock Exchange for good and not simply historical reasons. In terms of regulatory development, its framework of 'self-regulation' can be seen as providing a basic model for the system finally implemented under the Financial Services Act 1986 for all investment businesses: it involved a rulebook with which Stock Exchange members had to comply in their dealings together with a tradition of effective monitoring and enforcement. As will be seen,[57] it has maintained its monitoring role

2-19

---

48 By virtue of paragraph 2(2)(b) of Schedule 4 FSA 1986. Usually through compliance with listing requirements.

49 By virtue of paragraph 2(4) of Schedule 4 FSA 1986.

50 By virtue of paragraph 2(5) of Schedule 4 FSA 1986.

51 By virtue of paragraph 3(1) of Schedule 4 FSA 1986. And see SIB Guidance Release No 2/96 (published in March 1996), further.

52 By virtue of paragraph 5 of Schedule 4 FSA 1986.

53 Or 'RIEs'.

53a See paragraph 1-74, above, in relation to Tradepoint Financial Networks.

54 Known as the 'LSE'. It is an investment exchange whose members trade in UK government bonds and UK and international equities and bonds. The LSE also provides services for the settlement of trades in UK equities and, as will be seen in Part 4 of this Chapter, below, is the competent authority for the listing of securities in the UK. For some background discussion, see Patricia D Jackson,'Change in the Stock Exchange and regulation of the City', (1986) 7(3) Bus LR 90–96.

55 Known as the 'LIFFE', pronounced 'life' rather than like the river in Ireland. This is an investment exchange whose members trade in financial futures and options. See 'Airborne in the busy world of futures' by Sarah Cunningham, *The Times*, 14 September 1996. LIFFE merged with the London Commodities Exchange on 16 September 1996.

56 Known as 'OMLX', the London Securities & Derivatives Exchange Limited.

57 In Chapter 8.

in relation to potential cases of insider dealing. Since implementation of the Financial Services Act 1986, however, most of the regulatory role of the London Stock Exchange in relation to the activities of its members has been taken over by relevant SROs[58] and its main function now is that of an investment exchange.

INVESTMENT BUSINESS

The basic prohibition

2-20   Section 3 of the Financial Services Act 1986[59] is arguably its pivotal provision. It provides that no persons may carry on or purport to carry on investment business in the UK unless they are authorised or exempted persons. 'Investment business' is defined[60] as meaning the business of engaging in one or more of the activities which fall within the paragraphs of Part II of Schedule 1 to the Financial Services Act 1986 and are not excluded by Part III of that Schedule.

Territorial scope

2-21   The Financial Services Act 1986 is only concerned with the regulation of investment business in the UK. Section 1(3) provides that, for the purposes of the Act, a person carries on investment business in the UK if he either:

- carries on investment business from a permanent place of business maintained by him in the UK;[61] or

- engages in the UK in one or more of the activities set out in Part II of Schedule 1 which are not excluded by Parts III or IV of that Schedule and his doing so constitutes the carrying on by him of a business in the UK.[62]

---

58 Initially by TSA and the AFBD (and, to a small extent, by FIMBRA) and now mainly by the SFA.

59 Which is entitled 'Persons entitled to carry on investment business'.

60 In s 1(2) FSA 1986 and see also SI 1995/3271. Careful note must also be taken of the Investment Services Regulations 1995 (SI 1995/3275) which give effect to EEC Council Directive 93/22 on investment services in the securities field and to Provisions of EEC Council Directive 93/6 on the capital adequacy of investment firms and credit institutions.

61 Section 1(3)(a) FSA 1986.

62 Section 1(3)(b) FSA 1986.

The basic questions

To establish whether or not a person is or may be carrying on investment business in the UK, there are essentially four questions which need to be addressed. They are as follows:

2-22

- Are there any 'investments' or underlying investments involved in what is being done or proposed to be done?
- If there are, are any 'investment activities' involved or likely to be involved?
- If there are, are any of the 'exclusions' applicable?
- If not, is or will the activity be engaged in by way of business?

If there is an overseas element in any proposed arrangements, to fall under the Financial Services Act 1986 any investment activities which will be involved will have to be carried on from a permanent place of business maintained in the UK or otherwise constitute the carrying on of a business in the UK.[63]

2-23

'Investments'

Underlying 'investments' for these purposes are categorised in Part I of Schedule 1 to the Financial Services Act 1986.[64] Part I was drafted in very wide terms and lists 11 categories of 'investment'. These include 'shares',[65] 'debentures',[66] certain 'instruments entitling to shares and securities' and also 'certificates representing securities'.[67] 'Government and public securities'[68] are included as are 'options', 'futures' and 'contracts for differences'.[69] Finally, 'rights' to and 'interests' in anything which is itself an 'investment' falling within any other paragraph of Part I of Schedule 1 will also amount to a separate 'investment'.[70]

2-24

In considering whether investments are likely to arise or be involved in any particular situation, reference should always be made to Part I of Schedule 1 and to the supplemental and clarificatory notes set out therein which, effectively, form part of the legislation.

2-25

---

63 See s 1(3)(a) and (b) FSA 1986 and also paragraphs 2-21 and 2-22 above.

64 This is because s 1(1) FSA 1986 provides that, in the Act unless the context otherwise requires, 'investment' means any asset, right or interest falling within any paragraph in Part I of Schedule 1 to the Act. And see also SI 1995/3271.

65 By virtue of paragraph 1 of Schedule 1 FSA 1986.

66 By virtue of paragraph 2 of Schedule 1.

67 By virtue of paragraphs 4 and 5 of Schedule 1.

68 By virtue of paragraph 3 of Schedule 1.

69 By virtue of paragraphs 7, 8 and 9 of Schedule 1, respectively, and see SIB Guidance Releases 3/88 (issued in March 1988) and 1/96 (issued in February 1996), further.

70 By virtue of paragraph 11 of Schedule 1 FSA 1986.

'Investment activities'

2-26   The relevant 'investment activities' are listed in Part II of Schedule 1 to the Financial Services Act 1986. They are as follows:

- *Dealing in investments.*[71] This involves persons in buying, selling, subscribing for and also in underwriting investments or offering or agreeing to do those things, either as principal or as agent. It is an activity engaged in, for instance, by market makers and also by the 'treasury' departments of large companies.[72] Paragraph 28(1)(d) of Schedule 1[73] gives a fairly extended meaning to the terms 'buying' and 'selling'. It provides that, for the purposes of Schedule 1, references to those terms are to be taken as including references to any acquisition or disposal for valuable consideration. Paragraph 28(2) then provides that, in the case of an investment consisting of rights under a contract (or other arrangements), a 'disposal' is to be taken as including[74] assuming the corresponding liabilities under the contract (or arrangements) or surrendering, assigning or converting those rights. In the case of any other investment, a 'disposal' includes issuing or creating the investment or granting the rights or interests of which it consists.[75] For the purposes of this activity, references to an 'offer' also include references to an invitation to treat.[76]

- *Arranging deals in investments.*[77] Generally speaking, this activity involves a person making or offering or agreeing to make arrangements with a view to another person 'dealing' in a particular investment or with a view to a person who participates in the arrangements 'dealing in investments'. It does not apply to a person by reason of arrangements made by him with regard to a transaction to which he will himself be a party as principal or as an agent for one of the parties.[78] In such a case, however, paragraph 12 of Schedule 1 might be in point.

- *Managing investments belonging to another.*[79] Without wishing to state the obvious, this is the investment activity engaged in, for instance, by professional investment managers.

---

71 See paragraph 12 of Schedule 1.
72 Which invest the surplus funds of those companies. Normally, this will only involve them in the investment activity of 'dealing in investments'.
73 In Part V of Schedule 1 which is entitled 'Interpretation'.
74 By virtue of paragraph 28(2)(a) and (c) of Schedule 1.
75 By virtue of paragraph 28(2)(b) of Schedule 1.
76 By virtue of paragraph 28(1)(c) of Schedule 1.
77 See paragraph 13 of Schedule 1.
78 By virtue of note (1) to paragraph 13 of Schedule 1 FSA 1986.
79 See paragraph 14 of Schedule 1.

- *Giving investment advice.*[80] This activity involves giving, or offering or agreeing to give, to persons in their capacity as investors or potential investors 'advice on the merits'[81] of their purchasing, selling, subscribing for or underwriting an investment or exercising any right conferred by an investment to acquire, dispose of, underwrite or convert an investment. To fall within this activity, advice needs to be specific to an investment[82] as opposed to general or generic advice.[83] Neutral information,[84] in the absence of any express or implied recommendation or endorsement, is unlikely to amount to investment advice. Each case must, however, be considered on its own facts.

- *Establishing, operating or winding-up a collective investment scheme.*[85] This last investment activity should always be borne in mind in 'joint venture' situations[86] and reference must be made to the definition of 'collective investment scheme' contained in s 75(1)–(3) of the Financial Services Act 1986 and also to the restrictions on promoting such schemes imposed on authorised persons by s 76 of that Act.

'Excluded activities'

Once it has been established that an investment activity is involved in a particular situation, the application of each of the 'excluded activities' contained in Part III of Schedule 1 to the Financial Services Act 1986 should be considered. If there is an overseas element to what is going on, attention should also be paid to Part IV of Schedule 1.[87] If there is no such element, perhaps the most important of the 'exclusions' in Part III are the following:

2-27

---

80 See paragraph 15 of Schedule 1.

81 Which expression is thought to require a recommendation of some sort.

82 For instance, 'Buy shares in A N Other plc'.

83 For instance, 'Buy equities'.

84 For instance, 'A N Other plc seems to have had a good year'.

85 See paragraph 16 of Schedule 1 and see the Financial Services Act 1986 (Uncertificated Securities)(Extension of Scope of Act) Order 1996 (SI 1996/1322) which has added a new paragraph 16A to Schedule 1 FSA 1986, with effect from 15 July 1996. It is concerned with the sending on behalf of another person of dematerialised instructions relating to an investment. See SI 1995/3272 and paragraph 1-79, above, further.

86 Perhaps the best legislative definition of the expression 'joint venture' may be taken from the definition of 'joint enterprise' which is contained in paragraph 31 of Schedule 1. That paragraph provides that a joint enterprise means '...an enterprise into which two or more persons ("the participators") enter for commercial reasons related to a business or businesses (other than investment business) carried on by them; and where a participator is a body corporate and a member of a group each other member of the group shall also be regarded as a participator in the enterprise'.

87 Which contains 'Additional Exclusions For Persons Without Permanent Place Of Business In United Kingdom'. See also SI 1995/3275.

- For *'dealing as principal'*.[88] This paragraph contains an exclusion from paragraph 12 of Schedule 1. Generally speaking, its effect is that a person will only be regarded as 'dealing in investments' in transactions which he enters into as principal[89] in certain limited circumstances. For instance, if he holds himself out as engaging in the business of buying investments with a view to selling them.[90] This exclusion can be applicable to the own-account 'treasury' activities of companies.

- In respect of *'groups'* and *'joint enterprises'*.[91] The effect of this paragraph is that certain dealings between and activities involving bodies corporate in the same group and also participators in the same joint enterprise[92] will not amount to investment activities. Subject in each case to its terms, this exclusion can apply to dealing,[93] to arranging deals,[94] to managing investments[95] and to the giving of investment advice.[96] In each case, if the exclusion is applicable, the relevant paragraph within Part II of Schedule 1 is not regarded as applying to the activities in question.

- In respect of *'employees' share schemes'*.[97] This paragraph contains an exclusion from 'dealing' and from 'arranging deals in investments'.[98] It is headed 'Employees' share schemes' but is drafted quite widely as excluding the application of the relevant paragraphs to anything done by a company or certain other persons for the purpose of enabling or facilitating transactions in the shares or debentures of that company between or for the benefit of its *bona fide* employees or

---

88 See paragraph 17 of Schedule 1 FSA 1986.

89 Which is to say, for himself (for his own account).

90 See paragraph 17(1)(b) of Schedule 1 and see SIB Guidance Release 1/88 (issued in March 1988), further.

91 See paragraph 18 of Schedule 1 and SI 1996/1322.

92 For these purposes, a 'joint enterprise' is defined by paragraph 31 of Schedule 1 as meaning 'an enterprise into which two or more persons ("the participators") enter for commercial reasons related to a business or businesses (other than investment business) carried on by them; and where a participator is a body corporate and a member of a group each other member of the group shall also be regarded as a participator in the enterprise'. A 'body corporate' is defined by s 207(1) FSA 1986 as including a body corporate constituted under the law of a country or territory outside the UK whilst a 'group', in relation to a body corporate, is defined as meaning that body corporate, any other body corporate which is its holding company or subsidiary and any other body corporate which is a subsidiary of that holding company.

93 That is to say, to paragraph 12 of Schedule 1.

94 To paragraph 13 of Schedule 1.

95 To paragraph 14.

96 To paragraph 15.

97 See paragraph 20 of Schedule 1.

98 That is to say, from the application of paragraphs 12 and 13 of Schedule 1.

former employees or the holding of such securities by or for the benefit of any such persons.[99] Whether or not this exclusion should be regarded as being capable of applying beyond employee share schemes to other 'corporate' arrangements[100] is debatable. It also has other limitations and reference must be made to its precise terms.

- In respect of *the sale of a body corporate*.[101] This paragraph contains an exclusion from 'dealing', 'arranging deals in investments' and/or 'the giving of investment advice' for the purposes of or in connection with the acquisition or disposal of a majority of shares[102] in a body corporate. The acquisition and/or disposal must, however, be between parties each of whom is a body corporate, a partnership, a single individual or a group of certain connected individuals.

- In respect of *advice given or arrangements made in the course of a profession or business not otherwise constituting investment business*.[103] This paragraph contains an exclusion from the investment activities of 'arranging deals in investments' and/or 'giving investment advice'[104] in the course of carrying on any profession or business not otherwise amounting to investment business. The arrangements made or advice given must, however, be a 'necessary' part of other advice or services made or given in the course of carrying on that profession or business and will not be regarded as such if remunerated separately from the other advice or services. In practice, it is usually the determination of what exactly is 'necessary' in a given case which normally excludes the application of this 'exclusion'.

'Overseas persons'

Part IV of Schedule 1 to the Financial Services Act 1986 contains further exclusions in relation to certain investment activities carried on by 'overseas persons'.[105] Generally speaking, for these purposes, 'overseas

2-28

---

99 The precise group of such 'persons' is set out in paragraph 20(2)(a) and (b) of Schedule 1 FSA 1986.

100 Such as corporate personal equity plans and/or cheap corporate share dealing arrangements. See, for instance, Gil Brazier, 'Managing Shares at Arm's Length'(1993) LS Gaz, 28 July, pp 20–24.

101 See paragraph 21 of Schedule 1.

102 By virtue of paragraph 21(1)(a) and (b), the shares in question must consist of or include shares carrying 75% or more of the voting rights attributable to share capital which are exercisable in all circumstances at any general meeting of the body corporate or the shares, together with any already held by the person acquiring them, must carry not less than that percentage of those voting rights.

103 See paragraph 24 of Schedule 1.

104 That is to say, from activities falling within paragraphs 13 and 15 of Schedule 1.

105 Part IV of Schedule 1 is entitled 'Additional Exclusions for Persons Without Permanent Place of Business in United Kingdom'. And see also SI 1995/3275.

persons' are persons not carrying on investment business from a permanent place of business maintained by them in the UK.[106] The further exclusions are, in essence, as follows:

- Paragraph 26 of Schedule 1 excludes certain 'dealings' or 'arrangements' made by an 'overseas person' with or through an authorised person or an exempted person acting in the course of the business in respect of which he is exempt. For these purposes, a transaction is entered into 'through' a person if he enters into it as agent or arranges for it to be entered into by another person as principal or agent.[107]

- Paragraph 27 of Schedule 1 excludes certain activities[108] involving or resulting from an approach made to or by an overseas person in certain circumstances, so long as there has been no contravention by the overseas person of s 56[109] or s 57[110] of the Financial Services Act 1986.

'By way of business'

2-29   To require regulation, as constituting investment business, the investment activity or activities in question must by carried on or be engaged in by way of business.[111] Unhelpfully, the Financial Services Act 1986 does not define what is meant by 'business'. The Securities and Investments Board has, however, made some reference to this area in guidance material[112] and, essentially, it seems that it is necessary to apply general common law concepts of what amounts to 'business' and also commonsense to reach an answer.

2-30   Commercial motivation is a major element of engaging in a business as is any likely resulting commercial benefit, whether direct or indirect.

---

106 By virtue of paragraph 26(1) of Schedule 1 and then s 1(3)(a) FSA 1986 and see also SI 1995/3275.

107 By virtue of paragraph 29 of Schedule 1.

108 In particular, those otherwise falling within paragraphs 12, 13, 14 and 15 of Schedule 1. And see SI 1996/1322.

109 Which 'regulates' the making of unsolicited calls. An 'unsolicited call' is defined by s 56(8) as meaning a personal visit or oral communication made without express invitation.

110 Which regulates the issue of 'investment advertisements' which are defined by s 57(2) as meaning any advertisement inviting persons to enter or offer to enter into an investment agreement or to exercise any rights conferred by an investment to acquire, dispose of, underwrite or convert an investment or containing information calculated to lead directly or indirectly to persons doing so.

111 This is because s 1(2) FSA 1986 provides that 'In this Act "investment business" means the business of engaging in one or more of the activities which fall within the paragraphs in Part II of that Schedule and are not excluded by Part III of that Schedule'. 'That Schedule' is of course Schedule 1 FSA 1986.

112 See, for instance, SIB Guidance Release 2/88 (March 1988 – 'Pensions Advice and Management') and also SIB Guidance Release 4/89 (December 1989 – 'The Financial Services Act 1986 and the Press: Authorisation and Exemption'). See also note 36 to Chapter 10, below, and *Morgan Grenfell & Co Ltd v Welwyn Hatfield DC* [1995] 1 All ER 1.

Carrying on an investment activity out of friendship or for largely philanthropic reasons would not necessarily be caught by the Financial Services Act 1986 whereas doing so for a fee or commission is likely to be caught. Frequency, repetition and/or continuity are further elements of carrying on a business. Carrying on an investment activity on rare or isolated occasions is perhaps unlikely to be regarded as being by way of business although it must be stressed that one-off activities can in certain circumstances be caught. In essence, it remains vital to consider all the circumstances of a particular case. It is hard to be more specific than that on this area.

Criminal sanctions for breach

Section 4 of the Financial Services Act 1986 provides that it is potentially a criminal offence for a person to carry on, or purport to carry on, investment business in contravention of s 3 of that Act.[113] The maximum penalty, on conviction on indictment, is imprisonment for a term not exceeding two years or a fine or a mixture of both of those penalties. On summary conviction, a person may be liable to imprisonment for a term not exceeding six months or to a fine not exceeding the statutory maximum[114] or to a mixture of both.

2-31

It is, however, a defence, in any proceedings brought against a person for breach of s 3, for him to prove that he took all reasonable precautions and exercised all due diligence to avoid the commission of the offence.[115]

2-32

Where such an offence is committed by a company[116] and is proved to have been committed with the consent or connivance of or to have been attributable to any neglect on the part of certain persons, those persons as well as the company shall be guilty of the offence and are liable to be

2-33

---

113 That is to say, to do so whilst neither authorised nor exempted for the purposes of the FSA 1986.

114 There is statutory limit on the size of a fine which a Crown Court may impose on an offender who has been convicted on indictment although, generally speaking, it is thought that it should be within the capacity of the offender to pay: see *R v Churchill (No 2)* [1967] 1 QB 190. On summary conviction, generally speaking, the maximum fines imposable are fixed by reference to a standard scale of fines (at different levels) which was introduced by s 37 of the Criminal Justice Act 1982. For each level, the standard scale specifies the maximum fine which the magistrates may impose for an offence at that level. At the moment, the highest sum on the standard scale corresponds with what is known as the 'prescribed sum' which is the maximum fine which can be imposed by the magistrates following conviction for an either-way offence listed in Schedule 1 to the Magistrates' Courts Act 1980. The 'statutory maximum' referred to in s 4(1)(b) FSA 1986 is defined by s 74 of the Criminal Justice Act 1982 as 'the prescribed sum within the meaning of s 32 of the Magistrates' Courts Act 1980'. See also s 17 CJA 1991.

115 See s 4(2) FSA 1986.

116 Indeed, where any offence under the FSA 1986 is so committed.

proceeded against and punished accordingly.[117] The 'persons' in question include any director, manager, secretary or other similar officer of the body corporate as well as any person purporting to act as such. The list of 'persons' also includes a 'controller' of the company.[118] Where the affairs of a body corporate are managed by its members, such members are treated as directors for the purposes of the attribution set out above in relation to any acts or defaults connected with their functions of management.[119] There is a similar application to partnerships and unincorporated associations.[120]

Civil sanctions for breach

2-34   Section 5 of the Financial Services Act 1986[121] provides for the civil sanction of contract unenforceability where agreements are entered into in the course or as a result of the carrying on of unauthorised investment business. Essentially, in certain circumstances, it may render certain agreements unenforceable against the other party. A further effect is that the investor in question may also be entitled to recover any money or other property paid or transferred by him under the agreement together with compensation for any loss sustained by him as a result of having parted with it.[122] The compensation recoverable will be such as the parties may agree or as the court may determine on the application of either party.[123]

2-35   The two circumstances in which an agreement may be unenforceable are set out in s 5(1)(a) and (b) of the Financial Services Act 1986. The first scenario is where the agreement in question is entered into by a person in the course of carrying on unauthorised investment business.[124] The second is where it is entered into by an authorised or an exempted person in respect of the investment business in the course of which he enters into the agreement but this occurs as a result of anything said or done by a person carrying on unauthorised investment business.[125]

---

117 By virtue of s 202(1) FSA 1986. In relation to the 'consent' necessary, see *Attorney-General's Reference (No 1 of 1995)* [1996] The Times Law Report, 30 January 1996, CA. In considering s 96(1) Banking Act 1987 the necessary *mens rea* for 'consent' was that a defendant would need to be proved to know the material facts which constituted the offence by the body corporate and to have agreed to its conduct in its business on the basis of those facts.

118 Which expression is defined for the purposes of the FSA 1986 by s 207(5) of the Act.

119 See s 202(2) FSA 1986.

120 See s 202(3) and (4).

121 Entitled 'Agreements made by or through unauthorised persons'.

122 See s 5(1) FSA 1986.

123 By virtue of s 5(2) FSA 1986.

124 Section 5(1)(a).

125 Section 5(1)(b)(i) and (ii).

Section 5(7) sets out the agreements to which s 5 applies. They are   **2-36**
any agreements the making or performance of which by the party
seeking to enforce them, or from whom money or other property is
recoverable under s 5, constitutes an activity within paragraphs 12–16 of
Schedule 1 to the Financial Services Act 1986[126] which is not excluded by
any of paragraphs 17–27 of Schedule 1.[127]

The court does, however, have discretion under s 5(3) to allow an   **2-37**
agreement to be enforced despite the conditions in s 5(1) applying, or for
money or property paid or transferred under the agreement to be
retained, if the conditions in s 5(3) are satisfied. Generally speaking, it
will need to be just and equitable for the agreement to be enforced or, as
the case may be, for the money or property paid or transferred under it
to be retained.[128] If the agreement has been entered into by a person in
the course of carrying on unauthorised investment business,[129] s 5(3)
provides that the person so mentioned must have reasonably believed
that his entering into the agreement did not amount to unauthorised
investment business.[130] If the agreement was entered into by an
authorised person but as a result of anything said or done by a person in
the course of carrying on unauthorised investment business,[131] s 5(3)
provides that the authorised person must not know that the agreement
was so entered into.[132]

Section 6 of the Financial Services Act 1986[133] empowers the   **2-38**
Secretary of State[134] to apply for a court order[135] in the event of a
contravention or likely contravention of s 3.[136] The court can order the

---

126 See paragraph 2-26 above, with regard to 'investment activities'.
127 See paragraphs 2-27 and 2-28 above, with regard to 'excluded activities'.
128 See s 5(3)(c) FSA 1986.
129 Which is to say, in the circumstances set out in s 5(1)(a).
130 Section 5(3)(a).
131 Which is to say, in the circumstances set out in s 5(1)(b).
132 Section 5(3)(b).
133 Entitled 'Injunctions and restitution orders'.
134 In practice, this means the Securities and Investments Board.
135 A restitution order or an injunction.
136 Obviously, through the carrying on of unauthorised investment business.

person at fault and anyone else who appears to the court to have been knowingly concerned in the contravention[137] to take steps to restore the

---

137 Which, following *Securities and Investments Board v Pantell SA and Others (No 2)* [1991] 3 WLR at 857, may include any lawyers involved. That case, and its predecessor *Securities and Investments Board v Pantell SA and Another* [1990] 1 Ch at 426, contains important judgments on the statutory rights of action and *locus standi* under the FSA 1986 of the SIB, the chief 'watchdog' of the UK financial services and investment industry. When the FSA 1986 entered the statute book on 7 November 1986, it was clear that when fully operative, following appropriate delegation of authority by the Secretary of State, it would provide the SIB with wide-ranging statutory rights of action through the courts to seek both *ex ante* measures (such as injunctive relief) and *ex post facto* measures (such as restitution orders) for the protection of investors. What was then unclear (before most of the FSA 1986 came into force on 29 April 1988) was the extent to which the SIB would and, indeed, could seek to exercise those rights of action.

The case of *SIB v Pantell SA and Another* [1990] was the first brought under the FSA 1986 and demonstrated the SIB's willingness to use its statutory powers to protect investors. It concerned the activities of a Swiss company, Pantell SA, and its associates and the basic question before the court was whether, by sending advertisements (recommending shares in a particular company) from outside the UK to persons within the UK, the defendants were carrying on unauthorised investment business in the UK and, in doing so, were also acting in contravention of the various promotional restrictions contained in the FSA 1986. These provisions in the FSA 1986 (namely, ss 3 and 57, for instance) were relevant because neither Pantell nor its associates were authorised or exempted for the purposes of the FSA 1986. The Vice-Chancellor took the view that there was a strongly arguable case that the activities of Pantell (in circularising and dealing with customers in the UK) were in breach of s 3 of the FSA 1986 notwithstanding the fact that those activities were conducted from outside the UK.

On that basis, he considered an application by the SIB for a *Mareva* injunction restraining the defendants from dealing with assets in the UK pending final determination by the court of further relief sought by the SIB pursuant to s 6 of the FSA 1986. The *Mareva* injunction was granted: *held* – the statutory right of action conferred on the SIB by s 6 was as much a right of action as any normal common law right of action and that the SIB therefore had sufficient *locus standi* to apply for relief.

The claim against Pantell was subsequently amended to join its solicitors as the third, fourth and fifth defendants, in which it was contended that the solicitors had knowledge of the nature of the business carried on by Pantell, that it was being carried on in contravention of the FSA 1986 and that investors were paying money to Pantell for investment purposes. On that basis, by reason of their knowledge of these matters, it was alleged that the solicitors were 'knowingly concerned' in the various breaches by Pantell and their associates of the FSA 1986 sufficient for the purposes of ss 6(2) and 61(1). In particular, it was said that the solicitors operated a Pantell bank account in the UK, assisted in the distribution of advertisements and also paid cheques from UK investors into that bank account. The SIB sought an order against the solicitors that they should themselves pay such sums as would make good any losses suffered by UK investors, but the solicitors applied to have the claim against them struck out on the basis that, on the true construction of the relevant provisions, the SIB was not entitled to the relief claimed and accordingly the claim disclosed reasonable cause of action.

The case was heard by Sir Nicolas Browne-Wilkinson V-C in *SIB v Pantell SA and Others (No 2)* [1991] who felt that ss 6 and 61 of the FSA 1986 were more than mere machinery enabling the SIB to enforce the individual rights of investors in that they provided for a statutory rescission of unlawful transactions. Under the relevant provisions, the court could order repayment by the person at fault of sums paid to him under the unlawful transaction (whether or not such sums were capable of being identified as a separate fund of money) and the provisions appeared to provide that the same order could be made against a third party 'knowingly concerned'. The words of the provisions were general and contained nothing to limit their effect to identifiable property. *Held*: that, under ss 6(2) and 61(1) of the FSA 1986, the court had jurisdiction to order the solicitors (if they had been 'knowingly concerned' in a relevant contravention by Pantell) to pay to investors any sums paid to Pantell.

parties to the position they were in before the transaction was entered into.[138] The court may also order a wrongdoer to make a payment to any person suffering loss having regard to the profits made as a consequence of the contravention.[139]

Section 61 of the Financial Services Act 1986[140] also provides for court orders where there is a reasonable likelihood[141] that a person will contravene the provisions listed therein[142] or a contravention has already taken place if there is a reasonable likelihood of it being continued or repeated[143] or if there are steps which could be taken for remedying a contravention.[144] It can be seen that there is a degree of overlap between s 61 and s 6.

2-39

SECURITIES LAW

'Securities'

Generally speaking, for these purposes, the expression 'securities' means any shares or debentures and the like which may be issued by a company and either listed[145] or offered to others for purchase or subscription. Until quite recently, the legal regime governing unlisted securities has been far from clear when compared with that applying to listed securities.

2-40

The legislative background

In 1985, most of the legislation governing company law[146] was consolidated in the Companies Act 1985[147] and in three shorter 'satellite' Acts: they were the Business Names Act 1985,[148] the Company Securities (Insider Dealing) Act 1985[149] and the Companies Consolidation

2-41

---

138   See s 6(2) FSA 1986.
139   See s 6(3)–(6).
140   Which is entitled 'Injunctions and restitution orders'.
141   See s 61(1)(a) FSA 1986.
142   Which include ss 47, 56 and 57 FSA 1986 and also SIB and/or SRO Rules.
143   See s 61(1)(b).
144   See s 61(1)(c).
145   Essentially, on the Official List of the Stock Exchange in London.
146   Namely, the Companies Acts 1948–1983.
147   1985 c 6.
148   1985 c 7.
149   1985 c 8.

(Consequential Provisions) Act 1985.[150] The Companies Act 1989[151] which followed made amendments to existing company law and to other intervening legislation[152] and also added certain new provisions. The law governing public issues of securities required a company to issue a prospectus if it wished the public to buy its shares. Further provisions then applied controlling the contents, publication and subsequent registration of that prospectus and this was not changed significantly by the consolidation process outlined above. In the interim, however, EC law had reared its ugly head.

The European dimension

2-42   In 1984, the Stock Exchange (Listing) Regulations 1984,[153] which came into full operation on 1 January 1985, adopted and gave effect as part of UK law to three EC Directives: the Admissions Directive,[154] the Listing Particulars Directive[155] and also the Interim Reports Directive.[156] In combination, these Directives were designed to impose and provide for a minimum and equivalent standard of investor protection throughout the EC and also, it has been said, for greater interpenetration of national securities markets in the EC.

2-43   The Directives were underpinned by the fact that, in Europe, the listing of securities by a stock exchange was regarded as a process separate to and distinct from any offer which was made of them, whether for subscription or for purchase. This distinction[157] was given statutory form in the UK by the Financial Services Act 1986[158] which repealed the Stock Exchange (Listing) Regulations 1984.[159]

The Financial Services Act 1986

2-44   In Parts IV and V, the Financial Services Act 1986 was intended to provide the framework for the regulation of both listed and unlisted

---

150   1985 c 9.

151   1989 c 40.

152   Such as the FSA 1986.

153   SI 1984/716.

154   79/279/EEC.

155   80/390/EEC.

156   82/121/EEC.

157   Between offers for sale of unlisted securities which are not to be the subject of an application for listing on the Stock Exchange and issues of securities which are intended to be admitted to the Official List of the Stock Exchange.

158   1986 c 60.

159   See s 212(3) of and Part II of Schedule 17 FSA 1986.

securities in the UK. The legislative 'chapeau' to that Act provides that it is 'An Act ... to make new provision with respect to the official listing of securities, offers of unlisted securities, takeover offers and insider dealing ...' 'Securities' law would thus be removed from the ambit of the Companies Act 1985.[160] Although the supervision of listing and related matters has continued to be dealt with by the Stock Exchange,[161] Part V of the Financial Services Act 1986[162] never came into force.[163] Initially, the 'prospectus' provisions of the Companies Act 1985 continued to apply to such offers although they were also repealed with effect from 19 June 1995.[164] Part IV[165] has, however, been in force for some time now.

Further consultations and European impositions

During the Spring of 1994, it became apparent that the Treasury[166] was going to consult on an alternative scenario to replace the prospectus provisions of Part III of and Schedule 3 to the Companies Act 1985. Consult they did,[167] highlighting the EC Prospectus Directive[168] as being the main cause of changes required in this area of UK law. That Directive requires a prospectus to be published by an offerer when transferable securities are offered to the public for the first time, provided they have not already been admitted to official listing.[169] It also provides minimum contents requirements for any such prospectus.[170] The purpose of the Directive was to co-ordinate the requirements for the drawing-up, scrutiny and distribution of such prospectuses. Its scope is not however unrestricted. It does not apply to certain types of offer[171] nor to transferable securities of certain types.[172] These parameters directed the

2-45

---

160   1985 c 6. But see Brazier, 'The problem with securities law' (1994) NLJ, 1 April , pp 469–471) in which the author commented that 'To the uninitiated, the statutory framework of "securities" law is ... unclear and is thus potentially misleading to those unaware of its development and current state.'

161   See paragraphs 2-45 to 2-60, below.

162   Which was entitled 'Offers of Unlisted Securities'.

163   And was in fact repealed with effect from 19 June 1995: see paragraph 4 of Schedule 2 to the Public Offers of Securities Regulations 1995 (SI 1995/1537).

164   By virtue of art 2 of the Financial Services Act 1986 (Commencement) (No 13) Order 1995 (SI 1995/1538).

165   Which is entitled 'Official Listing of Securities'.

166   The 'branch' of the government with responsibility for securities law.

167   See HM Treasury, Draft Regulations and Consultation Document, 'Revised Implementation of the EC Prospectus Directive', July 1994.

168   The full title of which is Council Directive of 17 April 1989 coordinating the requirements for the drawing-up, scrutiny and distribution of the prospectus to be published when transferable securities are offered to the public (89/298/EEC).

169   See arts 1 and 4 of 89/298/EEC.

170   See, for instance, Sections II and III of 89/298/EEC, generally.

171   For instance, where transferable securities are offered to persons in the context of their trade, profession or occupation: see art 2.1(a) and art 2.1 generally.

172   For instance, transferable securities offered in connection with a take-over bid or a merger: see art 2.2(d) and (e) and art 2.2 generally.

extent to which the government sought to implement the Directive in the UK through changes to the regime outlined above.[173]

Revised implementation

2-46   Until June 1995, such implementation relied on Part IV of the Financial Services Act 1986 and the Listing Rules of the London Stock Exchange[174] where admission to official listing on the Exchange was sought for the securities offered. For all other offers of securities, the government continued to rely on Part III of the Companies Act 1985, on the Companies Act 1985 (Mutual Recognition of Prospectuses) Regulations 1991,[175] and on corresponding Northern Ireland legislation.

2-47   Initially,[176] the government intended to revise UK prospectus law by completing the repeal of Part III of the Companies Act 1985 and replacing it, in respect of offers of unlisted securities, by detailed regulations made under Part V of the Financial Services Act 1986 which would also reflect the provisions of the Directive.[177] However, the result of responses received in further consultation convinced the government that there might be a more effective way forward than through the proposed use of Part V of the Financial Services Act 1986 which, it was said, would have resulted in an extremely complex set of regulations leading to additional costs for issuers in having to obtain professional advice and would have failed to produce a body of law which was clear and readily enforceable.[178]

The 'more effective way'

2-48   That 'more effective way' reached the statute book in 1995 in the form of four statutory instruments which came into force on 19 June 1995. The Public Offers of Securities Regulations 1995[179] contain detailed provisions concerning prospectuses offering unlisted securities to the public. Made under s 2(2) of the European Communities Act 1972,[180] it also makes certain amendments to the Financial Services Act 1986. These

---

173   In paragraph 2-44.

174   Commonly known as the 'Yellow Book'.

175   SI 1991/823.

176   And see, also, paragraph 2-44, above.

177   Namely, 89/298/EEC. And see, also, the DTI consultative document, 'Listing Particulars and Public Offer Prospectuses – Implementation of Part V of the Financial Services Act 1986 and Related EC Directives' July 1990.

178   See the HM Treasury Consultation Document of July 1994 (cited in Note 167, above) at page 6.

179   SI 1995/1537. And see also the Investment Services Regulations 1995 (SI 1995/3275).

180   1972 c 68.

include amendments to Part IV in relation to listed securities and to s 58 in relation to investment advertisements. Made under s 58 of the Financial Services Act 1986, the Financial Services Act 1986 (Investment Advertisements) (Exemptions) (No 2) Order 1995[181] contains exceptions from the approval requirement otherwise imposed by s 57 of the Financial Services Act 1986 in respect of investment advertisements concerning public offers of securities[182] and also in respect of advertisements required or permitted to be published by exchange or market rules.[183] In combination with the Financial Services Act 1986 (Investment Advertisements) (Exemptions) Order 1995,[184] the 1995 No 2 Order also consolidates and replaces the provisions of the five 'exemptions' orders previously made under s 58 of the Financial Services Act 1986.[185] The fourth of the 1995 statutory instruments, made under s 211 of the Financial Services Act 1986, was the Financial Services Act 1986 (Commencement) (No 13) Order 1995[186] which effectively repealed Part III of and Schedule 3 to the Companies Act 1995.

The statutory framework for listed securities

Part IV of the Financial Services Act 1986 governs listed securities. Generally speaking, it was enacted and brought into force in two stages: certain provisions with effect from 12 January 1987 and the remainder by 16 February 1987.[187] It provides the statutory framework enabling listing rules to be made. It has, however, been amended in certain respects by virtue of the Public Offers of Securities Regulations 1995.[188]

2-49

Prior to the coming into operation of the Stock Exchange (Listing Regulations) 1984,[189] the requirements of the Stock Exchange 'Yellow Book'[190] had no statutory basis. They were simply the private requirements of the Stock Exchange in London, albeit with some statutory consequences. Since Part IV came into force, the requirements of the Yellow Book have been statutory requirements which the Stock Exchange is empowered to make by virtue of s 142(6) of the Financial

2-50

---

181   SI 1995/1536.
182   See Art 14 of SI 1995/1536.
183   See Art 11 of SI 1995/1536.
184   SI 1995/1266.
185   Namely, SIs 1988 316 and 716, 1990 27 and 1992 274 and 813 all of which were revoked. But see note 137 to Chapter 10, above.
186   SI 1995/1538, c 33.
187   See SI 1986/2246. See also SI 1988/740 in relation to parts of s 154 FSA 1986.
188   See reg 17 and Schedule 2 to the Public Offers of Securities Regulations 1995.
189   SI 1984/716.
190   Containing 'the Listing Rules'.

Services Act 1986.[191] Where any action is to be taken with regard to listed securities or securities which are to be listed, the requirements of Part IV of the Financial Services Act 1986 and of the Yellow Book must be complied with.

2-51   Generally speaking, the requirements vary according to what is intended, the nature of the issuer and the nature of the proposed issue of securities. Where an application for admission to the Official List has been made, in respect of securities which are to be offered to the public in the UK for the first time before admission, publication of a prospectus will be required and that prospectus will require the approval of the Stock Exchange.[192] Other securities of a company, for which official listing in the UK is sought, require listing particulars to be approved by the Stock Exchange and published in accordance with the publication requirements of the Yellow Book.[193] In achieving that end, they need to comply with the contents provisions of the Yellow Book which are designed to ensure that listing particulars[194] present a fair and accurate picture of the securities they describe. Listing particulars are roughly equivalent to the prospectus and the purpose of the two documents is similar.

2-52   That is to say, such documents should provide potential investors with sufficient information to enable them to come to an informed decision as to whether or not to invest. A prospectus will normally make an offer or extend an invitation to treat in respect of securities and will, perhaps more obviously, be more of a marketing document than listing particulars. Previously, it was harder to generalise on this because, for instance, a document offering securities in connection with an application for listing might be described as a 'prospectus' and yet contain 'listing particulars'.

2-53   Until approved by the Stock Exchange, neither listing particulars nor a prospectus must be published. Contravention by a person who is not an authorised person for the purposes of the Financial Services Act 1986 can amount to a criminal offence by virtue of s 154 of the Financial

---

191   Section 142 (entitled 'Official listing') contains some general and clarificatory provisions relating to Part IV of the FSA 1986. Section 142(6) provides that 'The International Stock Exchange of the United Kingdom and the Republic of Ireland Limited ... may make rules (in this Act referred to as "listing rules") for the purposes of any of the following provisions'. With effect from 8 December 1995, the Irish Stock Exchange separated from the London Stock Exchange. The registered company name for the latter is now the London Stock Exchange Limited.

192   See s 144(2) FSA 1986, inserted by reg 17 and paragraph 2 of Schedule 2 to the Public Offers of Securities Regulations 1995. Whether securities are being offered to the public in the UK is to be determined in accordance with Schedule 11A FSA 1986, inserted by virtue of reg 17, paragraph 3(2) of Schedule 2 and Schedule 3 POS Regulations 1995.

193   See s 144(2A) FSA 1986, also inserted by reg 17 and paragraph 2 of Schedule 2 POS Regulations 1995.

194   And prospectuses required by s 144(2) FSA 1986.

Services Act 1986,[195] but not s 57.[196] This is because s 58(1)(d) of the Financial Services Act 1986 provides that the general restriction on investment advertisements contained in s 57 does not apply to advertisements governed by s 154 or which consist of or any part of listing particulars, supplementary listing particulars, prospectuses, supplementary prospectuses or any other document required or permitted to be published by the Yellow Book.[197] The Yellow Book provides that s 154 applies (but only when listing particulars etc are or are to be issued) to formal notices, offer notices, mini-prospectuses and other advertisements for the purpose of announcing the admission of securities to listing or which are required to be issued in order to obtain listing. It does not cover, for instance, press releases or draft listing particulars nor does it apply to pathfinder listing particulars.

As the kind of documents to which s 154 does not apply (such as press **2-54** releases, draft listing particulars or pathfinder listing particulars) are likely to be investment advertisements,[198] s 57 of the Financial Services Act 1986 will be applicable to them unless one of the exceptions applies. For instance, proofs and pathfinder or draft listing particulars may be excepted by virtue of s 58(1)(d)(ii) of the Financial Services Act 1986[199] if they are specifically permitted to be published by the Yellow Book. They may also be excepted if article 11 of SI 1995/1266 applies to them[200] or if Articles 8 to 10 of SI 1995/1536 apply.[201] Otherwise, s 57 will apply and the advertisements in question will need to be issued or approved by an authorised person or a criminal offence will be committed.

Where listing rules require the publication of a prospectus,[202] it is not **2-55** lawful to offer the securities in question to the public in the UK before

---

195 Entitled 'Advertisements etc in connection with listing applications'. Extended by s 154A FSA 1986, inserted by reg 17 and paragraph 2 Schedule 2 POS Regulations 1995.

196 Section 57 FSA 1986 contains restrictions on issuing, or causing to be issued, 'investment advertisements' in the UK. Essentially, it introduced an approval requirement. Section 57(1) provides that they must either be issued by an authorised person or, alternatively, their contents must be approved by an authorised person before they may be issued. Section 57(3) provides that breach of s 57 may result in the commission of a criminal offence. 'Investment advertisements' are defined by s 57(2).

197 Section 58(1)(d)(ii) FSA 1986 was extended to prospectuses etc by reg 17 and paragraphs 5 and 6 Schedule 2 POS Regulations 1995.

198 Because they will contain information likely to lead people to make an investment. See s 57(2) further.

199 As amended; see note 197 above. That section contains 'Exceptions from restrictions on advertising'.

200 Generally speaking, if they are issued by an unauthorised person to persons sufficiently expert to understand the risks involved.

201 If the document in question may reasonably be regarded as being directed only at informing or influencing certain persons.

202 By virtue of s 144(2) FSA 1986, inserted by reg 17 and paragraph 2(1) Schedule2 POS Regulations 1995.

the time of publication of the prospectus.[203] Contravention by a person who is not an authorised person for the purposes of the Financial Services Act 1986 can amount to a criminal offence.[204] Also, any such contravention may be actionable at the suit of a person suffering loss as a result, subject to the defences applicable to actions for breach of statutory duty.[205]

2-56   One further point to be noted in this context is that s 47 of the Financial Services Act 1986[206] is generally applicable and can therefore apply to documents, and the like, issued pursuant to Part IV of the Financial Services Act 1986. Section 47 imposes criminal sanctions in respect of misleading statements and practices.

2-57   The provisions governing who is responsible for listing particulars, supplementary listing particulars, prospectuses and supplementary prospectuses,[207] and relating to the compensation of investors,[208] are also contained in Part IV of the Financial Services Act 1986. It should be noted that these provisions apply in relation to prospectuses and supplementary prospectuses as they do in relation to listing particulars.[209]

2-58   Section 152 lists five categories of person responsible for listing particulars or prospectuses. These include the issuer of the securities to which the document relates.[210] Where the issuer is a body corporate, they include each person who is a director of that body at the time the document is submitted to the Stock Exchange and also each person who has authorised himself to be named, and is named, in the document as a director or as having agreed to become a director of that body either immediately or at a future time. Also regarded as responsible are any persons who accept and are stated in the document as accepting responsibility for (or for any part of) the document and each person not falling within any of the above categories who has authorised the contents of (or any part of) the document.

2-59   Section 150 of the Financial Services Act 1986 then sets out the basis for compensation of an investor who has acquired securities. It provides

---

203   See s 156B(1) FSA 1986, inserted by reg 17 and paragraph 2(4) Schedule 2 POS Regulations 1995.

204   By virtue of s 156B(3) FSA 1986.

205   See s 156B(5) FSA 1986 and cf s 62 FSA 1986 further.

206   Section 47 is entitled 'Misleading statements and practices'. See Chapter 10 of this book, further.

207   See s 152 ('Persons responsible for particulars').

208   See ss 150 and 151.

209   By virtue of s 154A FSA 1986, inserted by reg 17 and paragraph 2(3) Schedule 2 POS Regulations 1995.

210   And for these purposes, 'issuer' is taken as including a reference to the person offering or proposing to offer the securities in question. See s 154A(b) FSA 1986, inserted by reg 17 and paragraph 2(3) Schedule 2 POS Regulations 1995.

that the person or persons responsible for the relevant listing particulars or prospectus shall be liable to pay compensation to any person who has acquired any of the securities and has suffered loss in respect of them as a result of any untrue or misleading statement in or omission from that document of anything required to be included by virtue of ss 146 or 147 of the Financial Services Act 1986.[211] Section 150 is expressly stated not to affect any liability which any person may incur apart from s 150.[212]

Section 151 of the Financial Services Act 1986[213] contains certain 'defences' to any liability to pay compensation on the basis of s 150.   **2-60**

Section 151(1) provides that a person will not incur any liability under s 150(1) for any loss in respect of securities caused by a statement or omission if he satisfies the court that, at the time when the document in question was submitted to the Stock Exchange, he reasonably believed (having made such enquiries, if any, as were reasonable) that the statement was true and not misleading or that the matter whose omission caused the loss was properly omitted and: **2-61**

- that he continued in that belief until the time when the securities were acquired;[214] or
- that they were acquired before it was reasonably practicable to bring a correction to the attention of persons likely to acquire the securities in question;[215] or
- that before the securities were acquired he had taken all such steps as it was reasonable for him to have taken to secure that a correction was brought to the attention of those persons;[216] or
- that he continued in that belief until after the commencement of dealings in the securities following their admission to the Official List and that the securities were acquired after such a lapse of time that he ought in the circumstances to be reasonably excused.[217]

Section 151(2) provides that a person shall incur no liability under s 150(1) for any loss in respect of securities caused by a statement purporting to be made by or on the authority of another person as an expert which is (and is stated to be) included in the document with the consent of that 'expert'. The person in question must, however, satisfy   **2-62**

---

211 See s 150(1) FSA 1986.
212 See s 150(4).
213 Section 151 is entitled 'Exemption from liability to pay compensation'.
214 Section 151(1)(a).
215 Section 151(1)(b).
216 Section 151(1)(c).
217 Section 151(1)(d).

the court that, at the time when the particulars were submitted to the Stock Exchange, he believed on reasonable grounds that the 'expert' was competent to make or authorise the statement and had consented to its inclusion in the form and context in which it was included and:

- that he continued in that belief until the time when the securities were acquired;[218] or

- that they were acquired before it was reasonably practicable to bring the fact that the expert was not competent or had not consented to the attention of persons likely to acquire the securities in question;[219] or

- that before the securities were acquired he had taken all such steps as it was reasonable for him to have taken to secure that that fact was brought to the attention of those persons forthwith;[220] or

- that he continued in that belief until after the commencement of dealings in the securities following their admission to the Official List and that the securities were acquired after such a lapse of time that he ought in the circumstances to be reasonably excused.[221]

2-63   For these purposes, an 'expert' is taken to include any engineer, valuer, accountant or other person whose profession, qualifications or experience give authority to a statement made by him.[222]

2-64   Section 151(3) provides (without prejudice to s 151(1) and (2)) that a person shall not incur any liability under s 150(1) for any loss in respect of any securities caused by any such statement or omission (as is mentioned in that section) if he satisfies the court that before the securities were acquired a correction (or, if appropriate, the fact that the expert was not competent or had not consented) had been published in a manner calculated to bring it to the attention of persons likely to acquire the securities in question[223] or that he took all such steps as it was reasonable for him to take to secure such publication and reasonably believed that it had taken place before the securities were acquired.[224]

2-65   There are three other 'exemptions' from liability otherwise incurred as a result of s 150 which are set out in s 151. They are as follows:

- A person shall not incur any liability under s 150(1) for any loss resulting from a statement made by an official person or contained in

---

218   Section 151(2)(a) FSA 1986.
219   Section 151(2)(b).
220   Section 151(2)(c).
221   Section 151(2)(d).
222   See s 151(7).
223   Section 151(3)(a).
224   Section 151(3)(b).

a public official document which is included in the document in question if he satisfies the court that the statement is accurately and fairly reproduced.[225]

- A person shall not incur any liability under s 150(1) or (3) if he satisfies the court that the person suffering the loss acquired the securities in question with knowledge that the statement was false or misleading, with knowledge of the omitted matter or of the change or the new matter (as the case may be).[226]

- A person shall not incur any liability under s 150(3) if he satisfies the court that he reasonably believed that the change or new matter in question was not such as to call for supplementary listing particulars or a supplementary prospectus.[227]

The statutory framework for unlisted securities

Until recently,[228] the public offer made only in the UK of unlisted securities for which official listing in the UK was not sought was governed by the 'prospectus' provisions of Part III of, and Schedule 3 to, the Companies Act 1985.[229] The intention was that public offers of unlisted securities which were not to be subject to an application for listing would be governed by Part V of the Financial Services Act 1986 when that Part V was brought into force. However, much time elapsed after the Financial Services Act 1986 entered the statute book[230] and Part V was finally repealed.[231]

2-66

Such offers are now subject to the Public Offers of Securities Regulations 1995[232] if no public offer or application for official listing is being made in any other EU Member State on the basis of the UK prospectus. For these purposes, a person is regarded as offering securities to the public in the UK if, to the extent that the offer is made to persons in the UK, it is made to the public and, for this purpose, an offer to any section of the public[233] is to be regarded as made to the public.[234] A person 'offers'

2-67

---

225   Section 151(4) FSA 1986.

226   Section 151(5).

227   Section 151(6).

228   19 June 1995.

229   1985 c 6.

230   On 7 November 1986.

231   With effect from 19 June 1995. By virtue of art 2 of SI 1995/1538.

232   SI 1995/1537. And see Investment Services Regulations 1995 (SI 1995/3275).

233   Whether selected as members or debenture holders of a body corporate or as clients of the person making the offer or in any other manner.

234   See reg 6 POS Regulations 1995.

securities if, as principal, he makes an offer which, if accepted, would give rise to a contract for the issue or sale of the securities[235] or if he invites a person to make such an offer, but not otherwise.[236]

2-68   Where securities which are not admitted to official listing and are not the subject of an application for listing[237] are offered to the public in the UK for the first time, the offerer must publish a prospectus[238] but before doing so must deliver a copy of it to the registrar of companies for registration.[239] The securities to which the Public Offers of Securities Regulations 1995 apply, in this context, are any investments falling within paragraphs 1, 2, 4 or 5 of Schedule 1 to the Financial Services Act 1986 which have not been admitted to official listing and are not the subject of an application for listing.[240] No advertisement, notice, poster or document[241] announcing a public offer of securities for which a prospectus is required by virtue of these provisions shall be issued or caused to be issued to the public in the UK by the person proposing to make the offer unless it states that a prospectus has or will be published and gives an address in the UK from which it can be obtained or will be obtainable.[242]

2-69   Regulation 13 of the Public Offers of Securities Regulations 1995 lists the categories of person responsible for a prospectus or supplementary prospectus. Primarily responsible will be the issuer of the securities to which the prospectus or supplementary prospectus relates.[243] Where the issuer is a body corporate, each person who is a director of that body corporate at the time when the prospectus or supplementary prospectus is published will be responsible[244] as will each person who has authorised himself to be named[245] in the prospectus or supplementary prospectus as a director or as having agreed to become a director of that body either immediately or at a future time.[246] Others responsible include the offerer of the securities, where he is not the issuer.[247] There

---

235   By him or by another person with whom he has made arrangements for the issue or sale of the securities.

236   See reg 5(a) and (b) POS Regulations 1995.

237   In accordance with Part IV FSA 1986.

238   Which complies, generally speaking, with reg 8 and Schedule 1 POS Regulations 1995.

239   See reg 4(1) and (2) POS Regulations 1995.

240   See reg 3 POS Regulations 1995.

241   Other than a prospectus.

242   See reg 12 POS Regulations 1995.

243   Reg 13(1)(a) POS Regulations 1995.

244   Reg 13(1)(b) POS Regulations 1995.

245   And is named.

246   Reg 13(1)(c) POS Regulations 1995.

247   Reg 13(1)(e) POS Regulations 1995. And see reg 13(1)(d) and (f)–(g) for the other categories of person responsible for the prospectus or supplementary prospectus.

are also provisions governing the payment of compensation for a false or misleading prospectus.[248]

A prospectus or supplementary prospectus prepared in accordance with the provisions outlined above[249] will be excluded from the approval requirement of s 57 of the Financial Services Act 1986 by article 14 of SI 1995/1536 which effectively replaced the previous exemption for prospectuses required by Part III of the Companies Act 1985 which was 'tucked away' in paragraph 8 of Schedule 15 to the Financial Services Act 1986. Article 14 provides that s 57 does not apply to an investment advertisement which is a prospectus or supplementary prospectus issued in accordance with Part II of the Public Offers of Securities Regulations 1995.

2-70

Mutual recognition

There may be circumstances in which an issuer of securities making a public offer within the scope of the Prospectus Directive,[250] but not seeking official listing in the UK, may wish to use the UK prospectus for marketing securities or to obtain official listing in another EC Member State. Depending on the circumstances of such a case, it may be possible for that issuer to take advantage of mutual recognition provisions in the Listing Particulars Directive[251] or the Prospectus Directive[252] enabling such use although the prospectus will then be regulated through 'pre-vetting' under Part IV of the Financial Services Act 1986[253] and the Yellow Book rather than by compliance with the Public Offers of Securities Regulations 1995. The publication of such a prospectus will be excluded from the approval requirement of s 57 of the Financial Services Act 1986 by s 58(1)(d)(ii) of the Financial Services Act 1986.

2-71

---

248 See regs 14-15 POS Regulations 1995. And see, also, *Possfund Custodian Trustee Ltd and Another v Diamond and Others* [1996] 2 All ER 774 and Times Law Report, 18 April 1996, Ch D, in which the question as to whether those responsible for the issue of a prospectus owed a duty of care to subsequent purchasers of the shares in question in the market was considered. Mr Justice Lightman took the view that, if the purpose of the prospectus was also that of informing and encouraging subsequent purchasers and this was established, it was arguable that a duty of care was owed to those purchasers.

249 See paragraphs 2-66 to 2-69, above.

250 89/298/EEC.

251 80/390/EEC.

252 89/298/EEC. See, for instance, art 21 entitled 'Mutual recognition'.

253 See, generally, s 156A FSA 1986, inserted by Schedule 2 paragraph 2(4) POS Regulations 1995.

Other offers of securities

2-72 There may be other offers of securities for which official listing is not sought which may not amount to public offers.[254] The Public Offers of Securities Regulations 1995 will not be applicable to such offers. Instead, as any marketing documents relating to such securities will inevitably be inviting persons to acquire them, they will be investment advertisements[255] and subject to the approval requirement of s 57 of the Financial Services Act 1986 and any relevant exemptions from that requirement contained in or provided by virtue of s 58 of that Act.[256]

THE 'POLITICS' OF REGULATION

2-73 'Politics' is an emotive word.[257] Its use introduces other concepts such as the acquisition and then maintenance of power by a state government. Ideally, these matters should have no place in determining effective policy in relation to protecting the interests of the investing public. But that would be naive to hope for in real life. Politics, and its conceptual baggage, has intruded into the education of our children, the level of 'state' assistance given to the poor and into the healing and general care of our sick; in fact, into every area where votes are to be won and lost because, at the end of the day, in a democracy the level of votes determines where the power to govern resides, albeit until the next relevant election.

2-74 On that basis, in coming to political decisions, governments are usually pragmatic. They may need to compromise between what common-sense and good advice dictates should be done and what may affect votes. For instance, in regulating the 'City', successive Conservative governments have usually taken care not to alienate their traditional corporate supporters. In risk-prone areas, such as banking and financial services, governments may also deem it prudent to distance themselves from direct daily involvement in the regulation and supervision of what

---

254   Such as where securities are offered to more than fifty persons or to persons in the context of their trades, professions or occupations: see reg 7(2)(a) and (b) POS Regulations 1995 and reg 7 generally for offers of securities which are deemed not to be offers to the public.

255   See s 57(2) FSA 1986.

256   In particular, see SIs 1995 1266 and 1536.

257   It is defined by the *Oxford English Dictionary* (New Compact Edition, 1991) as being 'the science and art of government'. For some background reading, see Professor JAG Griffith, *The Politics of the Judiciary* (Fontana). Also Anthony Sampson, *The Changing Anatomy of Britain* (1981). For more contemporary comment, see Simon Jenkins, *Accountable to None – the Tory Nationalisation of Britain* (Penguin).

is done. The history of financial services and securities regulation UK illustrates aspects of those political 'devices'.

Such regulation has, in fact, advanced over the years in a relatively haphazard fashion. In the years preceding enactment of the Financial Services Act 1986, there was no comprehensive regulation of the financial services and securities industry as it affected investors. Instead, there was a combination of piecemeal statutory intervention[258] and a measure of industry self-regulation.[259] There was no central agency with overall and independent control over the investment sector.[260] In the early 1980s, however, rapidly developing investment markets, the desired harmonisation of the relevant laws of EU Member States and a number of scandals in the investment sector led to calls for a comprehensive review of the law on investor protection. For once, the government agreed.

2-75

The review was carried out by Professor LCB Gower who recommended a widescale overhaul of the regulatory regime. Although initially favouring the creation of a central agency, the 'Gower' recommendations were essentially for a comprehensive system of regulation to enhance investor protection within a statutory framework based as far as possible on self-regulation but subject to a measure of 'governmental' supervision and intervention. They were largely accepted and the Financial Services Bill was published in December 1985. Although the subject of intensive lobbying by interested parties, the Bill remained essentially intact and led to the Financial Services Act 1986 which received the royal assent on 7 November 1986. This is the Act which provides the statutory framework for regulation of the financial services industry in the UK.

2-76

That framework is, however, a classic example of how, over recent years, the government has sought to organise yet distance itself from quasi-governmental public bodies and institutions whilst retaining a very real measure of control over their basic policies and day-to-day activities. The Financial Services Act 1986 contained many powers exercisable by the relevant Secretary of State. But many such functions were delegated to the Securities and Investments Board, which became the chief investment industry 'watchdog' in the UK. One of the main functions of the SIB is to 'recognise' and then supervise bodies[261] which may admit persons to membership thereby authorising them to conduct investment business in the UK. Such members are then subject to the rules of the body in question governing the conduct of investment

2-77

---

258 The main example being the Prevention of Fraud (Investments) Act 1958 and its system of 'licensed dealers'.

259 For instance, by the London Stock Exchange.

260 In contrast, for example, to the Securities and Exchange Commission in the USA.

261 Such as self-regulating organisations or 'SROs'.

business and related matters. The 'chain' of control, however, stretches back and up to the Secretary of State and to the government. The rationale for this 'hands-off' approach to regulation by the government can easily be the subject of cynical speculation. If something slips through the regulatory net,[262] there are many intervening stages, bodies and individuals before the 'buck' has finally to stop with the government.

2-78   The same apparently muddled yet probably deliberate approach exists in relation to insider dealing in the UK. There is no one body with overall responsibility for all aspects of its regulation. The London Stock Exchange continues to maintain an effective monitoring role over securities trading. Yet it is HM Treasury which is responsible for insider dealing 'policy' issues and the DTI which formally investigates and prosecutes alleged instances of the offence. Over the years since insider dealing first became a criminal offence in the UK in 1980, this division of labour and responsibility has surely contributed to the fact that the relevant legislation has not been enforced with any conspicuous success. Since 1980, over one hundred cases are said to have been reported to the DTI by the Stock Exchange. Yet only 50 or so have resulted in prosecution and only 25 or so have produced a conviction.

2-79   The problem[263] is likely only to have been aggravated by the recent practice of the DTI[264] in passing cases of alleged insider dealing on to the Securities and Futures Authority[265] for further investigation and action. Although the SFA has wide powers in respect of its member firms and their employees,[266] and could effectively prevent wrongdoers from working in the UK securities industry, this expansion of its role merely adds to the existing confusion. It is also a tacit admission by the DTI that the cases passed to the SFA might not produce a conviction if prosecuted through the criminal courts and that the legislative regime in respect of insider dealing, as it presently stands, is therefore not effective.

2-80   There are many advantages in involving professional market regulators more directly in the fight against insider dealing. They are much more likely to be aware of market participants and of new market

---

262   For instance, the activities of a businessman plundering the pension funds of his company. And see 'Accountable to nobody' by Simon Jenkins in *The Times*, 15 May 1996 for a devastating critique of governmental policy and regulatory practice in relation to the public utilities: compare and contrast.

263   Outlined in paragraph 2-78, above.

264   As reported in *The Times* Business News of 14 August 1995 (see 'SFA steps up war against insider deals' by Jon Ashworth) at p 40.

265   Which is the self-regulating organisation which regulates securities business (which amounts to investment business) under the aegis of the Financial Services Act 1986.

266   See Chapter 9 below, further.

practices. It is, however, questionable whether the SFA is the best regulator for this job. Those involved in monitoring securities trading at the London Stock Exchange have much more experience in identifying insider dealing. If professional regulators are to have a more significant role to play, it would make considerable sense to centralise the regulation of insider dealing in the UK and to charge the Stock Exchange with investigating and prosecuting as well as regulating and continuing to monitor potential insider dealing. Given the necessary independence and effective funding, it would also be sufficiently 'distant' from the government not to spoil the essentially 'hands-off' approach which has been adopted to the administration of government and regulation generally. It remains to be seen whether the centralisation of financial services, banking and also insurance regulation will figure high on the actual agenda of any new government.[267]

---

267 See 'Why the Mafia cannot regulate the Mafia' by Melvin Marckus, *The Times*, 15 January 1994 and 'Financial watchdogs need more bite with their bark' by Robert Miller, *The Times*, 14 March 1995, in relation to the Smith Report on financial services regulation in the UK published on behalf of the Treasury and Civil Service Select Committee of the House of Commons. See also 'Exchange could lose watchdog powers' by Robert Miller, *The Times*, 14 March 1996, which reported the suggested creation of a new Trading and Markets Authority to centralise much of 'City' regulation. Specific regulatory proposals favoured by the Labour Party at the present time include:(1) the introduction of a new Financial Services Act (so improvements can be made to the existing system); (2) making the SIB directly responsible for financial services regulation (retaining its present position without importing US-style SEC characteristics) to reduce the present multiplicity of regulations (and remove the fiction of 'self-regulation'); (3) the possibility of setting up a new body to be responsible for market surveillance; and (4) giving regulators greater powers over insider dealing. These points (and many others) were made by Labour's City Spokesman, Alistair Darling MP, in a conference speech to the ABI delivered on 8 May 1996. For more general comments on the style which might be adopted by a new Labour government, in relation to corporate development, see 'Labour begins to show how it means business' by Philip Bassett, *The Times*, 18 June 1996. This outlines the current thinking of the party and is based upon a party document entitled 'A new industrial Policy for Britain'. For a reaffirmation of the present Conservative government, see House of Commons Official Report, 20 December 1994, at columns 1593–96 (*per* Mr Anthony Nelson MP, Minister of State, Treasury).

CHAPTER 3

WHAT IS INSIDER DEALING?

INTRODUCTION

Press notoriety

If a straw poll was taken involving those reasonable men and women on the Clapham omnibus, most (if not all) of them would have some idea of what constitutes 'insider dealing'. Putting to one side the fact that insider dealing seems to have been a problem from the earliest days of the share 'market' which became the London Stock Exchange,[1] the notoriety this practice enjoys is probably due to the fact that at periodic intervals over the years, cases of alleged insider dealing have been reported in lurid fashion in the press.[2] It is unfortunate that subsequent

---

1   See para 1-41, above, for mention of insider dealing in the early days of the share and stock market which subsequently became the Stock Exchange in London.

2   For an example of restrained and informative comment, see 'A case to answer at Caradon', *The Times*, 19 January 1996, in relation to trading in shares of Caradon in September 1995. See also 'Insider alert after heavy trade in Blenheim shares' by John Nissé, *The Times*, 1 July 1996. Other cases of alleged or implied insider dealing reported or referred to in the press over recent years have included the following:

(a)   In May 1993, there may have been insider dealing in the shares of Tiphook (the container and trailer leasing transport group) two days before a profits warning was issued which sent its shares into what *The Times* reported on 8 May 1993 as being '... a nosedive'. The incident prompted Paul Myners, the Chairman of Gartmore Investment Management, to call (in a letter to the *Financial Times*) for a more robust approach to the investigation and prosecution of insider dealing in the City. The Surveillance Unit of the Stock Exchange was believed to have investigated the price movement and to have concluded that the price fall was in line with the transport sector as a whole. Shares in Tiphook had been the subject of 'bear raids' in the past whereby speculators attempted to drive their price downwards to make a profit by selling shares short.

(b)   In January 1994, Hogg Group (the insurance broker) became the subject of alleged insider dealing when heavy trading in its shares preceded a profits warning, the second such warning issued by Hogg in four months or so. Apparently, three million Hogg shares changed hands on one day just before the warning was issued when normal trading levels in Hogg shares were between 100,000 and 250,000 shares. Generally speaking, trading statements and profits warnings are thought to be a useful way in which companies can keep the market up-to-date about their progress. The problem, however, is where potential 'insiders' are able to make use of that information before it becomes 'public' knowledge.

(c)   In April 1994, there had been heavy trading for almost a month in both the ordinary shares and other securities of LASMO, the indebted oil company. This trading took place in the context of market rumours that a takeover bid was ...

reports of successful prosecutions have been much thinner on the ground and perhaps that is as telling a comment as any on the question of whether insider dealing is readily enforceable as a criminal offence. Insider dealing is, however, a known quantity.

THE MISCHIEF OF INSIDER DEALING

A general definition

3-02   A very generalised attempt at defining the criminal offence of 'insider dealing' would be along the following lines; a case of insider dealing in securities will usually involve the buying or selling of certain securities relating to a company by a person connected with that company[3] who, in doing so, is in possession of specific information which relates to those securities and is not generally known but which would be likely, if made public, to have a significant effect on the market price of the securities. There have, of course, been closely worded statutory definitions.[4] The mischief which insider dealing law is aimed at preventing, however, is clear. Those close to a company must not be allowed to abuse their position by making use of information in their possession, which concerns securities of that company, to some personal advantage.

2[cont] about to be made for LASMO. In fact, those rumours and the trading which occurred led the Takeover Panel to demand a statement from the stake-builder and prospective bidder which revealed itself to be Enterprise Oil which admitted that it was considering making a bid for LASMO. The internecine struggle which followed was interesting to say the least. Enterprise did not offer cash for LASMO. Instead, it offered 'junk', a package consisting of convertible 'A' shares with minimal dividend rights together with a batch of speculative warrants. LASMO retaliated by criticising the accounting policies used by Enterprise which led the Takeover Panel to rule that LASMO should refrain from repeating its allegation that Enterprise was in breach of UK accounting standards.

(d) In May 1994, the share price of Portals group (the bank note printer) jumped from 44p to 679p on one day, a Tuesday. On the following Friday, the Takeover Panel elicited a statement from the company that it was actually in bid talks with De La Rue. The share price promptly jumped another 99p. The buying of shares in Portals was believed to have been carried out by persons termed 'small fringe brokers' although on whose behalf it was not known and could only be guessed at.

3 Such as a director, shareholder, employee or professional adviser. But see 'City has the last word on insider dealing' by Paul Ham, *The Sunday Times*, 18 June 1995, which argues that 'small' private investors are more likely to be caught insider dealing than 'City' professionals.

4 See, for historical interest, ss 9–13 and then ss 1 and 2 of the Company Securities (Insider Dealing) Act 1985 (1985 c 8). The latest will be explored in Chapter 5.

Some basic examples of insider dealing

A realistic hypothetical scenario in which insider dealing could occur   **3-03**
might involve a director of a merchant bank advising a company in the
process of mounting a takeover of another company. The fact of the
announcement of a takeover offer[5] could well have an immediate effect
in pushing up the value of shares in the target company and perhaps
also in the bidding company. If the merchant banker in question had
acquired some of those shares in advance of the bid announcement, at
the pre-bid price, he would be indulging in a spot of insider dealing if he
disposed of them following the announcement of the bid.[6]

Another scenario might involve the imminent announcement by a   **3-04**
company of a particularly profitable year. Such news is likely to force up
the market value of shares in the company, making them more
expensive to acquire but also more profitable to sell. Conversely, the
news may relate to the fact of an imminent profits warning by a
company which would normally have the effect of reducing the value of
its securities, making them cheaper to acquire but also less valuable to
sell. In either scenario, a shareholder in possession of this information
(such as a director of the company) may be tempted to take advantage of
it (whether, as the case may be, by buying some more or selling existing

---

5   Through the posting of a bid.
6   Some prosecutions involving facts similar to this hypothetical scenario include
     the case of *R v Titheridge & Titheridge* (1983) unreported, but see (1983) 4 Co Law
     117. In that case, a company called Joseph Stocks & Sons (Holdings) Limited was
     the object of a takeover bid. Mrs Titheridge was secretary to the chairman of the
     merchant bank which was advising the bidding company. She passed
     information to her husband who dealt in securities of Joseph Stocks in December
     1980. Both Mr and Mrs Titheridge pleaded guilty to insider dealing and were
     convicted. They were each ordered to pay a £4,000 fine. Another related case
     which resulted in prosecution was *R v Jenkins* (1987) unreported but see, for
     instance,'Fine for insider dealer', *The Guardian*, 18 July 1987. In that case the
     private secretary to the chairman of British and Commonwealth Shipping plc
     dealt and attempted to deal on the basis of information which was not at the
     relevant times available to the public. On one occasion, the information related to
     a potential bid for another company; on the other occasion, it related to internal
     management changes at British and Commonwealth Shipping plc. The offences
     both occurred in the Autumn of 1986. The defendant pleaded guilty to both
     charges and was fined £10,000. He was also ordered to pay the sum of £2,000 in
     costs. See also *R v Morrisey & Staines* (1994) unreported but see 'Two accountants
     fined £1,500 each for insider dealing', *The Times*, 18 January 1984. See also para 1-
     02 above. A final example along the above lines may be found in the case of *R v
     Robinson & Robinson* (1987) unreported (but see Ashe and Counsell, 'Insider
     Trading – The Tangled Web' (1990), Fourmat Publishing (at 22) where Mr
     Robinson received information about a potential takeover bid for Mercantile
     House Holdings plc from his brother-in-law who was chairman of that company.
     Robinson then acquired 5,000 shares in Mercantile House in January 1987. He
     pleaded guilty to insider dealing and was fined £1,000.

securities), either to protect or augment the existing value of his holding.[7]

3-05   There are, of course, many other matters capable of having an effect on the share price of a company. A pharmaceutical company might discover a vaccine against the virus (or viruses) causing AIDS or perhaps a cure for cancer. A mining company might discover precious metals or oil on recently acquired land. The pension funds of a group of companies may have been pilfered by directors to shore-up the failing businesses of the group. All or any of these scenarios may have an effect on the price or value of related securities.

Some cases of insider dealing

3-06   One of the best-known cases of insider dealing in the UK concerned an adviser to a company involved in a takeover.[8] That adviser was a man called Geoffrey Collier who was then head of securities at City of London finance house Morgan Grenfell which had been retained by a client to advise on a takeover bid. When the bid was about to be launched, in the autumn of 1986, Mr Collier arranged the acquisition in London on his own behalf of shares of the target company. He did so through a company registered in the Cayman Islands prior to the announcement of the bid and was subsequently convicted on pleading guilty to insider dealing, his prison sentence of 12 months being suspended for two years. He was fined £25,000, ordered to pay £7,000 in costs and was subsequently also expelled from membership of the London Stock Exchange. Apparently, he only stood to profit in the amount of £15,000 as a result of what he did.

3-07   A further example achieved greater notoriety. It involved Ivan Boesky, who worked as a risk arbitrageur in the US. Risk arbitrageurs became prevalent in the 1980s. They would acquire holdings of shares in companies

---

7   Some prosecutions involving facts similar to these scenarios include the case of *R v Reardon-Smith* (1985) unreported who was a director of a company about to go into liquidation. Just before that stage, in May 1985, Reardon-Smith sold shares in the company. He pleaded guilty to insider dealing and was fined £3,000. Another similar case was *R v Cross* [1991] BCLC 125 CA, [1990] 91 Cr App R 115 CA. Mr Cross had been managing director of Wordplex plc but sold shares in that company shortly before a new issue of shares had the effect of bringing down their price. Initially, he was convicted of insider dealing and fined £7,000. On appeal, however, that conviction was quashed. And see 'When is share dealing criminal?'(1991) 12(18) Co L Dig 156.

8   See the case of *R v Collier* (1987), unreported but see 'Collier's Rise and Fall', *The Independent*, 2 July 1987. In that case the offences in question were committed in October and November 1986. In proceedings brought in the USA by the SEC, Mr Collier admitted the charges laid against him and consented to the issue of permanent injunctions under s 10(b) and r 10b-5 of the Securities Exchange Act 1934. See also 'Bang goes a Scandal', *Sunday Times*, 16 November 1986 and 'Mischief that may stop the Markets Heart', *Financial Times*, 2 July 1987.

in the hope that the market value of those shares would rise enabling them to turn a tidy profit on the disposal of the shares. A common scenario might again have involved the acquisition of shares in a company in anticipation of a takeover. If the takeover went ahead, the arbitrageur could either dispose of his shares at the bid price or, alternatively, retain them in the hope of exercising influence over the company following the takeover. Ivan Boesky had claims to be one of the most successful of this breed of speculator in securities. In corporate terms, he was often in the right place at the right time and many thought this was due to his superior market analysis. However, subsequently, in many cases it turned out to have been due to the receipt of inside information from a number of informants, one of whom[9] subsequently informed on Mr Boesky. Boesky was convicted and sentenced to imprisonment for three years. He also paid over $100 million in settlement to the Securities and Exchange Commission in the US. Approximately half that amount represented a fine while the other half represented the return of ill-gotten gains. If that makes the reader sympathetic on behalf of Mr Boesky, he or she should be aware that Boesky is alleged to have made a minimum profit from insider dealing of $50 million over a period of five years or so. Some newspaper reports at the time estimated his profit to be in the region of $200 million. Also, Boesky profited further in that he came to an agreement with the Securities and Exchange Commission[10] which enabled him to dispose of part of his own portfolio of holdings prior to the public announcement of the charges laid against him. The disposal proceeds are said to have amounted to well over $400 million.

MARKET INFORMATION

The value of information

What may be gleaned from the activities of Geoffrey Collier (in the UK) and Ivan Boesky (in the US)[11] is the potential value of accurate and timely securities-related information and the effect its presence and use

3-08

---

9   Dennis Levine, a New York banker. And see various Press reports at the time on the activities of Boesky: for instance, *The Sunday Times* of 23 November 1986, entitled 'Secret World of the Inside Stealer'. See also 'The Levine Case: getting tough on insider trading' by Stephen A Weiner and John F Pritchard (1986) 1(2) BJIB & FL 29–31. More recently see 'Viewpoint on a decade of upheaval', by Ivan Fallon, *The Sunday Times*, 25 September 1994.

10   After his activities had been detected. It is interesting that there seems to have been a degree of revisionism in the US in relation to the corporate 'players' of the 1980s. For instance, see 'Playback: the Conspiracy to Destroy Michael Milkon and his Financial Revolution' by David Fischel (1995). See also 'King of junk bonds pays campus dues' by Ben Macintyre, *The Times*, 9 October 1993.

11   See paras 3-06 and 3-07 above.

...may not always lead to power and influence but, as has been ...ed, its prompt use can sometimes give rise to a tidy[12] profit.

...act of world news

3-09   Relevant information may include matters of international concern such as one country declaring war on another[13] or, perhaps, where a country refuses to allow the inspection of its nuclear facilities by the relevant international authorities.[14] However, probably of greater significance in recent times has been the announcement of economic difficulties. The effect of such news on worried securities markets has been dramatic. Perhaps the most striking example of this led to the so-called 'Black Monday' crash which took place in October 1987.[15] In that instance, it is thought that widely reported news of economic policy differences between the US and Germany was primarily responsible for triggering the worldwide market crash which occurred.

The impact of corporate information

3-10   On a national level,[16] specific corporate information is the life-blood of any securities market because it can and does have a direct effect on the price of the securities to which it relates. In many instances, such information will relate to matters of corporate economics; for instance, profit forecasts or warnings.[17] It may relate to internal reorganisations within companies and could, for instance, detail any comings and goings amongst board directors or other senior employees. Finally, it could

---

12   Albeit, potentially, ill-gotten.

13   Whether an explicit verbal declaration or one implicit through action such as the invasion of Kuwait by Iraq, which led to the Gulf War.

14   For instance, the repeated refusals of North Korea in 1993–94 to allow the full inspection of its nuclear sites thereby denying the relevant international authorities the opportunity to determine whether it was attempting to manufacture nuclear weapons.

15   The so-called 'Black Monday' took place on 19 October 1987 when, in the USA, the Dow Jones industrial average fell over 500 points on the day which was significantly more than the worst one day fall during the 'Great Crash' of 1929. For press coverage at the time see, for instance, *Financial Times* of 24 October 1987 (entitled 'The Message of the Markets').

16   Which, so far as having an effect on the UK is concerned, probably includes Western Europe and possibly also the US. And see 'Guidance on the dissemination of price sensitive information', reissued by the London Stock Exchange in February 1995 and presently being reprinted.

17   How the company has weathered the recession or has had a good or a bad year and the like. And see 'A case to answer at Caradon', *The Times*, 19 January 1996, in relation to the activities (or alleged activities) of securities analysts and public relations firms.

relate to external matters, such as the trading or development pl
the company or its ideas for expansion.[18]

In a developed economy, where the securities markets are efficient, **3-11**
some economists[19] have argued that all information concerning the
financial position or prospects of a company will be fully and quickly
reflected in the value[20] of its securities. Where this is the case, it should
be safe for investors to assume that the market price accurately reflects
the true value of the securities in question. Those economists contend
that this ensures the efficient allocation of capital throughout the
relevant securities market.

'INSIDERS'

The actions of insiders

In the context of insider dealing, what an 'insider' will try to do is to buy or **3-12**
sell (or suggest that others buy or sell) securities when he is in possession of
information which may alter their price;[21] but he will do so before such
information has been made public and has therefore had a chance to have
any such effect. Such information will usually relate in particular to the
company in question. Its value will depend on its precise nature, exactly
who is aware of it and what they are then prepared to do.

Potential insiders

In the first instance, the most usual 'insiders' are persons employed by or **3-13**
connected with a company. They may be directors, other employees or
shareholders of that company. Other persons may also find themselves in
the position of having unpublished price-sensitive information.

---

18 Through takeovers, mergers and the like. And see 'Rich Relations in the City' by
    Sarah Whitebloom, *The Spectator*, 20 July 1996, in relation to the city 'PR' industry
    and 'Leaking all over the Square Mile' by Brian Basham, *The Spectator*, 3 August 1996.

19 Who support the economic theory known as the 'efficient capital markets'
    hypothesis. For more on this area see, for instance, Gilson and Kraakman, 'The
    Mechanisms of Market Efficiency'(1984) 70 Va L Rev 549.

20 Signified, in market terms, by the so-called 'market' price.

21 So-called 'price-sensitive information'.

Professional advisers[22] or the bankers to a company[23] are more than likely to come into possession of information which they could use to their advantage, by dealing for their own account in the shares of the company, if they were permitted to do so by insider dealing law.

3-14   But, what about others who may not be so closely connected with the company? What about an investment manager working in another part of the financial conglomerate which owns a merchant bank which is acting for the company in relation to a takeover? Should he (or his clients) be prohibited from benefiting if he becomes or is made aware of what is going on? If others are to be prohibited, the answer seems to be that he should also be prevented if, in regulatory terms, there is to be a 'level playing-field'. Taking this scenario a little further, what about the lawyers acting for the merchant bank which is advising the company about that takeover? Or those persons even further removed from the company, such as the executive officers of the Takeover Panel who answer initial queries about a potential takeover which is subsequently staged or perhaps even the designers involved in producing the takeover documentation or the printers who print that documentation? If a level playing-field is to be preserved, those people should also be prevented from profiting from being well-informed. But, as a matter of market policy, should insider dealing be prohibited?

SHOULD INSIDER DEALING BE PROHIBITED?

Market egalitarianism

3-15   If a securities market is to be efficient, it must be properly equipped to ensure that the price of securities accurately reflects their value. It might be

---

22 Such as employees of the merchant bank acting for a company in relation to a potential takeover. Consider the position of investment analysts: see *Mackie* v *HM Advocate* [1994] SCCR 277 HCJ and 'A moral code for insiders' by Neil Gow, NLJ 1994, 144 (6638) at 321. Also that of auditors: see *Caparo Industries plc* v *Dickman* [1989] 2 WLR 316 CA and 'Insider Dealing – Auditors Liability', prepared by City solicitors Slaughter & May, (1989) 3 (6) *Corporate Briefing* 142–144. But see also [1990] 2 AC 605 in which the House of Lords held that liability for economic loss due to negligent mis-statement or advice was given to a known recipient for a specific purpose of which the matter was aware and upon which the recipient had relied and acted to his detriment. There was no reason in policy or principle why auditors should be deemed to have a special relationship with non-shareholders contemplating investment in a company in reliance on its published accounts even where the affairs of the company were such as to render it susceptible to a takeover. In the case, the auditors had therefore not owed any duty of care to the plaintiff with regard to the acquisition of the company's shares. As to auditors, see also s 109 FSA 1986 and SI 1994/526, further.

23 Who lend it money to enable it to develop a new invention. And see paras 30 and 31 of the February 1995 guidance reissued by the London Stock Exchange.

thought that part of that equipment should include the means of preventing or, at least, of discouraging persons who are 'in the know' with unpublished price-sensitive information from taking unfair advantage of their informed position. A 'level playing-field' should be preserved, whereby information is promptly 'made public'[24] and 'insiders' are deterred from abusing their position, if a modern securities market is to preserve credibility. If that is achieved, all investors are then able to deal on the market on an equal footing. Everyone has equal access to all material information. This is the 'ideal' position in what has sometimes been described by economists as the theory of market egalitarianism.

Market efficiency

However, the idea that securities markets should operate on the basis of complete equality between investors and potential investors[25] is generally thought to be too idealistic to be workable in practice.[26] A requirement as to the immediate disclosure of all information would be too all-embracing. The market would be swamped with trivial material. Although most feel that 'insiders' should not be allowed to take unfair advantage of inside information, and investors should have prompt and easy access to important corporate information, there will always be people with informational advantages and disadvantages. This will be so however prompt or wide-ranging is any sensible requirement as to disclosure. Some investors will have greater experience or intuitive ability than others whilst some will simply ensure they always take the very best advice available. But what can be done? The answer seems to be that abuses can be minimised by requiring the prompt disclosure of material information to the market. Laws[27] can also be enacted to discourage persons from taking unfair informational advantages and to punish those who fail to comply. With this approach, market efficiency[28] and the promotion of public confidence in the market is the goal as opposed to market perfection which, in practice, must be impossible to attain.

3-16

---

24 Through disclosure to the market.
25 And between buyers and sellers of securities.
26 See Note 19 above. See also Carlton and Fischel, 'The Regulation of Insider Trading' (1983) 35 Stan L Rev.
27 Whether primary or secondary legislation.
28 Ensuring investor protection.

A 'level playing-field'

3-17   An informed layman would say that the effective dissemination of
material corporate information coupled with the prohibition of insider
dealing was essential for an efficient and credible securities market.
'City' commentators, politicians and regulators[29] continue to speak of
the need to ensure that London is a 'clean' place to do business or that
business may be attracted elsewhere. That argument was obviously
accepted by our law-makers some time ago because, since 1980,
legislation has been in place which has made insider dealing a criminal
offence.[30] It also seems to have been accepted without obvious challenge
by companies whose shares are traded in the UK.

3-18   That is because volatile, or even just unexpectedly variable, share prices
do not create good 'press' for a company. If, instead, price variability is
linked with rumours about the activities of insiders close to the decision-
makers of a company, market participants will be wary about dealing in its
shares. Such a situation is likely to lower the reputation of the company
amongst market analysts and this will cause problems if the company
wishes to raise money through share issues and the like. This is therefore
another strong argument in favour of prohibiting insider dealing. However,
the view that insider dealing should be made subject to the criminal law has
not always been held and, indeed, may not be wholly valid today.

An economist's view

3-19   In the 1960s, some economists and others propounded the view
essentially that there was nothing wrong with insider dealing. In 1966,
for instance, Professor Manne[31] argued that insider dealing was
beneficial in economic terms and ought not to be prohibited. To many
people, insider dealing remains a 'victimless' crime in that it will
usually be hard to establish a direct connection between the activities
of an insider and the position of an investor who, as a result of those

---

29 See, for instance, para 16.7 in Chapter 16 (entitled 'Current Challenges') on p 102 of
    the review document issued by the Securities and Investments Board in May 1993.
    That document was entitled 'Financial Services Regulation – Making the Two Tier
    System Work' and contained the report of Andrew Large, the Chairman of the SIB,
    following the request by the Chancellor of the Exchequer in July 1992 that he
    undertake a review of the regulatory system in place under the Financial Services
    Act 1986. Reference was made to the 'professional markets', which went on as
    follows: 'They need a different style of regulation to retail markets. But regulators
    cannot neglect them. Systemic risks to the financial health of the industry need to
    be avoided. Clean markets need to be maintained.'

30 See Chapter 4, below, for an account of the move towards insider dealing
    regulation, through legislation, in the UK. But see Nicholas Bourne, 'Should
    insiders end up inside?'(1987) 5 (3) Co L Dig 67–70.

31 In a book entitled *Insider Trading and the Stock Market* (1966).

activities, pays more or receives less[32] for dealing in securities. In some cases, it may be possible[33] for securities to be bought or sold between individuals in direct transactions. In those circumstances, if one of the contracting parties dealt on the basis of inside information, the other could perhaps be regarded as a victim of insider dealing. However, direct acquisitions or disposals are not the norm today.

Most transactions are conducted by and through intermediaries[34] pursuant to the facilities and rules but also subject to the supervision of a relevant securities market. This tends to remove any direct personal contact that might previously have been present[35] and makes it harder to identify a 'victim' of insider dealing. It is also difficult to quantify the 'loss' which would be suffered by such an investor. Although he would not be able to take advantage of fully up-to-date information which may affect the price of the securities with which he is concerned, he would probably have dealt in any event being unaware of the existence of the insider unless dealing by that person had an immediate and noticeable effect on the price of the securities. In doing so, he may have to pay more or receive less for those securities, but that will not usually be caused by any identifiable individual 'insider'. It will simply be the result of movements in the market price of the securities and, as most investment advertising is now required to warn with due prominence,[36] the price of securities can go up as well as down. Investors take the risk of the price moving against them when they deal. Without a connecting link between the insider and the 'outsider',[37] it is hard to see the outsider as a victim of any potential crime committed by the insider. Also, any brokers and market makers involved are professionals and should be well able to look after themselves.

3-20

Some economists[38] have argued that insider dealing actually benefits a securities market because it ensures that the market price of affected securities moves[39] in the appropriate direction.[40] In essence, those economists are saying that a securities market with active insiders ensures accuracy in the pricing of the securities so traded. Insider

3-21

---

32 That is to say, suffers a quantifiable loss. But note the view of the government that 'Insider dealing is not a victimless crime ...', *per* Mr Anthony Nelson MP (Minister of State, Treasury). See House of Commons Official Report, 20 December 1994, at column 1593.

33 Particularly where small 'private' companies are involved.

34 Usually both brokers and market makers.

35 Between buyer and seller.

36 See, for instance, rr 5-9 to 5-15 (inclusive) of the Rules of the Securities and Futures Authority.

37 Being the person not in possession of any inside information.

38 Including Professor Manne. See, for instance, *Insider Trading and the Stock Market*, (1966) at pp 77–110.

39 Either up or down.

40 In accordance with a fully informed view of the value of the securities.

dealing is said to move prices towards a level which correctly reflects the actual position of a company[41] at a given point in time. Economists also argue that insiders have little to gain in delaying the disclosure of information to the market.[42] Indeed, unless very close to a company, it would seem that they are rarely in a position where they are able to influence the timing of any such disclosure. So long as an insider has time to deal on the basis of his (or her) inside knowledge, he would normally want the information in question to be made public as soon as possible thereafter, enabling the price of the securities to be affected so fixing any profit from the transaction. In the long run, it is therefore suggested that investors may actually benefit from the activities of insiders.

3-22   A consequence of the arguments summarised above is that the prohibition of insider dealing may itself inhibit the flow of information to the market more than its occurrence. Insiders[43] may well not deal. The fact that insider dealing is prohibited may lead the insider[44] to keep his information to himself. In passing, it might be thought that this could make at least some insider dealing more likely because the suppressed information might thereby become more valuable. In any event, the flow of information into the public domain may be restricted. Individuals may be less likely to seek to acquire corporate information if a prohibition against insider dealing may prevent them from making use of it. Likewise, speculators may be discouraged from active market participation which would deny investors the beneficial stabilising effect which speculators are said to have of decreasing price volatility and of encouraging the flow of information into the market.[45] Price volatility may be reduced because speculators[46] are thought to buy when securities are cheap and to sell when they are expensive, thereby pushing prices into a narrower range.

3-23   It has also been argued that insider dealing should be permitted because it is a way of rewarding the entrepreneurial skills of employees.[47] It enables them to take advantage of their knowledge to augment their remuneration without this falling as an additional burden on their employers. In short, if it is permitted, insider dealing can, in certain circumstances, amount to a form of employee benefit. On paper this sounds a little far-fetched because it would depend on the occurrence, on a fairly regular basis, of circumstances in which relevant employees came to possess inside information. At best, even in boom times, this could only

---

41   And the value of its stock.
42   See Manne, *op cit*, pp 104 and 105.
43   In possession of relevant information.
44   Who may, for instance, be a company director.
45   See, for instance, Wu, 'An economist looks at s 16 of the Securities Exchange Act 1934' (1968) 68 Colum L Rev 260.
46   Perhaps stereotypically.
47   See Manne, *op cit*, pp 131–158.

remain an inefficient way of remunerating employees. Also, there would be a real risk that those in charge of decision-making at a particular company might be encouraged to engage in activities designed to alter its share price to their advantage. At best, this approach is an impractical justification for insider dealing.

In the short term, the 'benefit' to investors of active insider dealing on a market on which they also deal is a little hard to appreciate. For instance, its effect in ensuring a more accurate market price for securities has not been proven conclusively. Insider dealing might be a factor in nudging prices in a particular direction as the up-to-date position of a company becomes known to the market. But, in many cases, the disclosure of that information would have occurred regardless of any related insider dealing. It is therefore unclear whether permitting insider dealing *per se* would be likely to have much effect on the accuracy of share values.

3-24

On a more particular level, the effect of insider dealing on those values will not necessarily benefit an outsider who deals in ignorance of the inside information or the insider dealing which has taken place. He will not be able to deal on the basis of the price that would have been quoted had the inside information been made public. Although the decision to deal will still be his, and the price may move in favour of the transaction he effects,[48] he will be dealing in the absence of information which should have been made public. As such, he can easily be regarded as a victim, albeit indirectly, of a situation which the market should prevent.

3-25

It might be thought reasonable to assume that few investors[49] would deal with any confidence or frequency on an exchange where the activities of insiders reined unchecked or were only partially checked. However, in the UK, where insider dealing is a matter for the criminal law, there seems to be little evidence that the activities of insiders[50] have had much effect on public confidence in the City and the way it is regulated. Likewise, there seems no real evidence that those running companies whose securities have been the subject of alleged or established insider dealing have been regarded as possessing significantly less

3-26

---

48 For instance, it may increase when what he wants to do is to sell his holding.

49 Particularly private individuals.

50 And there is, apparently, a small incidence of insider dealing on the Stock Exchange in London to the extent that there have been a number of successful prosecutions.

an those whose companies have escaped.[51] Over recent years, has been caused over instances of alleged malpractice in ...te governance[52] or where investors have suffered notwithstanding the protections of the Financial Services Act 1986[53] than where the securities of a company may have been subject to insider dealing.

The 'moral' position

3-27   Although there may be some doubt as to whether insider dealing should be prohibited, if one accepts some of the economic arguments outlined above, there are many 'moral' arguments in favour of its regulation. In a regulatory environment where there are great 'political' concerns to ensure the protection of investors, it is unconscionable that insiders should be allowed to operate unchecked even if their activities may not necessarily be to the direct detriment of all potential investors. If they are allowed to make use of their inside knowledge, there would be no 'level playing-field' whereby all investors operate, relatively speaking, on the same basis. Also, the fact that insider dealing is regarded as dishonest behaviour may well be a reflection of the long-standing common law concern to prevent unjust enrichment and to forestall situations where people with fiduciary or quasi-fiduciary obligations are able to take advantage of their favoured position. Perhaps, more than anything else, that is why insider dealing remains prohibited.

---

51   The most that seems to occur is the odd sly comment in the financial Press. An example occurred (from *The Times* 'Business News' on 17 May 1994) in relation to dealing in the shares of the Portals group. The price of those shares jumped 44 pence on one day after a spate of buying by so-called 'fringe brokers'. By the end of the same week, after the intervention of the Takeover Panel, Portals was forced to admit that it was involved in bid talks with another company, De La Rue. The Pennington column in *The Times* commented that '... disregarding a mass outbreak of telepathy, those dealers, presumably, knew something, and that something constituted a leak. *Cui bono?* Well, the potential bidder looks the most embarrassed and the least pleased, which could allow tentative conclusions to be drawn by the uncharitable ... if somebody wanted to strengthen their hand in the negotiations or force the price higher by selective leaks into the market ...'

52   Directors tampering with pension fund surpluses and the like.

53   See Chapter 2, above, for more detail on the Financial Services Act 1986.

CHAPTER 4

THE MOVE TOWARDS INSIDER DEALING REGULATION IN THE UK

INTRODUCTION

Early moves

It will be seen, as this chapter develops, that the legislation prohibiting insider dealing took quite a long time in arriving on the statute book in the UK given that the basic mischief it was intended to prevent had been recognised and commented on as being undesirable for many years. Whatever the 'economic' arguments[1] in favour of or against it, insider dealing has been prevalent as a 'City' practice for some time.[2] The extent to which this contributed to the length of time it took a succession of governments to make it subject to the criminal law can only be speculated upon. If it did, it would not be the first time that 'City' opposition has prevented, or at least delayed, the elected government of the day[3] in taking action against dubious 'market' practices.[4]

4-01

Directors' duties

It was explained earlier[5] that, over recent years, insider dealing has usually involved the directors of a company or those people otherwise closely connected with its management and control or their advisers. In becoming 'insiders', they have used information in their possession as a basis for the prudent acquisition or disposal of shares in the company.[6]

4-02

---

1 See paras 3-19 to 3-23 in Chapter 3 above for an outline of some of the arguments put forward by economists in favour of insider dealing.

2 See Chapter 1 above for some discussion of the historical origins and development of insider dealing in the UK.

3 Particularly a Conservative government.

4 A comparatively recent example of 'City' opposition occurred in the run-in to what became known as 'Big Bang' when the basic distinction between 'brokers' and 'jobbers' was abolished along with fixed minimum commission. See Chapter 1, above, further.

5 See para 3-02 in Chapter 3 above for an attempted definition of the basic 'mischief' of insider dealing.

6 A recent example of alleged insider dealing concerned the writer and former Conservative Member of Parliament, Jeffrey Archer. He was one of the subjects of an investigation in 1994 by the Department of Trade and Industry into suspected insider dealing in the shares of Anglia Television, a company of which his wife was a non-executive director. No further action was taken against him. See House of Commons Official Report, 20 December 1994, at columns 1591–98 and also Chapter 8, below, further.

However, before enactment of the Companies Act 1980, provided the securities market trading activities of such people did not breach the fiduciary and certain other duties of care which they owed in the circumstances, generally speaking, they were not prohibited. The directors of the company owed duties to the company and not to its individual shareholders nor, for instance, to applicants for shares.[7] Generally speaking, the fiduciary duties of the directors of a company are to exercise their powers *bona fide* for the purposes for which they were conferred and for the benefit of the company[8] as a whole. Also, they must not put themselves in a position in which their duties to the company and their personal interests may conflict.[9]

The common law

4-03   An early authority for some of the propositions set out in para 4-02 above is the case of *Percival v Wright* (1902).[10] In that case, the directors of a company bought shares from Z. However, they did not disclose to him that negotiations were being conducted for the sale of all the shares in the company at a higher price than that being asked by Z. Those negotiations proved to be abortive but Z sued to have his sale of shares set aside on the grounds that the directors ought to have disclosed the negotiations to him. The court however held that the sale was binding since the directors were under no obligation to disclose the negotiations to Z. Although clearly wrong by the standards of today,[11] what was done was not prohibited at the time notwithstanding the fact that the directors were in possession and dealt on the basis of information which was not widely known but which would, if made public, have had a material effect on the market price of the securities in question.

GOVERNMENTAL DELIBERATIONS

Some learned committees and consultative documents

4-04   The Companies Act 1948[12] was based, to a large extent, on the Report in

---

7   See the case of *Percival v Wright* [1902] 2 Ch 421, discussed in para 4-03, below.

8   Including its shareholders as a body.

9   See, for instance, *Aberdeen Railway Company v Blaikie Bros* [1854] 1 Macq 461 at 471 and *Hindle v John Cotton Ltd* (1919) 56 SLR 625 at 631.

10   [1902] 2 Ch 421.

11   Set by insider dealing legislation if not morality.

12   Companies Act 1948 (11 & 12 Geo 6, c 38).

1945 of the Cohen Committee[13] which sat to review the state of com
and related law at the time. So far as share dealing by directors and
insider dealing was concerned, the Cohen Committee favoured the
imposition on company directors of disclosure requirements relating to
the shares they owned in the companies which employed them as
directors.[14] The Report also highlighted the use of nominee companies
and nominee shareholdings as ways of concealing insider dealing.
Unfortunately, this usage has continued over the years, particularly
through companies registered outside the UK. At the time, nothing
much in terms of the regulation of insider dealing occurred as a direct
and immediate result of the Cohen Report. Instead, more time passed.

Many of the more important proposals for the reform of company **4-05**
law in the last few decades were made by the Jenkins Committee which
reported in 1962.[15] One of the recommendations made by that
Committee[16] was that a director, who in any transaction relating to the
securities of his employing company[17] made improper use of a
particular item of confidential information which might be expected to
have a significant effect on the value of those securities, should be liable
to compensate a person suffering loss as a result of his action unless the
information in question was known to that person. Another
recommendation was that dealing by directors in options relating to the
listed securities of their employing companies should be prohibited.[18]
Unfortunately, although some of the recommendations made by the
Jenkins Committee were implemented and became law relatively
quickly in a number of later statutes,[19] the recommendation relating to
insider dealing was not one of them although, to be fair, an attempt was
made in the Companies Bill 1973.[20] This followed a report in 1972 by
Justice, the law reform organisation, which suggested that insider
dealing should be made a criminal offence.[21] The Stock Exchange and

---

13 The Cohen Report (1945), the Report of the Committee on Company Law
    Amendment, Cmnd 6659.

14 See Cmnd 6659 at paras 86 and 87. See also ss 323–329 of the Companies Act 1985
    ('Share dealings by directors and their families').

15 The Jenkins Report (1962), the Report of the Company Law Committee, Cmnd 1749.

16 1962 Cmnd 1749 at para 99(b).

17 Or of another company in the same group.

18 See s 323 Companies Act 1985 for the present prohibition.

19 Such as the Companies Act 1967 which amended the Companies Act 1948 in a
    number of areas. For instance, amendments were made to provisions governing
    company accounts so that the accounts of a subsidiary had to disclose the name of
    its ultimate holding company. Also, the Companies Act 1976 which enacted some
    of the provisions contained in the Companies Bill 1973 and also made amendments
    concerning the filing of company accounts and the keeping of accounting records.

20 Clauses 12–16 of the Companies Bill 1973 set out provisions which would have
    made insider dealing a criminal offence.

21 Justice, *Insider Trading* (1972), noted by Kay (1973) MLR 185.

the Takeover Panel had also issued a joint statement in 1973 recommending criminal sanctions. The Conservative government went with the flow.

4-06   The Conservative government White Paper on Company Law Reform[22] was presented to Parliament in July 1973. In it, the government announced its intention to introduce a new Companies Bill. Amongst the reasons given for this proposal was the fact that many of the recommendations made by the Jenkins Committee, which were not included in the Companies Act 1967, were still relevant and important. This included the view that existing arrangements for uncovering and dealing with commercial crime and other malpractices had proved to be inadequate. It was therefore proposed that insider dealing should be made a criminal offence.[23] The White Paper accepted that unfair benefits could be obtained by share dealing on the basis of confidential and price-sensitive information that was not available to the general 'investing' public. It stated that the object of any legislation should be to ensure that 'insiders' in possession of price-sensitive information[24] refrained from dealing until the information had properly been made generally available.

4-07   In many ways, the White Paper may have been influenced by the New South Wales Securities Industry Act 1970 and, in particular, by s 75A of that Act.[25] In passing, that provision was repealed and extended by the New South Wales Securities Industry Act 1975,[26] ss 112–114 of which were based upon clauses 12, 15 and 16 of the Companies Bill 1973.

4-08   The definition of 'insider' suggested by the Conservative government White Paper[27] was one including directors, employees, major shareholders and the professional advisers of a company together with close relations of those persons. It suggested that dealing in the securities of a company by anyone who was an 'insider' who, by reason of his relationship with the company or its officers, had information which he knew to be price-sensitive should be guilty of a criminal offence unless he could show that his primary intention in dealing in the securities at that particular time was not to make a profit or to avoid a loss.[28]

---

22   (1973) Cmnd 5391.

23   (1973) Cmnd 5391 at para 15.

24   Being information which, if generally known, would be likely to have a material effect on the price of the relevant securities.

25   See further the Securities Industry Act 1970 (NSW), s 75A.

26   Securities Industry Act 1975 (NSW), which repealed and extended the Securities Act 1970 (NSW). Sections 112–114 of the 1975 Act seem based on clauses 12, 15 and 16 of the UK Companies Bill 1973.

27   Paragraph 18 of (1973) Cmnd 5391

28   Paragraph 15 of (1973) Cmnd 5391.

The White Paper also reinforced the recommendation as to compensation which was made by the Jenkins Committee[29] and suggested that the legislation should confer a civil remedy on persons who could establish that they had suffered identifiable loss through the misuse of materially significant information.[30] Finally, the law should ensure that any insider who abused his position could also be held accountable to the company for any profit accruing from his actions.[31]

4-09

ABORTIVE LEGISLATION

The Companies Bill 1973

It was intended that Clauses 12–16 of the Companies Bill 1973[32] would give substantive effect to the recommendations as to insider dealing set out in the Conservative government White Paper. The Bill had a first reading in the House of Commons on 18 December 1973. However, it was lost when Parliament was dissolved on 7 February 1974. The Labour government which was elected decided not to reintroduce the Bill. Instead, they instigated their own review of company law which was also to consider the supervision of securities trading.

4-10

Further deliberations

The conclusions of that review were set out in the Labour Party Green Paper on the Reform of Company Law 1974[33] which was published in May 1974. Amongst other matters, the Green Paper criticised existing supervision of the City in its reliance upon self-regulation.[34] It concluded that self-regulation had failed to work. The Department of Trade[35] was too passive and was also inadequately staffed. The securities market for quoted companies was the responsibility of the Stock Exchange which, unfortunately, was also responsible for formulating its own rules. As the membership of its various committees was largely made up of securities industry professionals, there was a

4-11

---

29   Paragraph 19 of (1973) Cmnd 5391.

30   *ibid.*

31   Paragraph 20 of (1973) Cmnd 5391.

32   See Note 20 above.

33   The Labour Party Green Paper on the Reform of Company law, entitled 'The Community and the Company'. This was a Report of the Working Group of the Labour Party Industrial Policy Sub-Committee published in May 1974. The author is indebted to the Information Resource Centre of the Labour Party for help in tracking down details of that Paper.

34   For instance, by the Stock Exchange and the Takeover Panel.

35   Which was the responsible government department.

strong fear that the Stock Exchange was run by the industry more in the interests of those professionals than of investors. In particular, it was felt that it was unable to police the securities markets effectively, thereby preventing insider dealing.

4-12   The basic conclusion was that the case for a new Companies Commission was overwhelming. It would be a new public supervisory body taking over the Companies and Insurance Division of the Department of Trade. Day-to-day control of the Stock Exchange would though remain with its Council which would be responsible for the rules of the Exchange in consultation with the Commission.[36]

4-13   As for insider dealing, the authors of the Green Paper agreed with the objectives of clauses 12–16 of the Companies Bill 1973. They also agreed with the various categories of 'insider' suggested by the Conservative government White Paper.[37] They did, however, show some concern that the trustees of company pension schemes should be included as potential 'insiders', where appropriate.[38] The Green Paper proposed that a criminal offence should be committed by any person who possessed information of a price-sensitive nature, who knew or could reasonably be expected to know that it was 'inside' information and who used it for the purpose of dealing in securities to make a profit or to avoid a loss.[39] That basic provision would be reinforced by placing restrictions on the rights of certain persons, such as directors, likely to come into contact regularly with inside information in relation to their dealings with the securities concerned. It would be an offence for them to communicate price-sensitive information to third parties with the intention that those third parties might engage in dealing or if there were circumstances for supposing that they might.[40]

4-14   The maximum penalty suggested by the Green Paper for insider trading was to be imprisonment for seven years.[41] Also, it proposed that there should be a civil remedy by means of which an aggrieved party would have the right to have the transaction of which he complained reversed and it was thought that it might also be appropriate to have the insider account to the company for any profit obtained by him as a result of his dealing.[42] As something of an afterthought, it would also be ensured that Stock Exchange practice would be amended to enable both principals to any transaction to be identified more easily.[43]

---

36 See pages 18–21, 22–25 and also 36 of the Green Paper, further.
37 See note 27 above.
38 See section 8(2) on page 35 of the Green Paper, further.
39 *Ibid.*
40 *Ibid.*
41 See section 8(3) on page 35 of the Green Paper, further.
42 See section 8(3) on page 35–6 of the Green Paper, further.
43 See section 8(4) on page 36 of the Green Paper.

LEGISLATIVE PROHIBITION

The Companies Act 1980

Notwithstanding the impetus given to the proposed prohibition of **4-15**
insider dealing by the above, it still took some time before it became a
criminal offence. In 1977, the Takeover Panel and the Stock Exchange
issued a further joint statement which emphasised the need for
companies participating in or subject to takeovers to take care to see that
insider dealing did not occur. The Stock Exchange also issued its Model
Code for Securities Transactions by Directors of Listed Companies
which set out certain basic standards of good practice.[44] Finally, the
Labour government introduced a Companies Bill which provided for
criminal penalties and a civil remedy in certain relevant circumstances.
As before, that Bill was lost on the dissolution of Parliament.

Insider dealing did not become a criminal offence in the UK for the **4-16**
first time until the enactment of the Companies Act 1980.[45] The relevant
provisions of that Act were largely welcomed by the City as a means of
restricting an aspect of securities market behaviour which self-regulation
did not seem able to control. However, those practitioners familiar with
the problems inherent in bringing successful criminal prosecutions could
see the likely difficulties underlying an offence which required a
significant number of matters to be established. If anything, time has
only served to reinforce the reservations expressed about the new
legislation in 1980.

\ Part V of the Companies Act 1980 contained 11 separately **4-17**
identifiable offences involving insider dealing. They could, however, be
divided into three basic criminal offences: *first*, where an individual in
possession of insider information (who became known as an 'insider') or
an individual who received information from an insider (who became
known as a 'tippee') dealt in securities;[46] *secondly*, where either an
insider or a tippee counselled or procured another person to deal in
securities;[47] and, *thirdly*, where an insider or a tippee communicated
insider information to a third party if the recipient was likely to use that
information for dealing or for counselling or procuring another person
to deal.[48] As might be expected, the starting point for considering

---

44 See Chapter 9, below.
45 The Companies Act 1980 (1980 c 22). Part V of that Act made insider dealing a
criminal offence. The relevant provisions came into force on 23 June 1980 by virtue
of the Companies Act 1980 (Commencement) Order 1980 (SI 1980/745).
46 See s 68 of the CA 1980 in relation to the offence of 'dealing' in securities.
47 See s 68 of the CA 1980 in relation to the offence of 'procuring others to deal' in securities.
48 See ss 68 and 69 of the CA 1980 in relation to the 'communication of information' to
third parties.

whether an offence of insider dealing had been committed in any given case required an analysis of whether an 'insider' was involved in what was done and whether a person could be regarded as an insider had to be determined by reference to the circumstances in which that person was in possession of unpublished price-sensitive information.[49]

The Company Securities (Insider Dealing) Act 1985

4-18   The law relating to insider dealing in company securities was consolidated in the Company Securities (Insider Dealing) Act 1985[50] which entered the statute book on 11 March 1985 and came into force on 1 July 1985.[51] As with the enactments it consolidated, the object of this legislation remained the same: generally speaking, to prohibit certain individuals from dealing in company securities in relation to which they were in possession of inside information. A breach of that general prohibition remained a criminal offence.[52]

4-19   Four categories of individual were subject to the prohibitions imposed by the Act if, generally speaking, they were in possession of inside information.[53] In summary, 12 distinct offences were constituted by the Act, each being made up of a number of elements which needed to be established if a conviction was to be secured.[54] The Act was subsequently amended by the Financial Services Act 1986[55] and **4-20** repealed by the Criminal Justice Act 1993.[56]

As insider dealing was made a criminal offence,[57] the burden of proof required to secure a conviction was a high one. This has remained the case. Generally speaking, it is for the prosecution to prove the guilt of the accused beyond any reasonable doubt. The accused does not have to prove anything. On indictment,[58] the jury will be told by the judge that, unless they are satisfied beyond reasonable doubt on all the evidence that the accused in question committed the offence charged, they must acquit him.[59]

---

49   See ss 68 and 73 of the CA 1980 in relation to the categories of 'insider'.

50   The Company Securities (Insider Dealing) Act 1985 (1985 c 8) (hereafter 'CS(ID)A 1985').

51   See s 18 of the CS(ID)A 1985.

52   With the criminal penalties set out in s 8(1)(a) and (b) ('Punishment of contraventions') of the CS(ID)A 1985 cf s 72 CA 1980.

53   See ss 1(1), 1(5), 2, 1(3), 1(6) and 2(1)(a) of the CS(ID)A 1985.

54   See ss 1, 2, 4 and 5 of the CS(ID)A 1985.

55   Part VII of the FSA 1986 contained provisions relating to insider dealing. In particular, ss 177 and 178 set out provisions dealing with investigations into insider dealing.

56   By s 79(14) and Schedule 16 to the Criminal Justice Act 1993 (1993 c 36).

57   By the Companies Act 1980.

58   In the Crown Court.

59   In *Ferguson v R* [1979] 1 All ER 877, the formulation 'You must be satisfied beyond reasonable doubt so that you feel sure of the defendant's guilt' was suggested.

THE EC DIRECTIVE ON INSIDER DEALING

A co-ordinating regime

On 13 November 1989, the Council of the European Community adopted a Directive designed to co-ordinate the prohibition of insider dealing throughout the Member States of the EC. Thankfully, that directive is not a particularly long document. It is, however, important and led to a restatement of the law on insider dealing in the UK. To use its full name, the directive may be cited as the Council of the European Communities Directive of 13 November 1989 co-ordinating regulations on insider dealing.[60]

4-21

The purpose of the Directive

The purpose and rationale of the Directive was to ensure the provision of minimum standards for insider dealing laws throughout the European Community. Some of its provisions were mandatory; others were not.

4-22

Timescale and effect

Article 14 of the Directive provided for Member States to take any measures necessary to comply with its provisions before 1 June 1992.[61] Implementation by the UK led to the amendment and restatement of the law on insider dealing contained in Part V[62] of the Criminal Justice Act 1993.[63] That Act brought about the repeal of the previous statement of the UK law of insider dealing which, subject to certain amendments,[64] was set out in the Company Securities (Insider Dealing) Act 1985.[65]

4-23

---

60 Council Directive (EEC) 89/592 of 13 November 1989. For general reference and further discussion, see Stephen JD Ross, 'Insider trading: UK perspective within an EC framework' (1992) 4(10) CM 78-80 and also Michael Ashe, 'The Directive on Insider Dealing',(1992) 13 (1) Co Law 15–19.

61 Article 14(1) of Council Directive (EEC) 89/592.

62 Entitled 'Insider dealing'.

63 Criminal Justice Act 1993 (1993 c 36).

64 By the FSA 1986.

65 (1985 c 8). But see Peter King, 'Insider dealing v the Criminal Justice Act 1993' (1994) 7(7) CM 54. See also Charles Abrams, 'Insider dealing – the new regime'(1994) 1 (1) EFSL 7–10.

Introductory and explanatory material

4-24   The various recitals to the Directive set out one of the main arguments for prohibiting insider dealing.[66] One of the basic objectives of European Economic Community 'legislation'[67] has been the establishment and subsequent 'functioning' of the internal market.[68] The recitals state that the 'secondary market in transferable securities' plays an important role in the financing of 'economic agents'.[69] However, for that 'secondary market' to play its role effectively, every measure must be taken to ensure that it operates smoothly and this depends, to a large extent, on the confidence which the market inspires in investors.

4-25   The factors on which investor confidence depends include the basic feeling that investors are all placed on an equal footing[70] and that they will all be protected against the improper use of inside information. The recitals emphasise that, by benefiting certain investors as opposed to others, insider dealing is likely to undermine that confidence and may therefore prejudice the smooth operation of the market in question.

4-26   On that basis, the recitals state that necessary measures should therefore be taken to combat insider dealing. However, given that in some European countries there were no rules or regulations prohibiting insider dealing and that the rules or regulations of those Member States which did prohibit it often differed considerably as to how they achieved that end, the Council of the EC felt it was advisable for co-ordinated rules to be adopted at 'a Community level in this field'.[71] The hope was that such an approach would make it possible to combat trans-frontier insider dealing more effectively through co-operation between the various competent authorities. The recitals then make some interesting points about activities which should *not* amount to insider dealing. It is said that, since the acquisition or disposal of transferable securities necessarily involves a prior decision to acquire or to dispose taken by the person who undertakes one or other of those operations, the carrying out of the acquisition or disposal does not in itself constitute the use of inside information. Insider dealing involves taking advantage

---

66   The recitals are not numbered or otherwise referred to in the Directive with any legal precision.

67   Such as Council Directive (EEC) 89/592.

68   Article 100a(1) of the Treaty which established the European Economic Community states that the Council shall adopt measures for the approximation of the provisions laid down by law, regulation or administrative action in Member States which have as their object the establishment and functioning of the internal market.

69   Generally, the 'secondary market in transferable securities' is a global expression which refers to any means by which securities are capable of being transferred in the EC.

70   The so-called 'level playing-field'.

71   So provided by the ninth recital.

of inside information. The mere fact that market-makers[72] w
information confine themselves to pursuing their normal b
buying or selling securities or that stock brokers with inside in
confine themselves to carrying out an order should not in itsel
case necessarily be deemed to constitute the use of suc̲ ̲.ı̲s̲ı̲u̲e̲
information.

Also, the process of carrying out transactions with the aim of   **4-27**
stabilising the price of new issues of securities or secondary offers of
transferable securities should not in itself be deemed to constitute the
use of inside information. The recitals go on. Estimates developed from
or based on publicly available data cannot be regarded as inside
information and a transaction carried out on the basis of any such
estimate should not therefore constitute insider dealing. Finally, the
communication of inside information to an authority to enable it to
ensure that insider dealing does not take place should not be prohibited
by insider dealing law.[73]

The meaning of 'inside information' •

The Directive defines 'inside information' as meaning information of a   **4-28**
precise nature which has not been made public. It must relate to one or
several issuers of transferable securities or to one or several transferable
securities and be such that, if it was made public, it would be likely to
have a significant effect on the price of the transferable security or
securities in question.[74]

The meaning of 'transferable securities'

For the purposes of the Directive, 'transferable securities' also have a   **4-29**
specific definition.[75] They are said to mean any one or more of the
following:

- shares and debt securities, as well as securities equivalent to shares and
  debt securities;
- contracts or rights to subscribe for, acquire or dispose of shares and debt
  securities or their equivalent;
- futures contracts, options and financial futures in respect of shares and
  debt securities or their equivalent; and, finally

---

72   Or bodies authorised to act as contrepartie.
73   These points are all taken, consecutively, from the recitals to Council Directive
     (EEC) 89/592 of 13 November 1989 which are not numbered.
74   By virtue of art 1(1) of Council Directive (EEC) 89/592.
75   Set out in art 1(2).

- index contracts in respect of shares and debt securities or their equivalent.

4-30   To be 'transferable securities', however, securities falling within any one or more of the categories set out above must also have been admitted to trading on a market which is regulated and supervised by authorities recognised by public bodies, which operates regularly and which is accessible directly or indirectly to the public.[76]

The 'dealing' and 'tippee' prohibitions

4-31   The Directive provides that each Member State must prohibit certain stated persons who have inside information from taking advantage of it, in full knowledge of the facts, by acquiring or disposing of transferable securities of the issuer or issuers to which that information relates.[77] The prohibition must be applicable to the person in question whether the acquisition or disposal is for his own account or for the account of a third party and whether it is effected directly or indirectly.[78]

4-32   Generally speaking, the persons to be subjected to the 'dealing' prohibition[79] are persons who possess inside information by virtue of certain factors:

- their membership of the administrative, management or supervisory bodies of the issuer of transferable securities;[80]

- their holding in the capital of the issuer of transferable securities;[81] or

- their access to inside information through the exercise of their employment, profession or other duties.[82]

4-33   The basic 'dealing' prohibition[83] must be made applicable to any acquisition or disposal of transferable securities effected through a professional intermediary[84] although each Member State may provide that it will not apply to acquisitions or disposals effected without the involvement of a professional intermediary outside a market as referred to in para 4-30 above.[85] It must, however, be imposed by Member States

---

76   *ibid.*

77   Article 2(1).

78   *ibid.*

79   Set out in para 4-31 above. These are the persons a layman would regard as potential 'insiders' in relation to a company.

80   A common example would be a company director.

81   A shareholder, for instance.

82   For instance, a corporate finance executive of a merchant bank which is acting for a company.

83   Contained in art 2 of Council Directive (EEC) 89/592.

84   Article 2(3).

85   *ibid.*

on other persons[86] who, with full knowledge of the facts, possess inside information the direct or indirect source of which could only be one of the so-called 'insiders' referred to in para 4-32 above.[87]

The Directive also provides that where the 'persons' referred to above[88] are companies or some other type of legal person, the basic prohibition against insider dealing shall apply to the 'natural' persons[89] who take part in any decision to carry out a transaction for the account of the 'legal' person concerned.[90]

4-34

The 'disclosure' or 'tipping' prohibitions

The Directive goes on to provide that Member States shall prohibit any of the persons subject to the basic prohibition[91] who possesses inside information from disclosing that inside information to any third party unless such disclosure is made in the normal course of the exercise of an employment, profession or duties.[92] Also, each Member State must prohibit such persons from recommending or procuring a third party, on the basis of that inside information, to acquire or dispose of transferable securities admitted to trading on its securities markets.[93]

4-35

General exemptions

These prohibitions should not, however, apply to transactions carried out in pursuit of monetary, exchange-rate or public debt-management policies by a sovereign State, by its central bank or by any other body designated to that effect by the state or by any person acting on their behalf.[94] Member States were also able to extend this exemption to their 'federated states' or similar local authorities in respect of the management of their public debt.[95]

4-36

---

86 That is to say, other than those referred to in para 4-32 above.
87 Article 4 of Council Directive (EEC) 89/592.
88 By virtue of para 4-32.
89 That is to say, the individuals.
90 By virtue of art 2(2) of Council Directive (EEC) 89/592.
91 Imposed by art 2.
92 Article 3(a).
93 Article 3(b).
94 Article 2(4).
95 *ibid.*

ial scope

the territorial scope of the prohibitions,[96] the Directive provides ley must be imposed by each Member State at least to actions undertaken within its territory to the extent that the transferable securities concerned are admitted to trading on a market of a Member State.[97] Each Member State shall regard a transaction as carried out within its territory if it is carried out on a regulated market[98] situated or operating within that territory.[99]

4-38

Home-State provisions

Each Member State may adopt provisions which are more stringent than those laid down by the directive or additional provisions, provided that those provisions are applied generally.[100] In particular, it may extend the scope of the basic prohibition against dealing which is laid down in art 2 of the Directive.[101] It may also impose the prohibitions set out in para 4-35 above on persons falling within para 4-33 above.[102]

4-39

Home-State competent authorities

Each Member State must designate the administrative authority or authorities competent, if necessary in collaboration with other authorities, to ensure that the provisions adopted as a result of the directive are applied. The directive does not oblige Member States to establish a single 'statutory' body, such as the Securities and Exchange Commission in the US, to administer and enforce insider dealing law. Instead, a number of bodies may be employed in collaboration. But, the competent authorities have to be given all supervisory and investigatory powers necessary for the exercise of their functions again, where appropriate, in collaboration with other authorities.[103] Also, each Member State must provide that all persons employed or formerly employed by the competent authorities are to be bound by professional secrecy. Information covered by professional secrecy is not to be divulged to any person or authority except by virtue of provisions laid down by law.[104]

---

96 Being those provided for by arts 2, 3, and 4.
97 Article 5.
98 As referred to in Article 1(2).
99 Also, art 5.
100 Article 6.
101 And outlined in paras 4-31 to 4-34 above.
102 Also art 6.
103 Article 8(1) and (2).
104 Article 9.

Member State co-operation

The Directive then sets out extensive provisions governing the co-operation   **4-40**
which should take place between competent authorities in Member States.
They must, for instance, co-operate with each other whenever necessary for
the purpose of carrying out their duties.[105] To that end, they must
exchange any information required for that purpose although information
thus exchanged will be covered by the obligation of professional secrecy to
which the persons employed or formerly employed by the competent
authorities receiving the information are subject.[106]

The competent authorities may refuse to act on a request for   **4-41**
information where communication of that information might adversely
affect the sovereignty, security or public policy of the State addressed.[107]
They may also refuse where judicial proceedings have already been
initiated in respect of the same actions and against the same persons
before the authorities of the State addressed or where final judgment has
already been passed on such persons for the same actions by the
competent authorities of the State addressed.[108]

The authorities which receive information pursuant to the provisions   **4-42**
outlined above[109] may use it only for the exercise of their functions
under this directive for ensuring that the insider dealing provisions
which are adopted are subsequently applied and in the context of
administrative or judicial proceedings specifically relating to the exercise
of those functions.[110] However, where the competent authority
communicating information consents, the receiving authority may use it
for other purposes and may even forward it to the competent authorities
of other Member States.[111] The Directive also provides that the
European Community may, in conformity with the treaty establishing
the EEC, conclude agreements on insider dealing related matters with
non-EC Member States.[112]

Penalties for insider dealing

Finally, the Directive provides that it is up to each Member State to   **4-43**
determine the penalties to be applied for infringement of the measures

---

105 Article 10(1).
106 Also art 10(1).
107 Article 10(2)(a).
108 Article 10(2)(b).
109 In para 4-40 and 4-41 above.
110 Article 10(3).
111 *Ibid*.
112 Article 11.

taken pursuant to the directive.[113] The penalties must, however, be 'sufficient' to promote compliance with those measures.[114] Accordingly, this left Member States free to choose whether to impose criminal or civil sanctions, or a mixture of both, for breach of the law relating to insider dealing.

Listed companies

4-44 Where the transferable securities of a company have been listed and admitted to trading on a regulated market,[115] the Directive also provides that the company must inform the public as soon as possible of any major new developments in its sphere of activity which are not public knowledge and which may, by virtue of their effect on the assets and liabilities or financial position or on the general course of the business of the company, lead to substantial movements in the price of its shares.[116] Companies may, however, be exempted from this requirement by the competent authority or authorities in a Member State if the disclosure of particular information is such as to prejudice the legitimate interests of the company.[117]

THE PRESENT POSITION

The Criminal Justice Act 1993

4-45 After a process of consultation,[118] Part V of the Criminal Justice Act 1993[119] was enacted. Amongst other matters, its purpose was 'to

---

113 Article 13.

114 *ibid*.

115 As referred to in art 1(2) of the Directive and outlined in para 4-30 above.

116 This is by virtue of para 5(a) of Schedule C in the Annex to Council Directive (EEC) 79/279 which is applied by art 7 of Council Directive (EEC) 89/592. Council Directive 79/279/EEC, of 5 March 1979, was the Directive co-ordinating the conditions for the admission of securities to official stock exchange listing.

117 *ibid*.

118 Initially by the Department of Trade and Industry. This included, in December 1989, a consultative document entitled 'The Law on Insider Dealing' which proposed certain alterations to insider dealing law in the UK. Responsibility for insider dealing 'policy' is now with the Treasury. In relation to the need for public consultation, see Bill Knight, 'Insecure Law for Dealers' (1992) 6 (38) *Lawyer* 5.

119 1993 c 36 and see Appendix to this book for the relative substantive provisions. For an overview, and related discussion, see Eva Lomnicka, 'The new insider dealing provisions: the Criminal Justice Act 1993, Part V' (1994) JBL 173–188 and also Geoffrey Morse, 'Insider dealing: the new rules' (1993) 6 (12) FSLL and Sup 1F 8i–ii.

implement provisions of the Community Council Directive No 89/592/EEC and to amend and restate the law about insider dealing in securities'.[120] It was brought into force with effect from 1 March 1994[121] and will now be examined in detail.

---

120 From the legislative *'chapeau'* to the Criminal Justice Act 1993.

121 See also Insider Dealing (Securities and Regulated Markets) Order 1994 (SI 1994/187). For some background discussion, see Colin Mercer, 'Corporate law and finance in 1994 – a busy year', (1995) 16(1) Bus LR 2–3. Also Keith Wotherspoon, 'Insider dealing – the new law: Part V of the Criminal Justice Act 1993' (1994) 57(3) MLR 419–433. The parliamentary deliberations relating to Part V CJA 1993 are reported in *Hansard* as follows:

House of Lords

Second Reading	3 Nov 92: 539 HL Official Report (5th Series) at column 1347.
Committee Stage	19 Nov 92: 540 HL O R at 721.
Report Stage	3 Dec 92: 540 HL O R at 1469.
Third Reading	10 Dec 92: 541 HL O R at 317.

House of Commons

Second Reading	14 Apr 93: 222 HC O R (6th Series) at 859.
Statement by	
Sec of State	13 May 93: 224 HC O R at 939.
Committee Stage	25 May 93: HC O R S C B (Criminal Justice Bill).
Remaining Stages	29 Jun 93: 227 HC O R at 837.

CHAPTER 5

THE DEFINITIONAL BACKGROUND TO INSIDER DEALING

INTRODUCTION

The mischief of insider dealing was explored earlier.[1] To permit insider dealing would enable people close to a company to benefit from the possession of information about the company which results from their proximity but which is not widely known. The restatement of the law governing insider dealing contained in Part V of the Criminal Justice Act 1993[2] is based, in legislative terms, on a number of important definitions which must be applied in sequence to any consideration of a potential offence. Although the use of complicated definitions is thought by many to be user-inimical,[3] requiring the definitions to be consulted at the same time and in order to understand the main operative provisions, thankfully the definitions applicable to the offence of insider dealing are relatively precise. They are contained, mostly, in ss 54–60[4] of the Criminal Justice Act 1993.

5-01

INFORMATION IS THE KEY

Information

The offence of insider dealing is based upon the misuse of information which relates to securities.[5] 'Information', has been defined succinctly as 'Knowledge communicated concerning some particular fact, subject or event'.[6]

5-02

---

1   See Chapter 3 *et seq* above.
2   1993 c 36.
3   That is to say, the opposite of being user-friendly.
4   Entitled 'Interpretation'. And see Alistair Alcock, 'Insider dealing – how did we get here?' (1994) 15(3) Co Law 67–72.
5   'Securities' for these purposes are securities to which Part V of the Criminal Justice Act 1993 applies. Section 54(1) CJA 1993 provides that Part V *per se* applies to any security which falls within any paragraph of Schedule 2 to the CJA 1993 and also satisfies any conditions made applicable to it by any order made by the Treasury for the purposes of s 54(1). In Part V of the CJA 1993, and in this book unless otherwise indicated, any reference to a 'security' is a reference to a security to which Part V is applicable.
6   From the *Compact Oxford English Dictionary* (2nd edn, 1991).

nside information

5-03   The important expression 'inside information' is defined[7] essentially as meaning information which has four basic characteristics:

- The *first* is that it must relate to particular securities or to a particular issuer, or to particular issuers of securities and not to securities generally, or to issuers of securities generally.[8] For the purposes of Part V of the Criminal Justice Act 1993, it is provided that an 'issuer', in relation to any securities, means any company, public sector body or individual by which or by whom the securities have been or are to be issued.[9] It is further provided, for the purposes of Part V of the Act, that information shall be treated as relating to an issuer of securities which is a company not only where it is about the company but also where it may affect the business prospects of the company.[10]

- The *second* is that the information must be specific or precise.[11] As the Criminal Justice Bill [Lords] passed through the parliamentary process, the expression 'specific or precise' led to much discussion when it was considered by Standing Committee B. The Economic Secretary to the Treasury made it clear that the '… purpose … is to ensure that inside information does not include information which is mere rumour …'.[12] He pointed out that the provision was derived from an element of the definition of 'inside information' in the

---

7   By s 56 CJA 1993, for the purposes of ss 56 and 57 CJA 1993. This provision was said by the Economic Secretary to the Treasury to be '… central to this part of the Bill …'. See the House of Commons Official Report of Standing Committee B, 10 June 1993, at column 172. All subsequent references are to *Hansard* reports. See Note 121 to Chapter 4, above, and Note 6 to Chapter 6, below, further.

8   Section 56(1)(a) CJA 1993.

9   Section 60(2) CJA 1993.

10   Section 60(4) CJA 1993. The terms 'company' and 'public sector body' are themselves defined by s 60(3)(a) and (b) CJA 1993. It should be noted that the potential breadth of s 60(4) caused concern as the CJA 1993 passed through the legislative process. Mr Peter Ainsworth (MP for Surrey, East) wondered whether it might result in information about an entire market sector being treated as 'inside information'. He also thought its breadth '… could have a severe impact on the whole process of analysts' briefings …'; see the report of Standing Committee B, 10 June 1993, at columns 196–197. The Economic Secretary to the Treasury, Mr Anthony Nelson, made it clear that the inclusion of this provision was a deliberate attempt to ensure that the expression 'relates to particular … issuers' in s 56(1)(a) CJA 1993 was not interpreted too narrowly by the courts thus preventing information from being 'inside information' which, while not relating to particular issuers, was nonetheless price-sensitive. Without this 'business prospects' provision, there was a risk that information of concern to a company (such as an important regulatory decision or perhaps whether a customer was about to go out of business) would not be inside information. He also made it clear that companies (and stock analysts) operating in accordance with existing good 'stock exchange' practice had nothing to fear from the new legislation; see the report of Standing Committee B, 10 June 1993, at columns 197–199.

11   Section 56(1)(b) CJA 1993.

12   *Per* Mr Anthony Nelson, the Economic Secretary to the Treasury. See the report of Standing Committee B, 10 June 1993, at column 173.

relevant insider dealing directive.[13] However, it is said that the government had been concerned '... that "precise" alone might be interpreted narrowly by the courts, so "specific", which is employed in existing legislation, has been added ...'[14] Some further guidance was also given. In the context of a takeover bid, 'specific information' might be the fact that a bid was going to be made whilst 'precise information' would be the price at which the bid was going to be made. 'Precise information' will thus be narrow, exact and definitive and thus capable of a narrow interpretation[15] whilst the use of 'specific' kept the integrity of what was required by the directive[16] and already provided for by existing legislation. The expression as a whole was therefore thought to comply with the directive and to conform with existing legislation.[17] To go further and widen the scope of the information which was capable of being 'inside information' '... would run the serious risk of improperly, unduly and unreasonably inhibiting the analytical relationships and

---

13 Council Directive (EEC) 89/592 of 13 November 1989 co-ordinating regulations on insider dealing. Part of the definition of 'inside information' in art 1(1) of that directive refers to '... information ... of a precise nature ...'

14 See the report of Standing Committee B, 10 June 1993, at column 173.

15 'Precise' need not necessarily refer to figures. It could refer to a date, an event or a fact. *Per* the Economic Secretary to the Treasury. See the report of Standing Committee B, 10 June 1993, at column 175. But see 'Putting the pieces together – insider liability' in (1994) 15(3) Co Law 88.

16 See the report of Standing Committee B, 10 June 1993, at column 174. Certain scenarios were considered by Standing Committee B in the context of 'specific or precise' information:

  (i)   An analyst might have lunch with a company chairman. After lunch, on leaving the restaurant, they see a battered car. If the chairman says that he will not be buying a new car this year, would that be 'specific or precise' information if the analyst thinks, as a result, that the company must be doing badly? Although it was a question of judgment in individual cases, the Economic Secretary to the Treasury thought not. The information would not be specific about the prospects of an issuer and would not necessarily indicate that something was wrong with the company. It would be neither specific nor precise. See the report of Standing Committee B, 10th June 1993, at column 174. The scenario was suggested by Mr Alistair Darling, MP for Edinburgh, Central.

  (ii) At such a lunch, the company chairman might say to the analyst that 'our results will be much better than the market expects or knows'. Such information would not be precise because the chairman did not disclose what the results were going to be. It would, however, be specific because he would be saying something about the results of the company. *Per* the Economic Secretary to the Treasury, Mr Anthony Nelson. See the report of Standing Committee B, 10 June 1993, at column 175.

  (iii) If, alternatively, the company chairman disclosed that the profits were going to be at a certain level which was unknown to the market, that information would be precise rather than specific. *Per* the Economic Secretary to the Treasury. See the report of Standing Committee B, 10 June 1993, at column 175.

17 *Per* Mr Anthony Nelson, the Economic Secretary to the Treasury. See the report of Standing Committee B, 10 June 1993, at column 175.

assessment of companies that are much in the interest of investors in the financial markets as they are in the companies that want to encourage such relationships.'[18]

- The *third* is that the information has not been made public.[19]

- The *fourth*, more generalised, characteristic for the information in question is that it must be such as would be likely to have a significant effect on the price of any securities if it was made public.[20] In passing, for these purposes, 'price' is specifically said to include 'value'.[21] The requirement that the effect be 'significant' was thought necessary to ensure that the prohibition of insider dealing applied only in respect of major matters such as impending takeovers, imminent profits forecasts and dividend announcements out of line with expectations and not in respect of information likely to have only a trivial effect on the price of securities.[22] If that requirement was not imposed, it was thought likely that there would be many technical breaches of this legislation which would 'either lead to a host of prosecutions where there is no real mischief or the law would fall into disrepute'.[23] It was also possible that meetings between company management, fund managers and analysts would be inhibited if information which was likely to have any effect on the price of relevant securities could amount to 'inside information'.[24]

Information as an insider

5-04   In very general terms, the offence is based upon the actions of a person who has 'information as an insider'. For the purposes of Part V of the Act a person has 'information as an insider' if and only if it is 'inside

---

18   See also James E Tolan, 'The legal liability of security analysts' (1987) 2 (4) BJIB & FL 157–161 and then Michael Pescod and Emma Robarts, 'In line with market expectations? Analysts' briefings and brokers' lunches' (1993) 4(6) PLC 27–31.

19   Section 56(1)(c) CJA 1993. The expression information 'made public' is itself defined by s 58 CJA 1993.

20   Section 56(1)(d) CJA 1993.

21   Section 56(3) CJA 1993.

22   *Per* the Economic Secretary to the Treasury, Mr Anthony Nelson. See the report of Standing Committee B, 10 June 1993, at column 177.

23   *ibid*.

24   See, generally, the report of Standing Committee B, 10 June 1993, at columns 177–179. On the overall definition of 'inside information', the Economic Secretary to the Treasury commented as follows: 'Having consulted widely on the matter, complied with the directive and gone no further than existing legislation, I believe that we have struck the right balance and have a reasonable definition'.

information'[25] and he knows that it is inside information[26] and, also, that he has the information from an 'inside source' and he knows that he has the information from an inside source.[27] It has also been made clear that for these purposes, the 'person' will be an individual as opposed to a company '... because ultimately it will always be individuals who misuse inside information ...'.[28]

Information from an inside source

For the purposes of para 5-04 above, a person has information from an inside source[29] if and only if he has it through being a director, employee or shareholder of an issuer of securities[30] or through having access to the information by virtue of his employment, office or profession.[31] A person is also regarded as having information from an inside source if the direct or indirect source of his information is a person from one of the categories referred to earlier in this para 5-05.[32]

5-05

---

25 See s 57 CJA 1993 generally, which is entitled 'Insiders'. Essentially, this provision defines the persons to whom the legislation applies. 'Inside information' is defined by s 56(1) CJA 1993 and described in para 5-03 above.

26 Section 57(1)(a) CJA 1993.

27 Section 57(1)(b) CJA 1993.

28 *Per* Mr Anthony Nelson, the Economic Secretary to the Treasury. See the report of Standing Committee B, 10 June 1993, at column 189. See, also, s 61(1) CJA 1993 which outlines penalties on conviction.

29 And, in general terms, is thus an 'insider'.

30 Section 57(2)(a)(i) CJA 1993. It was made clear by the Economic Secretary to the Treasury that the definition of those persons having 'information as an insider', should include those such as shareholders, who 'own' a company and who are therefore likely to be privy to information which is significant, precise and market-sensitive. Not all such persons will be tempted into insider dealing but they might be and are therefore covered by this definition. See the report of Standing Committee B, 10 June 1993, at column 190.

31 Section 57(2)(a)(ii) CJA 1993. Whether a person has such access will be a question of fact. A person will be an 'insider' if he obtains information *qua* employee during the course of his employment just as if he did so as a director or shareholder. See the comments of the Economic Secretary to the Treasury in the report of Standing Committee B, 10 June 1993, at column 190.

32 Section 57(2)(b) CJA 1993. It will be noted that these provisions do not carry forward the definitional concept of being 'connected with the company' which was used in the Company Securities (Insider Dealing) Act 1985 (see s 9 and also, for instance, s 1(1) CS(ID)A 1985). The reason given for this change was that it reflected the provisions of the insider dealing directive (Council Directive (EEC)89/592 of 13 November 1989) and also because '... it is quite possible for someone to have direct access to price-sensitive information without being connected to a company ...'. See the comments of the Economic Secretary to the Treasury in the report of Standing Committee B, 10 June 1993, at column 190.

THE RELEVANT SECURITIES

5-06   Part V of the Criminal Justice Act 1993 is concerned with insider dealing in securities. The 'securities' to which it applies are those falling within any paragraph of Schedule 2 to the Criminal Justice Act 1993[33] which also satisfy any conditions made applicable to them under an order made by the Treasury for those purposes.[34] Such an order was made on 1 February 1994 and took effect on 1 March 1994.[35] The underlying intention is therefore clear that modifications may be made to the various categories of 'securities' which are set out in Schedule 2, should they be necessary, without the need for further primary legislation. The Treasury may by order amend Schedule 2,[36] so legislative flexibility is thereby built-in to Part V.[37] This was justified on the basis that the terms on which securities are admitted to formal markets differ widely and because of the need to ensure that it is possible to apply this legislation to situations where there is a ready trade in securities related to those traded on formal markets.[38] It may always be necessary to amend the legislation to reflect the development of new securities.[39]

5-07   Schedule 2 to the Criminal Justice Act 1993[40] contains categories of securities similar to although *prima facie* not as wide-ranging as the categories of 'investments' set out in Part I of Schedule 1 to the Financial Services Act 1986. It must be read in conjunction with any relevant orders made by the treasury.[41] This approach was adopted because it was not the intention of the government to 'catch' transactions in all securities falling within Schedule 2 to the Criminal Justice Act 1993.The purpose of the legislation was said to be that of ensuring confidence in

---

33   Section 54(1)(a) CJA 1993.

34   For the purposes of s 54(1). Section 54(1)(b) CJA 1993. And see Alistair Alcock, 'Insider Dealing' (1995) 16(1) Co Law 21–23.

35   See, generally, the Insider Dealing (Securities and Regulated Markets) Order 1994 (SI 1994/187).

36   Section 54(2) CJA 1993.

37   Section 64(1) CJA 1993 provides that, where Part V contains a power to make an order, it shall be exercisable by statutory instrument. By virtue of s 64(3), any such order may make different provision for different cases and may contain such incidental, supplemental and transitional provisions as the Treasury considers expedient. But s 64(2) is explicit in providing that no such order may be made under Part V unless a draft of the order has first been laid before and approved by a resolution of each House of Parliament. An affirmative resolution is therefore required; cf s 205A of the Financial Services Act 1986.

38   *Per* the Economic Secretary to the Treasury, Mr Anthony Nelson. See the report of Standing Committee B, 10 June 1993, at column 164–165.

39   Again, see the report of Standing Committee B, 10 June 1993, at column 165.

40   Headed 'Securities'.

41   Pursuant to s 54(2) CJA 1993. In particular, it must be read in conjunction with SI 1994/187 (as subsequently amended).

the 'market' in its broadest sense. Accordingly, as will be seen from paras 5-08 to 5-15 below, only transactions in securities that are 'market related' are made subject to this legislation. Essentially, the intention was that the legislation should apply to any 'security' falling within the overall scope of any paragraph in Schedule 2, which is traded on a 'regulated market'.[42] 'Regulated markets' for these purposes, are any markets established under the rules of any one of a number of 'specified' investment exchanges.[43]

Shares

Shares and stock in the share capital of a company are capable of being 'securities' for the purposes of insider dealing law.[44] They are of course 'investments' for the purposes of the Financial Services Act 1986.[45] 'Company' for the purposes of Part V of the Criminal Justice Act 1993 is taken to mean any body, whether or not it is incorporated and wherever it is incorporated or constituted, which is not a 'public sector body'.[46] A 'public sector body' is defined as meaning the government of the UK, of Northern Ireland or of any country or territory outside the UK.[47] Alternatively, it can be a local authority in the UK or elsewhere,[48] the Bank of England,[49] the central bank of any sovereign State[50] or any international organisation the members of which include the UK or another Member State.[51] To be 'securities' falling within Schedule 2 to

---

42 *Per* the Economic Secretary to the Treasury, Mr Anthony Nelson. See the report of Standing Committee B, 10 June 1993, at column 165.

43 See art 9 of SI 1994/187. The investment exchanges in question are specified in the schedule to that order as amended by SI 1996/1561. They include overseas investment exchanges which are recognised for the purposes of the Financial Services Act 1986 and the exchanges in other member states on which relevant securities are traded. The regulated markets which are regulated in the UK for the purposes of Part V of the CJA 1993 are any market established under the rules of the London Stock Exchange Limited, LIFFE Administration & Management, Tradepoint Financial Networks plc and OMLX, the London Securities and Derivatives Exchange Limited: see art 10(a)–(c) of SI 1994/187 as amended. See also Alistair Alcock, 'Insider Dealing' (1995) 16(1) Co Law 21–23. It should be noted that the Irish Stock Exchange separated from the London Stock Exchange with effect from 8 December 1995. The new registered company of the former is the Irish Stock Exchange Limited whilst the latter is the London Stock Exchange Limited. See also the Insider Dealing (Securities and Regulated Markets)(Amendment) Order 1996 (SI 1996/1561). SIs 1994/187 and 1996/1561 may be found in Appendices B and C to this book.

44 Paragraph 1 of Schedule 2 to the CJA 1993.

45 See para 1 of Schedule 1 to the FSA 1986.

46 Section 60(3)(a) CJA 1993.

47 Section 60(3)(b)(i) CJA 1993.

48 Section 60(3)(b)(ii) CJA 1993.

49 Section 60(3)(b)(iv) CJA 1993.

50 Section 60(3)(b)(v) CJA 1993.

51 Section 60(3)(b)(iii) CJA 1993.

the Criminal Justice Act 1993, any such stocks or shares must however be officially listed in a 'State within the European Economic Area'[52] or be admitted to dealing on or have their prices quoted on or under the rules of a regulated market.[53] The intention of course is that transactions in other shares, such as those in private companies, should not be subject to this legislation[54] and it may be that arrangements such as vendor placings will fall outside its scope.[55] The requirement that 'securities' must be listed, admitted to dealing or have their prices quoted etc, applies in relation to any security purporting to fall within any paragraph of Schedule 2 to the Criminal Justice Act 1993.[56]

Debt securities

5-09   Subject to the 'listing' requirement referred to in para 5-08 above, 'debt securities' may also be 'securities' for these purposes.[57] This category covers any instrument creating or acknowledging indebtedness which is issued by a company or public sector body. This includes, in particular, debentures, debenture stock, loan stock, bonds and certificates of deposit. For the purposes of Part V, an 'issuer' in the context of debt securities would be any company or public sector body by which the securities have been or are to be issued.[58]

---

52   For these purposes, a 'State within the European Economic Area' means a State which is a member of the European Union and the Republic of Iceland, the Kingdom of Norway and the Principality of Liechtenstein: See art 2 of SI 1994/187.

53   See art 4 of SI 1994/187. And see Nick Orosz, 'Insider dealing and the Euromarkets' I (1994) 13(1) IFL Rev 18–30.

54   *Per* the Economic Secretary to the Treasury, Mr Anthony Nelson. See the report of Standing Committee B, 10 June 1993, at column 164.

55   During the consideration of the Criminal Justice Bill [Lords] by Standing Committee B, Mr Peter Ainsworth asked the Economic Secretary to the Treasury to clarify the position of vendor placing. Mr Ainsworth said that when a broker was arranging a vendor placing, he would normally have agreements to deal with a number of people (a number of placees, the vendor and the company that was issuing shares to the vendor). As such arrangements would be subject to the shares in question being admitted to the Official List of the Stock Exchange, Mr Ainsworth assumed '... that such a situation is not covered by the Bill. Therefore, the Bill in no way affects the ability of brokers to continue to conduct vendor placing in the way that they do at present ...'. The most the minister felt able to confirm, in responding, was that the shares '... would not be securities until they were listed'. See the report of Standing Committee B, 10 June 1993, at columns 165-166.

56   See art 4 of SI 1994/187.

57   Paragraph 2 of Schedule 2 to the CJA 1993. And see art 4 of SI 1994/187, and John Belton, 'Insider Trading and the distressed debt market' (1995) 16 (4) Co Law 110–111.

58   Section 60(2) CJA 1993.

Warrants

The third category of 'securities' is that of 'warrants'. For these purposes, a warrant is described as being 'any right, whether conferred by warrant or otherwise, to subscribe for shares or debt securities'.[59] The corresponding category of 'investments' in the Financial Services Act 1986[60] contains a clarificatory 'Note' which says that 'It is immaterial whether the investments are for the time being in existence or identifiable'.[61] The 'investments' so referred to can only be the investments to which the warrant or other instrument entitles the holder to subscribe. The absence of such a provision in relation to the warrants subject to Part V perhaps indicates that those warrants may need to relate to securities which are in existence and/or identifiable. For the purpose of the Criminal Justice Act 1993, warrants may be 'securities' if they satisfy the 'listing' requirement.[62] Alternatively, they may be 'securities' for these purposes if the rights they confer are rights to subscribe for any share or debt security of the same class as a share or debt security which satisfies the 'listing' requirement.[63] The underlying intention is that securities such as warrants should be subject to this legislation only if related to 'market traded securities'.[64] One exception was, however, mentioned in that it was '... intended that the legislation will apply to all derivatives which are traded on the London International Financial Futures Exchange because of the important role that LIFFE plays in the United Kingdom's financial markets, even though in the case of the exchange's short-term interest rate contracts, there is no underlying security'.[65]

5-10

Depository receipts

The fourth category of 'securities' is entitled 'depositary receipts'. It relates to the rights under any depositary receipt[66] and a 'depositary receipt', for these purposes, is defined as meaning a certificate or other record and whether or not in the form of a document which is issued by or on behalf of a person who holds any relevant securities of a particular

5-11

---

59 Paragraph 3 of Schedule 2 to the CJA 1993.
60 In para 4 of Schedule 1 to the FSA; this category is entitled 'Instruments entitling to shares or securities'.
61 Note (1) to para 4 of Schedule 1 to the FSA.
62 See art 4 of SI 1994/187.
63 See art 5 of SI 1994/187.
64 See the report of Standing Committee B, 10 June 1993, at column 165.
65 *Per* the Economic Secretary to the Treasury, Mr Anthony Nelson. See the report of Standing Committee B, 10 June 1993, at column 165.
66 Paragraph 4(1) of Schedule 2 to the CJA 1993.

issuer and which acknowledges that another person is entitled to rights in relation to the relevant securities or relevant securities of the same kind.[67] For these purposes, 'relevant securities' are said to mean shares, debt securities and warrants[68] and depositary receipts may be 'securities' for the purposes of the Criminal Justice Act 1993 if they satisfy the listing requirement[69] or, alternatively, if the rights they confer are in respect of any share or debt security which satisfies the listing requirement.[70]

Options

5-12   The fifth category of 'securities' is entitled 'options'. It relates to any options to acquire or dispose of any security falling within any other paragraph of Schedule 2 to the Criminal Justice Act 1993.[71] For 'options' to be 'securities' for the purposes of the Criminal Justice Act 1993, they will need to satisfy the listing requirement referred to above.[72] Alternatively, the option will need to relate to any share or debt security which satisfies the listing requirement[73] or to any depository receipt which satisfies the listing requirement or relates to shares or debt securities which satisfy that requirement.[74] The legislative intention behind these provisions was to ensure that '... all derivatives of shares and debt securities that are themselves covered by the legislation are also within the ambit of the legislation. This means that it will apply to, for example, exchange-traded and over-the-counter options in a listed company's shares. It is important that the legislation does that to close off an avenue which could otherwise be exploited by the unscrupulous.'[75]

Futures

5-13   The sixth category is entitled 'futures'. These are said to be rights under a contract for the acquisition or disposal of relevant securities under

---

67 Paragraph 4(2)(a) and (b) of Schedule 2 to the CJA 1993.

68 Paragraph 4(3) of Schedule 2 to the CJA 1993.

69 See art 4 of SI 1994/187.

70 Article 6 of SI 1994/187. See, also, the report of Standing Committee B, 10 June 1993, at column 165, *per* Mr Anthony Nelson.

71 Paragraph 5 of Schedule 2 to the CJA 1993.

72 See art 4 of SI 1994/187.

73 Article 7(a) of SI 1994/187.

74 Article 7(b) of SI 1994/187.

75 *Per* Mr Anthony Nelson, the Economic Secretary to the Treasury. See the report of Standing Committee B, 10 June 1993, at column 165.

which delivery is to be made at a future date and at a price agreed when the contract is made.[76] For these purposes, the references made to a future date and to a price agreed when the contract is made are said to include references to a date and a price determined in accordance with the terms of the contract.[77] Also, the expression 'relevant securities' is said to cover any securities falling within any other paragraph of Schedule 2 to the Criminal Justice Act 1993.[78] For 'futures' to be 'securities' for the purposes of the Criminal Justice Act 1993, they will need either to satisfy the listing requirement[79] or the alternative condition set out in para 5-12 above.[80]

Contracts for differences

The seventh and final category is entitled 'contracts for differences'.[81]   **5-14**
These are described as being rights under a contract which does not provide for the delivery of securities but whose purpose or pretended purpose is to secure a profit or to avoid a loss by reference to fluctuations in one of three areas:

- a share index or other similar factor connected with relevant securities;[82]

- the price of particular relevant securities;[83] or

- the interest rate offered on money placed on deposit.[84]

For these purposes, the expression 'relevant securities' is said to   **5-15**
mean any security falling within any other paragraph of Schedule 2 to the Criminal Justice Act 1993.[85] For 'contracts for differences' to be 'securities' for the purposes of the Criminal Justice Act 1993, they must either satisfy the listing requirement[86] or the purpose or pretended purpose of the contract must be to secure a profit or avoid a loss by reference to fluctuations in the price of any shares or debt securities

---

76 Paragraph 6(1) of Schedule 2 to the CJA 1993.
77 Paragraph 6(2)(a) of Schedule 2 to the CJA 1993.
78 Paragraph 6(2)(b) of Schedule 2 to the CJA 1993.
79 See art 4 of SI 1994/187.
80 See art 7(a) of SI 1994/187.
81 Paragraph 7(1) of Schedule 2 to the CJA 1993.
82 Paragraph 7(1)(a) of Schedule 2 to the CJA 1993.
83 Paragraph 7(1)(b) of Schedule 2 to the CJA 1993.
84 Paragraph 7(1)(c) of Schedule 2 to the CJA 1993.
85 Paragraph 7(2) of Schedule 2 to the CJA 1993.
86 See art 4 of SI 1994/187.

satisfy the listing requirement[87] or in an index of the price of such shares or debt securities.[88]

PRICE, INFORMATION AND SECURITIES

5-16 The expression 'price-affected securities' is a constituent part of those provisions in Part V of the Criminal Justice Act 1993 which detail the basic offence of insider dealing.[89] The expression 'price-sensitive information' is relevant to certain of the defences which may be applicable to an individual charged with insider dealing.[90] For the purposes of Part V, securities are 'price-affected securities' in relation to inside information and inside information is 'price-sensitive information' in relation to securities if and only if the information would, if made public, be likely to have a significant effect on the price of the securities.[91] For these purposes, 'price' is said to include 'value'.[92]

5-17 It does, however, remain difficult to say, in any general sense, what will characterise 'price-sensitive' information. It is not, for instance, considered feasible to define any theoretical percentage movement in a share price which will make an item of information price-sensitive. It is usually necessary to consider a variety of factors relevant to each specific case. In addition to the information itself, these may include the existing price and volatility of the shares in question and also the prevailing

---

87 See art 8(a) of SI 1994/187.

88 See art 8(b) of SI 1994/187. For recent discussion of the effect on the use of contracts for differences, see Colin Mercer and Helen Shilling, 'Pre-offer moves: contracts for differences', (1995) 9 (6) *Corporate Briefing* 2–5 and Roddy Martin, 'Markets: contracts for differences',(1995) 6(4) ICCLR C87–88; both articles relate to the use of contracts for differences in the failed bid by Trafalgar House plc for Northern Electric plc in March 1995, during which Swiss Bank Corporation (advising Trafalgar) had acquired derivatives relating to shares in all the other regional electricity companies in the belief that a bid for one would push up the prices of all the others in the sector. Northern Electric complained to the Takeover Panel that this had been done in secret and with inside information. Although that complaint was rejected by the panel, the SIB and the Panel are engaged in consultation and a review of the position with a view to stamping out any misuse of inside information during a takeover bid. Essentially, their approach seems to be that a firm should not use derivatives to enable a customer to buy or sell and indirect stake where it knows or has reason to believe that, as a result of inside information, the customer cannot properly buy or sell such an indirect stake on the open market. Watch this space.

89 Section 52 CJA 1993.

90 Which are set out in s 53 CJA 1993.

91 Section 56(2) CJA 1993.

92 Section 56(3) CJA 1993.

market conditions.[93] Generally speaking, the more specific the information,[94] the greater the risk that it may be price-sensitive.[95] ⸙

In practice, in conjunction with their advisers, most companies are able to assess whether and the extent to which an event or fact known to the company will have a significant effect on its reported earnings per share, its pre-tax profits and any borrowings or other potential factors which may affect the share price of the company.[96] Those companies whose securities are listed on the Stock Exchange in London are under a general obligation[97] to disclose information where there are major new developments which may lead to a substantial movement in the price of their listed securities. This is both to keep the public informed of the position of the company and also to avoid the creation of a false market. Such disclosure must normally be effected by means of an announcement to the Company Announcements Office of the Stock Exchange.[98]

---

93 See para 8 of the 'Guidance on the dissemination of price sensitive information' document issued by the London Stock Exchange in February 1994 and para 4 of the document reissued in February 1995. It is understood that the document is presently being reprinted. See, for instance, the problems which resulted when details of a price review by the Electricity Regulator were leaked in July 1995. There was frantic trading in relevant shares and the Stock Exchange ordered the regulator to publish his review early. See Martin Waller, 'Shares yo-yo after power price leak', *The Times*, 7 July 1995. This led to an enquiry and the subsequent publication by the Exchange of 'Guidelines for the Control and Release of Price-Sensitive Information by Industry Regulations'. See also Christine Buckley, 'Tough new guidelines for industry regulators', *The Times*, 3 January 1996. See also Jon Ashworth, 'Former Rec Chief faces insider trial', *The Times*, 27 June 1996.

94 Particularly financial information such as sales and profits figures.

95 See para 10 of the Stock Exchange February 1994 guidance document and para 6 of the February 1995 reissue.

96 See para 9 of the Stock Exchange February 1994 guidance document, and para 5 of the February 1995 reissue.

97 See Chapter 9, below, ('Continuing Obligations') of the Listing Rules. The Listing Rules also indicate many events which must be announced to the market because they may be price-sensitive. These include dividend announcements, board appointments or departures, profit warnings, share dealings by directors or substantial shareholders, acquisitions and disposals above a certain size, annual and interim results, preliminary results, rights issues and other offers of securities. See para 9 of the Stock Exchange February 1994 guidance document, and para 5 of the February 1995 reissue, further. In particular, in other areas, judgement will necessarily be required by companies and their advisers. See also Frank Kane, 'Exchange guidelines clear but irrelevant', *The Guardian*, 26 February 1994.

98 The Company Announcements Office of the London Stock Exchange, which operates the Regulatory News Service (RNS) provided by the London Stock Exchange. See pp 14 and 15 of the Stock Exchange February 1994 guidance document and p 13 of the February 1995 reissue, further. RNS is an electronic information dissemination service for the receipt, validation and publication of regulated announcements provided by companies in compliance with the continuing obligations of listing. The purpose of the RNS is to ensure that announcements which may well have a significant effect on the price of relevant securities or market activity generally are validated and communicated to the market promptly and effectively. There have, however, been many recent grumblings over delays with the RNS and its technical shortcomings. See, for instance, 'Time is money even in the City', *The Times* (Pennington column), 24 May 1996.

INFORMATION MADE PUBLIC

The basic position

5-19   Reference has already been made[99] to circumstances in which information may have been or may be 'made public' in the context of insider dealing law and this area of the legislation was much debated during the consultations and discussions which preceded and followed its framing in the Criminal Justice Bill.[100] For these purposes, the expression 'made public' in relation to information is to be construed in accordance with the provisions of s 58 of the Criminal Justice Act 1993 although it is made clear that those provisions are not to be regarded as being exhaustive as to the meaning of that expression.[101] Essentially, s 58 contains two main elements. The first describes certain circumstances in which information is definitely to be regarded as having been made public.[102] These include where it is published in accordance with the rules of a regulated market for the purpose of informing investors and their professional advisors.[103] The second element provides that, where certain circumstances apply, information may be regarded as having been made public.[104] One instance is where the information may be acquired only by persons exercising diligence or expertise.[105] The rationale behind this second element was to set out circumstances in which information may be treated as having been made public because it was felt that, unless such instances were made clear, information might well be considered not to have been made public.[106]

---

99 See, for instance, para 5-18 above.

100 The Economic Secretary to the Treasury, Mr Anthony Nelson, commented that '... when information has and has not been made public is the single issue that has caused most concern to the organisations with which the government have been discussing the Bill'. See the report of Standing Committee B, 10 June 1993, at column 182.

101 See s 58(1) CJA 1993 and also the comments of the Economic Secretary to the Treasury, Mr Anthony Nelson, in the report of Standing Committee B, 10 June 1993, at column 187 where he said: 'It is in the interest of the investors in the market as well as companies with listed shares to conform with established ways of making information public ... Listed companies should publish their information in accordance with the rules of that regulated market as soon as possible. The Stock Exchange has urged them to do so, and the government believe that it is essential for them to do so ...'. See also Charles Abrams, 'Insider Dealing – the new regime (Part 2)' (1994) 1(2) EFSL 38–42.

102 Section 58(1) and (2) CJA 1993.

103 Section 58(2)(a) CJA 1993 and see para 5-21 below.

104 Section 58(1) and (3) CJA 1993.

105 Section 58(3)(a) CJA 1993.

106 *Per* the Economic Secretary to the Treasury, Mr Anthony Nelson. See the report of Standing Committee B, 10 June 1993, at columns 180-181 and also 184.

Whether or not information has been made public will be a matter of   **5-20**
fact. The importance of such a fact was well put as follows: 'If someone
possesses inside information and intends to make it public, but deals in
the meantime, that is insider dealing. If that person is in receipt of inside
information and makes it public so that it is in the public domain when
he deals, that is not insider dealing. It is a question of whether the
dealing falls on one side or the other of information having been made
public ...'[107] The point at which information becomes public is crucial
because that determines, in the context of insider dealing law, whether
the action taken before or after is legal or illegal.[108]

Disclosure to the market

Information is to be regarded as made public if it is published in   **5-21**
accordance with the rules of a 'regulated market' for the purpose of
informing investors and their professional advisers[109] and this is
regarded as an established way of making information public. For the
purposes of insider dealing law, a 'regulated market' is said to mean any
market, however operated, which is identified as a regulated market for
the purposes of Part V of the Criminal Justice Act 1993 by an order made
by the Treasury.[110] Having made such an order, certain markets have
been identified as regulated markets for these purposes and this
includes the London Stock Exchange.[111] Accordingly, information which
a listed company is obliged to and does have published through the
Company Announcements Office of the London Stock Exchange will
then be regarded as having been made public. To emphasise the point,
once information has been made public, it is not capable of being 'inside

---

107 *Per* the Economic Secretary to the Treasury, Mr Anthony Nelson. See the report of
  Standing Committee B, 10 June 1993, at columns 180–181 and also 186.

108 See the comments of the Economic Secretary to the Treasury, Mr Anthony Nelson in
  the report of Standing Committee B, 10 June 1993, at columns 180–181 and 187.

109 Section 58(2)(a) CJA 1993. And see paras 1 and 2 of the guidance document reissued
  by the London Stock Exchange in February 1995.

110 Section 60(1) CJA 1993. And see Alistair Alcock, 'Insider Dealing' (1995) 16(1) Co
  Law 21–23.

111 See art 9 and 10 and the Schedule to the Insider Dealing (Securities and Regulated
  Markets) Order 1994 (SI 1994/187) as amended by SI 1996/1561. See also para 5-07
  and note 43 above. Generally speaking, 'regulated markets' are markets established
  under the rules of a number of specified investment exchanges. In relation to
  markets regulated in the United Kingdom, those investment exchanges are the
  London Stock Exchange Limited, Tradepoint Financial Networks plc, LIFFE
  Administration & Management and OMLX, the London Securities and Derivatives
  Exchange Limited. And see the Insider Dealing (Securities and Regulated Markets)
  (Amendment) Order 1996 (SI 1996/1561), effective from 1 July 1996.

information' and so insider dealing law should not prevent persons dealing in the relevant securities.[112]

Public records [113]

5-22   Information is regarded as made public if it is contained in records which by virtue of any enactment are open to inspection by the public.[114] The expression 'by virtue of any enactment' was inserted deliberately to exclude publication in obscure non-statutory records, such as local parish registers. It should not therefore be possible for someone to arrange for information to be published somewhere in a parish register in rural Kent and then to rely on that information as having been made public. The obvious examples of registers which are present by virtue of an enactment are the companies and patent registries. Information which may be obtained from Companies House by making a company search against a company registered in the UK, obtainable by anyone on payment of a small fee, will be regarded as having been made public.[115] Material published in the *Official Gazette* would also be regarded as having been made public.[116]

Information already publicised

5-23   Information is also to be regarded as having been made public if it is derived from information which has already been made public.[117] Although whether or not information has been made public *ab initio* will be a matter of fact, the wording of this provision is rather vague.[118] What

---

112 See art 10 of SI 1994/187 and SI 1996/1561, further. But see Charles Abrams, 'The London Stock Exchange and insider dealing' (1995) 2(3) EFSL 79–80, and Laurence Garside, 'What shall we tell them?' (1994) 114/1212 *Accountancy* 83.

113 See s 56(1)(c) CJA 1993. However, '... there is everything to stop them or make them cautious about so doing before the information is in the public domain, unless they have one of the defences'. *Per* the Economic Secretary to the Treasury, Mr Anthony Nelson. See the report of Standing Committee B, 10 June 1993, at columns 180–181 and also 183.

114 Section 58(2)(b) CJA 1993. See the report of Standing Committee B, 10 June 1993, at column 183.

115 See Part XXIV ('The Registrar of Companies, His Functions and Offices') of the Companies Act 1985; in particular, s 709 ('Inspection, etc of records kept by the registrar').

116 See the comments of the Economic Secretary to the Treasury, Mr Anthony Nelson in the report of Standing Committee B, 10 June 1993, at column 183.

117 Section 58(2)(d) CJA 1993.

118 For instance, as to when and how information will be 'derived' from information already made public. What will have to be shown? See the comments of Alistair Darling MP, from the report of Standing Committee B, 10 June 1993, at column 181.

does seem clear is that such information need not necessarily be in writing. It may be derived from public information and thus made public by other means, such as orally.[119]

Information readily available to market professionals

Information is to be regarded as made public if it can be readily acquired   **5-24**
by those likely to deal in any securities to which the information relates.[120] It will also be regarded as made public if it can be readily acquired by those likely to deal in any securities of an issuer to which the information relates.[121] For these purposes, an 'issuer' in relation to any securities is said to mean any company, public sector body or individual by which or by whom the securities have been or are to be issued.[122] This category will cover information readily available to brokers and market makers and will include, for instance, information that others are dealing in a particular way. If a third party decided also to deal, on that basis and without knowing why the others were dealing in that way, that information would be regarded as having been made public.[123]

Other factors

There are certain other factors the presence of which will not prevent   **5-25**
information being treated as having been made public.[124] It should be emphasised that these situations will not necessarily mean that information has been made public. The provisions '... are there to lend comfort to those who might otherwise think that such circumstances definitely meant that information had not been made public ...'[125] Therefore, information may still be regarded as having been made public[126] even though:

---

119 *Per* the Economic Secretary to the Treasury, Mr Anthony Nelson. See the report of Standing Committee B, 10 June 1993, at column 183.

120 Section 58(2)(c)(i) CJA 1993. And see paras 20–25 of the guidance document reissued by the London Stock Exchange in February 1995, in relation to analysts.

121 Section 58(2)(c)(ii) CJA 1993.

122 Section 60(2) CJA 1993.

123 This point was raised by Mr Mike O'Brien (MP for Warwickshire North) and clarified by Mr Anthony Nelson, the Economic Secretary to the Treasury. See the report of Standing Committee B, 10 June 1993, at column 183.

124 See s 58(3) CJA 1993.

125 *Per* Mr Anthony Nelson, the Economic Secretary to the Treasury. See the report of Standing Committee B, 10 June 1993, at column 183.

126 The key word is 'may'. This means that a judgment will need to be made by the court as to whether information has been made public. See the report of Standing Committee B, 10 June 1993, at column 184.

- It can be acquired only by persons exercising diligence or expertise.[127] Whether information will be regarded by the court as having been made public by virtue of this provision will depend on the circumstances. It is unlikely that information published in some obscure journal will be so regarded unless, for instance, the journal related to one of the recently privatised utility sectors and the information concerned securities in a relevant company.[128]

- It is communicated to a section of the public and not to the public at large.[129] The presence of this situation 'may' mean that information has been made public, depending on the circumstances. It is not a mandatory situation where information 'must' be regarded as having been made public. If it was, the 'section of the public' might, for instance, be a group of stock market analysts who were inadvertently given inside information and it would mean that they could deal freely.[130]

- It can be acquired only by observation.[131] *Prima facie*, this provision does seem a little curious. It will though be for the court to decide whether, in all the circumstances, the information in question has been made public. The fact of a factory chimney smoking at night might be regarded as public information if a court took the view that people could see the smoking chimney and conclude that the factory was working overtime. It will though depend on all the circumstances.[132]

- It is communicated only on payment of a fee.[133] In itself, the payment of a fee does not necessarily have the effect of making information public. If it did, those wishing to deal on the basis of inside information would simply pay for that information. However, this provision ensures that the mere fact of a fee being paid in return for the communication of information does not prevent information from being regarded as having been made public. It will simply be one of the circumstances for the court to take into consideration.[134]

---

127 Section 58(3)(a) CJA 1993.

128 See the comments of the Economic Secretary to the Treasury, Mr Anthony Nelson, in the report of Standing Committee B, 10 June 1993, at columns 183–184.

129 Section 58(3)(b) CJA 1993.

130 This would not be desirable and this was made clear by the Economic Secretary to the Treasury, Mr Anthony Nelson. See the report of Standing Committee B, 10 June 1993, at column 182.

131 Section 58(3)(c) CJA 1993.

132 The 'factory chimney' example was used by the Economic Secretary to the Treasury, Mr Anthony Nelson. See the report of Standing Committee B, 10 June 1993, at column 184.

133 Section 58(3)(d) CJA 1993.

134 See the comments of the Economic Secretary to the Treasury, Mr Anthony Nelson. See the report of Standing Committee B, 10 June 1993, at column 182.

- It is published only outside the UK.[135] If, for instance, information is published in one of the major overseas newspapers but not in the UK, it might well be regarded as having been made public. To take an example of more restricted publication, it is unlikely to be so regarded if published only in the *'Tonga Evening News'* unless, for example, it related to a Tongan mining company or another local company.[136]

Whether, in any specific case, information will be regarded as having been made public will depend on the facts and circumstances of that case. However, the existence of any of the factors set out in para 5-25 above will not prevent it being so regarded. What is clear is that it is unlikely to be regarded as made public if publication takes place in an obscure journal or if 'public' records are hidden away at home or abroad 'in ... an unstatutory register ...'.[137]   **5-26**

PROFESSIONAL INTERMEDIARIES

Relevance

As will be seen shortly,[138] the expression 'professional intermediary' is important to the structure of insider dealing law. This is because the offence of insider dealing may be committed where there is dealing in securities in circumstances involving such a person. Generally speaking, the prohibition of insider dealing applies to deals on 'regulated markets'. If dealing takes place 'off-market', it will only be covered by this prohibition if it involves a professional intermediary. The scope of the prohibition was thus set to prevent its avoidance through dealings in securities not traded on a regulated market.[139] As to the extent of that scope, it was made clear that the principal concern of those framing this legislation, and thus implementing the insider dealing directive,[140] was   **5-27**

---

135 Section 58(3)(e) CJA 1993.

136 See the comments of the Economic Secretary to the Treasury, Mr Anthony Nelson in the report of Standing Committee B, 10 June 1993, at columns 183–184.

137 *Per* the Economic Secretary to the Treasury, Mr Anthony Nelson. See the report of Standing Committee B, 10 June 1993, at column 187.

138 In Chapter 6, below.

139 The example of such securities quoted by the Economic Secretary to the Treasury was that of Eurobonds listed in Luxembourg. He said those bonds were securities to which this legislation applies but that they were not traded on a regulated market. 'Trading, which is predominantly based in London, generally involves market makers who act as principals in the transactions ...'. See the report of Standing Committee B, 10 June 1993, at column 192.

140 Council Directive (EEC) 89/592 of 13th November 1989 co-ordinating regulations on insider dealing and see art 2(3) of that Directive.

'... the fairness and integrity of established regulated markets and cases where people deal through a professional intermediary ...'.[141] It was not thought feasible to go further than that and attempt to catch dealing off-market which was not effected through professional intermediaries. 'To do so would be difficult and complex, would result in much more legislation, would be highly controversial and would cause much difficulty ... It is not at all evident that there will be many cases where people deal off-market and not through professional intermediaries ...'.[142]

Meaning

5-28 For these purposes, a 'professional intermediary' is defined[143] as meaning a person who carries on a business consisting of a particular activity and who holds himself out to the public or to any section of the public[144] as being willing to engage in any such business.[145] It also means someone employed by such a person to carry out such an activity.[146] The 'activities' in question are those of acquiring or disposing of securities,[147] whether as principal or as agent, or acting as an intermediary between persons taking part in any dealing in securities.[148]

---

141 *Per* Mr Anthony Nelson, the Economic Secretary to the Treasury. See the report of Standing Committee B, 10 June 1993, at column 193.

142 *Per* the Economic Secretary to the Treasury, Mr Anthony Nelson. See the report of Standing Committee B, 10 June 1993, at column 193.

143 By s 59 CJA 1993. The expression was used, for instance, in art 2(3) of Council Directive (EEC) 89/592 but the government considered that a detailed definition was required. See the report of Standing Committee B, 10 June 1993, at column 192.

144 Including a section of the public constituted by persons such as himself. The full expression 'professional intermediary' was used both to conform with Council Directive (EEC) 89/592 and to ensure that, for example, if a deal was done over the telephone, BT or Mercury did not find themselves acting as an 'intermediary' for these purposes. See the comments of the Economic Secretary to the Treasury in the report of Standing Committee B, 10 June 1993, at column 192.

145 Section 59(1)(a) CJA 1993.

146 Section 59(1)(b) CJA 1993.

147 That is to say, securities to which Part V CJA 1993 is applicable. See s 54 and Schedule 2 CJA 1993.

148 Section 59(2)(a) and (b) CJA 1993. Whether or not a merchant bank involved in the sale or purchase of a business would be regarded as a 'professional intermediary' for these purposes would depend upon whether it was also acting as an intermediary in 'dealing' transactions. See the comments of the Economic Secretary to the Treasury, Mr Anthony Nelson in the report of Standing Committee B, 10 June 1993, at column 192. And see Harriet Creamer, 'Insider Dealing – a new approach' (1993) PLC 21–23 and 25–28 which discusses the effect of these new provisions on 'corporate finance' activities.

Limitations

A person is not however to be treated as carrying on a business   **5-29**
consisting of an activity referred to in para 5-28 above if the activity in
question is merely incidental to some other activity not so referred to[149]
or merely because he occasionally carries on one of those activities.[150]

Reliance on a professional intermediary

For the purposes of the offence of insider dealing,[151] a person dealing in   **5-30**
securities is regarded as relying on a professional intermediary if and
only if a person who is acting as a professional intermediary carries out
an activity referred to in para 5-28 above in relation to that dealing.[152]

---

149 Section 59(3)(a) CJA 1993.
150 Section 59(3)(b) CJA 1993.
151 See Chapter 6 below and s 52(3) CJA 1993.
152 Section 59(4) CJA 1993.

CHAPTER 6

THE BASIC OFFENCE OF INSIDER DEALING

INTRODUCTION

The basic provisions

The offence of insider dealing is set out in s 52 of the Criminal Justice Act 1993.[1] There are three forms which the offence may take: that of acquiring and/or disposing of securities; that of encouraging another to do so; and that of disclosing information.[2] Generally speaking, any relevant acquisition or disposal of securities must take place in certain stated 'circumstances'.[3] Although that single provision contains all three forms of the offence, it relies heavily on many of the definitions examined in Chapter 5 above.[4] Section 52 also has effect subject to various 'defences' to the offence which are set out in s 53 and also in Schedule 1 to the Act.[5]

6-01

Before going on to examine these matters in detail, it may be helpful to mention the legislative intention and approach underlying these provisions.[6] During the proceedings of the House of Commons Standing

6-02

---

1   1993 c 36.

2   See ss 52(1),(2)(a) and (2)(b) CJA 1993.

3   Set out in s 52(3) CJA 1993.

4   See Chapter 5, above, for a detailed examination of the more important definitions on which the operative provisions of Part V CJA 1993 (such as s 52) are based.

5   These defences are examined in detail in Chapter 7, below, But see also Nicholas Walmsby, 'Insider dealing: the well-connected's crime' (1993) 8(12) JIBL 508–12.

6   In very general terms, the courts departed from the old 'literal' approach to statutory construction some time ago. Since then, the judiciary has adopted a 'purposive' approach. That is to say, the courts now seek to discover the true parliamentary intention underlying the words used in legislation. Those words are then construed so as to give effect to, rather than to thwart, the intentions of Parliament. In doing so, however, there was a general 'exclusionary' rule to the effect that references by the courts to parliamentary material, as an aid to statutory construction, were not permissible.

     However, in the comparatively recent case of *Pepper (Inspector of Taxes) v Hart* and related appeals [1993] AC 593 and also [1993] 1 All ER 42, the House of Lords held (with Lord Mackay LC dissenting) that the exclusionary rule could be relaxed, subject to any question of parliamentary privilege, so as to permit reference to parliamentary materials where (a) the legislation was ambiguous or obscure or the literal meaning led to an absurdity; (b) the material relied on consisted of statements by a minister or other promoter of the Bill which led to the enactment of the legislation together, if necessary, with such other parliamentary material as was necessary to understand such statements and their effect; and (c) the statements relied upon were clear. ... *[continued overleaf]*

Committee B, which considered the 'Criminal Justice Bill [Lords]',[7] the Economic Secretary to the Treasury[8] said that the Bill '... rewrites the law on insider dealing ... The proposals ... will bring our law into line with the EC directive on the subject[9] which requires all Member States to make insider dealing illegal ...'.[10] Later, he commented thus on the 'difficult balancing act' which the government had had to perform in formulating the Bill: 'Not only must we crack down on insider dealing but we must be seen to be doing so effectively and must send the right deterrent messages to the financial services industry. Furthermore, we must not inhibit unreasonably the legitimate practices and expertise of those in the City of London and the financial services industry in general ...'.[11]

6-03   As for the detailed provisions of the Bill, the minister said that the government was:

> ... not trying to go well beyond the proposals of the directive or the existing law under the Company Securities (Insider Dealing) Act 1985. Some elements ... add to the existing law, but only where we must comply with the directive ... We are tightening the law, in the sense that we are clarifying and improving it, and making the definition of offences more certain. Hon Members will dispute with us whether we are achieving our aim. It is extremely difficult ... to

---

6   [cont'd] In some incisive passages on the above points, Lord Browne-Wilkinson commented (at pp 65–66 in the above-mentioned report) that 'Textbooks often include reference to explanations of legislation given by a minister in Parliament, as a result of which lawyers advise their clients taking account of such statements and judges when construing the legislation come to know of them'. Accordingly, with that blessing and given the nature of the point decided, detailed reference is made in this Chapter 6, and elsewhere in the book, to relevant parliamentary material. See also *Pickstone v Freemans plc* [1989] AC 66, *Melluish (HMIT) v BMI (No 3) Ltd* [1995] STC 964 and *Three Rivers District Council and Others (No 2) v Governor and Company of the Bank of England* [1996] 2 All ER 363, QBD.

The insider dealing provisions which became Part V of the CJA 1993 received detailed scrutiny by Standing Committee B of the House of Commons. In that context, they were subject to a degree of exegesis by the then Economic Secretary to the Treasury, Mr Anthony Nelson, who spoke for HM Government in the debate before the Standing Committee. Certain of his explanations and examples were cited in Chapter 5, *ante*, and are referred to elsewhere in the main text. For these purposes, the more relevant sittings (all in 1993) of Standing Committee B took place on Tuesday 25 May (the first sitting), Tuesday 8 June (the third sitting), on the morning and afternoon of Thursday 10 June (the fourth and fifth sittings) and on Tuesday 15 June (the sixth sitting). The Bill received the Royal Assent on Tuesday 27 July 1993.

7   When enacted on 27 July 1993, the Criminal Justice Bill [Lords] became the CJA 1993.

8   Then Mr Anthony Nelson.

9   Council Directive (EEC) 89/592 of 13 November 1989 co-ordinating regulations on insider dealing. See Chapter 4, above, further.

10   See the report of House of Commons Standing Committee B sitting on 10 June 1993 to consider the Criminal Justice Bill [Lords], at column 133.

11   See the report of Standing Committee B, 10 June 1993, at column 149.

devise the perfect definition that encapsulates all situations, but we are attempting to do that. Our approach has been to improve considerably the basis of the previous legislation ...[12]

PRELIMINARY DEFINITIONAL MATTERS

The 'dealing circumstances'

Sections 52(1) and (2)(a) of the Criminal Justice Act 1993 refer to the **6-04** occurrence of 'dealing' in securities taking place in certain 'circumstances' which are set out in s 52(3) of the Act. Those circumstances[13] are threefold:

- that the acquisition or disposal in question occurs on a 'regulated market';[14] alternatively,

- that the person dealing relies on a professional intermediary;[15] or, finally,

- that the person dealing is himself acting as a professional intermediary.[16]

The purpose of s 52(3) of the Criminal Justice Act 1993, and of **6-05** making two of the three forms of the offence referable to dealing in these circumstances, was to set certain limits to the ambit of the basic prohibition. The Economic Secretary to the Treasury made the position of the government clear at the Committee stage where he said that 'The great worry is about activities on the market. We are concerned with protecting investors who go to the market expecting it to be free and fair, and a market of integrity. Market activities will be within the scope of the Bill by ... being either on-market or dealt with through professional

---

12   See the report of Standing Committee B, 10 June 1993, at columns 151 and 152.

13   Which bring into play many of the definitions explained in Chapter 5, above.

14   Section 52(3) CJA 1993. Essentially, for these purposes, a 'regulated market' is a market (however operated) which is identified as such (whether by name or by reference to prescribed criteria) by an order made by the Treasury. See s 60(1) CJA 1993 and also the Insider Dealing (Securities and Regulated Markets) Order 1994 (SI 1994/187) which came into force on 1 March 1994 as amended by SI 1996/1561. Article 9 of that Order provides that any market established under the rules of one of the investment exchanges listed in the Schedule to the Order will be a 'regulated market' for the purposes of Part V of the Criminal Justice Act 1993. Article 10 provides that the regulated markets which are regulated in the UK for these purposes are any market established under the rules of the London Stock Exchange Limited, Tradepoint Financial Networks plc, LIFFE Administration & Management and OMLX, the London Securities and Derivatives Exchange Limited. See SI 1994/187 and Note 43 to Chapter 5, above, further. See also the Insider Dealing (Securities and Regulated Markets) (Amendment) Order 1996 (SI 1996/1561).

15   Section 52(3) CJA 1993. See s 59 CJA 1993 and Chapter 5 above, further.

16   *ibid.*

intermediaries'.[17] The intention was to prevent a person with inside information from circumventing the prohibition by dealing off-market instead of on-market.[18] That was not desirable. Accordingly, where transactions are conducted through a professional intermediary off-market, they are still capable of falling within the scope of the legislation.[19] But the government did not wish to go 'a bridge too far' and prohibit transactions off-market involving no professional intermediary. As the minister made clear, 'We could decide to go that far – some countries such as Belgium and Luxembourg have extended their law further. We choose to stay within the ambit of the directive. Going much further off-market would be unnecessary because there is no great clamour for it'.[20]

'Dealing in securities'

6-06   For the purposes of the provisions governing insider dealing contained in Part V of the Criminal Justice Act 1993, a person is regarded as 'dealing in securities' in two main circumstances:

- *first*, if he acquires or disposes of the securities, whether as principal or as an agent;[21] or

- *secondly*, if he procures directly or indirectly an acquisition or disposal by any other person.[22]

6-07   The basic purpose of these provisions, which are central to the offence of insider dealing, is to specify where, when and how 'dealing' may take place. The intention of the government was to define 'dealing' widely, 'in a way which catches a wide range of transactions to prevent creating loopholes which could be readily exploited by a determined insider ...'.[23]

6-08   The acquisition of securities of course encompasses the acquisition of legal title to the securities.[24] 'Acquire', in relation to a security, is,

---

17 See the report of Standing Committee B, 10 June 1993, at column 200.

18 For these purposes, 'off-market' transactions are transactions in securities which are effected otherwise than on a 'regulated market'.

19 See s 52(3) CJA 1993.

20 See the report of Standing Committee B, 10 June 1993, at column 200.

21 Section 55(1)(a) CJA 1993.

22 Section 55(1)(b) CJA 1993.

23 *Per* Mr Anthony Nelson, the Economic Secretary to the Treasury, from the report of Standing Committee B, 10 June 1993, at column 168.

24 For instance, through entry as a member on the register of members maintained by a company. By virtue of s 352 of the Companies Act 1985, every company is obliged to keep a register of its members and to enter in that register certain particulars specified by that section. It is the register of members, and not a share certificate, that is the effective document of title to shares. A share certificate is merely an acknowledgment on the part of the company in question that the name of the person mentioned in it is duly recorded in the register of members.

however, defined more widely for these purposes. It is said to include agreeing to acquire the security in question.[25] This ensures, for instance, that a person is not able to avoid the legislation if he agrees to buy securities but then disposes of his rights, making a profit, without having taken legal title to the securities.[26] 'Acquire', in relation to a security, is also said to include entering into a contract which creates the security.[27] This was thought necessary to ensure not only that dealing in existing securities falls within the legislation but also, perhaps mainly in relation to dealing in derivatives such as options, entering into a contract which has the effect of creating a new security.[28]

The disposal of securities, of course, encompasses the disposal of legal title to the securities. 'Dispose', in relation to a security, is also defined more widely for these purposes. It is said to include agreeing to dispose of the security[29] and also the bringing to an end of a contract which created the security.[30] The inclusion of an agreement to dispose of a security covers situations[31] where the person making a disposal may not have formal legal title to the securities in question. The reference to the bringing to an end of a contract which created a security was thought necessary, particularly in the area of index contracts and other contracts for differences, to ensure that where a person terminates such a contract he is to be regarded as disposing of the security.[32]

6-09

The width of the definition of 'dealing in securities' may be seen in the way it encompasses acquisitions or disposals by a person, whether effected as principal or as an agent for another.[33] This was intended to ensure, for instance, that the legislation applies as much to an agent who deals in order to make a profit or avoid a loss for his principal as it does to a person who deals for his own account.[34]

6-10

The same width can also be seen in the way a person may be regarded as dealing in securities in situations in which he procures, whether directly or indirectly, another person to acquire or dispose of securities.[35] For these purposes, a person is said to procure an

6-11

---

25 Section 55(2)(a) CJA 1993.

26 See the report of Standing Committee B, 10 June 1993, at column 168.

27 Section 55(2)(b) CJA 1993.

28 See the report of Standing Committee B, 10 June 1993, at column 168.

29 Section 55(3)(a) CJA 1993.

30 Section 55(3)(b) CJA 1993.

31 For instance, as mentioned in para 6-08, above. And see 'Bankers in the dock', *The Times* (Pennington column), 30 April 1996 in relation to the recent deliberations of the Financial Law Panel on insider trading.

32 See the report of Standing Committee B, 10 June 1993, at column 168.

33 Section 55(1)(a) CJA 1993.

34 See the report of Standing Committee B, 10 June 1993, at column 168.

35 Section 55(1)(b) CJA 1993.

acquisition or a disposal of a security if the security is acquired or disposed of by a person who is his agent,[36] his nominee[37] or, simply, a person who is acting at his direction in relation to the acquisition or disposal.[38] Also, these provisions are not to be regarded as being exhaustive as to the circumstances in which one person may be seen as procuring an acquisition or disposal of securities by another.[39]

6-12   Without the breadth of meaning introduced by provisions such as these, there are many ways in which a person could distance himself and yet still benefit from dealing in securities based on inside information. In essence, he could get someone else to do the dealing for him, such as an agent or a nominee.[40] Another obvious way would be to route the dealing through a company; particularly a company of which the person was the sole shareholder.[41] As sole shareholder, he could use his influence and control over the company to ensure it dealt in the securities in which he was interested. Although any profit made or loss avoided by the dealing would of course accrue to the company, the sole shareholder would benefit through the increased profitability of the company. As a company is a legal 'person' for these purposes, in this factual scenario it would be regarded as 'a person acting at the direction' of the sole shareholder who would thus be dealing in securities by virtue of the provisions outlined above.[42]

6-13   As it is provided that those provisions[43] are not exhaustive as to the circumstances in which one person may be regarded as procuring an acquisition or a disposal, in practice there are likely to be many other ways in which one person may procure another to deal. One scenario is important enough to be worthy of immediate comment and that is where a person has handed over the management of his investment portfolio to another. Depending on the circumstances, the investor may be considered to have procured particular dealings subject to the discretion exercisable by the investment manager. If, however, the investor has given a general direction to the manager to manage all his affairs and to deal in securities as he (the investment manager) thinks fit, it is unlikely that he would be regarded by the courts as having directed and accordingly procured dealings in particular securities.[44]

---

36   Section 55(4)(a) CJA 1993.
37   Section 55(4)(b) CJA 1993.
38   Section 55(4)(c) CJA 1993.
39   Section 55(5) CJA 1993.
40   That is the point of s 55(4)(a) and (b) CJA 1993.
41   This example was given by the Economic Secretary to the Treasury. See the report of Standing Committee B, 10 June 1993 (afternoon sitting), at column 171.
42   In particular, by virtue of s 55(4)(c) CJA 1993.
43   In s 55(4) CJA 1993.
44   *Per* the Economic Secretary to the Treasury. See the report of Standing Committee B, 10 June 1993, at columns 171 and 172.

THE BASIC OFFENCES

'Securities' and territorial extent of provisions

There are three forms of the offence of insider dealing and they will each be considered in turn. For these purposes, it should however be remembered that 'securities' are essentially any of the securities set out in Schedule 2 to the Criminal Justice Act 1993 provided they satisfy any conditions made applicable to them by any relevant order made for these purposes by the Treasury.[45] It should also be noted that the provisions contained in Part V of and also in Schedules 1 and 2 to the Criminal Justice Act 1993 extend, in terms of their application, to the UK and not merely to England and Wales.[46]

6-14

The 'dealing' offence

This is the *first form* of the offence of insider dealing. An individual who has information as an insider will be guilty of insider dealing if, in the 'dealing' circumstances outlined in paras 6-04 and 6-05 above, he deals in securities that are price-affected securities in relation to the information.[47] Whether or not this form of the offence of insider dealing has been committed in any given case will therefore depend upon the satisfaction of a number of requirements.

6-15

The offence *per se* can only be committed by an *individual*.[48] Although, in some circumstances, a company employing such an individual may itself incur criminal liability, this will not be a direct result of the application of Part V of the Criminal Justice Act 1993. A registered company is, of course, a corporation, a legal 'person',[49] with the advantage of limited liability. Generally speaking, only the company will be liable for its debts. Shareholders are only liable to the extent of making full payment for their shares. A company may, however, be vicariously liable for its employees in the same way a human employer would be liable. In addition, a company is also identified with its controlling officers. The acts and states of mind of its directors and

6-16

---

45 See s 54 and also Schedule 2 CJA 1993. See, also, arts 3 to 8 of the Insider Dealing (Securities and Regulated Markets) Order 1994 (SI 1994/187). With effect from 1 March 1994, arts 4–8 of that Order have set out conditions affecting securities to which Part V of the Criminal Justice Act 1993 is applicable.

46 See s 79(2) CJA 1993. The United Kingdom consists of England, Scotland, Wales and Northern Ireland.

47 Section 52(1) CJA 1993. See also s 52(3) CJA 1993.

48 See ss 52(1) and also (2) CJA 1993. Compare ss 47(1) and (2) of the Financial Services Act 1986 which refer to 'Any person ...'.

49 See the definition of 'person' in the Interpretation Act 1978.

senior managers, when they are acting as such, may be imputed to the company.[50] There are therefore circumstances in which a company could be guilty of an offence connected with insider dealing by an individual. For instance, a securities firm which instructed one of its junior dealers to execute transactions which it knew would involve insider dealing might be guilty of incitement. Similarly, if the company, through its directors, agreed that the junior dealer could commit insider dealing, it might be guilty of conspiracy. In similar circumstances, a company might also commit offences involving misleading statements and market practices by virtue of s 47 of the Financial Services Act 1986.[51]

6-17   The individual in question must have *'information as an insider'*.[52] The meaning of that expression is derived from the application of two further definitions, those of 'inside information' and where a person has 'information from an inside source'. A person is regarded as having 'information as an insider' if and only if it is and he knows that it is 'inside information'[53] and he has it and knows that he has it from an inside source.[54] As has been explained,[55] in general terms, 'inside information' is specific information about securities which has not been made public but which would have a significant effect on their price if it was made public.[56] Essentially, an individual has 'information from an inside source' if and only if he has a sufficiently close relationship with an issuer of securities.[57] He may be a director, an employee or a

---

50 See, for instance, the case of *JCR Haulage Ltd* [1944] KB 551. In that case, senior officers of a company, including its managing director, were indicted for conspiracy to defraud and the indictment was upheld by the Court of Appeal. Effectively, the state of mind of the managing director and his colleagues was imputed to the company so that their fraud was regarded as the fraud of the company. But see, also, *Meridian Global Funds Management Asia Ltd v Securities Commission* [1995] 3 All ER 918 and Times Law Report, 29 June 1995 at p 34, where the Judicial Committee of the Privy Council (*per* Lord Hoffmann) held that whenever a servant of a company had authority to do an act on its behalf, knowledge of that act would not necessarily be attributed to the company. It was a question of construction in each case as to whether the particular rule required that the knowledge that an act had been done, or the state of mind with which it was done, should be so attributed.

51 See Chapter 10, below. See, also, s 202(1) of the Financial Services Act 1986 which, essentially, provides that where an offence under the FSA 1986 committed by a body corporate is proved to have been committed with the consent or connivance of or to be attributable to any neglect on the part of any director or other senior officer of the body corporate, he as well as the body corporate shall be guilty of that offence and liable to be proceeded against and punished accordingly.

52 See Chapter 5, above, for a fuller discussion of the meaning of the expression 'information as an insider' which is defined in s 57(1) CJA 1993.

53 Section 57(1)(a) CJA 1993.

54 Section 57(1)(b) CJA 1993.

55 In Chapter 5, above.

56 See s 56(1)(a)–(d) CJA 1993, further.

57 See s 57(2) CJA 1993.

shareholder of that issuer[58] or he may have access to the information by virtue of his employment, office or profession.[59] He may also have 'information from an inside source' where the direct or indirect source of his information is one of the persons referred to above.[60]

The individual must also *'deal in securities'* that are 'price-affected securities' in relation to the information and the dealing must take place in *the 'dealing' circumstances.* The extended meaning of 'dealing in securities' for these purposes was examined in paras 6-06 to 6-13 above whilst the 'dealing' circumstances were outlined earlier in paras 6-04 and 6-05 above. The securities must be *'price-affected securities'* in relation to the relevant information. As has been examined earlier,[61] securities are 'price-affected' in relation to inside information if and only if the information would, if made public, be likely to have a significant effect on the price of the securities.[62] For these purposes, the 'price' must be taken as including the 'value' of securities[63] and will be the price at which they may be bought or sold on a relevant market such as the Stock Exchange in London. A significant effect on that price will be one which would, if made public, cause it to increase or decrease significantly.[64]

6-18

When the various requirements outlined in paras 6-14 to 6-18 above have been satisfied by the circumstances of a particular case, the individual who has so dealt in securities may be guilty of insider dealing. There are, however, a number of further points to explore if he is to be regarded as falling within *the territorial scope of the offence* of insider dealing.[65] For instance, he will not be guilty of the 'dealing' offence unless he was within the UK at the time he is alleged to have done any act constituting or forming part of the alleged dealing.[66] The

6-19

---

58 Section 57(2)(a)(i) CJA 1993. For some discussion of some important areas, see 'Rights issues, rumps and insider dealing', by City solicitors Freshfields, (1992) 7 (7) BJIB & FL 348–49.

59 Section 57(2)(a)(ii) CJA 1993.

60 That is to say, falling within s 57(2)(a) CJA 1993. See s 57(2)(b) CJA 1993.

61 In Chapter 5, above.

62 Section 56(2) CJA 1993.

63 Section 56(3) CJA 1993.

64 See Chapter 5, above, and the 'Guidance on the dissemination of price sensitive information' document reissued by the London Stock Exchange in February 1995, further. Some examples of information in relation to securities which, if made public and depending always upon the precise circumstances, could have a significant effect on the price of those securities might include the following:
- the hope/fear of a takeover or merger in relation to a company;
- bid speculation generally in relation to a company;
- imminent full or interim results for a company which happen to be good;
- an imminent profits warning in respect of a company.

65 See s 62(1) CJA 1993, generally.

66 Section 62(1)(a) CJA 1993. And see Charles Abrams. 'Insider dealing – the new regime (Part 2)' (1994) 1(2)EFSL 38–42.

'regulated market' on which the dealing is alleged to have occurred must be one identified in an order made by the Treasury, whether by name or by reference to criteria prescribed by the order, as being regulated in the UK for these purposes.[67] Finally, if relevant, the professional intermediary involved must have been within the UK at the time he is alleged to have done anything by means of which the offence is alleged to have been committed.[68]

The 'encouraging' offence

6-20 The *second form* of the offence of insider dealing has been regarded as being something of an anti-avoidance measure.[69] It was intended to prohibit a person with inside information from encouraging someone else to deal in securities in circumstances where that 'other' person might or might not have the same inside information. The offence will be committed where an individual, who has information as an insider, encourages another person to deal in securities that are price-affected securities in relation to the information whether or not this is known to that other person.[70] The encourager must, however, know or have reasonable cause to believe that the dealing would take place in the 'dealing' circumstances outlined in paras 6-04 and 6-05 above.[71]

6-21 The *effect* of this form of the offence is to prohibit encouragement to deal where the potential encourager knows or has reasonable cause to believe that the person receiving such encouragement will deal in the circumstances covered by the 'dealing' offence. Without a prohibition in these terms, it might have been possible for an individual to circumvent the legislation by saying to someone, 'Buy shares in ABC Limited off-market and do not make use of a stockbroker', knowing that the recipient of that encouragement would go and deal through his broker.[72] As with the 'dealing' offence, there are a *number of requirements* which need to be satisfied before such an individual could be found guilty of the offence.

---

67 Section 62(1)(b) CJA 1993. And see, also, the Insider Dealing (Securities and Regulated Markets) Order 1994 (SI 1994/187) and the Insider Dealing (Securities and Regulated Markets) (Amendment) Order 1996 (SI 1996/1561).

68 Section 62(1)(c) CJA 1993.

69 *Per* the Economic Secretary to the Treasury. See the report of Standing Committee B, 10 June 1993, at column 134.

70 Section 52(2)(a) CJA 1993.

71 *ibid*. See also s 52(3) CJA 1993.

72 Again, *per* the Economic Secretary to the Treasury. See the report of Standing Committee B, 10 June 1993, at column 134.

As with the 'dealing' offence,[73] this form of the offence can only be   **6-22**
committed by an individual[74] who has 'information as an insider'.[75]
That individual must 'encourage' another person to deal in securities.
'Encouragement' for these purposes is not defined by the Criminal
Justice Act 1993 but, in general usage, would require the individual to
induce the other to deal or otherwise to instigate the dealing.[76] As
before,[77] 'securities' for these purposes means securities falling within
Schedule 2 to the Criminal Justice Act 1993 which satisfy any conditions
made applicable by a relevant Treasury order.[78]

The relevant securities must be 'price-affected securities' in relation   **6-23**
to the information in question whether or not the other person knows
that they are price-affected securities.[79] The individual must, however,
know or have reasonable cause to believe that the dealing would take
place in the 'dealing' circumstances.[80] He will not, however, be guilty of
the 'encouraging' offence unless he was within the UK at the time when
he is alleged to have encouraged the dealing[81] or, alternatively, the
alleged recipient of the encouragement was within the UK at the time
when he is alleged to have received the encouragement.[82]

The 'disclosure' offence

The *third form* of the offence is also regarded as an anti-avoidance   **6-24**
measure.[83] It prohibits the disclosure of information which could be
used for insider dealing. An individual who has 'information as an
insider' may be guilty of insider dealing simply if he discloses the
information to another person, otherwise than in the proper

---

73 See paras 6-15 to 6-19, above.
74 See para 6-16, above.
75 See para 6-17 and Chapter 5, above.
76 From the *Compact Oxford English Dictionary*, 2nd edn, 1991.
77 See para 6-14, above.
78 Section 54(1) CJA 1993. See, also, the Insider Dealing (Securities and Regulated
    Markets) Order 1994 (SI 1994/187).
79 See para 6-18, above.
80 See paras 6-04 and 6-05, above. See paras 6-06 to 6-13 in relation to the meaning of
    'dealing in securities'. In relation to 'knowledge', it may include the state of mind of
    a person who shuts his eyes to the obvious: see *James and Son Ltd v Smee* [1955] 1 QB
    78 at 91. Also, where a person deliberately refrains from making enquiries the
    results of which he might not care to know, this may amount to actual knowledge
    of the facts in question: see *Westminster City Council v Croyalgrange Ltd* [1986] 2 All
    ER 353, HL. Whether a person has 'reasonable cause to believe' will be a question of
    fact to be established by evidence.
81 Section 62(2)(a) CJA 1993.
82 Section 62(2)(b) CJA 1993.
83 *Per* the Economic Secretary to the Treasury. See the report of Standing Committee
    B, 10 June 1993, at column 134.

performance of the functions of his employment, office or profession.[84] As with the two other basic forms of the offence, there are *a number of requirements* which need to be satisfied before an individual may have committed the offence.

6-25   As before, this form of the offence can only be committed by an individual[85] and he or she must have 'information as an insider'.[86] The offence is committed where such an individual 'discloses' the information to another person 'otherwise than in the proper performance of the functions of his employment, office or profession'. 'Disclosure', for these purposes, could be in writing but is more likely to be verbal. For instance, an investment analyst with the requisite information as an insider could leave work one evening and go for a drink. He could have one pint too many in a bar and then give a complete stranger the benefit of his inside information. This would seem to be all that is required for commission of the 'disclosure' offence.[87] There is no need for the recipient of the information to deal in securities; although, in practice, a resulting transaction is how the fact of disclosure is likely to come to light. But, if the recipient does 'deal', he may commit the 'dealing' offence.[88]

6-26   However, even if the fact of a relevant disclosure is established, the offence will only have been committed if the individual has disclosed the information otherwise than in the 'proper' performance of the functions of his employment, office or profession. The offence does not apply to someone who discloses information in the proper performance of the functions of his employment, office or profession. It is therefore clear that some of the disclosures which may be made by an individual in the course of his work may not be acceptable. For instance, it would not be in the 'proper performance' of his functions for an individual to disclose confidential information which he had been given in the course of his employment even if his intention was not that he or the recipient would benefit personally from the information but would instead make use of it for the financial benefit of

---

84 Section 52(2)(b) CJA 1993.

85 See para 6-16 above, further.

86 See para 6-17 above, further.

87 This example is cited by Mr Peter Ainsworth (MP for Surrey, East). See the report of Standing Committee B, 10 June 1993, at column 147.

88 Section 52 CJA 1993. This would depend, mainly, on whether the recipient would be regarded as having 'information as an insider' and, in particular, 'information from an inside source'. See ss 56 and 57 CJA 1993. And see *Re Attorney-General's Reference (No 1 of 1988)* [1989] 2 WLR 729, HL. For some relevant discussion, see Ebo Coleman, 'Securities regulation – involuntary recipients of inside information' (1990) 11(1) Co Law 18–19 and Takis Tridinas, 'The House of Lords rules on insider trading' (1989) 52 MLR 851–855. In relation to the position of 'tippees' under the legislation preceding Part V CJA 1993, see *R v Fisher* [1988] 4 BCC 360 and 'Insider dealing and tippees' (1988) 9(7) Co Law Dig 149.

his employer.[89] If, however, information is disclosed by an individual in the proper performance of his employment, office or profession, the 'disclosure' offence will not be applicable.[90]

The 'disclosure' offence will also be inapplicable if the individual falls outside its territorial scope. To be more precise, he will not be guilty of that offence unless he was within the UK at the time when he is alleged to have disclosed the information[91] or, alternatively, the alleged recipient of the information was within the UK at the time when he is alleged to have received the information.[92]

6-27

'GENERAL' AND 'SPECIAL' DEFENCES

Basis

Even if the necessary requirements for any of the three forms of the offence of insider dealing have been satisfied, the individual may still be able to take advantage of a number of defences.[93] There are some 'general' defences which are set out in s 53 of the Criminal Justice Act 1993. There are also some 'special' defences which are contained in Schedule 1 to that Act.[94]

6-28

---

89 *Per* the Economic Secretary to the Treasury. See the report of Standing Committee B, 10 June 1993, at columns 134 and also 155–156. Also, the 'disclosure' offence was initially framed in terms of 'disclosure in the performance of a duty'. See the report of Standing Committee B, 10 June 1993, at column 134. This reference was, however, removed because of concerns expressed that it would create a 'potentially significant loophole in the legislation'. Essentially, the concerns were that an insider and an accomplice might enter into a contractual relationship requiring the insider to disclose inside information to the accomplice. The insider would then have a duty under the contract to pass on that information and would accordingly be within the law when he did so.

90 Section 52(2)(b) CJA 1993. See the report of Standing Committee B, 10 June 1993, at column 156 where the Economic Secretary to the Treasury states, under pressure from Mr Alistair Darling (the MP representing Edinburgh, Central) that the '... adjective "proper" is well understood in the courts. It is difficult to define in every circumstance what will be within or without that term ...'.

91 Section 62(2)(a) CJA 1993.

92 Section 62(2)(b) CJA 1993.

93 Section 52(4) CJA 1993.

94 These matters are examined further in Chapter 7, below.

CHAPTER 7

DEFENCES TO THE OFFENCE OF INSIDER DEALING

INTRODUCTION

'Defences' and 'special defences'

Section 53 of the Criminal Justice Act 1993[1] provides 'defences' to the offence of insider dealing. *Prima facie*, it contains a number of relatively generalised provisions[2] which may be applicable where the individual in question has dealt in securities,[3] has encouraged another person to deal in securities[4] or has simply disclosed information to a third party otherwise than in the proper performance of the functions of his employment, office or profession.[5] The legislative intention, however, was that these provisions would, so to speak, 'particularise' the defences available and, in doing so, would thereby reflect '... the anxieties that have been put ... by practitioners since the introduction of the Bill, particularly about the need for greater certainty about the effect of the defences ...'.[6] Whether s 53, as enacted, is a successful reflection of those anxieties is a matter of opinion. However, putting that to one side for the moment, if any one of these defences is shown to be applicable in any given case, the individual in question will not be guilty of the criminal offence of insider dealing although it may be that other sanctions may be imposed upon him or against the firm employing him with regard to his actions.[7]

7-01

Schedule 1 to the Criminal Justice Act 1993 contains three supplemental 'special defences' which may be applicable in certain circumstances to individuals who would otherwise be guilty of the offence of insider dealing. The 'special defences' apply to the 'dealing'

7-02

---

1 1993 c 36.

2 Which offence is set out in s 52 of the Criminal Justice Act 1993 and examined in detail in Chapter 6, above.

3 See s 52(1) and then s 53(1) CJA 1993.

4 See s 52(2)(a) and then s 53(2) CJA 1993.

5 See s 52(2)(b) and then s 53(3) CJA 1993.

6 *Per* the Economic Secretary to the Treasury, Mr Anthony Nelson, talking about the Criminal Justice Bill [Lords]. See the report of Standing Committee B, 10 June 1993, at column 157.

7 For instance, under Chapters 2 and/or 7 of the Rules of the Securities and Futures Authority. And see paras 9-55 to 9-86, below, further.

and to the 'encouraging' forms of the offence; two of the defences are specific whilst the other is general. Section 53(4) of the Criminal Justice Act 1993 provides that the special defences shall have effect although the Treasury may by order amend Schedule 1.[8] The 'specific' special defences are capable of being applicable to market makers[9] and also in respect of price stabilisation[10] whilst the more 'general' specific defence relates to information, termed market information, which market participants necessarily possess when involved in major transactions.[11] The remainder of this Chapter examines these general and special defences in greater detail.

7-03   Significant concerns were expressed, as these provisions went through the legislative process, at the range of defences which would be available to defendants. It was said that the range was so wide that it might be difficult to secure convictions.[12] Because of the width of the provisions, there might be possible defences not envisaged by the government.[13] It might even be the case that fewer cases would be prosecuted because '... the prosecuting authorities will decide that there is no point in pursuing the cases because of the get-out clauses'.[14] These concerns were rejected by the government. The Economic Secretary to the Treasury commented that the first and third of the 'general' statutory defences already existed in the Company Securities (Insider Dealing) Act 1985, '... albeit in different words ...'. The second, so-called 'closed circle', defence was being added but was thought to be necessary. He went on:

> I reject the suggestion that the provision goes too wide ... the defences are reasonable. It is not possible to have an exhaustive definition to provide the certainty that we would all like. It is arguable that the more certainty there is, the more possibility of avoidance there may be. Our intention is not in any way to blur what is a defence and what is the offence and I hope and believe that we have got it about right...[15]

Only time will tell.

---

8   Section 53(5) CJA 1993.

9   See para 1 of Schedule 1 to the CJA 1993 which carried forward and replaced existing legislation. See, by way of comparison, s 3(1)(c) and (d) of the Company Securities (Insider Dealing) Act 1985.

10 See para 5 of Schedule 1 to the CJA 1993 which carried forward and replaced existing legislation. See, by way of comparison, s 6 of the Company Securities (Insider Dealing) Act 1985 as substituted by s 175 of the Financial Services Act 1986 with effect from 29 April 1988.

11 See paras 2–4 of Schedule 1 to the CJA 1993.

12 *Per* Mr Alistair Darling (MP for Edinburgh, Central). See the report of Standing Committee B, 10 June 1993, at column 160.

13 *ibid* at column 161.

14 *ibid* at column 162.

15 *Per* the Economic Secretary to the Treasury, Mr Anthony Nelson. See the report of Standing Committee B, 10 June 1993, at column 163.

DEFENCES TO 'DEALING IN SECURITIES'

Generally

There are three statutory 'defences' to the circumstances in which an individual may be guilty of insider dealing by virtue of 'dealing in securities'.[16] There is no 'dealing' offence if any one of these defences is applicable.

7-04

No expectation of relevant profit

The first is where the individual dealing is able to show that he did not, at the time, expect the dealing to result in a profit attributable to the fact that the information which he possessed was price-sensitive information in relation to the securities in question.[17] For these purposes, it is provided that the reference to a profit must be taken as including a reference to the avoidance of a loss.[18] Accordingly, the individual must be able to show that he did not, at the time, expect the dealing to result in a profit or in the avoidance of a loss which, in either case, was attributable to the fact that the information in question was price-sensitive information.[19]

7-05

Prima facie, this defence does not seem to be as straightforward as some of its legislative predecessors purported to be, on paper if not in practice.[20] Where it may be relevant, the individual in question will already have dealt in securities resulting in a profit, or in the avoidance of a loss, whilst in possession of price-sensitive information.[21] But the defence will only then be applicable if that individual is able to demonstrate that he did not, at the time of dealing, 'expect' the transaction to result in a profit or in the avoidance of a loss which would be 'attributable' to the fact that he possessed information that was price-sensitive to the securities in question. He may, for instance, have sold

7-06

---

16   They are set out in s 53(1)(a)–(c), inclusive, of the Criminal Justice Act 1993.

17   Section 53(1)(a) CJA 1993.

18   Section 53(6) CJA 1993.

19   Section 56(2) CJA 1993 provides that inside information is 'price-sensitive information' in relation to securities if and only if the information would, if made public, be likely to have a significant effect on the price of the securities.

20   Compare, for instance, s 3(1)(a) of the Company Securities (Insider Dealing) Act 1985 which provided, in effect, that an individual was not prohibited by reason of his having any information from 'doing any particular thing otherwise than with a view to the making of a profit or the avoidance of a loss (whether for himself or another person) by the use of that information'.

21   See s 56(2) CJA 1993. It is worth emphasising that 'price-sensitive information' in relation to securities is inside information which, if made public, would be likely to have a significant effect on the price of the securities.

shares whilst in possession of information which he expected to receive a favourable reaction from the market.[22] He will need to explain why he dealt but, in doing so, he will need to go further. The Economic Secretary to the Treasury said that: 'If it is a question of what the accused person can prove that he expected, that is a subjective test and he must persuade the court that his defence protects innocent behaviour only and that he did not intend to make a profit'.[23] The individual will need to demonstrate, presumably on a balance of probabilities,[24] that he did not expect the profit obtained or the loss avoided to be so attributable. Depending on the circumstances, this may or may not be difficult to establish.

The 'closed circle' defence

7-07 The second 'defence' may be in point where the individual is able to show that, at the time of dealing in the securities in question, he believed on reasonable grounds that the information had already been disclosed. For it to be applicable, however, that disclosure of information will need to have been effected widely enough to ensure that none of those taking part in the dealing were prejudiced by not having the information.[25]

7-08 Whether this defence may be applicable will depend upon the facts and circumstances of the case in question. For instance, what disclosure of information had taken place? What was the reason for the dealing? The provision does not specify what will be sufficient but it is thought that this defence may be applicable where the parties to a transaction were in contact with each other immediately prior to the dealing and all possessed information that could or could not then be made public.[26] It may therefore be of particular comfort to corporate financiers in ensuring that those involved in properly conducted transactions, such as underwriting an offer of listed securities, are not running the risk of being found guilty of insider dealing.[27] The legislative intention was that this defence would be concerned with such 'closed circles' as arise in corporate finance transactions where the counterparties to the transaction know the information on which they are agreeing the 'deal' and it is not more widely known outside that circle. If that information is inside information[28] and they would otherwise be prohibited from

---

22 See the report of Standing Committee B, 10 June 1993, at column 157.

23 *Per* the Economic Secretary to the Treasury, Mr Anthony Nelson. See the report of Standing Committee B, 10 June 1993, at column 163.

24 Rather than beyond any reasonable doubt.

25 Section 53(1)(b) of the Criminal Justice Act 1993.

26 See the report of Standing Committee B, 10 June 1993, at column 157.

27 *ibid.*

28 See s 56(1) CJA 1993.

doing the deal, this defence may enable them to proceed.[29] The provision was not intended to extend further.[30]

If the information in question is known outside the 'closed circle' to a transaction, it may have been 'made public' and there are, of course, stated circumstances in which information is regarded for these purposes as having been made public[31] and will therefore not be inside information.[32] If so, the individuals concerned with that information will not have information as insiders.[33] For instance, the information may be such that it can be acquired by persons exercising diligence or particular expertise.[34] If the information has been made public, insider dealing will not be an issue. If that has not occurred, insider dealing may be in point and that is when this 'closed circle' defence may be applicable. It is worth emphasising that it was aimed at the particular circumstances of underwriters and others involved in corporate finance transactions who possess information which might otherwise be regarded as inside information which is not generally known and is the basis on which they undertake a transaction in securities.[35] The question of whether the defence applies is, however, a matter separate from whether or not information has been made public.[36]

29　See the report of Standing Committee B, 10 June 1993, at column 158.

30　'The measure does not go beyond that.' *Per* the Economic Secretary to the Treasury, Mr Anthony Nelson. See the report of Standing Committee B, 10 June 1993, at column 158. And see Harriet Creamer, 'Insider dealing – a new approach' (1993) 4(9) PLC 21–23 and 25–28.

31　Which are set out in s 58(2) CJA 1993.

32　See s 56(1)(c) CJA 1993.

33　See s 57(1) CJA 1993.

34　See s 58(3)(a) CJA 1993 and Chapter 5, above.

35　*Per* the Economic Secretary to the Treasury, Mr Anthony Nelson. See the report of Standing Committee B, 10 June 1993, at column 159.

36　See the report of Standing Committee B, 10 June 1993, at columns 157–159 for the 'insurance policy' point raised by Mr Alistair Darling (MP for Edinburgh, Central) which was considered by the Economic Secretary to the Treasury, Mr Anthony Nelson. Essentially, the point concerned the possibility that the prohibition on insider dealing could be avoided by individuals 'planting' information prior to dealing in such a way as to enable them to contend that it had already been 'made public' for the purposes of s 58 CJA 1993 and, as such, could not be regarded as 'inside information' which is defined by s 56(1)(c) CJA 1993 as being information which has not been made public. See s 56(1) CJA 1993, further, for the other necessary characteristics of 'inside information'. Section 58(2)(b) CJA 1993 provides that information is to be regarded as made public if it is contained in records which, by virtue of any enactment, are open to inspection by the public and Mr Darling mentioned in this regard (reported at column 161) a parish register. Could such registers become the unlikely media through which at least some potentially price-sensitive information becomes a matter of public knowledge? See para 5-22, above, further.

Individual would have dealt anyway

7-10   The third 'defence' where the individual in question has 'dealt in securities' is where he is able to show that he would have done what he did even if he had not possessed the information.[37] For this defence to be applicable, the individual will therefore need to be able to demonstrate that he had a compelling reason or justification for dealing in the securities in question and that he, the individual, would have done so on that basis regardless of the inside information in his possession. Whether he is able to do so will depend on the facts and circumstances of the case.

7-11   It should be mentioned that this defence received significant criticism as these provisions went through the legislative process. It was said to be so wide as to be unjustifiable. Also, that this '... is the catch all − if everything else fails, the defendant can say that he has not done it ... I wonder whether that is right. The minister has said that he is open to suggestions. I strongly suggest that he dumps it ... I do not believe that it is of assistance.'[38]

7-12   The relevant provision[39] contains no guidelines as to what reasons for dealing may be sufficiently compelling. At the end of the day, this will be a matter for the courts to decide. Some scenarios have, however, been suggested by persons providing commentary on earlier insider dealing legislation.[40] These include situations where the individual in possession of inside information has to deal in order to pay outstanding bills or to meet medical fees or tax demands which relate to him or to his immediate family.[41] A further scenario which has been suggested is that of a trustee who possesses inside information. This defence may be available to him if he deals in price-affected securities on the basis of independent investment advice.[42] The implicit question for the courts would seem to be whether the circumstances in question were sufficiently compelling so that a reasonable man would have dealt whether or not he was in possession of inside information.

---

37   Section 53(1)(c) CJA 1993.

38   *Per* Mr Alistair Darling MP. See the report of Standing Committee B, 10 June 1993, at column 161.

39   Section 53(1)(c) CJA 1993.

40   Mainly in relation to s 3(1)(a) of the Company Securities (Insider Dealing) Act 1985.

41   See, for instance, Sugarman & Ashe, 'The Companies Act 1980' (1981) 2 Co Law 13 at p 19.

42   *Per* the Economic Secretary to the Treasury, Mr Anthony Nelson. See the report of Standing Committee B, 10 June 1993, at column 159.

DEFENCES TO 'ENCOURAGING ANOTHER TO DEAL IN SECURITIES'

Generally

There are also three statutory defences to the offence of insider dealing by an individual who 'encourages another person to deal in securities'.[43] They are analogous to the defences to 'dealing' which are outlined above.[44]

7-13

No expectation of profit

The first defence for the individual who has encouraged another to deal in securities is if he is able to show that he did not, at the time of encouraging the other person, expect the dealing which took place to result in a profit or in the avoidance of a loss which was attributable to the fact that the information in question was price-sensitive information in relation to the securities.[45] Whether this defence will be applicable in any given case will depend upon the relevant facts and circumstances and the individual will need to make his case on a balance of probabilities.

7-14

The 'closed circle' defence

The second defence differs slightly from its equivalent for 'dealing' in securities.[46] It will apply where the individual is able to show that, at the time, he believed on reasonable grounds that the information had been or would be disclosed widely enough to ensure that none of those taking part in the dealing would be prejudiced by not having knowledge of the information.[47] The slight difference is that the defence will still apply where, at the time of giving the encouragement, the information is not thought to have been disclosed but the individual is able to demonstrate that he had reasonable grounds for believing that it would be disclosed sufficiently.

7-15

---

43 These are set out in s 53(2)(a)–(c) CJA 1993, inclusive.

44 In paras 7-04 to 7-09, inclusive, above. See also s 53(1) (a)–(c) CJA 1993.

45 Section 53(2)(a) CJA 1993. Also s 53(6) CJA 1993. Additionally, see paras 7-05 and 7-06 above.

46 In s 53(1)(b) CJA 1993.

47 Section 53(2)(b) CJA 1993. See also paras 7-07–7-09 above.

7-16   Many have found the 'closed circle' defence 'slightly opaque' in its wording[48] and it was the subject of much discussion during the legislative process. Concerns were raised that it might not be sufficient to exclude dealings occurring during or resulting from significant corporate finance transactions where the individuals in question dealt on the basis of equality of information. Transactions such as rights issues or secondary offerings, requiring either underwriting or a placement where the shares issued were acquired by a merchant bank and then passed on, were mentioned. It was suggested[49] that what was required was a further defence to 'dealing' and 'encouraging', to the effect that there would be no offence of insider dealing if those taking part in the dealing were or would be in possession of the information.

7-17   This suggestion was rejected by the government on the grounds that the 'closed circle' defence was sufficient as it stood.[50] Where those persons taking part in a particular transaction possessed the relevant information, it was likely to have been disclosed sufficiently widely to ensure that none of those taking part in the dealing would be prejudiced by not having the information. In the context of corporate finance transactions, it was felt that there were circumstances where those taking part in the dealing but not directly involved in negotiating the transaction would not be prejudiced by not having the information. For instance, an employee of a financial institution might commit his employer to underwrite an offer, subject to board approval. The board of directors might then approve the deal on the basis of the recommendation of the employee without studying the offer document in any detail. In those circumstances, it was felt that there was no mischief in the board being unaware of all the details before any dealing took place. It was sufficient that the employee, a person taking part in the transaction, was so aware and this scenario was covered by the 'closed circle' defence.[51]

Individual would have encouraged another anyway

7-18   The third defence, where another person has been encouraged to deal in securities, is where the encourager is able to show that he would have

---

48   *Per* Mr Peter Ainsworth (MP for Surrey, East). See the report of Standing Committee B, 10 June 1993, at column 160.

49   *ibid.*

50   *Per* the Economic Secretary to the Treasury, Mr Anthony Nelson. See the report of Standing Committee B, 10 June 1993, at column 162.

51   See the report of Standing Committee B, 10 June 1993, at columns 162–163.

done what he did[52] even if he had not been in possession of the information.[53]

DEFENCES TO A 'DISCLOSURE OF INFORMATION'

Generally

There are two statutory defences in circumstances where the offence of insider dealing would otherwise have been committed by virtue of a disclosure of information.[54] The position differs slightly from the defences to the 'dealing' and to the 'encouraging' form of the offence because disclosure by an individual in the proper performance of the functions of his employment, office or profession does not amount to the 'disclosure' offence which requires disclosure 'otherwise' than in the proper performance of such functions. Also, the 'closed circle' defence to 'dealing' and to 'encouraging' is not applicable to 'disclosure' because that defence itself requires the parties to possess the same information.[55]

7-19

No expectation of dealing

The first available defence is where the individual is able to show that he did not, at the time of the disclosure, expect any person to deal in securities because of the disclosure in the circumstances mentioned in s 52(3) of the Criminal Justice Act 1993.[56] To reiterate, those circumstances occur where acquisitions or disposals[57] of securities take place on a regulated market[58] or where the person dealing relies on a professional intermediary[59] or is himself acting as a professional intermediary.[60] For this defence to be applicable, at the time of the disclosure, the individual therefore must not expect any dealing in securities to take place in those circumstances as a result of his disclosure. The disclosure must be for another purpose. Although this will be a matter for the courts to decide, the test is likely to be whether,

7-20

---

52   He would have encouraged the other to deal in the securities.
53   Section 53(2)(c) CJA 1993. And see, also, paras 7-10 and 7-12 above.
54   They are set out in s 53(3)(a) and (b) CJA 1993.
55   *Per* the Economic Secretary to the Treasury, Mr Anthony Nelson. See the report of Standing Committee B, 10 June 1993, at columns 159–160.
56   The so-called 'dealing circumstances'. See paras 6-04 and 6-05 above and s 53(3)(a) CJA 1993.
57   And see s 55(2) and (3) CJA 1993.
58   See s 60(1) CJA 1993.
59   See s 59 CJA 1993.
60   Section 52(3) CJA 1993.

in the circumstances, it would be reasonable for an individual to expect such dealing to take place as a result of the disclosure which is made.

7-21   An example of a scenario to which this defence might well be applicable can perhaps be drawn from a case[61] decided in the 1980s in the USA in which an investment analyst had become aware of certain unlawful practices allegedly carried on by a company[62] which, if true, would mean that its assets had been exaggerated, to say the least. In researching the true position, the analyst mentioned these allegations to certain of his own customers who responded by selling the shares they held in the company. The allegations were found to be true and the company subsequently went into receivership. The analyst was censured by the Securities and Exchange Commission although he was subsequently cleared by the Supreme Court. But, had he what he did in the UK and otherwise assuming the commission of the offence of insider dealing by virtue of his disclosures to his customers,[63] would he have been able to take advantage of this defence?[64] The case would probably depend upon the extent of his disclosures at the time. Provided he was not advising his customers to cut and run, and was merely investigating the allegations without seeking to spread them further, the courts might well be persuaded by the analyst that it was reasonable for him not to expect his customers to dispose of their shares forthwith. This defence might well therefore be applicable.

No expectation of profit

7-22   The second defence to 'disclosure' may apply where the person disclosing information did expect that dealing in securities would result from his disclosure. With this provision, he must, however, be able to show that he did not expect any such dealing to result in a profit attributable to the fact that the information was price-sensitive information[65] in relation to the securities.[66] For these purposes, the reference to 'a profit' must also be taken as including a reference to the avoidance of a loss.[67]

---

61   *Dirks v Securities Exchange Commission* (1982) 681 F 2d 824.
62   The company was called 'Equity Funding of America'.
63   Assuming of course that the disclosure was otherwise than in the proper performance of the functions of his employment; see s 52(2)(b) CJA 1993.
64   That is, of s 53(3)(a) CJA 1993.
65   See s 56(2) CJA 1993.
66   Section 53(3)(b) CJA 1993.
67   Section 53(6) CJA 1993.

THE 'SPECIAL DEFENCES' TO INSIDER DEALING

Generally

There are three scenarios which are thought to merit 'special defences' to   **7-23**
the crime of insider dealing. Two of the defences are specific and
concern the role of 'market makers'[68] and the question of 'price
stabilisation.'[69] The third is more general and relates to the possession of
a particular sort of information which is termed 'market information'.
These defences are set out in paras 1–5 of Schedule 1 to the Criminal
Justice Act 1993 and apply to the 'dealing' and to the 'encouraging'
forms of the offence.

'Market makers'

The purpose of this defence is to protect market makers carrying on their   **7-24**
business as such; holding themselves out, at all normal times, as being
willing to buy and sell and thus to make a market in those securities in
which they deal. The 'policy' rationale is that market makers should be
able to continue to quote two-way continuous prices so long as they act
in good faith.[70] Without this defence, market makers might well run the
risk of insider dealing by dealing in certain circumstances. Before
commenting on this specific defence,[71] there are a number of defined
terms which must first be mentioned.

For the purposes of this defence, a 'market maker' is defined[72] as   **7-25**
meaning a person who holds himself out at all normal times, in
compliance with the rules of a regulated market or an approved
organisation, as willing to acquire or dispose of securities and is
recognised as doing so under those rules. Regulated markets do not
recognise market makers. Instead, the market makers who deal on a
market are recognised as doing so under the rules of the market.[73]
'Securities', for these purposes, are of course securities falling within the
various categories set out in Schedule 2 to the Criminal Justice Act

---

68 Carrying forward the provisions in s 3(1)(c) and (d) of the Company Securities
(Insider Dealing) Act 1985.

69 Carrying forward the provisions of s 6 of the Company Securities (Insider Dealing)
Act 1985.

70 *Per* the Economic Secretary to the Treasury, Mr Anthony Nelson. See the report of
Standing Committee B, 15 June 1993, at column 216.

71 Contained in para 1 of Schedule 1 to the CJA 1993. But see also Alistair Alcock, 'In
defence of insider dealing' (1990) 140 NLJ 1470.

72 In para 1(2)(a) and (b) of Schedule 1 CJA 1993.

73 *Per* the Economic Secretary to the Treasury, Mr Anthony Nelson. See the report of
Standing Committee B, 15 June 1993, at column 216.

1993[74] and 'regulated markets' are markets designated by Treasury Order as such for the purposes of Part V of the Criminal Justice Act 1993.[75] Finally, for the purposes of this specific defence, an 'approved organisation' is said to mean an international securities self-regulating organisation approved under para 25B of Schedule 1 to the Financial Services Act 1986.[76]

7-26   This defence provides that an individual will not be guilty of insider dealing through dealing in securities or encouraging another person to deal[77] if he is able to show that he acted in good faith in the course of his business as a market maker[78] or his employment in the business of a market maker.[79] There is no requirement that the market maker must have acquired any relevant information that he possesses in the course of his business. How any information was acquired is immaterial.[80] This defence was also amended during the legislative process in an attempt to avoid any suggestion that it might be applicable to all the employees of a market maker, including those not involved directly in market making. The legislative intention was that it should only be applicable to the market making employees of a market maker.[81] Whether an individual will be able to demonstrate that he acted 'in good faith', to the satisfaction of the court, will depend on his situation and on the facts and circumstances of the particular case. This will be a 'judgmental' matter but 'in good faith' is said to be an expression familiar to the courts.[82]

---

74   See s 54(1) and (2) and Schedule 2 CJA 1993. See, also, the Insider Dealing (Securities and Regulated Markets) Order 1994 (SI 1994/187).

75   See s 60(1) CJA 1993. See, also, SI 1994/187 and the Insider Dealing (Securities and Regulated Markets)(Amendment) Order 1996 (SI 1996/1561).

76   Paragraph 1(3) of Schedule 1 CJA 1993. Paragraph 25B of Schedule 1 to the FSA 1986 provides a limited exclusion from investment business where the investment activity of arranging deals in investments is engaged in for the purposes of carrying out the functions of a body or association which is approved under that paragraph as an international securities self-regulating organisation. Such an activity engaged in by the organisation or by any person acting on its behalf is not regarded as constituting the carrying on of investment business in the UK and thus does not require authorisation for the purposes of the FSA 1986. See para 25B further.

77   See s 52(1) and (2)(a) CJA 1993. Also, see paras 6-15 to 6-23, above.

78   Paragraph 1(1)(a) of Schedule 1 CJA 1993.

79   Paragraph 1(1)(b) of Schedule 1 CJA 1993.

80   *Per* the Economic Secretary to the Treasury, Mr Anthony Nelson. See the report of Standing Committee B, 15 June 1993, at column 216.

81   *ibid.*

82   *ibid* at column 217.

'Market information'

The second 'special defence' to a charge of insider dealing relates to the possession by an individual of information which amounts to what is termed 'market information'.[83] This was envisaged as being a specific sort of information which market participants involved in major transactions would necessarily and inevitably possess.[84] An obvious example of market information could concern a person who has sold a large tranche of shares. Publication of that information might have an effect on the relevant share price as might the knowledge that someone intended to dispose of such a tranche.[85] The relevant provisions in fact contain two defences, where an individual might otherwise be guilty of insider dealing through dealing in securities or through encouraging another person to deal in securities, where the information in question amounts to market information.

7-27

For the purposes of this 'special defence', information which is 'market information' will also be inside information. 'Market information' is defined[86] as meaning information consisting of one or more of certain stated matters of fact which would seem to consist of an exclusive list. Those facts are as follows:

7-28

- that securities[87] of a particular kind have been or are to be acquired or disposed of or that their acquisition or disposal[88] is under consideration or is the subject of negotiation;[89]

- that securities of a particular kind have not been or are not to be acquired or disposed of;[90]

- the number of securities acquired or disposed of or to be acquired or disposed of or whose acquisition or disposal is under consideration or is the subject of negotiation;[91]

- the price or range of prices at which securities have been or are to be acquired or disposed of or the price or range of prices at which the securities whose acquisition or disposal is under consideration or the subject of negotiation may be acquired or disposed of;[92]

---

83 See paras 2–4 of Schedule 1 CJA 1993, inclusive.
84 *Per* the Economic Secretary to the Treasury, Mr Anthony Nelson. See the report of Standing Committee B, 15 June 1993, at column 216.
85 *ibid.*
86 In paras 4(a)–(e) of Schedule 1 CJA 1993.
87 See s 54 CJA 1993 and SI 1994/187.
88 See s 55(2) and (3) CJA 1993.
89 Paragraph 4(a) of Schedule 1 CJA 1993.
90 Paragraph 4(b) of Schedule 1 CJA 1993.
91 Paragraph 4(c) of Schedule 1 CJA 1993.
92 Paragraph 4(d) of Schedule 1 CJA 1993.

- the identity of the persons involved or likely to be involved in any capacity in an acquisition or disposal.[93]

7-29   The first defence[94] based upon the possession of market information provides that an individual will not be guilty of insider dealing by virtue of dealing in securities or through encouraging another person to deal in securities if he is able to show that the information which he had as an insider was market information[95] and that it was reasonable for an individual in his position to have acted as he did despite having that information as an insider at the time.[96] As these provisions went through the legislative process, the Economic Secretary to the Treasury commented that:

> the requirement that people must act in a reasonable manner, particularly in relation to the criminal law, is an objective assessment and is probably not susceptible to further or more precise definition. In deciding whether it would be reasonable to use market information in specific circumstances, a practitioner would do well to consult the regulations of the body under which he is authorised to conduct investment business or the rules of the market in which he is dealing...[97]

It is also provided that, in determining whether it was reasonable for an individual to do any act despite having market information at the time, certain factors shall in particular be taken into account.[98] Those factors stated are as follows:

- the content of the information;[99]
- the circumstances in which the individual first had the information and in what capacity;[100] and also
- the capacity in which he now acts.[101]

7-30   The second special defence based upon the possession of market information[102] sets out circumstances in which it is considered acceptable for an individual to use market information. It provides that an individual will not be guilty of insider dealing by virtue of dealing in securities or encouraging another person to deal if he is able to show that

---

93 Paragraph 4(e) of Schedule 1 CJA 1993.
94 Set out in para 2(1) of Schedule 1 CJA 1993.
95 Paragraph 2(1)(a) of Schedule 1 CJA 1993.
96 Paragraph 2(1)(b) of Schedule 1 CJA 1993.
97 See the report of Standing Committee B, 15 June 1993, at column 217.
98 See para 2(2) of Schedule 1 CJA 1993.
99 Paragraph 2(2)(a) of Schedule 1 CJA 1993.
100 Paragraph 2(2)(b) of Schedule 1 CJA 1993.
101 Paragraph 2(2)(c) of Schedule 1 CJA 1993.
102 Contained in para 3 of Schedule 1 CJA 1993.

he acted in connection with an acquisition or disposal which was under consideration or the subject of negotiation or in the course of a series of such acquisitions or disposals.[103] In doing so, he must show that he acted with a view to facilitating the accomplishment of the acquisition or disposal or the series of acquisitions or disposals.[104] It must also be the case that the information which the individual had as an insider was market information arising directly out of his involvement in the acquisition or disposal or series of acquisitions or disposals.[105]

7-31

The most obvious rationale for this defence is to enable persons involved in or contemplating takeovers and mergers to deal in securities[106] or to encourage others to do so without running the risk of being guilty of insider dealing. For instance, the directors of a company in the process of making an offer to acquire the share capital of another might want to encourage the acquisition of such shares by friendly parties in advance of the bid being posted. The potential bid would be inside information[107] and the securities in question would be price-affected securities in relation to that information.[108] In the absence of this special defence, an encouragement to deal in these circumstances would have the potential of making the directors guilty of insider dealing.[109]

Price stabilisation

The third 'special defence' relates to the securities market practice known as 'price stabilisation'. Generally speaking, this usually involves a 'stabilising manager' supporting the price of newly-issued securities for a limited period following their issue, while they are being offered to the public. The purpose is to ensure the success of the issue by keeping the price steady. The 'stabilising manager' is normally the securities house responsible for the new issue and stabilisation will involve it in

7-32

---

103 Paragraph 3(a)(i) of Schedule 1 CJA 1993.

104 Paragraph 3(a)(ii) of Schedule 1 CJA 1993. This provision echoes, albeit in different language, the defence provided by s 3(2) of the Company Securities (Insider Dealing) Act 1985.

105 Paragraph 3(b) of Schedule 1 CJA 1993.

106 And for the purposes of Part V CJA 1993, a person 'deals in securities' if he acquires or disposes of the securities (whether as principal or as agent) or he procures, directly or indirectly, an acquisition or disposal of the securities by any other person. See s 55(1) etc CJA1993.

107 See s 56(1) CJA 1993. The bid would relate to particular securities and would, if made public, be likely to have a significant effect on the price of those securities.

108 See s 56(2) CJA 1993. Because the information would, if made public, be likely to have a significant effect on the price of the securities.

109 See ss 52(2)(a) and 52(3) CJA 1993.

purchasing some of the newly-issued securities from the market to steady the price and prevent its decline.[110]

7-33　　The rationale for allowing stabilisation in controlled circumstances is twofold: to protect investors who might otherwise be affected by price fluctuations in respect of dealings following a new issue of securities and also to ensure the orderly distribution of securities.[111]

7-34　　As stabilisation involves the price of securities being maintained artificially, it is a form of market manipulation which can be a criminal offence under s 47(2) of the Financial Services Act 1986.[112] However, s 48(7) provides, generally speaking, that s 47(2) will not be regarded as contravened by anything done for the purposes of stabilising the price of investments if it is done in conformity with the Stabilisation Rules promulgated by the Securities and Investments Board and contained in Part 10 of the Financial Services (Conduct of Business) Rules 1990.[113] The purpose of those rules is to ensure the close regulation of stabilisation under the aegis of the Financial Services Act 1986. Where a person authorised to carry on investment business for the purposes of that Act takes action to stabilise the price of securities, he must comply with any applicable provisions of the Stabilisation Rules.

7-35　　For the purposes of this defence to insider dealing, 'the price stabilisation rules' mean rules which are made under s 48 of the Financial Services Act 1986 which make provision as to the circumstances and manner in which and the time when or the period

---

110 See Part 4 of and Appendix E to the Financial Services (Conduct of Business) Rules 1990 of the Securities and Investments Board (as updated and revised), further. As to amendments and restatements of those rules, see SIB Rules and Releases Nos 90 (18 October 1990), 140 (14 June 1994), 156 (25 May 1995) and 160 (24 November 1995).

111 See House of Commons Official Report (6th Series, Volume 103) for 30 October 1986, at columns 538–547 (where House of Lords amendments to the Financial Services Bill were being considered). Also, it has been said that stabilisation was originally excluded from the restrictions on insider dealing to ensure the Eurobond 'market' did not move away from the UK to a financial centre with a more relaxed attitude. See Ashe & Counsell, *Insider Trading* (1990, Fourmat Publishing) referring to Suter, *The Regulation of Insider Dealing In Britain* (Butterworths) at p 116 and also Rider, Abrams and Ferran, *Guide to the Financial Services Act 1986* (CCH Editions, 2nd edn) at para 730.

112 Generally speaking, market manipulation is made a criminal offence by s 47(2) of the FSA which provides that 'Any person who does any act or engages in any course of conduct which creates a false or misleading impression as to the market in or the price or value of any investments is guilty of an offence if he does so for the purpose of creating that impression and of thereby inducing another person to acquire, dispose of, subscribe for or underwrite those investments or to refrain from doing so or to exercise, or refrain from exercising, any rights conferred by those investments'. See Chapter 10, below, for a fuller treatment.

113 As updated and revised by the SIB. See note 110, above, further. See s 48(2)(i), (7), (7A), (8) and (9) of the FSA 1986.

during which action may be taken for the purpose of stabilising the price of investments of any specified description.[114]

In the absence of this defence, the actions of a stabilising manager would involve insider dealing. He would have information as an insider[115] and would be dealing in securities[116] that were price-affected securities[117] in relation to that information.[118] The defence, however, provides that an individual will not be guilty of insider dealing by virtue of dealing in securities or encouraging another person to deal if he shows that he acted in conformity with the price stabilisation rules.[119]

7-36

OTHER LIMITATIONS ON THE OFFENCE

Individuals acting on behalf of public sector bodies

The offence of insider dealing[120] does not apply to anything done by an individual acting on behalf of a 'public sector body' in pursuit of monetary policies or policies with respect to exchange rates or the management of public debt or foreign exchange reserves.[121] This provision is intended to apply only to 'official' activities in pursuit of monetary policy and the like. It is not intended to apply 'to anything done by any person acting on behalf of a public sector body in an official capacity'.[122] As such, this provision was welcomed, as the Criminal Justice Bill went through the legislative process, as being useful and also something which 'will reassure many people'.[123]

7-37

For the purposes of insider dealing law, the expression 'public sector body' is defined[124] as meaning any one of five 'bodies'. Those five bodies are listed as follows:

7-38

---

114 Paragraph 5(2) of Schedule 1 to the CJA 1993. See also s 48(2)(i) of the FSA 1986.

115 Probably on the basis of ss 56(1) and 57(1), (2)(a)(ii) of the CJA 1993.

116 Section 55 CJA 1993.

117 Section 56(2) CJA 1993.

118 Section 52(1) C J A 1993.

119 Paragraph 5(1) of Schedule 1 CJA 1993.

120 As set out in s 52 CJA 1993.

121 Section 63(1) CJA 1993.

122 *Per* the Economic Secretary to the Treasury, Mr.Anthony Nelson. See the report of Standing Committee B, 15 June 1993, at column 213.

123 *Per* Mr Alistair Darling (the MP for Edinburgh, Central) with obvious tongue in cheek. He went on: 'Unjustified and unkind comments were made last autumn, when the government had certain difficulties with the currency, which we need not discuss for the purposes of the debate. The amendments will be useful'. See the report of Standing Committee B, 15 June 1993, at column 213.

124 By virtue of s 60(3)(b) CJA 1993.

- the government of the UK, of Northern Ireland or of any country or territory outside the UK;[125]
- a local authority in the UK or elsewhere;[126]
- any international organisation the members of which include the UK or another Member State;[127]
- the Bank of England;[128] or
- the central bank of any sovereign State.[129]

---

125 Section 60(3)(b)(i) CJA 1993.
126 Section 60(3)(b)(ii) CJA 1993.
127 Of the EC. Section 60(3)(b)(iii) CJA 1993.
128 Section 60(3)(b)(iv) CJA 1993.
129 Section 60(3)(b)(v) CJA 1993.

CHAPTER 8

THE MONITORING, ENFORCEMENT AND PROSECUTION OF INSIDER DEALING

THE CRIMINAL SANCTION

The offence, the government and related matters

In 1990, in response to the Trade and Industry Select Committee, the Conservative Government stated its intention to retain criminal sanctions as the primary means of preventing and punishing insider dealing.[1] The Conservative government has continued to believe that 'criminal offences prosecuted in the courts should remain the primary means of action against insider dealers'.[2] For instance, as the Criminal Justice Bill[3] went through the legislative process, the Economic Secretary to the Treasury said that:

8-01

> Despite the relatively small number of convictions secured since 1980, I do not accept that our existing insider dealing legislation is a failure. Rather, it has played an important part in changing attitudes to the improper use of insider information, with the effect that insider dealing is now universally accepted as being wrong, which it was not when it was made illegal in 1980.[4]

---

1   In response to a suggestion that sanctions imposed by a civil regulator might provide an alternative 'civil' penalty for insider dealing, the point was made that 'The regulator's action would be to impose a sanction on the basis that it was in the public interest to penalise individuals who conducted themselves in a particular way. That is the classic reason for creating a criminal offence. The government accordingly believes that the criminal law remains appropriate'. That passage was quoted by the Economic Secretary to the Treasury, Mr Anthony Nelson. See the report of Standing Committee B, 15 June 1993, at column 207.

2   *Per* the Economic Secretary to the Treasury, Mr Anthony Nelson. See the report of Standing Committee B, 15 June 1993, at column 207. But see Alastair N Brown, 'The problem of insider dealing' (1995) 40 (4) JLSS 153–154. Also, 'How to tackle insider dealers', *The Times* (Pennington column), 21 May 1996.

3   Which became the CJA 1993.

4   *Per* the Economic Secretary to the Treasury, Mr Anthony Nelson. See the report of Standing Committee B, 15 June 1993, at column 206. It should, however, be mentioned that reports have appeared in the press that the DTI is now passing certain cases of alleged insider dealing to 'City' regulators (such as the SFA) in an attempt to widen the scope of investigations into possible market abuse. The SFA, of course, has significant powers exercisable in respect of its member firms and their employees. See, for instance, *The Times* Business News of 14 August 1995 ('SFA steps up war against insider deals' by Jon Ashworth) at p 40 and Chapter 9, below, further.

he Conservative government also believes that the standard of proof required in prosecutions for insider dealing should remain 'beyond all reasonable doubt' and should not be reduced to the standard required in civil litigation which is that of a 'balance of probabilities'. The Economic Secretary to the Treasury made the point that people were mistaken if they believed that changing the standard of proof which was required would substantially increase the number of convictions. He said that:

> an analysis of the evidence in past cases suggests that the real difficulty lies in establishing that someone possesses inside information, rather than with the burden of proof which applies to whether, for example, someone knows that information is inside information.[5]

8-03   For the moment, the Conservative government has rejected suggestions that the offence of insider dealing should be replaced or supplemented by specific 'civil' sanctions capable of being imposed by one of the 'City' regulators, such as the Securities and Investments Board or the Securities and Futures Authority. The Economic Secretary to the Treasury said that the government was not proposing to take any such approach. 'Why, for example, should "less serious" cases of insider dealing, which today would be prosecuted, be taken away from the courts when "less serious" cases of theft or fraud are not?'[6] He also emphasised that the possibility of civil sanctions, perhaps through the medium of bringing an action for damages, already existed under current law. Also, '... self-regulating organisations can take action where there is a breach of their rules. That is a civil course open to them, and fines can be imposed. The insider can also lose his job'.[7]

The Criminal Justice Act 1993

8-04   Section 61 of the Criminal Justice Act 1993 sets out the penalties for insider dealing and also the requirements for bringing prosecutions. It carries forward and reapplies the penalties which were available under the Company Securities (Insider Dealing) Act 1985[8] and the maximum

---

5   See the report of Standing Committee B, 15 June 1993, at column 207.

6   *ibid*. For some related discussion, see David A Bennett, 'What's wrong with insider dealing?' (1994) 5(9) ICCLR 299–301. Also Michael Ashe, 'Towards a civil penalty enforcement system in securities regulation' (1990) 5(7) BJIB & FL 291–292.

7   *ibid*. And see note 4 above, further. See also Alastair J Gordon, 'Let the victim bite back' (1993) (March) Bus LR 4–5 and 'Toothless act catches no crooks', *The Times* (Pennington Column), 2 November 1995. See, finally, the recent report on insider dealing by Norman Barry published by the Foundation for Business Responsibilities (June 1996), which suggest insider dealing should be decriminalised and replaced by a 'civil' action.

8   See s 8(1) of the Company Securities (Insider Dealing) Act 1985.

penalty of imprisonment for a term not exceeding seven years and an unlimited fine is said to reflect 'the seriousness with which the government regard the crime of insider dealing'.[9] The arrangements for bringing prosecutions also replicate similar provisions in the Company Securities (Insider Dealing) Act 1985[10] which were said to 'have effectively prevented vexatious actions'.[11] Essentially, prosecutions can only be brought by or with the consent of the Secretary of State for Trade and Industry or the Director of Public Prosecutions.[12] These matters are examined later in this chapter, the main purpose of which is to set out in general terms how a case of possible insider dealing in the UK, at the present time, might come to be detected, investigated and subsequently prosecuted.

The usual scenario

If there are unusual price movements or dealings in securities, these matters are likely to be noticed by the market surveillance group of the London Stock Exchange. This unit monitors the securities market by computer. If there is strong evidence of insider dealing, the case will be referred by the Stock Exchange to the Department of Trade and Industry which will consider what took place further. If necessary, inspectors may be appointed pursuant to ss 177–178 of the Financial Services Act 1986 or, more generally, pursuant to Part XIV of the Companies Act 1985. If appointed, such inspectors[13] have wide powers and may, for instance, examine on oath any person who they consider may be able to give information concerning insider dealing offences. In this regard, as the Criminal Justice Bill went through the legislative process, Economic Secretary to the Treasury commented that:

8-05

> Those are considerable powers and it was felt, certainly when the Company Securities (Insider Dealing) Act 1985 was passed, that they should remain vested in the Secretary of State, to reassure people that such powers of inquisition – as, legislatively, they are – would be exercised not lightly but properly in all cases ... That remains the case for the time being.[14]

---

9 *Per* the Economic Secretary to the Treasury, Mr Anthony Nelson. See the report of Standing Committee B, 15 June 1993, at column 206.

10 See s 8(2) of the Company Securities (Insider Dealing) Act 1985.

11 *Per* the Economic Secretary to the Treasury, Mr Anthony Nelson. See the report of Standing Committee B, 15 June 1993, at column 206.

12 Section 61(2) and (3) of the CJA 1993. There have been press reports that only four unrelated prosecutions have been brought under the CJA 1993. Provisions against five individuals with only one conviction resulting. See Jason Nissé, 'Insider alert after heavy trade in Blenheim shares', *The Times*, 1 July 1996.

13 Usually a chartered accountant and a Queen's Counsel.

14 See the report of Standing Committee B, 15 June 1993, at column 208. And see Nigel Read, 'Information and insiders – a case study' (1994) (May) IHL 26–27.

8-06   A prosecution may follow such investigation. With regard to criminal proceedings, the Economic Secretary to the Treasury commented that:

> The government expect that the arrangements for bringing prosecutions will continue as at present, with the majority of prosecutions being brought by the Secretary of State for Trade and Industry, but the stock exchange will be given permission to bring prosecutions where appropriate.[15]

He mentioned that this had already occurred. He also thought that it might be feasible for the Securities and Investments Board to prosecute in a case of insider dealing.[16]

8-07   However, to date, the government has steered clear of establishing a central agency charged with monitoring, investigating and subsequently prosecuting cases of insider dealing in particular and financial crime in general. In the first instance, they have expressed reluctance at delegating the 'fairly draconian' investigatory powers which are available to a 'non-governmental body'.[17] They doubt whether such a transfer of powers would enhance the number of prosecutions brought or convictions secured.[18] Also, they do not believe that there is any consensus, in the City or elsewhere, 'on the need for a substantial regulatory revision. There is no clear consensus about a replacement'.[19] The Economic Secretary to the Treasury went further and said:

> Unless it is clear what should replace the present system and there is consensus for such a change, I do not consider it responsible to embark lightly on primary legislation. If there are to be any changes in this sphere for the long term, it is important to get them right and not to lurch from one system of City regulation to another.[20]

MONITORING THE MARKETS

The role of the London Stock Exchange

8-08   The market surveillance group of the London Stock Exchange[20a]

---

15   *ibid* at column 206.

16   *ibid* at column 208.

17   *ibid*.

18   *ibid*.

19   *ibid* at column 209.

20   *ibid*.

20a Regulatory operations at the Stock Exchange were reported as being 'streamlined' in 1995–96. The supervision and surveillance groups were merged within the overall market regulation department under the aegis of the Exchange's Director of Market Services. There have been recent press reports of the Insider Dealing Unit of the Exchange. See Jason Nissé, 'Insider alert after heavy trade in Blenheim shares', *The Times*, 1 July 1996.

maintains a computer vigil over securities trading by means of which it is able to identify and investigate suspicious dealings. It is thought to investigate all dealings where there have been sharp price movements in the relevant securities and dealings prior to takeovers and mergers. The procedure adopted seems to be to invite and follow through all investigations in certain defined circumstances. Before computers were employed, surveillance was a matter of poring over hard-copy records to identify unusual dealing. Surveillance has grown in sophistication since then and, encouraged by the example of the New York Stock Exchange,[21] the London Stock Exchange has developed and improved its computer monitoring facilities since computerised trading was established in the 1980s, introducing an integrated monitoring and surveillance system called 'IMAS' to speed up investigations into unusual dealings.

The IMAS system is thought to consider all market transactions and to send out alerts when a share price moves unexpectedly or when a significant trade has an effect on the market. The surveillance group is thus able, for instance, to isolate and examine trades that occur outside fixed parameters which may therefore be suspicious. It can also investigate trades by reference to volume or to the securities houses that are involved. It can 'trail' particular trades back to identify the counterparties involved and the prices at which they dealt. Once so identified, a suspicious trade can then be checked back against a database of information concerning other suspicious trades from 1980[22] onwards. That database may provide information on particular individuals and their connections with particular companies and/or with the professional advisers of those companies. In conjunction with a company called Search-Space, the Exchange has also endeavoured to apply artificial intelligence software capable of analysing trading patterns and certain key happenings. Essentially, they have sought to limit the transactions they have to consider carefully to those which are thus 'thought' to have been the most suspicious. The purpose of this initiative is for the Exchange to be better equipped to provide clear cut evidence to those charged with investigating and prosecuting insider dealing.[22a] The Exchange is also to introduce a system of 24-hour trading suspensions or 'halts' when there are unexplained or suspicious movements in share prices.[22b] Before a halt

8-09

---

21 A number of computer systems have been used in the US to 'monitor' securities trading: 'ASAM', the powerful Automated Search and Match system used by the New York Stock Exchange; also 'ISIS', Intermarket Surveillance Information Systems, which has provided a database of deals in securities on American exchanges.

22 When insider dealing was first made a criminal offence.

22a See Frank Kane, 'Scourge of the insiders', *The Sunday Times*, 26 May 1996 which reports further the views and approach of the Director of Market Services of the Stock Exchange.

22b Reported to be introduced in August 1996. See Rufus Olins, 'Exchange cracks down on insider trading', *The Sunday Times*, 19 May 1996.

is imposed, the company or its broker will be given the choice to put out a statement or to provide an explanation as to what has occurred. Once a halt has been imposed, a company can ask for it to become a share suspension.

INVESTIGATIONS UNDER
THE FINANCIAL SERVICES ACT 1986

The Department of Trade and Industry

8-10   If the procedures outlined in paras 8-08 and 8-09 above indicate that an unusual transaction in securities may have involved insider dealing, the case will usually be referred by the Stock Exchange to the Department of Trade and Industry. Much less likely in practice would be for a person affected by or suspecting insider dealing to raise the matter with the DTI. In most cases, further investigation will be required before a prosecution will be feasible and there are a number of options open to the Secretary of State at this stage.

The investigative powers

8-11   Specific powers enabling the Secretary of State for Trade and Industry[23] to investigate suspected cases of insider dealing are contained in Part VII ('Insider Dealing') of the Financial Services Act 1986. The fact that there were no such powers in the original legislation[24] was a major deficiency which was not remedied promptly.[25]

The appointment of inspectors

8-12   If it appears to the Secretary of State that there are circumstances suggesting that an offence under Part V of the Criminal Justice Act 1993 may have been committed, he may appoint one or more competent inspectors to carry out such investigations as are requisite to establish whether or not any offence has been committed and to report the results

---

23   Who has recently gloried under the title of the President of the Board of Trade. In 1995, 43 cases were said to have been referred by the Exchange to the DTI. See Jason Nissé, 'Insider alert after heavy trade in Blenheim shares', *The Times*, 1 July 1996.

24   The Companies Act 1980.

25   Curiously, powers were included in the Companies Bill but were not enacted in the Companies Act 1980.

of their investigations to him.[26] The appointment of such an inspector[27] may specify the period during which he is to continue his investigation. It may confine that investigation to particular matters.[28] Also, at any time during the investigation, the Secretary of State may vary the appointment.[29] He may limit or extend the period during which the inspector is to continue his investigation. He may also, at that later stage, confine the investigation to particular matters. It seems that the Secretary of State is under no obligation to disclose why he wishes inspectors to investigate a particular case provided he acts in good faith in exercising his power to appoint them.[30] However, the fact that inspectors have been appointed is not always made public.

---

26   See s 177(1) FSA 1986. Also, see s 79(13) and paras 7, 9 and 10 in Part I of Schedule 5 to the CJA 1993 and the Criminal Justice Act 1993 (Commencement 5) Order 1994 (SI 1994/242). See Robert R Pennington, 'Insider dealing and the Financial Services Act 1986' (1987) 131 Sol Jo 206 and 208. For a measure of light relief see also Christopher Fiddes, 'With cat-like tread, the men from the Ministry come back to call on Lord Archer', *The Spectator*, 23 September 1995, p 28, for some discussion of these matters.

27   Who will usually be a senior barrister or Queen's Counsel and/or a chartered accountant. In relation to investigations under the Companies Act 1948, Lord Denning MR commented in *Norwest Holst Ltd v Department of Trade and others* [1978] 3 All ER 280, at 290d, that 'Ever since 1948 there has been a valuable provision of the Companies Act by which the Board of Trade can appoint inspectors to investigate the affairs of a company. Many investigations have been held by inspectors, usually one of Queen's Counsel, and the other an accountant'.

28   Section 177(2) FSA 1986.

29   Section 177(2A) FSA 1986. See also ss 74(1) and (2) Companies Act 1989.

30   See *Norwest Holst Ltd v Department of Trade and others* [1978] 3 All ER 280 CA and subsequently, where the principles discussed seem equally applicable to investigations under s 177 FSA 1986. In that case, inspectors were appointed by the Secretary of State for Trade under s 165 of the Companies Act 1948 to investigate the affairs of Norwest Holst Ltd, an engineering company. The company claimed that it knew of no facts or circumstances on which the Secretary of State could justify ordering an inquiry into its affairs. It asked him to disclose the circumstances and evidence on which he relied in exercising his discretion. The Secretary of State refused to give that information and the company brought proceedings claiming declarative and injunctive relief on the basis that the Secretary of State had not acted fairly or in accordance with the rules of natural justice by giving the company no opportunity to answer the complaints against it before appointment of the inspectors. The action failed at first instance and the company appealed.

It was, however, held on appeal that the decision of the Secretary of State to appoint inspectors was no more than an administrative decision, commencing an investigation at which those involved would have the opportunity to state their case. Lane LJ called this the administrative phase ([1978] 3 All ER at 296b). The decision to appoint inspectors did not commence a judicial or executive phase. There was therefore nothing under the rules of natural justice requiring the Secretary of State to give the company any prior opportunity to defend its position. The only requirement was that, in exercising his discretion, the Secretary of State should make his decision in good faith and there was no evidence to suggest that he had not done so. As Lord Denning MR commented, '... as long as the Secretary of State acts in good faith, it is not incumbent on him to disclose the material he has before him, or the reasons for the inquiry' ([1978] 3 All ER at 293a). The appeal was therefore dismissed.

Their powers

8-13   Once inspectors have been appointed, they have wide investigatory powers.[31] If they consider that 'any person' is or may be able to give information concerning any offence under Part V of the Criminal Justice Act 1993, they may require that person to produce to them any documents in his possession or under his control which appear to them to be relevant to the investigation.[32] The reference above to 'any person' should be noted. It means that the inspectors may investigate persons, such as journalists or bankers, who may not be insider dealers themselves but may possess information enabling transactions by insiders to be identified. The inspectors may require the person in question to attend before them[33] and may examine him on oath.[34] Any statement made by a person may be used in evidence against him.[35] They may otherwise require him to give them all assistance in connection with the investigation which he is reasonably able to give[36] and it shall be the duty of the person concerned to comply with that requirement.[37] For these purposes, 'document' includes information recorded in any form but, in relation to information recorded otherwise than in legible form, the power to require production includes power to require the production of a copy of the information in legible form.[38] A person who is convicted following a prosecution instituted as a result of an investigation by virtue of these provisions may be ordered to pay the expenses of the investigation to such extent as may be specified in the order and these shall be treated as including, in particular, such reasonable sums as the Secretary of State may determine in respect of general staff costs and overheads.[39]

Powers of entry

8-14   The Financial Services Act 1986 also contains specific powers of entry which may be utilised for the purposes of an insider dealing

---

31   Similar in most respects to those exercisable by inspectors appointed under Part XIV of the Companies Act 1985. See Andrew Crawford, 'Insider dealing provisions' (1987) 6(3) IFL Rev 44–45. For discussion of other investigatory powers in the FSA 1996, see Eva Lomnicka, 'Scope of Section 105 Powers of Investigation' (1989) JBL 418–421.

32   Section 177(3)(a) FSA 1986. See also s 79(13) and paras 7 and 9(2) of Schedule 5 CJA 1993.

33   Section 177(3)(b) FSA 1986.

34   Section 177(4) FSA 1986.

35   Section 177(6) FSA 1986.

36   Section 177(3)(c) FSA 1986.

37   Section 177(3) FSA 1986, generally.

38   Section 177(10) FSA 1986.

39   Section 177(11) FSA 1986.

investigation.[40] For instance, a Justice of the Peace may issue a warrant if satisfied, by information on oath given by or on behalf of the Secretary of State, that there are reasonable grounds for believing that an offence has been committed under Part V of the Criminal Justice Act 1993 and that there are on any premises documents relevant to the question of whether that offence has been committed.[41] No inspector need be in place for this power to be exercised and it may apply to 'any premises'. However, a warrant may also be issued by a Justice of the Peace if satisfied, by information on oath given by or on behalf of the Secretary of State or by a person appointed or authorised to exercise the investigatory powers outlined in para 8-13 above, that there are reasonable grounds for believing that there are on any premises documents whose production has been required under those powers but which have not been produced in compliance with such a requirement.[42] This power might well be in point if it is feared that documentary evidence of insider dealing is about to be destroyed. The relevant warrant will authorise a police constable, together with any other named person and any other constables, to enter the specified premises using such force as is reasonably necessary for the purpose[43] and to search for and take possession of, or take steps to preserve or prevent interference with, any documents appearing to be the documents in question.[44] Copies may be taken of those documents and any person named in the warrant may be required to provide an explanation of them or to state where they may be found.[45] Any person who intentionally obstructs the exercise of any rights conferred by such a warrant or who fails without reasonable excuse to comply with a requirement thereunder shall be guilty of an offence and liable to be fined.[46]

False or misleading information

It should be borne in mind that the 'person' in question will commit an offence if, in purported compliance with one of the requirements outlined

---

40   See s 199 FSA 1986, entitled 'Powers of entry'.

41   Section 199(1) FSA 1986. This subsection, and subsection (2), were inserted by virtue of s 76(1) and (2) of the Companies Act 1989, with effect from 21 February 1990. The reference to Part V of the CJA 1993 was inserted by virtue of s 79(13) and para 12 of Schedule 5 to the CJA 1993. For the purposes of s 199, 'documents' are said to include' information recorded in any form'. See s 199(9).

42   Section 199(2) FSA 1986. Note that a warrant under s 199 is valid for one month. Section 199(4) provides that it '... shall continue in force until the end of the period of one month beginning with the day on which it is issued'.

43   Section 199(3)(a) FSA 1986.

44   Section 199(3)(b) FSA 1986.

45   Section 199(3)(c) and (d) FSA 1986.

46   Section 199(6) FSA 1986.

in para 8-13 above, he furnishes information to the inspectors which he knows to be false or misleading in a material particular or if he recklessly furnishes information which is false or misleading in a material particular.[47] A person found guilty of such an offence may be liable, on summary conviction, to imprisonment for a term not exceeding six months or to a fine not exceeding the statutory maximum or to both.[48] On conviction on indictment, he may be liable to imprisonment for a term not exceeding two years or to a fine or to both.[49]

Restrictions

8-16   The potentially wide investigatory powers outlined in para 8-13 above are, however, constrained slightly because a person cannot be required to disclose any information or to produce any document which he would be entitled to refuse to disclose or produce on grounds of legal professional privilege in proceedings in the High Court.[50] Generally speaking, legal professional privilege may encompass confidential communications between a client and his legal advisers made to enable legitimate legal advice to be given or received or with reference to litigation which is taking place or is contemplated by the client.[51] Also, banking records may be excluded in that a person cannot be required to disclose any information or to produce any document in respect of which he owes an obligation of confidentiality by virtue of carrying on the business of banking unless the customer to whom the confidentiality is owed consents to the disclosure or production or the making of any such requirement was authorised by the Secretary of State.[52] Finally, where a person claims a lien on a document, its production by virtue of these provisions must be regarded as being without prejudice to his lien.[53]

---

47   Section 200(1)(b) FSA 1986, entitled 'False and misleading statements'.

48   Section 200(5)(b) FSA 1986.

49   Section 200(5)(a) FSA 1986.

50   '... or on grounds of confidentiality as between client and professional legal adviser in proceedings in the Court of Session'. See s 177(7) FSA 1986.

51   It will not cover communications made with the intention of furthering a criminal purpose and, in a criminal trial, the privilege is not absolute. See, for instance, *Halsbury's Laws of England* (4th edn, reissue), vol II(2) ('Criminal Law, Evidence & Procedure') at para 1163 (as subsequently amended).

52   Section 177(8)(a) and (b) FSA 1986. Substituted by s 74(1) and (4) CA 1989, with effect from 21 February 1990.

53   Section 177(9) FSA 1986.

Conduct of investigations

Once inspectors have been appointed under the Financial Services Act
1986 and an investigation has commenced, it is likely that it will be
conducted in a similar way and on a similar basis to an investigation
under the Companies Act 1985. Accordingly, the proceedings will be
regarded as 'administrative' in nature and not as having judicial or
quasi-judicial characteristics. Generally speaking, the inspectors will be
asked to establish the facts of what happened and, in the course of so
doing, to form certain views or conclusions. As Sachs LJ commented in
the Court of Appeal in the case of *Re Pergamon Press Ltd* (1970):[54]

8-17

> ... the inspectors' function is in essence to conduct an investigation
> designed to discover whether there are facts which may result in
> others taking action. It is no part of their function to take a decision
> whether action be taken, and *a fortiori*, it is not for them finally to
> determine such issues as may emerge if some action eventuates.[55]

In their deliberations, the inspectors must act fairly. If they are
disposed to condemn or criticise anyone in a report, it seems that they
should first give him an opportunity to correct or contradict the
allegations in question, to which end the provision of an outline of those
matters has been said to be sufficient.[56] Normally, a person in a position to
be criticised would have an opportunity to state his case when questioned
by the inspectors. It was, however, made clear by the Court of Appeal in
the case of *Maxwell v Department of Trade and Industry and others* (1974)[57]

8-18

---

54 [1970] 3 All ER 535. *Re Pergamon Press Ltd* concerned the refusal by the directors of a
company, who included the late Robert Maxwell, to give evidence to inspectors
appointed by the Board of Trade pursuant to s 165 Companies Act 1948. The
directors were concerned that any interim report by the inspectors might be
prejudicial to them in respect of proceedings brought against them in the US by a
corporate shareholder in the company. They wanted the opportunity to see
transcripts of evidence adverse to them and to cross-examine witnesses. The
inspectors would not allow this but made it clear that the directors would be given
the opportunity to answer allegations made against them. This did not placate the
directors who refused to co-operate further. It was left to the court to decide
whether the directors were justified in their refusal and the Court of Appeal held
that their refusal was unjustified.

55 [1970] 3 All ER 535 at p 540g.

56 *Per* Lord Denning MR [1970] 3 All ER 535 at p 539f.

57 [1974] 2 All ER 122. *Maxwell v Department of Trade and Industry and others* concerned,
in the words of Lord Denning MR at p 129g, an attempt by the late Robert Maxwell
'... to appeal from the findings of the inspectors to the courts'. Following on from
Re Pergamon Press Ltd, the inspectors completed their investigation and made two
interim reports and also a final report. Those reports were critical of Maxwell and
he responded with this action, claiming that many of the criticisms were made in
disregard of the rules of natural justice. The Court of Appeal held that he was not
entitled to the relief he sought. As Lord Denning MR said, still at p 129g:
'Parliament has given no appeal. So Mr Maxwell has tried to get round it by
attacking the conduct of the inspectors themselves. In this he has failed utterly. To
my mind the inspectors did their work with conspicuous fairness'.

that, having heard the evidence and reached their conclusions, the inspectors were under no obligation to put to a witness such of those conclusions as might be critical of him. All that was necessary was that the inspectors should put to the witness the points that they proposed to consider when he first came to give evidence. As Lord Denning MR commented:

> [t]he inspectors are doing a public duty in the public interest. They must do what is fair to the best of their ability. They will, of course, put to a witness the points of substance which occur to them – so as to give him the chance to explain or correct any relevant statement which is prejudicial to him. They may even recall him to do so. But they are not to be criticised because they may on occasion overlook something or other.[58]

Once the inspectors have heard the evidence, they are entitled to come to the final conclusions which would be set out in their report.

8-19 Subject to acting fairly, the inspectors should not be subject to any set rules of procedure and should be free to act at their own discretion. In particular, because the inspectors are not presiding over judicial proceedings, they are not obliged to allow persons they are investigating to peruse transcripts or statements made by others which may be adverse to them. Although legal advisers may attend meetings which their clients may have with inspectors,[59] the inspectors need not allow the cross-examination of other witnesses as this would turn the investigation into judicial or quasi-judicial proceedings. As Lord Denning MR said, the inspectors '... must be masters of their own procedure. They should be subject to no rules save this: they must be fair.'[60]

Failure to co-operate with an investigation

8-20 The inspectors have power to require any person who they consider is or may be able to give information concerning an offence under Part V of the Criminal Justice Act 1993 to produce relevant documents, to attend before them and otherwise to give them all reasonable assistance.[61] It is the duty of such a person to comply with that requirement.[62] If he refuses to comply or refuses to answer any question put to him by the inspectors[63] with regard to any matter relevant for establishing whether

---

58   [1974] 2 All ER 122 at p 129b.
59   As happened in the case described in Note 57 above, Robert Maxwell was accompanied by his solicitor.
60   [1970] 3 All ER 535 at p 540c. Inspectors have been given guidance by a handbook prepared by the Department of Trade and Industry.
61   See s 177(3)(a)–(c) of the FSA 1986.
62   Section 177(3) FSA 1986.
63   Appointed under s 177 FSA 1986.

or not any suspected offence has been committed, the inspectors may certify that fact in writing to the court and the court may then inquire into the case.[64]

In considering the matter, the court may hear any witness who may be produced on behalf of or against the alleged offender together with any statement which may be offered in defence.[65] If, after having done so, the court is satisfied the person did without reasonable excuse refuse to comply with the inspectors, it may take certain steps. The course it adopts will depend upon the nature of the case and the position of the individual in question. It may, for instance, punish him in like manner as if he had been guilty of contempt of court.[66] Alternatively, it may direct the Secretary of State to exercise his powers under the section in respect of the individual and the court may give such a direction notwithstanding that the offender is not within the jurisdiction of the court if it is satisfied that he was notified of his right to appear before the court and of the powers available to it.[67]

8-21

If such a direction is given by the court in respect of a person who is authorised to conduct investment business,[68] the Secretary of State may serve a notice on such a person which may achieve any one of a number of results.[69] It may cancel any authorisation of his to carry on investment business after the expiry of a specified period after the service of the notice.[70] It may disqualify him from becoming authorised to carry on investment business after the expiry of a specified period.[71] It may restrict any authorisation of his in respect of investment business during a specified period to the performance of contracts entered into before the notice comes into force.[72] It may prohibit him from entering into transactions of a specified kind or entering into them except in specified circumstances or to a specified extent.[73] It may prohibit him from soliciting business from persons of a specified kind or otherwise than

8-22

---

64 Section 178(1) FSA 1986.

65 Section 178(2) FSA 1986.

66 Section 178(2)(a) FSA 1986.

67 See s 178(2)(b) FSA 1986. This option is perhaps more likely to be adopted where the person in question is involved in the financial services industry.

68 For the purposes of the FSA 1986. See Chapter 2, above, further.

69 See s 204 FSA 1986, further, in relation to the service of notices under the FSA 1986.

70 Section 178(3)(a) FSA 1986. Section 178(4) FSA 1986 provides that the 'specified period' referred to in s 178(3)(a) and s 178(3)(c) will be such period as appears to the Secretary of State reasonable to enable the person on whom the notice is served to complete the performance of any contracts entered into before the notice comes into force and to terminate such of them as are of a continuing nature.

71 Section 178(3)(b) FSA 1986.

72 Section 178(3)(c) FSA 1986.

73 Section 178(3)(d) FSA 1986.

from such persons[74] or, finally, it may prohibit him from carrying on business in a specified manner or otherwise than in a specified manner.[75] A notice served on a person may be revoked at any time by the Secretary of State serving a revocation notice on him and the Secretary of State will revoke such a notice if it appears to him that the person in question has agreed to comply with the relevant request or to answer the relevant question.[76] However, if the original notice cancelled the authorisation of the person to carry on investment business,[77] the revocation of that notice will not have the effect of reviving the authorisation unless the person in question would, apart from the original notice, be an authorised person at the time of the revocation through membership of a recognised self-regulating organisation or through certification by a recognised professional body.[78] If, instead, he was authorised in some other way,[79] he will need to reapply for authorisation although it is provided that nothing in this provision[80] should be construed as preventing any person who has been subject to a 'cancellation' notice from becoming authorised again after revocation of the notice.[81] Presumably, though, the reason for the cancellation would prey on the minds of those assessing his 'fitness and properness' to return. It should also be borne in mind that, where the Secretary of State serves a notice or revokes such a notice, in respect of a person authorised or formerly authorised to conduct investment business whether directly by the Securities and Investments Board or through membership of a self-regulating organisation or certification by a recognised professional body, the Secretary of State must also serve a copy of the notice on that body.[82] It would then be open to that regulator to reconsider whether the person was 'fit and proper' to continue to conduct investment business.

8-23   If such a direction is given by the court in respect of a person who is not authorised to conduct investment business, the Secretary of State may direct that any authorised person who knowingly transacts investment

---

74 Section 178(3)(e) FSA 1986.

75 Section 178(3)(f) FSA 1986.

76 Section 178(7) FSA 1986. That is to say, if the person is now co-operating with the investigation.

77 See s 178(3)(a) FSA 1986, referred to in Note 70 above.

78 Section 178(8) FSA 1986. Also, see ss 7 *et seq* FSA 1986 in relation to authorisation through membership of a self-regulating organisation and ss 15 *et seq* in relation to authorisation through certification by a recognised professional body. See, also, Chapter 2, above.

79 Perhaps directly by the Securities and Investments Board. See ss 25 *et seq* FSA 1986 and Chapter 2, above.

80 That is to say, s 178(8) FSA 1986.

81 Section 178(8) FSA 1986.

82 Section 178(9) FSA 1986. See, also, Chapter 2, above.

business of a specified kind or in specified circumstances or to a specified extent with or on behalf of that unauthorised person shall be treated, generally speaking, as having contravened the rules of his regulator.[83] That regulator may be one of the self-regulating organisations or recognised professional bodies or the Securities and Investments Board. Such a contravention may then render the authorised person liable to disciplinary action by the regulator. There might also be civil liability at the suit of a person who suffers loss as a result of the contravention.[84]

The court may only invoke the procedures described in paras 8-21, **8-24** 8-22 or 8-23 above if satisfied that the 'alleged offender' had no reasonable excuse for refusing to co-operate with the inspectors.[85] Some statutory direction is given in this regard in that a person will not be regarded as having a 'reasonable excuse' for any such refusal in a case where the offence or suspected offence being investigated relates to dealing by him on the instructions or for the account of another where, at the time of his refusal, he did not know the identity of the other person or he was subject to the law of a country or territory outside the UK which prevented him from disclosing information relating to the dealing without the consent of that other person if he might have obtained that consent or otherwise obtained exemption from that law.[86] One area where the law prohibiting insider dealing has been less than wholly effective has been in relation to dealing by or through nominee companies registered outside the UK. It is thought that such companies have been widely used by insider dealers to preserve anonymity. The effect of the statutory 'direction' outlined above is that banks and others active in the securities markets have at least to make an effort to identify those for whom they really act and are not simply able to rely on foreign confidentiality requirements to deny information to inspectors.

The procedures outlined above were, to some extent, addressed by **8-25** the courts in *Re an inquiry under the Company Securities (Insider Dealing) Act 1985*.[87] In 1986, inspectors were appointed by the Secretary of State under s 177 of the Financial Services Act 1986 to hold an inquiry into suspected

---

83 Section 178(5) FSA 1986. Chapter V of Part I FSA 1986 is headed 'Conduct of investment business' but contains provisions relating to the making of rules in a number of areas including conduct of business rules, financial resources rules, cancellation rules, client money rules and also rules relating to unsolicited calls. See Chapter 2, above, further.

84 Section 178(5) FSA 1986. See ss 62 and 62A FSA 1986 in relation to civil rights of action for damages. See also the FSA 1986 (Restriction of Right of Action) Regulations 1991 (SI 1991/489).

85 Section 178(2) FSA 1986.

86 Section 178(6)(a) and (b) FSA 1986.

87 [1988] 1 All ER 203 HL. And see Eilis Ferran, 'Insider trading and public disclosure' (1988) 47(2) CLJ 160–162 and Pandyeotis Tridimas, 'The Financial Services Act and the detection of insider trading' (1987) 8(4) Co Law 162–166.

leaks of price-sensitive information about takeover bids from the Office of Fair Trading, the Department of Trade and Industry and the Monopolies and Mergers Commission. The case concerned a financial journalist who wrote two articles which appeared to have been based on leaked information. The inspectors requested that the journalist reveal the sources of his information but he refused. The matter was then certified for an inquiry by the court into his refusal. At first instance, Hoffmann J dismissed the application by the inspectors on the basis that the journalist had a 'reasonable excuse' for his refusal. The inspectors, however, appealed and the case came finally to be considered by the House of Lords. In dealing with such referrals, Lord Griffiths made clear that it was 'the duty of the High Court to satisfy itself on evidence placed before it of the necessity that the source should be revealed, and it must not act as a rubber stamp to support the view of the inspectors'.[88] He also felt that s 10 of the Contempt of Court Act 1981, which was said to have established and recognised that, in the interests of a free and effective press, it was in the public interest that a journalist should be entitled to protect his sources unless some other overriding public interest required him to reveal them, had no direct application to a reference to the court under s 178. In the case, however, it was agreed by the parties that whether the journalist had a 'reasonable excuse' for refusing to answer questions from the inspectors depended on whether he was entitled to rely on the public interest in protecting his source and the test to be applied depended on the true construction of s 10.[89] It was held that, on a true construction of s 10, a person could be in contempt of court for refusing to disclose his source of information if the disclosure was necessary for the prevention of crime generally rather than a particular identifiable future crime. Since the purpose of the inquiry by the inspectors was to expose the leaking of official information and to consider measures to prevent future leaks and insider dealing, and since on the evidence the information of the journalist was necessary for that purpose, the journalist could not rely on s 10 for protection but was required to reveal his sources. Otherwise he could be committed for contempt.

The results of an investigation

8-26   During an investigation, the inspectors shall make such interim reports to the Secretary of State as they think fit or as he may direct. On its conclusion, they shall make a final report to him.[90]

---

88   [1988] 1 All ER 203 at 210h.

89   See [1988] 1 All ER 203 at 207c–j and 208a–c. See also *Halsbury's Laws of England* (4th edn, reissue), Volume II (2)('Criminal Law, Evidence & Procedure') at para 1163 (as subsequently amended).

90   Section 177(5) FSA 1986.

If the Secretary of State thinks fit, he may direct the inspectors to take   **8-27**
no further steps in the investigation or only to take such further steps as
are specified in the direction. Where an investigation is the subject of
such a direction, the inspectors shall make a final report to the Secretary
of State only when the Secretary of State directs them to do so.[91]

Restrictions on the disclosure of information

The general purposes of an investigation by inspectors include the   **8-28**
unearthing and also the validation of relevant information about its
subject-matter. Certain restrictions are, however, imposed on the use
and disclosure of that information once so obtained.[92] Those restrictions
relate to 'restricted information' which is defined for these purposes as
information obtained by a person, known as the 'primary recipient', for
the purposes of or in the discharge of his functions under the Financial
Services Act 1986 or any rules or regulations made thereunder, whether
or not obtained through any requirement to supply it made under those
provisions.[93] Information obtained by inspectors pursuant to an
investigation would thus be 'restricted information'. Information is not,
however, to be so regarded if it has already been made available to the
public through being disclosed in any circumstances in which or for any
purpose for which disclosure is not precluded by these provisions.[94] For
these purposes, 'primary recipient' includes inspectors appointed or
authorised to exercise any powers under s 177 of the Financial Services
Act 1986 as well as the Secretary of State.[95] It also includes any officer or
servant of any such person.[96]

Information obtained by an inspector, as a 'primary recipient', which   **8-29**
is 'restricted information' and which relates to the business or other
affairs of any person must not be disclosed by him or by any person
obtaining the information directly or indirectly from him without the
consent of the person from whom he obtained the information or, if
different, the person to whom it relates.[97] In the absence of appropriate

---

91 Section 177(5A) FSA 1986. Inserted by ss 74(1) and 74(3) Companies Act 1989 with
effect from 21 February 1990. See Frank Kane, 'DTI to drop Anglia TV and Saatchi
inquiries', *The Sunday Times*, 10 December 1995 in relation to the winding down of
investigations.

92 See Part VIII FSA 1986.

93 Section 179(2) FSA 1986.

94 Section 179(4) FSA 1986.

95 Section 179(3)(h)(a) FSA 1986.

96 Section 179(3)(i). Paragraphs (h) and (i) were amended by virtue of ss 75(1) and 212
and Schedule 24 CA 1989, with effect from 21 February 1990.

97 Section 179(1) FSA 1986. And see House of Commons Official Report, 20 December
1994, at column 1596 (*per* Mr Anthony Nelson, Minister of State, Treasury) in
relation to the publication reports and the confidentiality of information.

consent, this provision can prevent the publication of reports received by the Secretary of State and any person contravening it is guilty of an offence and liable, on conviction on indictment, to imprisonment for a term not exceeding two years or to a fine or to both.[98]

8-30   There are, however, certain stated circumstances in which these provisions will not prevent the disclosure of otherwise 'restricted information'.[99] These circumstances include the following:

- where disclosure is with a view to the institution of or otherwise for the purposes of criminal proceedings[100] which may obviously be relevant where possible insider dealing has been investigated;

- where disclosure is with a view to the institution of or otherwise for the purposes of any civil proceedings arising under or by virtue of the Financial Services Act 1986[101] and also where it is for the purpose of enabling or assisting a recognised self-regulating organisation or recognised investment exchange to discharge its functions as such;[102]

- where disclosure is for the purpose of enabling or assisting any inspector appointed or authorised to exercise any powers under s 177 of the Financial Services Act 1986 to discharge his functions;[103] and also for the purpose of enabling or assisting an 'overseas regulatory authority' to exercise its regulatory functions.[104]

8-31   By virtue of these provisions, it can be seen that otherwise 'restricted information' unearthed by inspectors may be disclosed for a wide range of regulatory purposes. In addition, the Secretary of State has power, by order, to designate 'public or other authorities'.[105] In doing so, these provisions will not then prevent the disclosure of information for the purposes of enabling or assisting any such designated authority to discharge any functions specified in the order.[106]

---

98 See s 179(6)(a) and (b) FSA 1986.

99 See s 180 FSA 1986, generally.

100 Section 180(1)(a) FSA 1986.

101 Section 180(1)(b) FSA 1986.

102 Section 180(1)(n) FSA 1986.

103 Section 180(1)(p) FSA 1986.

104 Section 180(1)(q) FSA 1986. This paragraph was inserted by virtue of ss 75(2), (3)(e) and (f) CA 1989, with effect from 21 February 1990 (certain purposes) and 25 April 1991 (otherwise).

105 Section 180(3) and (4) FSA 1986. Amended by s 75(2),(5) CA 1989 with effect from 21 February 1990.

106 Some 'designated authorities' for these purposes include the London Stock Exchange (see the Financial Services (Disclosure of Information) (Designated Authorities) Order 1986 (SI 1986/2046)) and the Panel on Takeovers and Mergers (see the Financial Services (Disclosure of Information) (Designated Authorities No 2) Order 1987 (SI 1987/859)).

INVESTIGATIONS UNDER THE COMPANIES ACT 1985

The powers of the Secretary of State

There are a number of investigatory powers conferred on the Secretary of State by the Companies Act 1985.[107] Although they are not specific to the investigation and detection of insider dealing, such wrongdoing may be discovered as a result of their use. Some involve the formal appointment of inspectors whilst others do not.

8-32

To obtain information as to share ownership

This power enables information to be obtained about share ownership in circumstances in which it is not considered necessary to appoint inspectors to investigate the matter. If it appears to the Secretary of State that there is good reason to investigate the ownership of any shares in or debentures of a company, and that it is unnecessary to appoint inspectors to do this, he may require any person whom he has reasonable cause to believe to have or to be able to obtain any information as to the present and past ownership of those securities to give to him any such information.[108] Although principally aimed at other matters, this provision could unearth information relevant to potential insider dealing. There needs to be a 'good reason' for such an investigation and it is thought that this requires that it should be in the public interest.

8-33

One scenario to which this provision may be applicable is the investigation of shareholdings in a company prior to a potential takeover. For these purposes, the information which may be required can include the names and addresses of persons 'interested' in the shares or debentures and of any persons who act or have acted on their behalf in relation to those securities.[109] A person is deemed to have an 'interest' in shares or debentures if he has any right to acquire or dispose of them or of any interest in them or to vote in respect of them. Also, if his consent is necessary for the exercise of any of the rights of other persons interested in them or if other persons interested in them can be required or are accustomed to exercise their rights in accordance with his instructions.[110]

8-34

---

107 1985 c 6. As subsequently amended by the Companies Act 1989 (hereafter 'CA 1989').
108 Section 444(1) Companies Act 1985(hereafter 'CA 1985').
109 Also s 444(1) CA 1985.
110 Section 444(2) CA 1985.

8-35   If the Secretary of State experiences difficulty in finding out the relevant facts about any shares or debentures,[111] whether issued or to be issued, he may by order direct that the securities will until further order be subject to the restrictions of Part XV of the Companies Act 1985.[112] If securities are made subject to Part XV, they are essentially 'frozen': any transfer of those securities is void and no voting rights are exercisable in respect of them; no further shares may be issued in respect of them and, except in a liquidation, no payment may be made of any sums due from the company whether in respect of capital or otherwise.[113] Generally speaking, once 'frozen', an order may only be made by the Secretary of State or the court directing that the securities are no longer subject to the restrictions if they are satisfied that the relevant facts about the shares have been disclosed to the company and no unfair advantage has accrued to any person as a result of the earlier failure to make that disclosure.[114] These provisions could prevent someone from realising a profit or avoiding a loss in respect of securities and may therefore be of relevance in the context of insider dealing.

8-36   An offence is committed by any person who fails to give information required of him under these provisions or who, in giving information, makes any statement which he knows to be false in a material particular or who recklessly makes any statement which is false in a material particular. Such a person may be liable to imprisonment or to a fine or to both.[115]

To require the production of documents

8-37   The Secretary of State may also, at any time, give directions[116] to a company requiring it, at such time and place as may be specified in the directions, to produce specified documents if he thinks there is good reason for doing so.[117] The Secretary of State may also at any time, if he thinks there is good reason for doing so, authorise an officer of his, or some other competent person, to require a company to produce to him

---

111 Section 445(2) CA 1985 provides that, apart from s 445(1A), s 445 ('Power to impose restrictions on shares and debentures') applies in relation to debentures as it does in relation to shares.

112 Section 445(1) CA 1985.

113 See Section 454(1)(a)–(d), as subsequently amended, and Part XV CA 1985, further.

114 See s 456(3)(a) and s 456 CA 1985, generally.

115 Section 444(3) CA 1985.

116 Generally speaking, directions given by the Secretary of State must be specific. See *R v Secretary of State for Trade, ex p Perestrello* [1980] 3 All ER 28.

117 Section 447(2) CA 1985, as subsequently amended by the CA 1989. For these purposes, 'documents' are defined by s 447(9) as including information recorded in any form. If illegible, the power to require its production includes power to require the production of a copy of it in legible form: again, s 447(9) CA 1985.

any documents which he or that other person may specify.[118] In exercising these powers, the Secretary of State or such officer may require production of the documents in question from any person who appears to be in possession of them.[119] If, however, that person claims a lien on the documents, any production will be without prejudice to the lien.[120] These powers to require the production of documents include power, if the documents are produced, to take copies of them or extracts from them and also to require an explanation of them from the person producing them or from any other person who is a present or past officer or employee of the company.[121]

The powers outlined in para 8-36 above are reinforced by the fact **8-38** that a search warrant may also be obtained. A Justice of the Peace may issue such a warrant if satisfied, on information on oath given by or on behalf of the Secretary of State or a person appointed or authorised to exercise these powers, that there are reasonable grounds for believing that there are on any premises documents whose production has been required but which have not been produced in compliance with that requirement.[122] If issued, a warrant will authorise a constable and any other person named in it and any other constables to enter and search the premises specified in the information and to take possession of any documents appearing to be the documents in question.[123] Such a warrant will remain in force for one month after its issue[124] and any documents recovered may be retained for three months or, if within that period criminal proceedings to which the documents are relevant are commenced, until the conclusion of those proceedings.[125] Any person who intentionally obstructs the exercise of any rights conferred by a warrant issued pursuant to these provisions or who fails without reasonable excuse to comply with any requirement to explain the documents or to state where they may be found is guilty of an offence and liable to be fined.[126] An officer of the company will also be guilty of an offence if he destroys, mutilates or falsifies documents affecting or relating to the affairs or property of the company or is privy to such acts although he will have a defence if he is able to prove that he had no

---

118 Section 447(3) CA 1985, as subsequently amended by the CA 1989.

119 Section 447(4) CA 1985, as subsequently amended by the CA 1989.

120 Also s 447(4) CA 1985.

121 Section 447(5)(a)(i) and (ii) CA 1985, as subsequently amended by the CA 1989.

122 Section 448(1) CA 1985. Section 448 was substituted by the CA 1989 with effect from 21 February 1990.

123 Section 448(3) CA 1985. Section 448(10) provides that, for these purposes, 'documents' include 'information recorded in any form'.

124 Section 448(5) CA 1985.

125 Section 448(6)(a) and (b) CA 1985.

126 Section 448(7) CA 1985.

intention of concealing the state of affairs of the company or of defeating the law.[127] A person guilty of such an offence will be liable to imprisonment or to a fine or to both.[128]

8-39   If documents are not produced, the Secretary of State or his officer may require the person who was required to produce them to state, to the best of his knowledge and belief, where they are.[129] If the requirement to produce them or to provide an explanation is not complied with, the company or the other person on whom the requirement was imposed will be guilty of an offence and liable to be fined.[130] It is, however, a defence if such a person is able to prove that the documents were not in his possession or under his control and that it was not reasonably practicable for him to comply with the requirement.[131] Any person who, in purported compliance with a requirement to provide an explanation, provides or makes an explanation or statement which he knows to be false in a material particular or who recklessly provides or makes an explanation or statement which is so false is guilty of an offence and liable to imprisonment or a fine or to both.[132]

8-40   Finally, there are restrictions on the extent to which information or documents relating to a company obtained by virtue of these provisions can be disclosed. Generally, unless the company in question consents in writing, the material cannot be disclosed except to a 'competent authority' unless publication or disclosure is required for any one of a number of stated purposes which include the institution of criminal proceedings[133] and the institution of or otherwise for the purposes of proceedings under the Company Directors Disqualification Act 1986.[134] A person who publishes or discloses information or documents in breach of these restrictions will be guilty of a criminal offence and liable

---

127 Section 450(1) CA 1985, as subsequently amended by the CA 1989.

128 Section 450(3) CA 1985.

129 Section 447(5)(b) CA 1985, as subsequently amended by the CA 1989.

130 Section 447(6) CA 1985, as subsequently amended by the CA 1989.

131 Section 447(7) CA 1985, as subsequently amended by the CA 1989.

132 Section 451 CA 1985.

133 Section 449(1)(a) CA 1985, as subsequently amended by the FSA 1986 and the CA 1989.

134 1986 c 46. Section 449(1)(ba) CA 1985, as inserted by the Insolvency Act 1985 and amended by the Insolvency Act 1986. According to figures released by the DTI in February 1996 (see 'Business Round-up', *The Times*, 21 February 1996), disqualification orders against unfit directors rose from 355 in 1994 to 633 in 1995, taking the number of directors banned in the last 10 years to more than 3,000. This was reported as reflecting a tougher stance being taken against so-called 'bad bosses'. The periods of disqualification imposed have tended to be longer where criminal proceedings have also been brought against the person in question (see Jon Ashworth, 'Venables faces penalty threat as DTI cries foul in the boardroom', *The Times*, 1 December 1995).

to imprisonment or a fine or to both.[135] For these purposes, 'competent authorities' include the Secretary of State, the Securities and Investments Board and inspectors appointed to investigate insider dealing under the Financial Services Act 1986.[136]

To investigate the affairs of a company

The Secretary of State has power to appoint inspectors to investigate the affairs of a company and to report in such manner as he may direct, on application being made by the company.[137] If the company has a share capital, inspectors may also be appointed on the application of not less than 200 of its members or of members holding not less than one-tenth of the shares issued.[138] If the company does not have a share capital, inspectors may be appointed on application being made by not less than one-fifth in number of the persons on the register of members of the company.[139] Any such application must, however, be supported by such evidence as the Secretary of State requires for the purpose of showing that the applicant or applicants have good reason for requiring the investigation[140] and he may, before appointing inspectors, require security to be given, to an amount not exceeding £5,000, for payment of the costs of the investigation.[141]

8-41

The Secretary of State must appoint inspectors to investigate the affairs of a company, and report on them in such manner as he directs, if the court by order declares that there ought to be such an investigation.[142]

8-42

The Secretary of State may also make such an appointment if it appears to him, generally speaking, that there are circumstances suggesting impropriety which could, of course, include insider dealing.[143] For instance, it may be that the affairs of the company are being, or have been, conducted with intent to defraud its creditors or the creditors of any other person or otherwise for a fraudulent or unlawful purpose or in a manner which is unfairly prejudicial to some part of its members;[144] that any actual or proposed act or omission of the company,

8-43

---

135 Section 449(2) CA 1985.
136 Section 449(3) CA 1985, as subsequently amended, and see section 3 of this Chapter.
137 Section 431(1), (2)(c) CA 1985.
138 Section 431(1), (2)(a) CA 1985.
139 Section 431(1), (2)(b) CA 1985.
140 Section 431(3) CA 1985.
141 Section 431(4) CA 1985.
142 Section 432(1) CA 1985.
143 Section 432(2) CA 1985.
144 Section 432(2)(a) CA 1985. For these purposes, 'members' include any person who is not a member but to whom shares in the company have been transferred or transmitted by operation of law: see s 432(4) CA 1985.

including an act or omission on its behalf, is or would be so prejudicial or that the company was formed for any fraudulent or unlawful purpose;[145] that persons concerned with the formation of the company or the management of its affairs have in connection therewith been guilty of fraud, misfeasance or other misconduct towards it or towards its members;[146] or, that the members of the company have not been given all the information with respect to its affairs which they might reasonably expect.[147] Inspectors may be appointed in these circumstances on the basis that any report they may make is not for publication[148] and the power to appoint them is exercisable with regard to a body corporate notwithstanding that it is in the course of being voluntarily wound-up.[149]

8-44   If inspectors appointed under these provisions to investigate the affairs of a company think it necessary for the purposes of that investigation to investigate the affairs of another related body corporate,[150] they have the power to do so.[151] It is the duty of all officers and agents of the company[152] to produce to the inspectors all documents relating to the company, to attend before the inspectors when required to do so and, otherwise, to give the inspectors all assistance in connection with the investigation which they are reasonably able to give.[153] For these purposes, an inspector may examine any person on oath and may administer an oath accordingly.[154] An answer given by a

---

145 Section 432(2)(b) CA 1985.

146 Section 432(2)(c) CA 1985.

147 Section 432(2)(d) CA 1985.

148 Section 432(2A) CA 1985. Inserted by s 55 CA 1989 with effect from 21 February 1990.

149 Section 432(3) CA 1985.

150 Which is or was at the relevant time a subsidiary or holding company of the company in question or a subsidiary of its holding company or a holding company of its subsidiary. See s 433(1) CA 1985.

151 Section 433(1) CA 1985.

152 And, for these purposes, an 'agent' in relation to a company or other body corporate includes its bankers and solicitors and persons employed by it as auditors, whether or not those persons are officers of the company or other body corporate. See s 434(4) CA 1985.

153 Section 434(1)(a)–(c) CA 1985 as amended by the CA 1989.

154 Section 434(3) CA 1985.

person to a question put to him by inspectors may be used in evidence against him.[155]

If any person fails or refuses to co-operate with inspectors appointed under these provisions, the inspectors may certify that fact in writing to the court.[156] The court may then 'enquire into the case' and, after hearing any relevant witnesses and any statement which may be offered in defence, may punish the person in question as if he had been guilty of contempt of court.[157]

8-45

On the conclusion of their investigation, the inspectors will make a final report to the Secretary of State. During the investigation, they may also have made interim reports and will have done so if directed to do so by the Secretary of State.[158] The Secretary of State may, if he thinks fit, forward a copy of any such report to the registered office of the company.[159] He may also cause any such report to be printed and published.[160] If it appears to the Secretary of State, from any report made or information obtained from an investigation pursuant to these provisions, that any civil proceedings ought in the public interest to be brought by any body corporate, he may himself bring such proceedings in the name of and on behalf of the body corporate.[161] He will, though, indemnify the body corporate against any costs or expenses incurred by it in connection with any such proceedings.[162]

8-46

Generally speaking, the expenses of an investigation under these provisions will, in the first instance, be met by the Secretary of State but

8-47

---

155 Section 434(5) CA 1985. In the 'Guinness appeal' cases of *R v Saunders, R v Parnes, R v Ronson* and *R v Lyons* [1995] Times Law Report, 28 November 1995, CA, it was held that there was no unfairness in allowing the use in a criminal trial of evidence arising out of interviews conducted with the defendants by inspectors from the DTI. Ernest Saunders also took his case to Europe, and the European Commission on Human Rights had referred it to the European Court in Strasbourg. It was contended there on his behalf that he was denied a fair hearing at the initial criminal trial because of the use of DTI-obtained evidence and that this was in breach of art 6 of the European Convention on Human Rights which guaranteed the right to a fair trial. Although the Court of Appeal took the view that the jury at the trial were well justified in finding the defendants to have acted dishonestly, there are many with sympathy for the views contended on behalf of Mr Saunders concerning the use of evidence obtained by DTI inspectors.

156 Section 436(1) CA 1985.

157 Section 436(3) CA 1985.

158 Section 437(1) CA 1985.

159 Section 437(3)(a) CA 1985.

160 Section 437(3)(c) CA 1985. In some cases, this may take a considerable time. For instance, inspections were first appointed in June 1988 to investigate the affairs of Barlow Clowes gilt managers which collapsed with investors being owed some £190 million. Peter Clowes was sentenced to 10 years in prison in 1992 for his part in the collapse. The DTI report, however, was not published until July 1995, for a variety of reasons.

161 Section 438(1) CA 1985.

162 Section 438(2) CA 1985.

may be recovered from certain other persons.[163] For instance, a person convicted on a prosecution instituted as a result of an investigation may in the same proceedings be ordered to pay the costs of the investigation to such an extent as is specified in the order.[164]

To investigate company ownership

8-48   The Secretary of State also has power, where it appears to him that there is good reason to do so, to appoint inspectors to investigate and report on the ownership of any company and otherwise with respect to that company, '... for the purpose of determining the true persons who are or have been financially interested in the success or failure (real or apparent) of the company or able to control or materially to influence its policy.'[165] It is generally thought that there is a 'good reason' for an investigation where it would be in the public interest for it to take place. Although not specific to insider dealing, the exercise of this power could lead to the discovery of information relevant to unusual dealings and thus of possible insider dealing. The appointment of inspectors can define the scope of their investigation which can be limited to the investigation of matters connected to particular shares or debentures. The period over which the investigation is to extend may also be stipulated.[166] Subject to the terms of their appointment, the powers of the inspectors appointed extend to the investigation of any circumstances which suggest the existence of 'an arrangement or understanding which, though not legally binding, is or was observed or likely to be observed in practice and which is relevant to the purposes of the investigation.'[167]

8-49   If an application is made to the Secretary of State by members of a company, on the basis set out in para 8-40 above,[168] for the investigation of particular shares or debentures, then subject to certain provisions he shall appoint inspectors to conduct the investigation applied for.[169] However, he need not do so if he is satisfied that the application is vexatious[170] or where he considers he will have sufficient powers to

---

163 Section 439(1) CA 1985 and see s 439 CA 1985 generally.
164 Section 439(2) CA 1985.
165 Section 442(1) CA 1985.
166 Section 442(2) CA 1985.
167 Section 442(4) CA 1985.
168 See s 431(2)(a) or (b) CA 1985.
169 Section 442(3) CA 1985. Substituted by s 62 CA 1989 with effect from 21 February 1990.
170 Section 442(3A) CA 1985.

conduct the investigation himself under other relevant provisions.[171] Where inspectors are appointed, their terms of appointment shall exclude any matter where the Secretary of State is satisfied that it would be unreasonable for it to be investigated.[172] The Secretary of State may also require the applicants to provide security as to payment of the costs of the investigation, to an amount not exceeding £5,000.[173]

For the purposes of an investigation into company ownership, certain provisions applicable to an investigation of the affairs of a company are also applicable.[174] They will apply to officers and agents of the company and they will be capable of applying to all persons who are or have been, or whom the inspectors have reasonable cause to believe to be or have been, financially interested in the success or apparent success or failure of the company in question or any other body corporate whose membership is investigated with that of the company.[175] They will also apply to such persons able to control or to materially influence the policy of the company and any other person whom the inspector has reasonable cause to believe possesses information relevant to the investigation.[176] Finally, if it appears to the Secretary of State in connection with an investigation under these provisions that there is difficulty in finding out the relevant facts about any securities, he may order that they be subject to the restrictions of Part XV of the Companies Act 1985.[177]

8-50

To investigate share dealings

The Secretary of State may appoint inspectors to investigate and report to him if it appears to him that there are circumstances suggesting that certain contraventions may have taken place in relation to the shares or debentures of a company.[178] The contraventions in question relate to the prohibition on directors dealing in share options and also their duties to disclose shareholdings in their own company.[179] An investigation in respect of these provisions may discover insider dealing, although such discovery of course would not be its primary objective. The period for

8-51

---

171 Section 442(3C) CA 1985. Namely, s 444 CA 1985; and see paras 8-32 to 8-35 above.
172 Section 442(3A) CA 1985.
173 Section 442(3B) CA 1985.
174 Namely, ss 433(1), 434, 436 and 437 CA 1985. See paras 8-43 to 8-45 above.
175 Section 443(2)(a) CA 1985.
176 Section 443(2)(a) and (b) CA 1985.
177 Section 445(1) CA 1985. See para 8-34 above.
178 Section 446(1) CA 1985.
179 See ss 323, 324 (and Schedule 13) and 328(3)–(5) CA 1985.

ors are appointed may be limited and may be confined to ntures of a particular class.[180]

irposes of an investigation in relation to these provisions, provisions applicable to investigations into the affairs of a e also applicable[181] and they apply to officers of the company in question and of any relevant body corporate which is subject to the investigation.[182] Certain of the provisions[183] also apply to authorised persons and to officers (whether past or present) of a body corporate which is authorised to conduct investment business for the purposes of the Financial Services Act 1986.[184]

PROSECUTION AND PENALTIES

The decision to prosecute

8-53   Once a case of alleged insider dealing has been investigated and thereby substantiated, a decision will have to be taken as to whether or not those concerned should be prosecuted. Basically, proceedings for offences under Part V of the Criminal Justice Act 1993 may not be instituted in England and Wales except by or with the consent of the relevant Secretary of State[185] or the Director of Public Prosecutions.[186] In relation to proceedings in Northern Ireland, either the Secretary of State or the Director of Public Prosecutions for Northern Ireland must consent to proceedings being brought.[187] As these provisions went through the parliamentary process, it was emphasised that:

> these arrangements for bringing prosecutions ... replicate the provisions in our existing legislation, which have effectively prevented vexatious actions ..| The government expect that the arrangements for bringing prosecutions will continue as at present, with the majority of prosecutions being brought by the Secretary of State for Trade and Industry ...[188] |

---

180 Section 446(2) CA 1985.

181 Namely, ss 434 to 437 CA 1985; and see paras 8-43 to 8-45 above.

182 Section 446(4) CA 1985.

183 Namely, ss 434 to 436 CA 1985.

184 Section 446(4)(a) and (c) CA 1985. Substituted by s 212(2) and para 21 of Schedule 16 to the FSA 1986 with effect from 29 April 1988. And see s 446(4) CA 1985 further.

185 The Secretary of State for Trade and Industry; recently glorying in the title of the President of the Board of Trade.

186 Section 61(2)(a) and (b) CJA 1993.

187 Section 61(3) CJA 1993.

188 *Per* Mr Anthony Nelson, the Economic Secretary to the Treasury. See the report of Standing Committee B on the Criminal Justice Bill [Lords], 15 June 1993, at column 206. But see R Bosworth Davies, 'Dealing with the insider dealers' (1990) 11(3) Co Law 42 and Gil Brazier, 'Let market men track the crooks', *The Times*, 8 March 1994.

The penalties for insider dealing

On summary conviction, an individual guilty of insider dealing may be liable to a fine not exceeding the statutory maximum or imprisonment for a term not exceeding six months or to both.[189] On conviction on indictment, such an individual may be liable to a fine or imprisonment for a term not exceeding seven years or to both.[190] As these provisions went through the Parliamentary process, it was emphasised that they 'carried forward the maximum penalty available under the existing legislation ... which ... reflects the seriousness with which the government regard the crime of insider dealing ...'.[191]

8-54

Contract enforceability

Unlike cases involving the carrying on of unauthorised investment business,[192] no contract is void simply because one of the parties was an insider dealer. Likewise, no contract is made unenforceable by reason only of the commission of offences involving insider dealing.[193] This has the effect that where a deal by an insider is part of a series of transactions relating to a particular tranche of securities, his involvement will not prevent settlement of those transactions.[194] This provision was intended to replicate a provision in the Company Securities (Insider Dealing) Act 1985[195] and to reflect 'the fact that there would be enormous difficulties and potential damage to innocent parties in unravelling transactions simply

8-55

---

189 Section 61(1)(a) CJA 1993.

190 Section 61(1)(b) CJA 1993.

191 See the report of Standing Committee B, 15 June 1993, again at column 206.

192 See s 5 ('Agreements made by or through unauthorised persons') of the FSA 1986, subsection (1) of which provides, essentially, that certain agreements which are entered into by a person in the course of carrying on unauthorised investment business or are entered into by a person who is an authorised or exempted person but in consequence of anything done or said by a person in the course of carrying on unauthorised investment business shall be unenforceable against the other party. That other party will be entitled to recover any money or other property paid or transferred by him under the agreement together with compensation for any loss sustained by him as a result of having parted with it. See s 5(7) in relation to the agreements to which s 5(1) is applicable. See Chapter 2, above, in relation to investment business and the need for authorisation.

193 Section 63(2) CJA 1993. See also 'Enforcing sales of shares by insider dealers', in relation to *Chase Manhattan Equities Ltd v Goodman* [1991] BCC 308 and *The Times*, 23 March 1991, Ch D, and the question of whether an agreement for the sale of shares tainted by insider dealing was enforceable, (1992) 5 (3) FSLL 1–3.

194 This example was given by the Economic Secretary to the Treasury, Mr Anthony Nelson. See the report of Standing Committee B, 15 June 1993, at column 213.

195 Which, in s 8(3), provided that 'No transaction is void or voidable by reason only that it was entered into in contravention of ss 1, 2, 4 or 5 [of the Company Securities (Insider Dealing) Act 1985]'.

an insider had been involved as part of a long chain of
ions ...' This provision is said to 'put these matters beyond
_____' [196]

Enforcement under the Financial Services Act 1986

8-56   Investigations into alleged insider dealing, by or at the instigation of the
Secretary of State,[197] may well unearth breaches by persons authorised to
conduct investment business of the rules of their particular regulator. Most
securities industry professionals are regulated by the self-regulating
organisation called the Securities and Futures Authority, either through
their own membership of that body or through employment by a member
firm.[198] In the context of insider dealing, it would be a rules breach if a
member firm failed to use its best endeavours to ensure that it did not
knowingly effect a transaction for a customer which was prohibited by
insider dealing legislation.[199] If such a breach occurred, the Securities and
Futures Authority could bring disciplinary proceedings against the
member firm.[200] Also, civil remedies might be available. For instance, a
private investor who suffered loss as a result of the contravention might be
able to found a claim for damages under s 62 of the Financial Services Act
1986[201] which, generally speaking, enables private investors to bring an
action against member firms if they suffer loss by reason of any Conduct of
Business Rules breach by the firm.[202]

8-57   Insider dealing might be unearthed by the Securities and Investments
Board[203] as a result of its own investigation into the affairs of a person
who appears to have been carrying on investment business. The SIB has
power[204] to investigate the affairs, or any aspect of the affairs, of any
person so far as relevant to any investment business which he is or was

---

196 *Per* the Economic Secretary to the Treasury, Mr Anthony Nelson. See the report of
  Standing Committee B, 15 June 1993, at column 214.

197 The Secretary of State for Trade and Industry; see Note 185 above.

198 For a more detailed explanation of the role of the Securities and Futures Authority,
  see Chapter 9 below.

199 Rule 5-46(2) of the SFA Rules. See rule 5-46, generally.

200 Under Chapter 7 of the SFA Rules.

201 Section 62(1) and (2) FSA 1986. See also s 62A FSA 1986, inserted by s 193(1) CA
  1989, and the Financial Services Act 1986 (Restriction of Right of Action)
  Regulations 1991 (SI 1991/489).

202 See Chapter 2, above, and also Chapter 9, below, further.

203 See Chapter 2, above, further.

204 Delegated to the Securities and Investments Board by the Secretary of State. See
  s 114(1),(2),(4) and (5) FSA 1986. It should also be noted that the functions of the
  Secretary of State in respect of these provisions have not been transferred to the
  Treasury. See generally the Transfer of Functions (Financial Services) Order 1992
  (SI 1992/1315).

carrying on or which he appears to be or have been carrying on where there seems good reason for doing so.[205] Generally, however, the SIB may not investigate the affairs of a member of a recognised self-regulating organisation unless the SRO has requested the investigation or it appears to the SIB that the SRO is unable or unwilling to investigate in a satisfactory manner.[206] The SIB may require the person whose affairs are to be investigated to attend before it at a specified time and place and to answer questions or furnish information with regard to any matter relevant to the investigation.[207] It may also require the production of specified documents[208] and any person who fails without reasonable excuse to comply with a requirement imposed under one of these provisions will be guilty of an offence and liable on summary conviction to imprisonment for a term not exceeding six months.[209]

The Securities and Investments Board has a number of other powers which may be relevant in the context of deterring insider dealing. It may prohibit an authorised person from disposing of or otherwise dealing with any assets or any specified assets and such a prohibition may relate to assets outside the UK.[210] Generally speaking, this power is not, however, exercisable in relation to authorised persons who are members of recognised self-regulating organisations.[211] Where a person authorised by the SIB contravenes its conduct of business or related rules,[212] it may publish a statement of that contravention.[213] Perhaps of greater relevance is the fact that the SIB may also issue a 'disqualification direction' disqualifying an individual from being employed by authorised or exempted persons[214] in connection with investment business where it appears to the SIB that the individual is not a fit and proper person to be so employed.[215] Any person who accepts or continues in any employment in contravention of a disqualification direction will be guilty of an offence and liable on summary conviction

8-58

---

205 Section 105(1) FSA 1986.

206 Section 105(2) FSA 1986.

207 Section 105(3) FSA 1986.

208 Section 105(4) FSA 1986.

209 Section 105(10) FSA 1986.

210 Section 66 FSA 1986.

211 See s 64(4) FSA 1986.

212 Generally speaking, rules or regulations made under Chapter V ('Conduct of Investment Business') of Part I FSA 1986. See s 60(1) FSA 1986 further. This includes conduct of business rules, financial resources rules, cancellation rules, notification regulations, client money regulations and unsolicited calls regulations.

213 See s 60 FSA 1986.

214 See Chapter 2, above.

215 See s 59 FSA 1986.

to be fined[216] and it is the duty of an authorised person to take reasonable care not to employ or continue to employ a person in contravention of such a direction.[217]

8-59   The SIB may also apply to the court for injunctive relief and for restitution orders, essentially to protect investors.[218] However, whether these powers would assist in the context of insider dealing would depend on the circumstances of a particular case and is perhaps debatable.

8-60   An injunction may be granted if the court is satisfied that there is a reasonable likelihood that any person will contravene conduct of business rules or similar provisions,[219] that any person has contravened such provisions and there is a reasonable likelihood that the contravention will continue or be repeated[220] or that such a contravention has taken place and there are steps that could be taken for remedying it.[221] If granted, the injunction may restrain the contravention or direct that persons knowingly concerned in the contravention take steps to remedy it.[222] A restitution order may be granted if the court is satisfied that profits have accrued to any person as a result of a contravention referred to above or that one or more investors have suffered loss or have otherwise been adversely affected as a result of that contravention.[223] Generally, the court may order the person concerned to pay into court or may appoint a receiver to recover from him such sum as appears to be just having regard to the profits, the extent of the loss or other adverse effect.[224]

---

216 Section 59(5) FSA 1986.

217 Section 59(6) FSA 1986.

218 See s 61 FSA 1986, generally

219 Section 61(1)(a) FSA 1986, which provides generally speaking for the grant of an injunction by the court on the application of the Securities and Investments Board if the court is satisfied that there is a reasonable likelihood that any person will contravene any provision of rules or regulations made under Chapter V of Part I FSA 1986 or the rules of a recognised self-regulating organisation, recognised professional body, recognised investment exchange or recognised clearing house to which the person is subject and which regulates the carrying on by him of investment business.

220 Section 61(1)(b) FSA 1986.

221 Section 61(1)(c) FSA 1986.

222 See s 61(1) FSA 1986, generally.

223 Section 61(3) FSA 1986.

224 See s 61(1), (4) FSA 1986, further.

INTERNATIONAL MATTERS

Global mischief

The problem for those charged with the prohibition of insider dealing is **8-61** not usually its detection. Odd movements in the price of securities are often *prima facie* evidence of the occurrence of insider dealing. The problem lies in the successful prosecution of those responsible; often cautious felons who may, for instance, have camouflaged their activities behind nominee companies registered outside the UK which may also have made use of bank accounts maintained in countries placing a high premium on customer confidentiality.

Formal and informal understandings

The US and the UK have been involved in attempts to overcome these **8-62** problems through increased international co-operation designed to avoid secrecy and confidentiality restrictions in the interests of stable and 'clean' markets. Informal agreements have, for instance, been reached with certain other countries on the exchange of relevant information.[225] Some important arrangements have been embodied in more formal memoranda of understanding, such as the agreement in 1986, relating to securities and futures, effectively between the US Securities and Exchange Commission, the US Commodity Futures Trading Commission and the UK Department of Trade and Industry.[226] That document contained the basis on which those regulators agreed to exchange information with a view to ensuring compliance with their respective legal regimes governing insider dealing, market manipulation[227] and the like. The Securities and Investments Board is also regarded as a signatory to that memorandum of understanding.[228] A further similar memorandum of understanding was entered into in April 1987 between the DTI and the Securities Bureau of the Japanese Ministry of Finance.

---

225 For instance, between the US and Switzerland and between the US and the Cayman Islands.
226 Entered into on 23 September 1986.
227 See Chapter 10, below, further.
228 By virtue of a supplementary memorandum entered into in November 1988.

Requests for assistance by overseas regulatory authorities

8-63   The Companies Act 1989 also contains specific powers[229] exercisable by the Secretary of State for the purpose of assisting an overseas regulatory authority which requests his assistance in connection with inquiries being carried out by it or on its behalf.[230] For these purposes, 'overseas regulatory authorities' are defined as authorities which, in a country or territory outside the UK, exercise certain functions including those corresponding to the Secretary of State under the Companies Act 1985 or the Financial Services Act 1986 and the Securities and Investments Board under the Financial Services Act 1986.[231]

8-64   The Secretary of State must not exercise the powers in question unless he is satisfied that the assistance requested of him is for the purposes of the regulatory functions of the overseas regulatory authority.[232] In deciding whether to exercise these powers, he may take into account in particular whether corresponding assistance would be given in that other country or territory to an authority exercising regulatory functions in the UK[233] and also whether it would be appropriate in the public interest to give the assistance sought.[234] He may consider the seriousness of the matter to which the inquiries relate, the importance to the inquiries of the information sought in the UK and whether the assistance could be obtained by other means.[235] The Secretary of State may decline to exercise these powers unless the overseas regulatory authority undertakes to make such contribution towards the costs of their exercise as the Secretary of State considers appropriate.[236]

8-65   The powers in question are similar in content to those examined earlier in this chapter. The Secretary of State may require any person to attend before him at a specified time and place and answer questions or otherwise furnish information with respect to any matter relevant to the inquiries;[237] such a person may be required to produce any specified documents which appear to the Secretary of State to relate to any matter relevant to the inquiries and otherwise to give him such assistance in

---

229 See Part III CA 1989 ('Investigations and powers to obtain information').
230 Section 82(1) CA 1989.
231 See s 82(2)(a)–(c) CA 1989, generally.
232 Section 82(3) CA 1989.
232 *ibid.*
233 Section 82(4)(a) CA 1989.
234 Section 82(4)(d) CA 1989.
235 Section 82(4)(c) CA 1989
236 Section 82(6) CA 1989.
237 Section 83(2)(a) CA 1989. And see paras 8-31 to 8-51, above, further.

connection with the inquiries as he is reasonably able to give.[238] The Secretary of State may examine a person on oath[239] and a statement by a person in compliance with a requirement imposed under these provisions may be used in evidence against him.[240] The Secretary of State may authorise an officer of his or any other competent person to exercise these powers on his behalf.[241]

A person may not be required to disclose information or produce a document which he would be entitled to refuse to disclose or produce on the grounds of legal professional privilege in proceedings in the High Court although a lawyer may be required to furnish the name and address of his client.[242] However, any person failing without reasonable excuse to comply with a requirement imposed on him by virtue of the powers described in para 8-64 above will commit an offence and may be liable on summary conviction to imprisonment for a term not exceeding six months or to a fine or to both.[243] Also, a person who in purported compliance with any such requirement furnishes information which he knows to be false or misleading in a material particular or who recklessly furnishes information which is false or misleading in a material particular will commit an offence. On conviction on indictment, such a person will be liable to imprisonment for a term not exceeding two years or to a fine or to both; whilst on summary conviction, he may be liable to imprisonment for a term not exceeding six months or to a fine not exceeding the statutory maximum or to both.[244]

8-66

Generally, information relating to the business or other affairs of a person which is supplied by an overseas regulatory authority in connection with a request for assistance or is obtained by virtue of the powers outlined in para 8-64 above may not, with certain exceptions, be disclosed by the primary recipient or by any person obtaining the information directly or indirectly from him without the consent of the person from whom the primary recipient obtained the information or, if different, the person to whom it relates.[245] One of the exceptions is that information may be disclosed to any person with a view to the institution of or otherwise for the purposes of criminal proceedings.[246] Any person contravening these provisions commits an offence and is

8-67

---

238 Section 83(2)(b) and (c) CA 1989.
239 Section 83(3) CA 1989.
240 Section 83(6) CA 1989.
241 Section 84(1) and see s 84 generally.
242 Section 83(5) CA 1989.
243 Section 85(1) CA 1989.
244 Section 85(2)(a) and (b) CA 1989.
245 Section 86(1) and (2) CA 1989.
246 Section 87(1)(a) CA 1989. See also s 86(2)(a) CA 1989.

liable on conviction on indictment to imprisonment for a term not exceeding two years or to a fine or to both; on summary conviction, the person may be liable to imprisonment for a term not exceeding three months or to a fine not exceeding the statutory maximum or to both.[247]

---

247 Section 86(5) CA 1989.

CHAPTER 9

OTHER CONSTRAINTS ON INSIDER DEALING

INTRODUCTION

As has been seen earlier,[1] the prohibition of insider dealing is continued by the Criminal Justice Act 1993.[2] There are however a number of additional factors which may also discourage or even prevent insider dealing. These range from the various equitable and fiduciary duties imposed on company directors, through certain obligations contained in relevant primary legislation,[3] to the 'Model Code' for transactions in securities by directors which is annexed to the 'listing' rules issued by the London Stock Exchange.[4] These additional 'factors' comprise a considerable amount of technical material and the purpose of this chapter is to provide an outline of the more important of these matters. If any seem relevant to a particular case, reference will need to be made to fuller legal treatments and also, wherever possible, to up-to-date source materials.

9-01

EQUITABLE OBLIGATIONS

The position of directors

Although a company is owned by its shareholders, its management[5] is vested in its board of directors. They may conduct its affairs themselves or through officers appointed by them. As such, directors are generally regarded as agents of the company. They therefore have a fiduciary relationship with the company[6] and standards of conduct and of acting *bona fide* and in good faith result from that relationship.

9-02

---

1 Namely, in Chapters 5–7, above.
2 1993 c 36.
3 Mainly, the Companies Act 1985 (1985 c 6).
4 Contained in an Appendix to Chapter 16 of those Listing Rules. See also R Bosworth-Davies, 'Policing insider dealing – the self-regulating regime' (1993) 14(5) Co Law at 112.
5 How its activities are carried on and supervised.
6 For a magisterial exposition of the principles and caselaw underlying the duties of directors, see LCB Gower, *Principles of Modern Company Law* (5th edn), Chapter 21.

9-03   These duties are owed by each director individually from when he becomes a director and they may not cease when that appointment has been terminated.[7] However, in the absence of other factors, such duties are owed to the company itself and not to its shareholders or potential shareholders.[8] As for 'other factors', fiduciary duties could be owed to shareholders if, for instance, they instructed the directors to participate on their behalf in commercial negotiations.[9] But it seems that the directors of a holding company do not owe fiduciary duties to a subsidiary company, where that subsidiary has an independent board of directors[10] but, generally speaking, any such fiduciary duties which are established are also owed by officers and managers authorised by the directors to act in a managerial capacity on behalf of the company.[11]

General fiduciary duties

9-04   There seems general agreement that four main fiduciary duties are generally applicable to company directors.[12] They must act in good faith in what they believe to be the best interests of the company.[13] They must not exercise the powers conferred upon them otherwise than for the purposes for which they were conferred.[14] They must not fetter their

---

7   See *Lindgren v L &P Estates Ltd* [1968] Ch 572, CA, although an argument that a 'director-elect' was in a fiduciary position to the relevant company was rejected. See also *Industrial Development Consultants Ltd v Cooley* [1972] 1 WLR 443 and *Canadian Aero Services Ltd v O'Malley* (1973) 40 DLR (3d) 371.

8   This proposition was established by the decision in the case of *Percival v Wright* [1902] 2 Ch 421 where the directors of a company bought shares from X but, in doing so, did not disclose to X that negotiations were taking place for the sale of all the shares of the company at a price higher than that being asked by X. X sued to have his sale set aside on the grounds that the directors ought to have disclosed the negotiations to him. It was held that the sale was binding as the directors were under no obligation to disclose the negotiations to X. Any fiduciary and other duties of care were owed to the company and not to individual shareholders such as X.

9   Such as those involving an offer for their shares. See *Briess v Woolley* [1954] AC 333, HL. In acting as agents for shareholders, directors would then be in breach of these additional fiduciary duties if they negotiated in their own interests as opposed to those of the shareholders

10   See *Lindgren v L & P Estates Ltd* [1968] Ch 572, CA.

11   See *Canadian Aero Service Ltd v O'Malley* (1973) 40 DLR (3d) 371. To justify the disqualification of a director, insider dealing must have some relevant factual connection with the management of the company in question. See *R v Goodman* [1994] 1 BCLC 349 CA. See also, generally, the Company Directors Disqualification Act 1986 (1986 c 46).

12   See pp 553 *et seq* of *Gower's Principles of Modern Company Law* (5th edn, 1992).

13   See *Re W & M Roith Ltd* [1967] 1 WLR 432. See also *Lonrho Ltd v Shell Petroleum* [1980] 1 WLR 627 HL where Lord Diplock said, at 634F, that '... it is the duty of the board to consider ... the best interests of the company. These are not exclusively those of its shareholders but may include those of its creditors'.

14   See *Howard Smith Ltd v Ampol Ltd* [1974] AC 821, PC.

discretion as to how they shall act in the future and, perhaps most important in the context of insider dealing, they must not put themselves in a position in which their own personal interests conflict or may conflict with those of the company.[15]

No conflict of interest

As the people in charge of the management of a company, its directors are perhaps the most likely of its personnel to come into contact with unpublished information which may affect the price of its securities. As such, in utilising that information, it is well established that they must not allow their personal interests to conflict with their duties to the company or they may be held liable to account for any profits that they make. A profit could, for instance, result from the sale by directors of securities in the company which they own. Essentially, without the informed consent of the company, its directors must not make use of corporate information for their own profit. If they do, they may be held liable to account for that profit, particularly if ownership of the company changes hands perhaps following a takeover.

9-05

An important case which illustrates this area of the law was the decision of the House of Lords in *Regal (Hastings) Ltd v Gulliver*.[16] The case concerned cinemas. Company Y owned one and its directors reached a decision to acquire two other cinemas before selling this business as a going concern. Company Z was formed with the intention that it should acquire a lease of the two cinemas. However, the potential lessor was suspicious and insisted either that the subscribed share capital of Company Z should amount, at least, to £5,000 or that the directors should give personal guarantees in relation to the lease. The original scheme was changed as Company Y could only subscribe £2,000 for shares in Company Z and the directors did not like the idea of giving personal guarantees. Under the new scheme, which the directors did not think to put to Company Y in general meeting for ratification, Company Y subscribed for 2,000 shares in Company Z whilst a further 3,000 were subscribed for by the directors and their friends. Subsequently, all the shares in Companies Y and Z were sold, with a profit accruing to the directors. However, the new owners of Company Y then caused it to bring an action against the old directors, requiring them to account for the profit that had accrued to them as a result of the share sale transaction as they had held a majority of the shares in Company Y.

9-06

---

15 See paras 9-05 to 9-08, below. And see *Meridian Global Finds Management Asia Ltd v Securities Commission* [1995] 3 All ER 918 and *The Times* Law Report, 29 June 1995, PC in relation to the attribution of knowledge to a company.

16 [1942] 1 All ER 378. Also, subsequently to say the least, [1967] 2 AC 134n.

Although this claim was rejected by the High Court and by the Court of Appeal, it was accepted by the House of Lords on the basis of case law relating to the position of trustees.[17] The former directors were liable to account for their profit once it was established that what they had done had resulted in a profit to themselves and was so related to the affairs of the company that it could properly be said to have been done in the course of their management and in the utilisation of their opportunities and special knowledge as directors of the company.[18] As decisions go, perhaps this was a trifle harsh and could be said to have been of benefit to the wrong people, namely the new owners and not the former shareholders of Company Y.[19]

9-07   The misuse of information to his profit by only one director, rather than the board as a whole, may lead his colleagues to cause the company to seek redress against him. This occurred in the case of *Industrial Development Consultants v Cooley*[20] where, in relation to a commercial project which had lapsed, the managing director of the company became aware that it was going to be revived. He concealed this information from his colleagues and left the company to join the project. In doing so, he was held to have misused corporate information and had to account for the profit he made from the arrangement. In essence, he should have disclosed this information to his colleagues and not taken advantage of it himself.

9-08   Disclosure to fellow directors and personal abstinence still seems the prudent course to take for any director in receipt of significant corporate information unless the company in general meeting has decided that the company will not make use of the information in question and has also decided that the director himself may do so in his personal capacity. If that is so decided, provided all up-to-date information relating to the matter was before the general meeting when the decision came to be made, the director should be able to proceed accordingly without being in breach of this fiduciary duty. However, it does seem that a board of directors cannot authorise the directors as a whole to utilise the information in their personal capacity although it might be able to authorise one (or a number) of them to do so provided the director in question takes no part in the deliberations which lead up to that decision and does not vote on it.[21] To be on the safe side, such a decision should

---

17   Such as *Keech v Sandford* (1726) Sel Cas Ch 61.

18   See the judgment of Lord MacMillan at [1967] 2 AC 153.

19   See *Gower's Principles of Modern Company Law* (5th edn, 1992), pp 562–567, for a more detailed critique of this decision.

20   [1972] 1 WLR 443.

21   See the decision of the Privy Council in *Queensland Mines Ltd v Hudson* [1978] 52 AJLR 379, PC.

also be submitted for ratification by the company in general meeting or by all the shareholders in the company who are entitled to vote.[22]

FURTHER STATUTORY MATTERS

Prohibitions, disclosure and discovery

The most important statutory 'matter' is of course Part V of the Criminal Justice Act 1993, by virtue of which insider dealing continues to be a criminal offence.[23] Other relevant provisions affect and may discourage or prevent insider dealing through prohibiting certain dealings by directors, by requiring the disclosure of certain dealings and by enabling companies to ascertain the identity of those holding their shares. At first glance, however, none of these provisions is particularly comprehensible and what follows attempts no more than an outline.

9-09

Prohibition on directors dealing in share options

It is an offence for a director of a company to buy certain rights relating to 'relevant shares' or 'relevant debentures'[24] and a person found guilty is liable to imprisonment or to a fine or to both.[25] This provision applies to a shadow director as it does to a director[26] and, for these purposes, 'relevant shares', in relation to a director of a company, means shares in the company or in any other body corporate which is the subsidiary or holding company of the company which have been granted a listing on a stock exchange whether in Great Britain or elsewhere.[27]

9-10

The rights in question are rights to call for delivery at a specified price and within a specified time of a specified number of relevant shares or a specified amount of relevant debentures;[28] rights to make delivery at a specified price and within a specified time of a specified number of relevant shares or a specified amount of relevant

9-11

---

22   See, further, *Gower's Principles of Modern Company Law* (5th edn, 1992), pp 569–570.
23   See Chapters 5–7, above.
24   See s 323 CA 1985.
25   Section 323(2) CA 1985.
26   Section 323(4) CA 1985.
27   Section 323(3)(a) CA 1985 and see s 323(3)(b) in relation to the meaning of 'relevant debentures'.
28   In 'market' terminology, this is a 'call' option. See s 323(1)(a) CA 1985.

debentures;[29] or an amalgamation of those rights.[30] Clearly, a director with or without inside information might contemplate the acquisition of such rights. These provisions, with the accompanying criminal sanction, should dissuade him. It is however provided that these provisions are not to be taken as 'penalising'[31] a person who buys a right to subscribe for shares in a body corporate or buys debentures that confer a right to subscribe for or of conversion into shares of that body corporate.[32]

9-12   These provisions also apply to the wife or husband and to the infant children of a director of a company, who are not themselves directors of the company, as they do to the director.[33] It is however a defence for a person charged under these provisions to prove that he or she had no reason to believe that his or her spouse or, if appropriate, parent was a director of the company in question.[34]

Duty of director to disclose shareholdings in own company

9-13   When a person becomes a director of a company, he must notify it in writing if he is interested in shares in or debentures of that company or another company in the same group.[35] The details which must be given are of the subsistence of his interests at that time[36] and of the number of shares and the amount of debentures in which each interest of his subsists.[37] A director is also under a continuing obligation to notify the company in writing of the occurrence of (i) any event in consequence of

---

29 And this is a 'put' option. See s 323(1)(b) CA 1985.

30 Potentially, the rights in question would confer both a 'put' and a 'call' option. See s 323(1)(c) CA 1985.

31 Which, presumably, means that they would not apply.

32 Section 323(5) CA 1985.

33 Section 327(1)(a) and (b) CA 1985.

34 Again, s 327(1) CA 1985.

35 Schedule 13 to the CA 1985 must be read in conjunction with ss 324(1) and (2): s 324(3) CA 1985. These provisions are contained in Part X of the Companies Act 1985 which is entitled 'Enforcement of fair dealing by directors'. Part I of Schedule 13 contains detailed provisions relating to whether a person has an interest in shares and/or debentures. For instance, the expression 'an interest in shares or debentures' is to be taken as including any interest of any kind whatsoever in shares or debentures (see para 1(1) of Schedule 13). Also, where property is held on trust and any interest in shares or debentures is comprised in the trust property, any beneficiary of the trust who does not otherwise have an interest in those securities is to be taken as having such an interest (see para 2 of Schedule 13).

36 Section 324(1)(a) CA 1985.

37 Section 324(1)(b) CA 1985. It should be noted that an obligation imposed on a person by virtue of s 324(1) to notify an interest must, if the person knows of the interest on the day on which he becomes a director, be fulfilled before the expiration of the period of 5 days beginning with the day following that day: para 14(1) of Schedule 13 CA 1985. Otherwise the obligation must be fulfilled before the expiration of the period of five days beginning with the day following that on which the existence of the interest comes to his knowledge: para 14(2) of Schedule 13.

whose occurrence he becomes or ceases to be interested in any such shares or debentures;[38] (ii) the entering into by him of a contract to sell any such shares or debentures;[39] (iii) the assignment by him of a right granted to him by the company to subscribe for shares in or debentures of the company;[40] and (iv) the grant to him by another group company of a right to subscribe for shares in or debentures of that other body corporate, the exercise of such a right granted to him and the assignment by him of such a right so granted.[41] Any such notification to the company must state the number or amount and class of the shares or debentures involved[42] but notification is not required where the occurrence of the relevant event comes to the knowledge of the person in question after he has ceased to be a director.[43] For the purposes of these provisions, an interest in shares or debentures of the spouse or infant child of a director of a company is treated as the interest of the director.[44]

A person who fails to discharge one of the obligations specified under para 9-13 above, will be guilty of an offence and liable to imprisonment or to a fine or to both[45] as will a person who in purported discharge of such an obligation makes a statement to the company which he knows to be false or recklessly makes a statement which is false.[46]

9-14

So far as companies are concerned, every company must keep a register for the purposes of the provisions outlined in paragraphs 9–13 and 9-14 above.[47] The procedure is this: whenever a company receives information from a director given by virtue of those provisions, it is obliged to enter that information, with the date of the entry, in the

9-15

---

38 Section 324(2)(a) CA 1985. See, also, para 17(1) of Schedule 13 CA 1985 for circumstances in which an obligation imposed by s 324 will not be discharged.

39 Section 324(2)(b) CA 1985. And see para 17(2) of Schedule 13.

40 Section 324(2)(c) CA 1985. And see para 18(1) of Schedule 13.

41 Section 324(2)(d) CA 1985. And see paras 18(2) and 19 of Schedule 13.

42 See s 324(2) CA 1985, generally. Also, para 15 of Schedule 13 provides that an obligation imposed on a person by that section to notify the occurrence of an event must, if at the time at which the event occurs he knows of its occurrence and of the fact that its occurrence gives rise to the obligation, be fulfilled before the expiration of the period of five days beginning with the day following that on which the event occurs: para 15(1). Otherwise, the obligation must be fulfilled before the expiration of a period of five days beginning with the day following that on which the fact that the occurrence of the event gives rise to the obligation comes to his knowledge: para 15(2).

43 Section 324(4) CA 1985. See also the Companies (Disclosure of Directors' Interests) (Exceptions) Regulations 1985 (SI 1985/802).

44 Section 328(1)(a) and (b) CA 1985.

45 Section 324(7)(a) CA 1985.

46 Section 324(7)(b) CA 1985.

47 Section 325(1) CA 1985. And see Part IV of Schedule 13 to the Companies Act 1985 which contains further provisions in relation to the required register of directors' interests.

register against the name of the director in question.[48] Whenever a company grants to a director a right to subscribe for shares in or debentures of the company, it is also obliged to enter in the register against his name the date on which the right was granted, when it is exercisable, the consideration for the grant and a description of the securities in question.[49] When any such right is exercised by a director, the company is obliged to enter that fact in the register against his name together with other relevant details of the securities.[50] Generally speaking, if these provisions are not complied with, the company and every officer of the company who is in default is liable to a fine and, for continued contravention, to a daily default fine.[51]

9-16   There is a further provision in relation to companies whose shares or debentures are listed on the London Stock Exchange.[52] When such a company is notified of any matter by a director in consequence of the above provisions and that matter relates to listed securities, the company must notify the London Stock Exchange of the matter and the exchange may publish any such information in such manner as it may determine.[53] Such notification must take place before the end of the next working day.[54] If there is any default in complying with these provisions, the company and every officer of it who is in default is guilty of an offence and liable to a fine and, for continued contravention, to a daily default fine.[55]

Duty of disclosure of interests in shares

9-17   There are further complicated[56] provisions relating to the disclosure of shareholdings elsewhere in the Companies Act 1985,[57] Intended to prevent takeovers by stealth, these may require notification to be made to a public company where a person to his knowledge acquires an interest in shares comprised in its 'relevant share capital' or where he

---

48   Section 325(2) CA 1985.
49   Section 325(3)(a)–(b) CA 1985.
50   See s 325(4) CA 1985.
51   See s 326 CA 1985.
52   Or on any other recognised investment exchange other than an overseas investment exchange within the meaning of the FSA 1986.
53   Section 329(1) CA 1985, generally.
54   Section 329(2) CA 1985.
55   Section 329(3) CA 1985.
56   To be honest, 'complicated' is something of an understatement.
57   In Part VI of the Companies Act 1985, entitled 'Disclosure of interests in shares'.

ceases to be interested in such shares[58] or becomes aware that he has acquired an interest in shares so comprised or has ceased to be interested in shares so comprised in which he was previously interested.[59] Generally, the 'relevant share capital' of a public company means the issued share capital of a class carrying rights to vote in all circumstances at general meetings of that company.[60]

The obligation of disclosure under the provisions outlined above arises where the person in question has a 'notifiable interest' immediately after the relevant time but not immediately before;[61] it also arises where the person had a notifiable interest immediately before the relevant time but not immediately after it or where he has such an interest immediately after but the percentage levels of his interest immediately before and after are not the same.[62] If a person has interests in shares which are 'material interests',[63] he will have a 'notifiable interest' at any time the aggregate nominal value of those shares is three per cent or more of the nominal value of the share capital.[64] He will have a notifiable interest at any other time the aggregate nominal value of his shares is 10 per cent or more.[65]

9-18

Where notification is required, the obligation must be fulfilled within the period of two days next following the day on which that obligation arises. It must be in writing to the company[66] and must specify the share capital to which it relates.[67] It should be noted that, for these purposes, a person is taken to be interested in any shares in which his spouse or infant child is interested.[68] Every public company is obliged to keep a

9-19

---

58   Section 198(1)(a) CA 1985. See, also, regs 2 and 3 of the Disclosure of Interests in Shares (Amendment) Regulations 1993 (SI 1993/1819).

59   Section 198(1)(b) CA 1985. See also s 198(3) and (4) CA 1985.

60   See s 198(2) CA 1985.

61   Section 199(4) CA 1985.

62   Section 199(5)(a) and (b) CA 1985. See regs 2, 4 and 5 of the Disclosure of Interests in Shares (Amendment) Regulations 1993 (SI 1993/1819). See also s 200 CA 1985, in relation to notifiable interests, which stipulates how the 'percentage levels' of an interest are to be calculated.

63   See s 199(2A) CA 1985 which provides that a 'material interest', for these purposes, is any interest other than certain specified interests which include 'an interest which a person authorised to manage investments belonging to another has by virtue of having the management of such investments under an agreement in or evidenced in writing': s 199(2A)(a) CA 1985. See regs 2 and 4 of SI 1993/1819.

64   Section 199(2)(a) CA 1985.

65   Section 199(2)(b) CA 1985.

66   Section 202(1) CA 1985, as amended by ss 134, 212 and Schedule 24 to the Companies Act 1989.

67   Section 202(2) CA 1985 and see s 202, further. See, also, regs 2 and 6 of SI 1993/1819.

68   Section 203(1) CA 1985.

register for the purposes of these provisions.[69] Whenever it receives information from a person in fulfilment of an obligation of disclosure, it must inscribe in the register within the next three days,[70] against the name of that person, the information and the date of inscription.[71]

9-20   The obligation of disclosure may also arise from an agreement between two or more persons in relation to the acquisition by any one or more of them of interests in shares of a particular public company which are comprised in the relevant share capital of that company.[72] These provisions will apply to such an agreement if it imposes obligations or restrictions on any one or more of the parties with regard to their use, retention or disposal of interests in shares of the company which are acquired pursuant to the agreement.[73] Once an interest in the shares of the target company has been so acquired, these provisions continue to apply to the agreement in question regardless of whether or not any further acquisition of interests in shares in the company takes place pursuant to the agreement, whether there is any change in the parties to the agreement or any variation of the agreement, provided the agreement continues to contain provisions imposing obligations or restrictions as outlined above.[74] These provisions do not apply to agreements which are not legally binding unless they involve mutuality in the undertakings, expectations or understandings of the parties. Also, they do not apply to an agreement to underwrite or sub-underwrite any offer of shares in a company provided the agreement is confined to that purpose and any matters incidental to it.[75] However, where these provisions do apply, for the purposes of the obligation of disclosure, each party to the agreement is taken to be interested in all shares in the target company in which any other party to it is interested apart from the agreement.[76]

9-21   A notification of an interest in the shares of a target company made by a person who is for the time being a party to an agreement to which the provisions outlined in para 9-20 above apply, must state that the person making the notification is a party to such an agreement, must include the names and addresses of the other parties to the agreement identifying them as such and must also give details of the shares in

---

69   Section 211(1) CA 1985.
70   Section 211(3) CA 1985.
71   Section 211(1) CA 1985.
72   See s 204(1) CA 1985.
73   Section 204(2)(a) and (b) CA 1985.
74   Section 204(4)(a)–(c) CA 1985.
75   Section 204(6) CA 1985.
76   Section 205(1) CA 1985.

question.[77] There are further complicated provisions obliging persons acting together in these circumstances to keep each other informed[78] and also governing circumstances in which a person may be regarded as becoming or ceasing to be interested in shares by virtue of the interest of another person.[79]

Investigations into share ownership by companies

Generally speaking, all a public company is likely to know about its shareholders is the names in which they are registered as members of the company. But as those names may well be the names of nominees acting on behalf of the beneficial owners, the company and its directors may know very little about the real owners of the company. If the disclosure provisions outlined in paras 9-13 to 9-21 above are complied with, a company will have some knowledge about the activities of its directors and substantial shareholders. Some companies have also taken the additional step of incorporating provisions in their articles of association enabling them to obtain information from their members. But what else can they do?

9-22

A public company[80] may serve what has come to be known as a '212 notice' with a view to obtaining further information. With regard to persons whom it knows or has reasonable cause to believe to be or, at any time during the immediately preceding three years, to have been interested in shares comprised in the relevant share capital of the company, it may require information from them. By notice in writing, it may require them to confirm or indicate whether or not they are or have been so interested and, where that is so, to give such further information as may be required.[81] Such a notice may require the person to whom it is addressed to give particulars of his own past or present interest in such shares held by him at any time during the three-year period.[82] Where the interest is a present interest and any other interest in the shares subsists or subsisted during the three-year period at a time when his own interest subsisted, he may be required to give such particulars with regard to that other interest as may be required by the notice.[83] Where the interest is a past interest, he may be required to give, so far as he

9-23

77 Section 205(4)(a)–(c) CA 1985. See also s 205(5) in relation to notification where a person has ceased to be a party to an agreement to which s 204 applies.
78 See s 206 CA 1985, as amended.
79 See s 207 CA 1985. See also s 210 CA 1985, as amended.
80 See s 1(3) CA 1985 as to the meaning of 'public company'.
81 Section 212(1)(a) and (b) CA 1985.
82 Section 212(2)(a) CA 1985.
83 Section 212(2)(b) CA 1985.

knows, details of the identity of the person who held that interest immediately upon his ceasing to hold it.[84]

9-24   A company may be required to exercise these powers[85] on the requisition of members of the company holding not less than one-tenth of the paid-up capital of the company carrying voting rights at general meetings of the company.[86] Such a requisition must state that the requisitionists are requiring the company to exercise these powers, must specify the manner in which they require the powers to be exercised and must give reasonable grounds for requiring the company to do so. It must be signed by the requisitionists and deposited at the registered office of the company.[87] On the deposit of such a requisition, the company must exercise these powers in the manner specified in the requisition[88] and, if it does not do so, the company and every officer of it who is in default is liable to a fine.[89] Once the company has carried out the investigation so requisitioned, it must cause a report of the information it has unearthed to be prepared and it must be made available at its registered office within a reasonable period after the conclusion of the investigation.[90] If the investigation is not concluded within three months, the company must prepare interim reports every three months.[91]

9-25   A notice given under the provisions outlined in para 9-23 above shall require any information it is seeking to be given in writing within such reasonable time as specified in the notice.[92] If a person fails to respond to a '212 notice', the company may apply to the court for an order directing that the shares in question be made subject to the restrictions of Part XV of the Companies Act 1985.[93] Such a person, or one who makes a statement which he knows to be false in a material particular or who recklessly makes any statement which is false in a material particular, will be guilty of an offence and liable to imprisonment or to a fine or to both.[94] However, a person will not be guilty of such an offence if he

---

84   Section 212(2)(c) CA 1985.
85   Under s 212 CA 1985.
86   Section 214(1) CA 1985.
87   Section 214(2)(a)–(c) CA 1985.
88   Section 214(4) CA 1985.
89   Section 214(5) CA 1985.
90   Section 215(1) CA 1985.
91   Section 215(2) CA 1985.
92   Section 212(4) CA 1985.
93   Section 216(1) CA 1985. Part XV CA 1985 is entitled 'Orders imposing restrictions on shares'.
94   Section 216(3) CA 1985.

proves that the requirement to give the information was frivolous or vexatious[95] or if he has for the time being been exempted by the Secretary of State from the operation of these provisions.[96]

Any information received by a company in response to such a notice must be entered against the name of the registered holder of the shares in question, in a separate part of its register of interests in shares, together with the fact that the requirement was imposed and the date on which it was imposed.[97] Entries in the register of interests of shares of a company may only be deleted in certain circumstances[98] and the register must be open to inspection without charge.[99]

THE LISTING RULES AND THE MODEL CODE

The Listing Rules and companies

Made pursuant to Part IV of the Financial Services Act 1986,[100] the Listing Rules of the London Stock Exchange govern the admission of securities to the Official List. Once listed, companies must comply with all Listing Rules applicable to them.[101] Observance of these continuing obligations is thought to have been of some use in preventing insider dealing and is said to be essential to the maintenance of an orderly market in securities. Amongst other matters, the Listing Rules attempt to ensure that all users of the London Stock Exchange have simultaneous access to the same information.[102] Any failure by a company to comply with any applicable continuing obligations may result in the Stock Exchange censuring the company[103] and publishing that fact[104] or suspending or, even, cancelling the listing of the

---

95 Section 216(4) CA 1985.

96 Section 216(5) CA 1985.

97 Section 213(1) CA 1985.

98 In accordance with s 217 CA 1985.

99 See s 218 CA 1985.

100 Sections 142–156 FSA 1986. See also the Public Offer of Securities Regulations 1995 (SI 1995/1537 and paras 2-45 to 2-60 in Chapter 2 above).

101 Paragraph 1.1 in Chapter 1 of the Listing Rules. See, for instance, Chapter 9 of the Listing Rules ('Continuing Obligations') which contains certain of the continuing obligations which a listed company must observe once any of its securities have been admitted to listing. Chapter 1 concerns 'Compliance With and Enforcement of the Listing Rules'. In considering these matters, readers should be mindful of the cautionary note expressed in the Preface of this book.

102 See the introductory material in the preface to Chapter 9 of the Listing Rules, ('Scope of chapter').

103 Paragraph 1.9(a) in Chapter 1 of the Listing Rules.

104 *ibid.*

securities in question or any class of those securities.[105]

The continuing obligations of companies

9-28   With regard to information, companies must provide the Stock Exchange, without delay, with all the information that the Exchange considers appropriate in order to protect investors or ensure the smooth operation of the market[106] together with any other information or explanations that the Exchange may reasonably require for the purpose of verifying whether listing rules are being and have been complied with.[107]

9-29   Listed companies are under a continuing general obligation of disclosure. Such a company must notify the Company Announcements Office of the Exchange, without delay,[108] of any major new developments in its sphere of activity which are not public knowledge and which may[109] lead to substantial movement in the price of its listed securities.[110] If, however, a company considers that disclosure to the public of any such information might prejudice its legitimate interests, the Exchange may grant a dispensation from the requirement to make the information public.[111]

9-30   Generally speaking, information that is required to be notified to the Company Announcements Office of the Exchange must not be given to a third party by the company before it has been so notified.[112] A company need not notify the Exchange of information about impending developments or matters in the course of negotiation and may give such information in strict confidence to its advisers and to persons with whom it is negotiating a transaction or with a view to raising finance. These persons may include prospective underwriters or placees of the securities company. The company must though advise such persons that

---

105 Paragraph 1.9(b). See paras 1.8 and 1.10 further, and see paras 1.19 to 1.21 (with regard to the suspension of listing) and paras 1.22 and 1.23 (with regard to the cancellation of listing).

106 Paragraph 1.2(b).

107 Paragraph 1.2(c).

108 Paragraph 9.15 in Chapter 9 of the Listing Rules provides that where a company is required by the rules to notify information to the Company Announcements Office at a time when that office is not open for business, the company must ensure that there is adequate coverage of the information by also distributing it to not less than two national newspapers in the UK and to two newswire services operating in the UK. However, a new electronic Direct Input Provider service was introduced in September 1996 to enable companies to make announcements more effectively.

109 By virtue of the effect of those developments on its assets and liabilities or financial position or on the general course of its business.

110 Paragraph 9.1(a). See para 9.2 also and regulation 3(1) of the Traded Securities (Disclosure) Regulations 1994 (SI 1994/188) in relation to securities not admitted to the Official List.

111 Paragraph 9.8.

112 Paragraph 9.6.

any information they receive is confidential and must be satisfied they are aware that they must not deal in the securities of the company before it has been made available to the public.[113] If, at any time, the necessary degree of confidentiality cannot be maintained or has been breached and the information in question is such that knowledge of it would be likely to lead to a substantial movement in the price of securities, the company must notify the Company Announcements Office by way of a warning announcement to the effect that it expects shortly to release information which may to lead to such a substantial movement in the price of its securities.[114]

Listed companies must notify the Company Announcements Office, without delay (by the end of the business day following receipt of the information by the company), of any information disclosed to them relating to certain major interests in their share capital.[115] The notification must also include the date on which the information was disclosed to the company and, if known, the date on which the transaction was effected.[116] A listed company must notify the Company Announcements Office of any information which is obtained by it pursuant to a '212 notice',[117] without delay (by the end of the business day following receipt of the information), where it has become apparent that an interest in shares exists or has been increased or reduced or has ceased to exist and that this should have but has not been disclosed to the company pursuant to ss 198 to 208 of the Companies Act 1985.[118] A listed company must also notify the Company Announcements Office of any information relating to interests in securities which is disclosed to it.[119] Amongst other matters, the notification must state the date on which the disclosure was made to the company, the nature of the transaction and the nature and extent of the interest of the director in the transaction.[120]

9-31

---

113 Paragraph 9.5.
114 Paragraph 9.4.
115 Pursuant to ss 198–208 CA 1985; and see paras 9-17 to 9-21, above.
116 Paragraph 9.11(a) and (b) of the Listing Rules.
117 See s 212 CA 1985 and paras 9-22 to 9-26, above.
118 Paragraph 9.12 of the Listing Rules.
119 Pursuant to s 324 CA 1985, as extended by s 328 CA 1985. See paras 9-13 to 9-16, above.
120 See paras 16.13–6.17 of the Listing Rules.

The Listing Rules and directors

9-32   Through the 'Model Code' for transactions in securities by directors, certain employees and persons connected with them, the Listing Rules have probably served to restrain those persons who might otherwise have been most easily tempted into insider dealing. Generally, the Listing Rules also impose obligations as to the disclosures a company must make about its directors[121] and set out certain requirements for transactions between a company and any of its directors.[122] It is provided that a listed company must ensure that its directors accept full responsibility, both collectively and individually, for its compliance with the Listing Rules.[123]

9-33   If a director fails to accept and discharge his responsibilities for the compliance by his company with the Listing Rules, the Stock Exchange may take one or more of the following steps:[124] it may censure the relevant director;[125] in the case of wilful or persistent failure by a director to discharge his responsibilities following such a censure, it may state publicly that in its opinion the retention of office by the director is prejudicial to the interests of investors;[126] and, if the director remains in office following a public censure by the Exchange, it may suspend or cancel the listing of the securities of the company or any class of its securities.[127] Unless the Exchange considers that the maintenance of the smooth operation of the market or the protection of investors requires otherwise, it will give advance notice to the parties concerned of any of the above steps which it proposes to take and will give them an opportunity to make representations to the Exchange.[128]

The Model Code

9-34   It is provided that a listed company must adopt by board resolution, and must take all proper and reasonable steps to secure compliance with, a 'dealing' code in terms no less exacting than those of the Model Code which is appended to Chapter 16 of the Listing Rules.[129] Most

---

121 In Chapter 16 ('Directors') of the Listing Rules.

122 And other related parties. See Chapter 11 of the Listing Rules.

123 Paragraph 16.2.

124 Through the Quotations Committee. See the introductory 'scope' material to Chapter 16 of the Listing Rules.

125 Paragraph 1.10 of the Listing Rules.

126 *ibid.*

127 *ibid.*

128 Paragraph 1.7. But see para 1.11 of the Listing Rules and any material published thereunder, further.

129 Paragraph 16.18 of the Listing Rules.

companies simply adopt the Model Code for these purposes, although they may impose more rigorous restrictions if they wish.[130] The company must, however, seek to secure compliance by its directors and by any employee of the company or director or employee of a subsidiary undertaking or parent undertaking of the company who, because of his office or employment, is likely to be in possession of unpublished price-sensitive information in relation to the company.[131]

The purpose of these provisions, and of the Model Code, is to ensure that directors and other prominent employees of the company[132] do not abuse, and do not place themselves under suspicion of abusing, price-sensitive information which they may have or be thought to have especially in periods leading up to an announcement of financial results by the relevant company.[133] For these purposes, it is provided that any information regarding transactions required to be notified to the Company Announcements Office of the London Stock Exchange in accordance with Chapters 10 and 11 of the Listing Rules will be regarded as being 'price-sensitive'.[134]   **9-35**

The basic prohibitions are threefold: (1) A director must not deal in any securities of the listed company at any time when he is in possession of unpublished price-sensitive information in relation to those securities.[135] (2) He must not deal in any securities of the listed company on considerations of a short-term nature.[136] (3) He must not deal in any securities of the listed company during what is referred to as a 'close period' which, in most cases, will be the period of two months immediately preceding the preliminary announcement of the annual results of the company.[137] If the company reports on a half-yearly basis, the period of two months immediately preceding the announcement of   **9-36**

---

130 Paragraph 16.19 of the Listing Rules.

131 Paragraph 16.18(a) and (b) of the Listing Rules. And see 'Restrictions on dealing: directors and connected persons' (1994) 5(9) PLC 5–6.

132 And certain persons 'connected' with them. See s 346 CA 1985, further.

133 See the Introduction to (which does not form part of) the Model Code.

134 See para 1(f) of the Model Code, further. Initially, the definition of 'unpublished price-sensitive information' set out in that paragraph of the Model Code (in subparas 1(f)(i)–(iv)) adopts the definition of 'inside information' given by ss 56(1)(a)–(d), 56(3) and 60(4) CJA 1993. However, it goes on to provide that it should be assumed, without prejudice to the generality of those provisions, that any information regarding transactions required to be notified to the Company Announcements Office in accordance with Chapters 10 or 11 of the Listing Rules and information of the kind referred to in certain other paragraphs of the Listing Rules will be regarded as being price-sensitive. The other paragraphs in question are listed at the end of para 1(f).

135 Paragraph 4 of the Model Code.

136 Paragraph 2 of the Model Code.

137 Or, if shorter, the period from the relevant financial year end up to and including the time of the announcement. See para 3(a) of the Model Code.

the half-yearly results will also be a 'close period'[138] whilst if it reports on a quarterly basis, the period of one month immediately preceding the announcement of those results will be such a period.[139]

9-37   In any event, a director must not deal in any securities of the listed company without advising the chairman (or one or more other directors designated for this purpose) in advance and receiving clearance. In his own case, the chairman (or other designated director) must advise the board in advance at a board meeting (or advise another designated director or directors) and receive clearance from the board (or the designated director(s)), as appropriate.[140] Written records of these matters must be kept by the company, which must give written confirmation to the director concerned that such advice and clearance (if any) have been so recorded.[141]

9-38   It is however provided that a director must not be given clearance to deal in any securities of the listed company during what is referred to as a 'prohibited period'. A 'prohibited period' for these purposes has a threefold definition. It is defined as meaning (1) any close period;[142] (2) any period when there exists any matter which constitutes unpublished price-sensitive information in relation to the securities of the company, whether or not the director has knowledge of such matter, and the proposed dealing would (if permitted) take place after the time when it has become reasonably probable that an announcement will be required in relation to that matter;[143] or (3) any period when the person responsible for the clearance otherwise has reason to believe that the proposed dealing will be in breach of the code.[144] A director may however be given clearance to sell, but not to purchase, securities in exceptional circumstances when he would otherwise be prohibited from doing so because the proposed sale would fall within a close period.[145] Clearance may not be given if the chairman or designated director is aware of any other reason under this code which would prohibit the director from dealing. As to what circumstances might be considered 'exceptional' for these purposes, the Model Code cites a pressing financial commitment on the part of the director that cannot otherwise be satisfied. It is however up to the chairman (or designated director), in

---

138 Paragraph 3(b) of the Model Code.
139 Paragraph 3(c) of the Model Code.
140 Paragraph 6 of the Model Code.
141 Paragraph 8 of the Model Code.
142 Paragraph 7(a) of the Model Code.
143 Paragraph 7(b) of the Model Code.
144 Paragraph 7(c) of the Model Code.
145 Paragraph 9 of the Model Code.

considering clearance, to take a view on whether the circumstances of a particular case ought to be considered exceptional.[146]

'Dealing', for these purposes, is defined as meaning any sale or purchase of or agreement to sell or purchase any securities. It is also said to encompass the grant, acceptance, acquisition, disposal, exercise or discharge of an option (whether a call or a put option or both) or other right or obligation (whether present or future, conditional or unconditional) to acquire or dispose of securities or any interest in securities.[147] The definition of 'dealing' set out above is a general definition and (*prima facie*) wide in ambit. For the avoidance of doubt, however, it is provided elsewhere[148] that certain transactions constitute 'dealings' for these purposes and are therefore subject to the code. These include (1) transactions involving the 'bed and breakfasting' of securities;[149] (2) dealings between directors and/or relevant employees of the company;[150] (3) off-market dealings;[151] and (4) transfers for no consideration by a director.[152] Given the width of the general definition of 'dealing', it is also provided that certain dealings are not subject to the code. These include (1) undertakings or elections to take up entitlements under a rights issue or other offer (including an offer of shares in lieu of a cash dividend);[153] (2) the take up of entitlements under a rights issue or other offer (including an offer of shares in lieu of a cash dividend);[154] (3) allowing entitlements to lapse under a rights issue or other offer (including an offer of shares in lieu of a cash dividend);[155] (4) the sale of sufficient entitlements nil-paid to allow take up of the balance of the entitlements under a rights issue;[156] and (5) undertakings to accept or the acceptance of a takeover offer.[157]

9-39

---

146 See para 9 of the Model Code, further.

147 Paragraph 1(b) of the Model Code.

148 In para 19 of the Model Code.

149 Paragraph 19(a) of the Model Code. 'Bed and breakfasting' normally involves a sale of securities with the intention of repurchasing an equal number of such securities soon afterwards.

150 Paragraph 19(b) of the Model Code. For these purposes, 'relevant employees' are defined by para 1(d) as meaning any employee of the listed company or director or employee of another group company who, because of his office or employment, is likely to be in possession of unpublished price-sensitive information in relation to the listed company.

151 Paragraph 19(d) of the Model Code.

152 Paragraph 19(e) of the Model Code and see para 19, further.

153 Paragraph 20(a) of the Model Code.

154 Paragraph 20(b) of the Model Code.

155 Paragraph 20(c) of the Model Code.

156 Paragraph 20(d) of the Model Code.

157 Paragraph 20(e) of the Model Code and see para 20, further.

9-40   So far as this may be consistent with his duties of confidentiality to the company, a director must seek to prevent persons connected[158] with him and also relevant investment managers[159] from dealing in securities of the listed company during a close period or at any time when the director is in possession of unpublished price-sensitive information in relation to those securities and would be prohibited from dealing by the code.[160] The director must advise all such connected persons and investment managers of the name of the listed company of which he is a director, of the close periods during which they cannot deal in the securities and of any other periods when the director knows that he is not himself free to deal in the securities by virtue of the code unless his duties of confidentiality to the company prohibit him from disclosing such other periods.[161] He must also advise the recipients of such information that they must tell him immediately after they have dealt in securities of the company.[162]

THE CITY CODE ON TAKEOVERS AND MERGERS

The relevance of the Code

9-41   In recent history, given the potential effect on the price of relevant securities, a takeover bid for a company has been one of the most likely scenarios for the occurrence of insider dealing. Although not directed specifically at that mischief, the 'Takeover Code'[163a] has sought 'principally to ensure fair and equal treatment of all shareholders in relation to takeovers'.[163] It provides an 'orderly framework' within which takeovers may take place. Issued and administered by the Panel on Takeovers and Mergers, the Code 'represents the collective opinion of those professionally involved in the field of takeovers as to good business standards and as to how fairness to shareholders can be achieved'.[164] It is thus a relevant factor and has the effect of being a further restraint on

---

158 Within the meaning of s 346 CA 1985.

159 Paragraph 11(b) of the Model Code provides, essentially, that a director must seek to prohibit any dealing in securities of the listed company at the times in question by an investment manager on his behalf or on behalf of any person connected with him where either he or any person connected with him has funds under management with that investment manager, whether or not on a discretionary basis.

160 See para 11 of the Model Code, generally.

161 Paragraph 12(a)–(c) of the Model Code.

162 Paragraph 12(d) of the Model Code.

163 See para (a) ('Nature and purpose of the Code') in s 1 of the Introduction to the City Code on Takeovers and Mergers. Section 1 is entitled simply 'The Code'.

163a Hereafter 'TC'.

164 Paragraph (a) in s 1 of the Introduction, TC.

insider dealing. It should, however, be mentioned that the deliberations of the Panel may be subject to judicial review by the court.[165]

Application and enforcement

Generally speaking, the Code applies to offers for all listed and unlisted public companies considered by the Panel to be resident in the UK, the Channel Islands or the Isle of Man.[166] It also applies to certain offers for private companies considered to be so resident.[167] The Panel is said 'normally' to consider a company to be so resident only if it is incorporated in the UK, the Channel Islands or the Isle of Man and has its head office and place of central management in one of those jurisdictions.[168]

9-42

9-43

It is provided that the Code is concerned with takeover and merger transactions of all relevant companies, however effected. These transactions include partial offers, offers by a parent company for shares in its subsidiary and certain other transactions where control of a company is to be obtained or consolidated.[169] Although the Code does not have the force of law, it is recognised by 'City' regulators essentially as representing 'best practice' in this area. They may require their members not to act in a takeover for any person unlikely to live up to that standard.[170] Also, if a person authorised to conduct investment business in the UK fails to comply with the Code, he may face the

---

165 See *R v Takeover Panel, ex p Datafin plc* [1987] 1 All ER 564. In that case, it was held that in the UK the proper place to resolve disputes in takeover bids was before the panel and the proper time was contemporaneously so matters could be dealt with speedily without undue delay, expense or distraction for those involved. Compare the position of the Insurance Ombudsman Bureau, a body whose powers are derived from contract. See *R v Insurance Ombudsman Bureau and Another, ex p Aegon Life Assurance Ltd* [1993] Times Law Report, 7 January 1994.

166 Paragraph (a) in s 4 ('Companies and Transactions to which the Code Applies') of the Introduction to the TC.

167 For instance, it also applies to offers for private companies considered to be resident in the UK, the Channel Islands or the Isle of Man when their equity share capital has been listed on the Stock Exchange at any time during the 10 years prior to the relevant date (see para 4(a)(i) of the Introduction, TC).

168 See para 4(a) of the Introduction,TC.

169 See para 4(b) ('Transactions') of the Introduction,TC.

170 See, for instance, rule 5-48 of the Conduct of Business Rules of the Securities and Futures Authority ('Support of Takeover Panel's Functions'). The days of the Panel and the Code remaining non-statutory may be limited due to the proposed 13th European Parliament Council Directive on Company Law concerning Takeover Bids. See Commission of the European Communities, com (95) 655 final, 7.02.96. This may, however, lead to more takeover litigation. See 'Let's kill all the lawyers ...', *The Times* (Pennington column), 20 June 1996 and 'The Takeover Panel and the Thirteenth Directive on Company Law Concerning Takeover Bids', issued by the Panel, June 1996. The author is grateful to the Panel for help in tracking down information on these matters.

sanctions of the self-regulating organisation of which he is a member. Ultimately, this may mean the withdrawal of that authorisation.[171]

9-44   In the context of insider dealing, there are a number of provisions in the Code which relate to the availability and use of information and the related responsibilities of those concerned in a takeover. The remainder of this section outlines some of those provisions.

Some general principles

9-45   The Code makes clear the impracticality of devising detailed rules to attempt to cover all the scenarios that can arise in takeovers.[172] Those concerned in takeovers, primarily the directors of bidding and target companies, must therefore adhere to the spirit as well as to the precise letter of the Code. That 'spirit' is enshrined, to a large extent, in some General Principles which are said to apply in circumstances not directly covered by the Rules of the Code. The financial advisers of offeror and offeree companies have particular responsibilities to ensure that the Code is complied with during the course of an offer and that the respective parties are aware of their obligations thereunder.[173]

9-46   It is provided that all shareholders of the same class of an offeree company must be treated similarly by an offeror.[174] As regards the availability of information during the course of an offer or when an offer is being considered, neither an offeror nor an offeree company nor one of their financial advisers may furnish information to some shareholders which is not made available to all the shareholders.[175] Shareholders must also be given sufficient information and advice to enable them to reach a properly informed decision and must have sufficient time to do so. No relevant information should be withheld from them[176] and care must be taken that statements are not made which may mislead shareholders or the market.[177]

---

171 See para 1(c) of the Introduction ('Enforcement of the Code').

172 See the Introduction to the General Principles TC.

173 See the Introduction to the General Principles TC.

174 General Principle 1TC.

175 General Principle 2 TC. This principle does not apply to the furnishing of information in confidence by a target company to a *bona fide* potential offeror or *vice versa*.

176 General Principle 4 TC.

177 General Principle 6 TC.

Secrecy

The Code emphasises the vital importance of absolute secrecy before any announcement relating to a bid is made. All the parties who are privy to confidential information concerning an offer or potential offer must treat that information as secret and may only pass it to another person if it is necessary to do so. The recipient must, however, be made aware of the need for secrecy.[178] At the beginning of discussions about a potential offer, the financial advisers in question must warn their clients of the importance of secrecy and security.[179]

9-47

Prohibited dealings

To prevent the abuse of confidential information, the Code also prohibits dealings of any kind in securities of a target company (including options and derivatives in respect of or referenced to such securities) by any person, not being the offeror, who is privy to confidential price-sensitive information concerning an offer or potential offer. Such dealings may not take place between the time when there is reason to suppose that an approach or an offer is contemplated and the announcement of the approach or offer or of the termination of the discussions.[180] No person who is privy to any such information may make any recommendation to any other person as to dealing in the relevant securities.[181] No such dealings may take place in securities of the offeror except where the proposed offer is not price-sensitive in relation to such securities.[182] Also, during an offer period, the offeror and persons acting in concert with it must not sell any securities in the offeree company except with the prior consent of the Takeover Panel and following 24 hours' public notice that such sales might be made.[183]

9-48

---

178 Rule 2.1 TC.

179 Note 1 to rule 2.1 TC.

180 Rule 4.1(a) TC; and see Statement 1996/13, issued by the Takeover Panel on 13 June 1996, in relation to 'Derivatives'. The Panel believes that public disclosure should be required with respect of derivative transactions by the parties to an offer, their associates and large share holders. See also the SIB Consultative Paper 'Equity-related Derivatives: Inside Information and Public Disclosure Issues' (also 13 June 1996).

181 Rule 4.1(b) TC.

182 Rule 4.1(c) TC.

183 Rule 4.2 TC. Where the Panel becomes aware of instances to which Part V CJA 1993 may be relevant, it will generally inform the DTI.

Equality of information to shareholders

9-49 Information about companies involved in an offer must be made equally available to all shareholders as nearly as possible at the same time and in the same manner.[184]

Restrictions following offers

9-50 The announcement of a takeover bid can have a dramatic effect on the share price of the companies concerned. It may increase or decrease, depending on how the market views the matter, which can encourage insider dealing and create a false impression of the position of the company in question. Conducting or defending such a bid can also affect companies commercially, not least because this ties down resources and can hinder management. It is not therefore surprising that the Code contains provisions which, in very general terms, prevent offers which have been withdrawn or have lapsed from being remade within a period of 12 months from the date of the withdrawal or the offer lapsing.[185] There are also restrictions on the offeror, or any person who acted or is acting in concert with the offeror, acquiring shares in the target company.[186] These restrictions may not apply if what is proposed receives the consent of the Panel.[187]

Financial advisers and conflicts of interest

9-51 The Code offers guidance on situations in which a merchant bank, or other financial adviser, may have the opportunity to act for a potential offeror or a target company in circumstances in which it possesses material confidential information about the other party. This may, for instance, be because it advised that other party on another matter or perhaps because it was otherwise involved in an earlier transaction. The information may even be unpublished price-sensitive information and may place the financial adviser in a position in which there is a conflict of interest. In some circumstances, such a potential conflict may be resolved by means of a 'Chinese wall' isolating the information within

---

183 Rule 4.2 TC. Where the Panel becomes aware of instances to which Part V CJA 1993 may be relevant, it will generally inform the DTI.

184 Rule 20.1 TC. See, also, General Principle 2 TC and the notes to rule 20.1.

185 See rule 35 TC, further.

186 See rule 35.1(a)(ii) and (iii) TC.

187 See rule 35.1(a) TC.

the organisation of the financial adviser.[188] If, however, that proves to be impossible, the financial adviser may have to decline to act for the company.[189] Guidance to the Code provides essentially that 'multi-service financial organisations' must arrange their affairs, where necessary, to ensure the total segregation of distinct operations[190] and also that those operations are conducted 'without regard for the interests of other parts of the same organisation or of their clients ...'.[191]

Rules governing substantial acquisitions of shares

Certain 'Rules Governing Substantial Acquisitions of Shares' are issued and administered by the Panel. They are aimed at restricting the speed with which a person may increase his holding of shares and rights over shares to an aggregate of between 15% and 30% of the voting rights in respect of a company. For instance, subject to certain exceptions, a person may not in any period of seven days acquire shares carrying voting rights in a company representing 10% or more of the voting rights if such acquisition when aggregated with any shares which he already holds would carry 15% or more but less than 30% of the voting rights of that company.[192]

9-52

These rules also require the accelerated disclosure of acquisitions of shares or rights over shares relating to such holdings. For instance, following such an acquisition, if a person comes to hold shares representing 15% or more of the voting rights in a company he must notify that acquisition and his total holding to the company and to the Company Announcements Office of the Stock Exchange not later than noon on the business day following the date of the acquisition.[193] He

9-53

---

188 If, for instance, the information in question is in the possession of the firm's market makers, an effective 'Chinese wall' would ensure that the firm's corporate financiers never came to know of it. For these purposes, a 'Chinese wall' essentially involves effective internal rules of confidentiality. It would be an established and effective arrangement which requires information obtained by a firm in the course of carrying on one part of its business of any kind to be withheld in certain circumstances from persons with whom it deals in the course of carrying on another part of its business. The expression can also be used to describe an established arrangement between different legal entities within the same group which requires information obtained by one group company to be withheld from persons with whom another group company carries on business.

189 See Appendix 3.2(a) TC.

190 In the example used in note 188 above, they would need to ensure the effective segregation of the market makers from the corporate financiers. See Appendix 3.2(b) TC.

191 See Appendix 3.2(b) TC.

192 See rules 1 and 2 of the Rules Governing the Substantial Acquisition of Shares (hereafter 'SARs'), further.

193 See rule 3(a) SARs, further.

must do the same if his holding already represents 15% or more of the voting rights and as a result of the acquisition is increased to or beyond any whole percentage figure.[194]

9-54   The rules apply to transactions in the shares of companies considered by the Panel to be resident in the United Kingdom, the Channel Islands, the Isle of Man or the Irish Republic if their shares are listed on the Stock Exchange. They do not, however, apply where the Takeover Code itself applies to the acquisition by a person of shares or rights over shares.[195]

THE SECURITIES AND FUTURES AUTHORITY

The significance of the Securities and Futures Authority

9-55   The significance of the Securities and Futures Authority[196] is that it is the main 'FSA'[197] regulator of the securities industry and thus regulates the investment business carried on by most securities industry professionals in the City of London. It was formed in April 1991 by the merger of The Securities Association[198] and the Association of Futures, Brokers and Dealers.[199] It is one of the so-called 'self-regulating organisations'[200] recognised by the Securities and Investments Board[201] and is thus able to provide authorisation for persons who apply to it and are accepted into membership. Such persons are then able to engage in the investment business for which they were authorised without being in breach of the Financial Services Act 1986.[202]

---

194 See rule 3(b) SARs, further.

195 See paras 1 and 2 ('Constitution' and 'Scope') of the Introduction to the SARs.

196 Known hereafter as the 'SFA'.

197 The Financial Services Act 1986. Essentially, s 3 FSA 1986 provides that no person may carry on investment business in the UK unless authorised to do so or otherwise exempted. See Chapter 2 above, further.

198 Known as 'TSA'.

199 Known as the 'AFBD'.

200 Or 'SROs'.

201 Well-known as the 'SIB'. Again, see Chapter 2, above, further.

202 Which breach can result in the imposition of both civil and criminal sanctions. See ss 4 and 5 FSA 1986 and Chapter 2, above, further.

The regulatory scope of the Securities and Futures Authority

The investment business which the SFA is capable of regulating has   **9-56**
brought together and now comprises the regulatory scope of its two
predecessor SROs.[203] It therefore covers dealing in investments,
arranging deals in investments and advising on deals in all types of
'investments'.[204] In the main, the SFA regulates stock broking, market
making and the related activities of sophisticated financial intermediaries.
Although the SFA can regulate investment management, this is unusual
and, in practice, a firm intending to act as an investment manager will
normally be expected to obtain authorisation through membership of the
Investment Management Regulatory Organisation.[205] However, if the
firm itself (or a subsidiary) is to provide the investment management of
securities in conjunction with other services capable of being regulated by
the SFA, principally to private customers, the firm (or the subsidiary)
may seek authorisation from the SFA.

The SFA does, however, make it clear that those activities   **9-57**
undertaken within corporate finance business which amount to
investment business, and thus require authorisation, do fall within its
regulatory scope. It is therefore likely that the majority of authorised
persons involved in the securities industry will be members of the SFA,
particularly stock brokers and merchant banks. The rules and
procedures of the SFA are geared towards the protection of investors
and the regulation of 'market' wrongdoing and are therefore of
relevance in the context of the prevention of insider dealing. To
appreciate those rules, it is however necessary to outline a number of
preliminary matters.

Membership of the Securities and Futures Authority

When a securities industry 'player', such as a stockbroker, first applied   **9-58**
for membership of a SRO,[206] it will have been investigated and will only
have been admitted into membership[207] on being found to be 'fit and
proper' to engage in the investment business proposed. Once so
admitted, and thus authorised to engage in investment business,
members of the SFA must comply with the Rules of the SFA. These

---

203 See para 9-55 above. See SFA rule 1-2 and Appendix 1 to the SFA Rules, further.
204 As categorised in Part I ('Investments') of Schedule 1 FSA 1986. And see para 5 of
    Appendix 1 SFA Rules.
205 Known acronymically as 'IMRO'. And see rule 1-2 SFA Rules.
206 Probably before 27 February 1988, which was chosen as the date by which all
    investment businesses had to apply for authorisation.
207 Probably of TSA, one of the two SRO predecessors of the SFA. And see Appendix 3
    to the SFA Rules.

contain provisions governing the relationship between the member firm and the SFA including the need for SFA members to have and to maintain adequate financial resources. They must also notify the SFA[208] on the occurrence of certain specified circumstances which include financial difficulties; changes in significant personnel and in those persons concerned with the investment business conducted by the firm; and also where changes are proposed to those persons 'controlling' the firm. There are also detailed provisions[209] governing the relationship between SFA members and their customers.

The SFA Rules in outline

9-59   There are a number of chapters to the SFA Rules together with further supplementary appendices. In the interests of user-friendliness there is also an index. It is unfortunate that the emphasis placed on closely defined expressions is to many, in the long-run, user-inimical. The contents of the chapters, in outline, are as follows:

- *Chapter 1* contains certain general rules relating to the SFA including its scope;[210] those circumstances in which *force majeure* may make it impracticable for a firm to comply with the SFA Rules[211] and a specific prohibition[212] against a firm entering into any contract or arrangement which is intended to indemnify or compensate it against any liabilities or consequences which will or may arise or be incurred as a result of non-compliance with the SFA Rules or any action which the SFA will or may take in relation to the firm or its employees. Rule 1-8 makes it clear that, save in certain circumstances,[213] the SFA must treat as confidential all information concerning the affairs of an applicant or a member firm.[214]

- *Chapter 2* sets out certain membership rules including the application procedure for membership of the SFA;[215] provisions relating to the registers of individuals maintained by the SFA;[216] and also the

---

208 Sometimes in advance. See, generally, Appendix 5 to the SFA Rules.

209 Termed 'Conduct of Business' or 'CoB' Rules. And see Appendix 38 to the SFA Rules.

210 In rule 1-2 SFA Rules, which is amplified by the contents of Appendix 1 to the SFA Rules.

211 Rule 1-6 SFA Rules.

212 In rule 1-7 SFA Rules.

213 See rule 1-8(2) SFA Rules which sets out the six general circumstances in which the SFA may disclose confidential information. See SI 1995/3275.

214 Including those of its officers, employees and customers. And see SFA Board Notice 298 (20 December 1995), further.

215 In rules 2-1 to 2-13 SFA Rules. And see SFA Board Notice 284.

216 In rules 2-24 to 2-41 SFA Rules.

specific notification requirements imposed upon members of the SFA.[217]

- *Chapter 3* sets out the financial rules applicable to SFA members which do not fall within the definition of 'investment firm' contained in the Investment Services Directive.[217a] The rules include the basic computation of financial resources[218] which a firm must at all times maintain in excess of its financial resources requirement and, in that context, the calculation of its primary financial resources requirement and the relevance of position risk and counterparty risk to the financial resources requirement of a firm. Chapter 3 contains the provisions relating to financial records and systems of internal control;[219] the requirements of financial reporting;[220] and also notification.[221] Rules 3-40 to 3-41 contain provisions relating to the form and content of financial reporting statements and accounting policies whilst rules 3-50 to 3-55 contain important provisions[222] relating to the appointment and duties of auditors. By virtue of rule 3-51, an SFA member must appoint an auditor who has been approved by the SFA for appointment under rule 3-51, who is also qualified in accordance with Rule 3-51(4).[223] Officers, employees or controllers of the firm, amongst others, will not be qualified for appointment as its auditors.[224]

- *Chapter 4* contains the rules relating to client money and the safekeeping of customers' investments and assets which apply to members of the SFA. Up to 30 June 1996, it contained specific SFA provisions relating to client money and setting out the extent of the continued application of the Financial Services (Client Money) Regulations 1991 and the Financial Services (Client Money) (Supplementary) Regulations 1991 to SFA members. For such persons, however, the existing Financial Services (Client Money) Regulations 1991 and the Financial Services (Client Money) (Supplementary)

---

217 In rules 2-42 to 2-55 SFA Rules. See, generally, Appendix 5 to the SFA Rules.

217aSee SFA Board Notice 240 (February 1995) which confirmed the application of the existing Chapter 3 financial rules from 31 December 1995 to member firms not covered by the Investment Services Directive (EEC Council Dir 93/22) and the Capital Adequacy Directive (EEC Council Dir 93/6).

218 See rule 3-62, rules 3-63 to 3-69 and then rules 3-70 to 3-74 SFA Rules, further.

219 Rules 3-10 to 3-13 SFA Rules.

220 In rules 3-20 to 3-23 SFA Rules.

221 In rules 3-30 to 3-32 SFA Rules.

222 Particularly in relation to the preservation of corporate and related pension fund assets.

223 For instance, through membership of the Institute of Chartered Accountants in England and Wales. See rule 3-51(4) further.

224 Pursuant to rule 3-51 SFA Rules.

Regulations 1991 were deleted on 30 June 1996. From that date, new SFA client money rules came into full effect having run in parallel from 1 February 1996.[224a]

- *Chapter 5* contains the 'Conduct of Business' or 'CoB' Rules which are applicable to the relationship between SFA members and their customers. Rule 5-46 sets out provisions relating to insider dealing. Other relevant rules are rule 5-25 which relates to underwriting whilst rule 5-47 governs the stabilisation of securities.

- *Chapter 6* sets out provisions relating to the handling by SFA members of complaints from customers and also gives brief details of the arbitration schemes which are available. The Consumer Arbitration Scheme relates to claims against SFA members by private customers whilst the Full Arbitration Scheme is available for members to use for disputes between themselves, whether or not arising out of investment business or passported investment business, and for customers whose claims exceed £50,000.

- *Chapter 7* contains the SFA enforcement rules. These include details of its monitoring and investigation powers,[225] its powers of intervention[226] and its disciplinary powers and procedures.[227]

- *Chapter 8* contains the commencement and transitional provisions relating to the rules of the SFA. Subject to those provisions,[228] the SFA Rules came into effect from 1 April 1992.

- *Chapter 9* contains expressions and words defined for the purposes of the Rules of the SFA. Many practitioners take the view that the SFA Rules overuse definitions to the extent that they are unhelpful.

- *Chapter 10* contains financial rules applicable to member firms falling within the definition of investment firm contained in the Investment Firm Directive. Those rules came into effect from 31 December 1995.[228a]

224a See SFA Board Notices 253 (for the initial proposals), 284 (in relation to changes prompted by implementation of EEC Council Directive 93/92) and 297 (20 December 1995, for confirmation of BN 253), further. See also SIB Consultative Paper No 95 (January 1996) at para 8. There have also been subsequent SFA client money developments. See SFA Board Notices Nos 298, 300, 311, 317, 318, 329, 330 and 347 (12 July 1996).

225 In rules 7-8 to 7-11 SFA Rules.

226 In rules 7-12 to 7-22 SFA Rules.

227 In rules 7-23 to 7-44 SFA Rules.

228 In particular, those set out in Schedule 1 to rule 8-3 SFA Rules. And see SFA Board Notice 298 (20 December 1995), further.

228a The firms have come to be called 'ISD firms', and 'Non-ISD firms'. The rules are the Financial (ISD) Rules. See SFA Board Notice 200 (August 1994) and particularly 249 (15 May 1995).

- Finally, there are also 38 supplementary appendices to the SFA Rules. These contain such material as guidance notes on the 'fit and proper person' test,[229] various guidance notes in relation to the financial rules[230] and also the 'Standards for Compliance with Regulatory Requirements'[231] which sets out the position of the SFA in relation to how a member firm should organise and control its internal affairs and have adequate arrangements to ensure there is compliance with the SFA Rules.

The SFA Conduct of Business Rules

It was envisaged that there would be a basic 'three-tier' structure to these rules which govern how a member firm must deal with and/or for its customers.

9-60

The *first tier* would comprise the 10 general Statements of Principle promulgated by the SIB. They may be found at the beginning of the SFA Rules. They were drafted very widely[232] and apply directly to the conduct of investment business and financial standing of all authorised persons. Breach of the principles does not give rise to actions for damages but is available to the SFA for the purposes of discipline and intervention. SFA member firms must observe high standards of integrity and fair dealing[233] and also high standards of market conduct.[234] They must deal fairly and thoroughly with their customers.[235] They must avoid or resolve conflicts of interest.[236] They must have and maintain adequate financial resources to meet their commitments and to withstand the risks to which their businesses are subject.[237] They must also co-operate with the SFA and must keep the SFA promptly informed of anything concerning the firm which might reasonably be expected to be disclosed to the SFA.[238] This requirement is additional to the specific notification requirements contained in Chapter 2 and elsewhere in the SFA Rules.

9-61

---

229 In Appendix 3 to the SFA Rules.

230 For instance, in Appendices 20 to 32 to the SFA Rules.

231 In Appendix 38 to the SFA Rules.

232 Which was deliberate. Compare the ambit of the General Principles to the Takeover Code. And see SFA Board Notice 298 (20 December 1995), further

233 Principle 1 (of the 10 Statements of Principle promulgated by the SIB on 15 March 1990).

234 Principle 3. For these purposes, see the Financial Services (Statements of Principle) (Endorsement of Codes and Standards) Instrument 1995 which endorsed the Takeover code for the purposes of Principle 3, with effect from 19 January 1995.

235 Principles 4 and 5.

236 Principle 6.

237 Principle 8.

238 See Principles 9 and 10. And note SFA Board Notice 298 (20 December 1995).

9-62   The *second tier* consisted of 40 'core conduct of business rules' also promulgated by the SIB,[239] which has power to 'designate' rules made in respect of certain stated matters[240] so as to make them applicable to members of SROs such as the SFA. These core rules were, however dedesignated in December 1994 in relation to the SFA and references to them as such are in the process of being deleted. The rationale was the perceived need for the SIB to allow SROs more flexibility in their use of rules and other mechanisms for ensuring observance of the necessary standard of investor protection.[240a] Dedesignation has no effect on their content of application to member firms and the core rules may still be found lurking in bold type[241] in the CoB Rules set out in Chapter 5 of the SFA Rules. Second-tier provisions were known as 'designated' rules and regulations. Examples of instruments which are designated are the Common Unsolicited Calls Regulations and provisions contained in the Financial Services (Client Money) Regulations 1991.

9-63   Second-tier rules were expanded (and occasionally clarified) by *third tier* provisions which have consisted of material specifically promulgated by the SFA as being of particular relevance or guidance as to the conduct of business of its member firms.

The customer relationship

9-64   Generally speaking, members of the SFA need only comply with the CoB Rules insofar as they are acting with or on behalf of 'customers'. The CoB Rules govern and regulate their relationship with customers. If a person is not a customer, generally speaking, the CoB Rules need not be complied with. Other matters, however, such as the potential application of s 47 of the Financial Services Act 1986,[242] would still be potentially applicable.

9-65   A 'customer' is defined[243] as meaning 'any person with or for whom a member firm carries on or intends to carry on any"'investment business" or other business for that person carried on in connection with that investment business'. Previously, the 'business' referred to was any

---

239 Pursuant to s 63A FSA 1986 ('Application of designated rules and regulations to members of self-regulating organisations').

240 Such as the conduct of business rules, the financial resources rules, the client money regulations and the regulations affecting unsolicited calls. See note 37a to Chapter 2, above, further.

240a See Andrew Large, 'Financial Services Regulation: Making the Two-Tier System Work', published by the SIB in May 1993, further. See also SIB Consultative Paper No 95 (January 1996) at paras 2–7.

241 Initially, they were followed by a reference such as '[cr 28]' which indicates the relevant core rule provision.

242 See Chapter 10, below.

243 In Chapter 9 of the SFA Rules.

'regulated business' or 'associated business'. For those purposes and others, 'regulated business' means[244] 'investment business'[245] which is business carried on from a permanent place of business maintained by a firm in the United Kingdom. 'Associated business' is defined[246] as meaning business carried on in connection with 'investment business'.

The definition of 'customer' does not include 'market counterparties.'[247] Market counterparties are persons dealing[248] with the SFA member in the course of investment business of the same description as that in which the SFA member is acting[249] and also certain specified 'professionals'[250] whom the SFA member has notified in writing that it will be treating them as market counterparties in accordance with the CoB Rules.[251] They will not then be regarded as customers and accordingly will not have the benefit of the customer protections built-in to the CoB Rules. **9-66**

The distinction between 'private' and 'non-private' customers is also important. 'Private customers' are defined as meaning 'customers who are individuals and who are not acting in the course of carrying on investment business'. Generally speaking, 'non-private customers' are persons who have elected to be treated as such in accordance with the SFA Rules and, except for certain purposes, are customers who are not private customers.[252] The effect of this distinction is that, again generally speaking, private customers[253] should be entitled to fuller protections under the CoB Rules than non-private customers.[253a] The investor protection rationale for this is that they are thought to be more at risk and thus to be more deserving of protection than large companies who are arguably more likely to be aware, having taken legal advice as to the consequences, of what they are doing. In the course of carrying on corporate finance work, SFA member firms will come into contact both with private customers and non-private customers. They may also deal with or for persons, such as their market counterparties, who need not be regarded as customers at all. **9-67**

---

244 See Chapter 9 of the SFA Rules, further.

245 See s 1(2) FSA 1986.

246 Again, in Chapter 9 of the SFA Rules, further.

247 But see para (b)(i) of the definition of customer in Chapter 9 of the SFA Rules.

248 As principal or as agent for an unidentified principal.

249 For instance, they may both be merchant banks or stockbrokers.

250 For instance, another SFA member.

251 But see rule 5-4 SFA Rules, further.

252 But see the precise definitions in Chapter 9 SFA Rules, further.

253 Which will include most members of the public.

253a But see SFA Board Notice 303 (19 February 1996) in relation to off-exchange derivatives transactions involving private customers.

Corporate finance business

9-68   There is a specific 'exclusion' from the definition of 'customer' in relation to 'corporate finance business'.[254] If it is applicable, it may enable an SFA member carrying on corporate finance business with or for a customer (or for its own account) to avoid having to treat third parties[255] as customers in the context of investment services provided to its customer. Essentially, this exclusion applies where it would be unreasonable to expect the firm to have a customer relationship with third parties because there would be too much of a conflict between the interests of those third parties and the interests of its original customer (or its own interests).

9-69   This treatment of 'corporate finance business' is, however, slightly more complicated than the similar exclusion which was contained in the Rules of The Securities Association.[256] It is no longer sufficient simply for the circumstances to be such that the investor cannot reasonably expect the firm to treat him as a customer or he indicates to the firm that he is not expecting to be so treated. Now, unless the firm is arranging underwriting commitments, there must be no material difference between the way the firm communicates or deals with the investor[257] and other similar people and the firm must clearly indicate to that investor that it is not acting for him[258] and thus he will not be treated as its customer. In fact, both of these requirements must be complied with before the exclusion will be satisfied and thus applicable.

9-70   The SFA Rules contain a specific definition of 'corporate finance business.'[259] It covers any investment services[260] provided by an SFA member firm to a number of persons, including:

- an issuer, holder or owner of 'investments,'[261] with regard to their offer, issue, underwriting, repurchase, exchange or redemption or the variation of the terms of the 'investments' or any related matter;

- any company in connection with a related takeover, merger or reorganisation; and

---

254 See para (b)(iii) of the definition of 'customer' in Chapter 9 of the SFA Rules.

255 Such as members of the public or shareholders in the company in question.

256 In rule 1090.02 in Chapter IV of the Rules of TSA.

257 ie, the person to be excluded from any need to be treated as a customer by the firm.

258 Because it is acting for someone else or on its own account.

259 Set out in Chapter 9. For some background reading, see 'Corporate Finance and Capital Market Rules' (a SIB Consultative Paper, February 1988).

260 Which is to say, any activities undertaken in the course of carrying on investment business.

261 For instance, shares or debentures.

- any shareholder or prospective shareholder of a company established or to be established in connection with a takeover.

In each particular case, reference must be made to the definition to ascertain whether a member of the SFA is or may be engaged in corporate finance business.

The effect of a member firm of the SFA carrying on 'corporate finance business' is that only certain specifically stated CoB Rules apply to customer relationships arising from that business. Those rules are set out in Table 5-1(5) in the CoB Rules. They include a number of provisions which are relevant to the prevention of 'market' misconduct,[262] which will be outlined shortly. The complete list is as follows: **9-71**

Rule	Subject
5-1	application
5-2	reliance on others
5-3	Chinese walls
5-5	classes of customer
5-7	inducements
5-9(1) to (3)	issue and approval of advertisements
5-12	issue or approval of advertisements for an overseas person
5-15	fair and clear communications
5-17	compliance procedures for unsolicited calls
5-18	standards of conduct for unsolicited calls
5-24	customers' rights
5-25	underwriting
5-29	material interest
5-30(1)	customers' understanding
5-31(1)	suitability
5-46	insider dealing
5-47	stabilisation of securities
5-48	support of Takeover Panel's functions
5-49	reportable transactions
5-51 to 5-54	compliance

As mentioned in para 9-71 above, a number of the rules set out in Table 5-1(5) are relevant to market conduct. The following paragraphs offer some commentary on those provisions. **9-72**

---

262 Such as rule 5-46 SFA Rules, which relates to insider dealing.

Chinese walls

9-73 Generally speaking, authorised persons are expected either to avoid any conflict of interest[263] but, where conflicts do arise, to ensure fair treatment for all their customers. Depending on the circumstances, they may achieve this by disclosure,[264] through 'internal rules of confidentiality', by declining to act for the customer or otherwise. 'Otherwise' might for instance encompass an automatic trading programme that takes any decision to deal, etc, away from the person with the conflict of interest. Such arrangements, however, can have their own problems.[264a] The expression 'internal rules of confidentiality' is perhaps the best way of summarising what is meant by a 'Chinese wall'. Essentially, a 'Chinese wall' is an established and effective arrangement which requires information obtained by a firm in the course of carrying on one part of its business to be withheld in certain circumstances from persons with whom it deals in the course of carrying on another part of that business. The expression can also be used to describe an established arrangement between different legal entities within the same group which requires information obtained by one group company to be withheld from persons with whom another group company carries on business.

9-74 SFA CoB rule 5-3(1) and(2) applies to 'Chinese wall' arrangements intended to have the effect that information should be withheld between different parts of a business or between different businesses. It does not state what form the arrangement should take, merely that it should be an established and effective arrangement in preventing the flow of information from one part of a firm to another or from one group company to another group company. Where such an arrangement is in place, for the purposes of the SFA CoB Rules, persons employed in the first part may withhold information from those employed in the second or information may be withheld between separate group companies, but only to the extent that the business of one of those parts involves investment or associated business.

9-75 Essentially, where a firm maintains a 'Chinese wall' between different parts of its business operations then, for the purposes of the SFA CoB Rules, information obtained by one part will not be imputed to the other part. This is contrary to the general legal presumption that information

---

263 By virtue of SIB Statement of Principle 6 and see paras 9-04 to 9-08 above, further, in relation to fiduciary duties generally.

264 Essentially, by fully disclosing the problem to a potential customer before acting for him. Also, in relation to the use of derivatives in the failed bid by Trafalgar House plc for Northern Electric plc in March 1995, see 'Behind the Chinese walls', *The Times* (Pennington Column), 14 June 1996.

264aParticularly if they cannot be amended or switched-off in times of market crisis. See 'Bankers in the dock', *The Times* (Pennington Column), 30 April 1996.

obtained by any one part of a body corporate[265] will be regarded as within the knowledge of the body corporate as a whole. So far as intra-group confidentiality is concerned, it is the general position that information obtained by one group company is not attributable to another unless both companies share the same employees. For the purposes of the SFA CoB Rules, information may be withheld but CoB rule 5-3(2) does not absolve a group company from having to comply with an obligation from outside the CoB Rules to transmit information to another group company. The protection offered through the use of a 'Chinese wall' only operates in terms of the application of the CoB Rules. It is not a device which is well recognised under general law as a way of managing conflicts of interest or problems of confidentiality. It does not alter any requirement to transmit information which may arise apart from the SFA CoB Rules.

Underwriting

Many corporate transactions involve the issue of shares by a company. In an offer for sale, such shares will be offered to the public. Where this is the case, the offer will normally be underwritten. That is to say, persons known as underwriters will agree to subscribe for the shares to the extent that they are not otherwise taken up. Accepting such an obligation[266] is not an investment opportunity for the financially unsophisticated.

9-76

Accordingly, rule 5-25 of the SFA CoB Rules is intended to protect customers in this area. It provides that, without the prior written consent of the customer, a firm must not execute transactions for a private customer or effect or arrange discretionary transactions for any customer under which the customer will incur obligations as an underwriter or sub-underwriter in connection with any form of issue of investments. This is stated as including any offer for subscription, any offer for sale or any placing of investments or any takeover offer where the consideration does or may consist of investments. The consent given by a customer may however be general or related to specific issues of investments. In the case of a private customer, it is likely that the customer would need to be specifically warned about the risks which he was taking by entering into any underwriting arrangement.[267]

9-77

---

265 As a body corporate is regarded as a separate and distinct legal person. See also Lynn Counsell, 'Chinese walls: a device not a solution', (1993) 1(3) IJRL&P 314–316. Also, in relation to the use of derivatives in the failed bid by Trafalgar House plc for Nortern Electric plc in March 1995, see 'Behind the Chinese Walls', *The Times* (Pennington column), 14 June 1996. And see rule 5-3(3) and (4) SFA CoB Rules, further.

266 And becoming party to an underwriting agreement.

267 See SFA CoB rule 5-30, which relates to the understanding of a customer.

Material interest

9-78   SIB Statement of Principle 6[268] provides that a 'firm should either avoid any conflict of interest arising or, where conflicts arise, should ensure fair treatment to all its customers by disclosure, internal rules of confidentiality, declining to act, or otherwise ...'. It goes on to provide that a 'firm should not unfairly place its interests above those of its customer ...'. Ideally, therefore, a firm should avoid any conflict arising. If, however, this is impractical or impossible to avoid, the firm must ensure fair treatment to its customers and Principle 6 suggests a number of ways. The problem may be solved if the firm makes full disclosure to the potential customer before acting. If a customer decides in any event to proceed, he may find it hard to complain about the position subsequently. It may be sufficient if the firm has in place adequate internal rules of confidentiality, such as a 'Chinese wall' separating different parts of its business. If not, it may well be the best course of action for the firm to decline to act for the customer although, in some circumstances, this might itself cause problems for the firm[269] in relation to existing customers.

9-79   Rule 5-29 of the SFA CoB Rules supplements and particularises Statement of Principle 6. It provides that where a member firm has a 'material interest' in a transaction to be entered into with or for a customer,[270] the member firm must not knowingly either advise, or deal in the exercise of a discretion, in relation to that transaction unless it takes reasonable steps to ensure fair treatment for the customer. For these purposes, a 'material interest' is defined negatively. In relation to a transaction, it does not include 'disclosable commission' on the transaction or goods or services which can reasonably be expected to assist in the provision of investment services to customers and which are provided or to be provided under a 'soft commission agreement'.

9-80   SIB Statement of Principle 6 has an ambit which appears to be deliberately wide in that it refers to 'any conflict of interest'. SFA CoB Rule 5-29(1) is more limited in that it only applies where a firm is entering into transactions and is limited to a material interest or a relationship giving rise to a conflict of interest in relation to such a transaction. Statement of Principle 6 refers to fair treatment for all customers whereas rule 5-29(1) is concerned with the particular customer in question. It requires the firm not to advise or deal unless it takes reasonable steps to provide fair treatment for the customer and the various approaches described under Principle 6 would then be relevant.[271]

---

268 Entitled 'Conflicts of interest'.

269 It might amount to a breach of fiduciary duty or breach of contract, etc.

270 Or where the firm has a relationship which gives rise to a conflict of interest in relation to such a transaction.

271 See para 9-78, above.

SFA CoB rule 5-29(2) goes on to suggest one approach which a firm **9-81** may take to enable it to act by ensuring fair treatment for a customer and that is by relying on a 'policy of independence'. If such a policy is to be relied upon, it must *both* require any relevant employee to disregard[272] any 'material interest' or conflict of interest when advising customers or dealing for them in the exercise of discretion *and* must be set out in writing and be known by the relevant employee.[273] If such a policy is to be relied upon by a firm in relation to private customers, it must first have disclosed to them in writing that it may give them advice or deal for them where it may have a material interest or conflict of interest and also that the relevant employee is required to comply with a policy of independence and to disregard any material interest or conflict of interest when making recommendations or arranging transactions. The SFA has however made it clear that, if the presence of a policy of independence is not itself sufficient to ensure fair treatment for customers, the firm should take other steps and this may include specific disclosure.

Insider dealing

There are specific SFA CoB Rule provisions relating to insider dealing. **9-82** SFA CoB rule 5-46(1) obliges a firm *not* to effect[274] an 'own account' transaction[275] when it knows[276] of circumstances which mean that it, its 'associate', or an employee of either would be prohibited from effecting that transaction by means of the legislation which makes insider dealing a criminal offence.[277] SFA CoB rule 5-46(2) provides that the member firm must use its best endeavours to ensure that it does not knowingly effect such a transaction for a customer which it knows would be so prohibited. On that basis, the SFA would be able to discipline a firm for entering into a transaction which it knows would be prohibited by the relevant legislation. Also, a breach of CoB rule 5-46 would mean that an investor who suffered any consequential loss might be able to found a claim for damages under s 62 of the Financial Services Act 1986 which, generally speaking, enables private investors to bring an action against

---

272 ie, not be influenced by.

273 And one way of satisfying this last requirement might be by inclusion in a service contract. See also SFA CoB rule 5-29(3).

274 Whether in the UK or elsewhere.

275 ie, a transaction effected or arranged by the firm in the course of carrying on either investment business or associated business and on its own account (for itself) or on the account of an associate acting on its own account. See the definition in Chapter 9 SFA Rules further.

276 ie, it acts with knowledge of.

277 Referred to as the 'statutory restrictions on insider dealing'. Formerly the Company Securities (Insider Dealing) Act 1985; now Part V of the CJA 1993.

member firms if they suffer loss by reason of any breach of the SFA CoB Rules by the firm. The ambit of these CoB Rule provisions is however limited by rule 5-46(3). A member firm will not be prohibited by them where the statutory prohibition only applies because of knowledge of the 'firm's own intentions'. A firm may also deal where it is a recognised market maker[278] with an obligation to deal in the securities in question.

Stabilisation of securities

9-83   'Stabilisation' essentially involves a stabilising manager supporting the price of newly-issued securities for a limited period following their issue. It is a form of permitted market manipulation and is therefore closely regulated. SFA CoB rule 5-47 provides that where a firm takes action for the purpose of stabilising the price of securities, it must comply with any applicable provisions of the 'statutory stabilisation rules' which means the Stabilisation Rules issued by the SIB and contained in Part 10 of the Financial Services (Conduct of Business) Rules 1990.[279] The rationale for allowing stabilisation in controlled circumstances is to protect investors who might otherwise be adversely affected by price fluctuations in respect of dealings in a new issue of securities. It is provided,[280] generally speaking, that the provisions prohibiting market manipulation[281] will not be regarded as contravened by anything done for the purposes of stabilising the price of investments if it is done in conformity with the Stabilisation Rules.

Support of Takeover Panel's functions

9-84   As a non-statutory body, the Takeover Panel does not have the disciplinary sanctions available to the SFA. However, the City Code on Takeovers and Mergers and the Rules Governing Substantial Acquisitions of Shares have been endorsed under SIB Statement of Principle 3, which means that SFA members have to comply with them as if they formed part of those Statements of Principle. The Panel also relies on regulators such as the SFA to support its functions and SFA CoB rule 5-48 provides

---

278 ie, a person who holds himself out as willing to buy/sell securities at prices specified by him and is recognised as doing so by a recognised investment exchange. And see SFA CoB rule 5-46(3), further.

279 Which are the CoB Rules issued by the SIB and are thus generally applicable to persons directly authorised by the SIB. And see Appendix 16 to the SFA Rules, further.

280 In s 48(7) FSA 1986.

281 See s 47(2) FSA 1986 and Chapter 10, below.

that a firm must not act or continue to act for a 'specified person'[282] or an agent acting for a specified person in connection with a takeover, a substantial acquisition of shares or a transaction subject to rule 8 of the Takeover Code[283] unless it has the consent of the Takeover Panel. Rule 5-48 goes on to provide that a member firm must render all such assistance as it is reasonably able to provide to enable the Panel to perform its functions and must provide to the Panel such information, documents and records as the Panel requests.

Reportable transactions

SFA CoB Rule 5-49 provides that member firms must report to the SFA by means of an 'approved reporting system'[284] all transactions within the regulatory scope of the SFA[285] which they effect[286] in all kinds of investments, except for those investments or transactions listed in rule 5-49(2). The purpose is to enable the SFA to keep a check on what business a firm is doing, what customers it is dealing with and how it is carrying on its business. From the reports which it receives, generally speaking, the SFA is able to monitor the extent to which a firm is complying with its rules. Reports must usually be made no later than the end of the business day following the date of the transaction. There are other specific provisions relating to trade reporting which are set out in rule 5-49.

9-85

Personal and other dealings

SFA CoB Rule 5-51 provides that a firm must take reasonable steps[287] to ensure that its officers and employees act in conformity with their own and its responsibilities under the Financial Services Act 1986, the SFA Rules and the provisions of Part V of the Criminal Justice Act 1993. To ensure that, and also to ensure propriety in personal dealings, a firm must give to every employee a written 'personal account notice' which contains certain requirements set out in rule 5-51(7). Where the business of the firm involves securities or derivatives relating to securities, the

9-86

---

282 Being a person named in a notice published by the Takeover Panel, essentially as being someone *not* to do business with. And see the Financial Services (Statements of Principle) (Endorsement of Codes and Standards) Instrument 1995. (SIB Rules Release 154, published on 19 January 1995.)

283 Rule 8 TC provides, essentially, for the disclosure of dealings by offerors and others.

284 For 'approved reporting systems' see Appendix 17 to the SFA Rules.

285 Whether transactions executed as principle or as agent.

286 Whether on or off-exchange. And note SFA Board Notice 298 (20 December 1995).

287 Including the establishment and maintenance of appropriate procedures.

notice must also contain a summary of Part V of the Criminal Justice Act 1993 and every employee must enter into a written undertaking with the firm[288] to observe these requirements.

---

[288] Usually separate from but forming part of his service contract. See Appendix 44 to the SFA Rules, further.

CHAPTER 10

OTHER 'MARKET' OFFENCES

INTRODUCTORY MATTERS

Other relevant legislation

This book is mainly, but not solely, concerned with the criminal offence of insider dealing. There are certain other 'market'-related offences and the Criminal Justice Act 1993[1] is not the only Act of Parliament which enables criminal sanctions to be imposed on persons involved in wrongdoing concerning securities and the securities 'industry' in the United Kingdom. Certain offences[2] continue to be set out in the Theft Act 1968.[3] As will be seen shortly, the Financial Services Act 1986[4] may also be relevant although that Act is primarily concerned with investor protection containing, as it does, the statutory framework for the regulation of the financial services industry in the UK.[5]

10-01

The common law

Statute is not, however, the only means by which those concerned with the securities industry may be punished for wrongdoing. We have seen earlier[7] that 'regulatory' and other sanctions may be applicable.[6] The old-established common law offence of conspiracy to defraud may also be relevant, although its use in this context in the future may well be curtailed by the greater particularity of certain of the more modern statutory offences.[8]

10-02

---

1   1993 c 36.
2   Such as theft, obtaining property or a pecuniary advantage by deception and false accounting.
3   1968 c 60. And see ss 1, 7, 15–17 TA 1968 and later in this Chapter 10 where mention will be made of certain of these offences.
4   1986 c 60.
5   See Chapter 2 above, further.
6   In Chapter 9, above. See also Chapter 2, above.
7   For instance, disciplinary proceedings brought against a recalcitrant member by an SRO such as the SFA.
8   Such as offences those contained in s 47 FSA 1986, which relate to the making of misleading statements (s 47(1)) and market manipulation (s 47(2)) and see later in this Chapter.

UNAUTHORISED INVESTMENT BUSINESS

The basic prohibition

10-03 Section 3 of the Financial Services Act 1986[9] provides that no person shall carry on, or purport to carry on, 'investment business' in the United Kingdom unless he is an authorised or an exempted person. That basic prohibition came into force on 29 April 1988[10] and any person who carries on, or purports to carry on, investment business in contravention is guilty of an offence.[11]

The relevance of 'investment business'

10-04 'Investment business', for these purposes, is defined[12] as meaning the business of engaging in one or more of the activities which fall within Part II of Schedule I to the Financial Services Act 1986 and are not excluded by Part III of that Schedule.

10-05 The Financial Services Act 1986 is only concerned with the regulation of investment business in the United Kingdom. For the purposes of that Act,[13] a person carries on investment business in the United Kingdom if he:

- carries on investment business from a permanent place of business maintained by him in the United Kingdom;[14] or

- engages in the United Kingdom in one or more of the activities set out in Part II of Schedule I which are not excluded by Parts III or IV of that Schedule and his doing so constitutes the carrying on by him of a business in the United Kingdom.[15]

10-06 On the basis set out in paras 10-04 and 10-05 above, in establishing whether a person is or will be carrying on investment business in the United Kingdom, there are essentially four questions which need to be answered:

- Are any 'investments' or underlying 'investments' involved in what is being done or is proposed to be done?[16]

---

9   Headed 'Persons entitled to carry on investment business'.
10 By virtue of the Financial Services Act 1986 (Commencement) (No 8) Order 1988 (SI 1988/740).
11 Section 4 FSA 1986 and see paras 10-11 to 10-14, below for further comment in relation to sanctions for breach of s 3 FSA 1986. And see 'Carrying on Investment Business in the UK' (a SIB Consultative Paper issued in March 1989).
12 In s 1(2) FSA 1986.
13 By virtue of s 1(3) FSA 1986.
14 Section 1(3)(a) FSA 1986.
15 Section 1(3)(b) FSA 1986.
16 See para 10-07, below.

- If so, are or will any 'investment activities' be involved?[17]
- If so, are any of the exclusions applicable?[18]
- If not, is or will the activity be engaged in by way of business?[19]

Underlying 'investments' for these purposes are categorised in Part I
of Schedule 1 to the Financial Services Act 1986. Part I is drafted in very
wide terms and lists 11 categories of investment. These include shares[20]
and debentures[21] and certain 'instruments entitling to shares or
securities'.[22] When considering whether investments are involved in a
particular situation, reference must always be made to Part I of
Schedule 1 and to the supplemental notes therein which effectively form
part of the legislation.

10-07

The relevant 'investment activities' are listed in Part II of Schedule 1.
They are as follows:

10-08

- *Dealing in investments.*[23] This involves buying, selling, subscribing for
  or underwriting investments or offering or agreeing to do so, either
  as principal or as an agent. For these purposes, the terms 'buying'
  and 'selling' are given a fairly extended definition.[24]

- *Arranging deals in investments.*[25] Generally speaking, this involves
  making, or offering or agreeing to make, arrangements with a view
  to another person dealing in investments. It does not apply to
  arrangements made by a person with regard to a transaction to
  which he will himself be a party as principal or as agent;[26] but, in
  that case, para 12 of Schedule 1 may apply.

- *Managing investments belonging to another person.*[27] Perhaps to state
  the obvious, this is the investment activity engaged in by
  professional investment managers.

- *Giving investment advice.*[28] This involves giving, or offering or
  agreeing to give, to persons in their capacity as investors or potential
  investors advice on the merits[29] of their purchasing, selling,

---

17 See para 10-08, below.
18 See para 10-09, below.
19 See para 10-10, below.
20 See Schedule 1 para 1, FSA 1986.
21 See Schedule 1 para 2, FSA 1986.
22 See Schedule 1 para 4, FSA 1986.
23 See Schedule 1 para 12, FSA 1986.
24 See Schedule 1 para 28(1)(d) and (2), FSA 1986.
25 See Schedule 1 para 13, FSA 1986.
26 See note (1) to Schedule 1 para 13, FSA 1986.
27 See Schedule 1 para 14, FSA 1986.
28 See Schedule 1 para 15, FSA 1986.
29 Which is to say, a recommendation of some sort.

subscribing for or underwriting an investment or exercising any right conferred by an investment to acquire, dispose of, underwrite or convert an investment. To fall within this paragraph, any such advice will need to be specific to an investment as opposed to being general or generic advice. Neutral information, in the absence of any express or implied recommendation or endorsement, is unlikely to amount to investment advice. Each case must, however, be considered separately, on the basis of its own facts.

- *Establishing etc collective investment schemes.*[30] This activity, which includes operating or winding-up a collective investment scheme, should be borne in mind particularly in 'joint venture' situations and reference should be made to the definition of 'collective investment scheme'[31] and also to the restrictions which are imposed on the promotion of such schemes by authorised persons.[32]

10-09   If it is established that an investment activity is involved in a particular situation, each of the 'excluded activities' set out in Part III of Schedule 1 will need to be considered.[33] If one of them is applicable, it may disapply the investment activity. If there is an overseas element, Part IV of Schedule 1 may be applicable.[34] It contains further exclusions in relation to certain investment activities carried on by 'overseas persons'[35] who, generally speaking, are persons without a permanent place of business in the United Kingdom.

10-10   To require regulation, as constituting investment business, the investment activities in question must be carried on or be engaged in by way of business. Unhelpfully, the Financial Services Act 1986 does not define what is meant by 'business' for these purposes.[36] Essentially, it is therefore necessary to apply general common law concepts of what amounts to 'business' and, also, a degree of commonsense to reach an answer. Commercial motivation is a major element of engaging in a business as is any resulting commercial benefit, whether direct or indirect. Carrying on an investment activity out of friendship or for

---

30   See Schedule 1 para 16, FSA 1986. And see Note 85 to Chapter 2 above and SI 1996/1322, further.

31   In s 75 FSA 1986.

32   See s 76 FSA 1986.

33   See Schedule 1 paras 17–25B, FSA 1986.

34   See Schedule 1 paras 26–27, FSA 1986.

35   See s 1(3)(a) FSA 1986.

36   Although, see some helpful guidance material issued by the SIB on Pensions Advice and Management. See Note 112 to Chapter 2, above. See *Morgan Grenfell & Co Ltd v Welwyn Hatfield DC* [1995] 1 All ER 1. The court considered that 'business' should be given a meaning which in ordinary parlance conformed to what would be seen as a 'business transaction' as compared to something of a more casual nature. See also *R v Wilson (Rupert)* (1996) Times Law Report, 14 August 1996, CA.

philanthropic reasons would not necessarily be caught[37] whereas doing so for a fee or commission is likely to be caught. Frequency, repetition and/or continuity are further elements of carrying on business. Carrying on an investment activity on rare or isolated occasions is perhaps unlikely to be regarded as being by way of business although it must be stressed that one-off activities may, in certain circumstances, be caught. In essence, it remains vital to consider all the circumstances of a particular case and it is therefore hard to set out general guidance on this area.

Basic sanctions for breach

It is a criminal offence for a person to carry on or purport to carry on investment business in contravention of the basic prohibition.[38] The maximum penalties, on conviction on indictment, is imprisonment for a term not exceeding two years or a fine or both.[39] On summary conviction, the possible penalties are imprisonment for a term not exceeding six months or a fine or both.[40] It is, however, a defence for a person accused with such an offence to prove that he took all reasonable precautions and exercised all due diligence to avoid commission of the offence.[41] If such an offence committed by a body corporate[42] is proved to have been committed with the consent or connivance, or to be attributable to any neglect on the part, of certain 'persons' they, as well as the company, shall be guilty of that offence and are liable to be proceeded against accordingly.[43] Those 'persons', for these purposes, are any director, manager, secretary or other similar officer of the body corporate or any person purporting to act in any such capacity[44] or a controller of the body corporate in question.[45] **10-11**

There are also civil sanctions for the carrying on of unauthorised investment business.[46] Essentially, in certain 'circumstances', certain 'agreements'[47] may be rendered unenforceable against an investor who may be entitled to recover any money or other property paid or transferred by him under the agreement together with compensation for **10-12**

---

37   Under and for the purposes of the FSA 1986.
38   Contained in s 3 FSA 1986. See para 10-03, above.
39   Section 4(1)(a) FSA 1986.
40   Section 4(1)(b) FSA 1986.
41   Section 4(2) FSA 1986.
42   Indeed, where any offence under the FSA 1986 is committed by a body corporate.
43   See s 202(1) FSA 1986, further.
44   Section 202(1)(a) FSA 1986.
45   Section 202(1)(b) FSA 1986.
46   Set out in s 5 FSA 1986. See Mark Lawson, 'The enforcement of "unenforceable" agreements under the Financial Services Act 1986' (1988) JBL 281–297.
47   The relevant 'agreements' are set out in s 5(7) FSA 1986.

any loss sustained by him as a result of having parted with it.[48] The 'circumstances' in question are where the agreement is entered into by a person in the course of carrying on unauthorised investment business[49] or by an authorised person but in consequence of anything said or done by a person carrying on unauthorised investment business.[50] The agreements to which these provisions apply are any agreements the making or performance of which by the party seeking to enforce them, or from whom money or other property is recoverable under these provisions, constitutes an investment activity[51] which is not covered by any of the so-called 'excluded activities'.[52] The court does, however, have discretion to allow an agreement to which these provisions apply to be enforced, or for money or property paid or transferred under it to be retained, if certain conditions[53] are satisfied.

10-13   In relation to the carrying on of unauthorised investment business,[54] the Secretary of State[55] may apply for a court order[56] where there is a reasonable likelihood that this will take place or where it has taken place and there is a reasonable likelihood that it will continue or that it will be repeated.[57] If satisfied that a person has entered into any transaction in this context,[58] the court can order the person at fault and anyone else who appears to the court to have been knowingly concerned in the contravention[59] to take such steps as the court may direct to restore the

---

48 See s 5(1) FSA 1986.

49 Section 5(1)(a) FSA 1986.

50 Section 5(1)(b) FSA 1986.

51 Falling within any paragraph of Part II to Schedule 1 FSA 1986.

52 Contained in Parts III or IV of Schedule 1 FSA 1986.

53 Set out in s 5(3) FSA 1986.

54 ie the s 3 FSA 1986 prohibition against the carrying on of unauthorised investment business.

55 Which in practice, in terms of the enforcement of s 6 FSA 1986, means the SIB. See s 114(1),(2) and (4) FSA 1986 but see also art 4 of, and para 1 of Schedule 2 to, the Financial Services Act 1986 (Delegation) Order 1987 (SI 1987/942).

56 Which is to say, a restitution order or an injunction.

57 Section 6(1)(a) and (b) FSA 1986.

58 ie in contravention of the s 3 FSA 1986 prohibition.

59 Which, after the decision of Sir Nicolas Browne-Wilkinson V-C in *SIB v Pantell SA and Others (No 2)* [1991] 3 WLR at 857, may include lawyers acting for the primary defendants. *Pantell (No 2)* followed *SIB v Pantell SA and Another* [1990] 1 Ch 426 and concerned an action brought by the SIB against two overseas companies which, it was alleged, were persons who had carried on unauthorised investment business in the UK causing loss to investors. The SIB joined as defendants certain solicitors who had acted for the original defendants, alleging that they were thus 'knowingly concerned' with the breaches in question of ss 3, 47, 56 and 57 FSA 1986. The SIB sought an order from the court that the solicitors should make good the loss suffered by the investors and it was confirmed that ss 6(2) and 61(1) FSA 1986 enabled the SIB to obtain orders for repayment of monies, not only from those directly concerned with relevant breaches of the FSA 1986 but also from third parties who could be said to be 'knowingly concerned' with such contraventions.

parties to the position they were in before the transaction was entered into.[60] The court may also order a wrongdoer to make such payment as appears to be just having regard to any profits which appear to have accrued and/or to the extent of any losses which have been incurred.[61]

Application may also be made[62] for an injunction or a restitution order where there is a reasonable likelihood that a person will contravene any one of certain provisions[63] or where such a contravention has taken place and there is a reasonable likelihood that it will continue or be repeated or if there are steps which could be taken for remedying the contravention.[64]

10-14

PROMOTIONAL OFFENCES

Introductory matters

In regulating the conduct of investment business, the Financial Services Act 1986 also contains certain promotional restrictions, both in relation to investment advertisements[65] and cold calling.[66] Compliance with these restrictions is underpinned by further provisions which impose criminal sanctions on the making of misleading statements and on courses of conduct creating a false or misleading impression in relation to investments.[67] These statutory provisions are of course additional, and without prejudice, to the application of any relevant common law considerations for those involved in promotion such as the need to avoid making negligent mis-statements or engaging in market practices which could amount to a conspiracy to defraud potential investors. When considering any promotional activity in relation to securities, it is therefore necessary to consider in particular whether it will involve the making of unsolicited calls, whether it will amount or give rise to the issue of an investment advertisement and whether it will involve an

10-15

---

60 Section 6(2) FSA 1986.

61 See s 6(3)–(7) FSA 1986, further.

62 As with s 6 FSA 1986, in practice, enforcement of s 61 FSA 1986 has been delegated to the SIB. See s 114(1),(2) and (4) FSA 1986 but see also arts 3 and 4 of, and paras 1, 7, 8 and 9 of Schedule 1 and para 2 of Schedule 2 to the Financial Services Act 1986 (Delegation) Order 1987 (SI 1987/942).

63 See s 61(1) FSA 1986. The provisions in question include ss 47, 56, 57 or 59 FSA 1986 and/or rules made by a recognised SRO.

64 See s 61(1) FSA 1986, further. Depending on the wrongdoing involved, there may well be a degree of overlap between ss 6 and 61 FSA 1986.

65 In s 57 FSA 1986.

66 In s 56 FSA 1986.

67 See s 47 FSA 1986 and paras 10-16 to 10-19 and 10-41 to 10-45 below.

activity which raises the need for authorisation under the Financial Services Act 1986.

Misleading statements and practices

10-16   Section 47 of the Financial Services Act 1986 contains two main categories of offence which must be borne in mind and may be applicable to promotional activities involving 'investments'.[68] Section 47(1)[69] covers misleading statements, promises or forecasts whilst s 47(2)[70] essentially concerns market manipulation.[71] The two offences are not mutually exclusive. A statement or concealment which falls within s 47(1) could also constitute a course of conduct creating a false or misleading impression as to the price or value of investments thereby falling within s 47(2).[72]

Breach of section 47

10-17   Breach of s 47 will amount to a criminal offence. The maximum penalties for conviction on indictment are imprisonment for a term not exceeding seven years or a fine or both.[73] On summary conviction, the maximum penalties are reduced to imprisonment for a term not exceeding six months or a fine not exceeding the statutory maximum or both.[74] No civil sanction of contract unenforceability is provided for under s 47[75] nor is a civil claim available to a private investor who might have suffered loss, on the basis of s 62 of the Financial Services Act 1986.[76] However, the fitness and properness of an authorised person, found guilty of an offence under s 47, to continue to engage in investment business would

---

68   Sections 47(1) and (2) both refer to 'investments', which is to say investments falling within Part I of Schedule 1 FSA 1986. Section 47(1) also refers to an 'investment agreement', which expression is defined by s 44(9) FSA 1986.

69   Which seems derived from s 13 (as amended) of the Prevention of Fraud (Investments) Act 1958 (hereafter 'PF(I)A 1958'). The PF(I)A 1958 was repealed by the FSA 1986: see s 212(3) and Part I of Schedule 17 FSA 1986.

70   Which had no PF(I)A 1958 counterpart. Previously, wrongdoing in this area was prosecuted (if at all) under the aegis of conspiracy to defraud. See, for instance, *Scott v Brown, Doering McNab & Co* [1892] 2 QB 724, CA, which concerned an illegal share transaction

71   Which is to say, conduct creating a false or misleading impression as to the market in or value of investments.

72   Which is dealt with later in this Chapter 10. See paras 10-41 to 10-45, below.

73   Section 47(6)(a) FSA 1986.

74   Section 47(6)(b) FSA 1986.

75   Compare s 5 FSA 1986 which provides for the unenforceability of certain agreements where investment business has been carried on in breach of s 3 FSA 1986.

76   See also, s 62A FSA 1986 and the Financial Services Act 1986 (Restriction of Right of Action) Regulations 1991 (SI 1991/489). Section 61 FSA 1986 may however be applicable, leading to an injunction or a restitution order.

clearly be in question.[77] Also, an aggrieved investor might have an action at common law. This could, for instance, be for loss suffered through reliance on a fraudulent or negligent mis-statement. The person at fault might also have committed a common law offence, such as conspiring to defraud investors.[78]

Misleading statements

This offence may be committed by any person[79] who:

- makes a statement,[80] promise or forecast which he knows to be misleading, false or deceptive or dishonestly conceals any material facts;[81] or

- recklessly makes (whether or not dishonestly) a statement, promise or forecast which is misleading, false or deceptive.

In either case, the maker of the statement, promise or forecast or the concealer of the material facts is guilty of this offence if this is done for the purpose of inducing, or if he is reckless as to whether it may induce, another person[82] to do or to refrain from doing certain things. Those things are to enter or offer to enter into or to refrain from entering or offering to enter into an investment agreement[83] or to exercise or refrain from exercising any rights conferred by an investment.[84] There is no need for the inducement to be successful. It is also sufficient if the intention is to induce a course of action by someone other than the person to whom the statement[85] was made or from whom facts are concealed.[86] For example, a statement made to an investment adviser with a view to inducing his clients to act would be caught.

---

77 And see ss 25–30 FSA 1986 although persons directly authorised by the SIB are in the minority and have been discouraged by the SIB, potential applicants being directed towards one of the SROs.

78 See later in this Chapter 10 in paras 10-46 to 10-53.

79 Who, it should be noted, need not be a director or other officer of the financial concern involved nor need the person be acting in the course of carrying on investment business.

80 For instance, in an advertisement.

81 And this requires dishonesty on the part of the maker of the statement.

82 Whether or not the person to whom the statement was made or from whom the facts were concealed.

83 See s 44(9) FSA 1986 which contains a definition of 'investment agreement' for the purposes of the FSA 1986.

84 See Part I of Schedule 1 FSA 1986 which sets out the various categories of 'investments' for the purposes of the FSA 1986.

85 etc.

86 See s 47(1) FSA 1986, generally. In the context of insider dealing, this offence could be committed by a person who conceals price-sensitive information from a counterparty to induce him to deal, if the concealment is dishonest.

Territorial scope

10-19 Some territorial limits on the scope of this offence are imposed by the legislation.[87] Thus, for an offence to have been committed under the provisions outlined in para 10-18 above, the statement, promise or forecast must be made in or from the United Kingdom, or the facts must be concealed in or from the United Kingdom;[88] the person on whom the inducement is intended to or may have effect is in the United Kingdom;[89] or the investment agreement is or would be entered into or the rights conferred by the investment are or would be exercised in the United Kingdom.[90] For the offence of market manipulation[91] to be applicable, the act in question must be done, or the course of conduct must be engaged in, in the United Kingdom,[92] or the false or misleading impression must be created in the United Kingdom.[93]

Investment advertisements

10-20 Section 57 of the Financial Services Act 1986 imposes a strict regime of control over the issue in the United Kingdom of 'investment advertisements'. Unless one of the exceptions provided under or by virtue of s 58 applies, an investment advertisement can only be issued or caused to be issued in the United Kingdom by an authorised person unless its contents have first been approved for issue by an authorised person.[94] An authorised person so involved will be subject to certain controls and guidelines in relation to the issue and approval of investment advertisements imposed on it by the rules of its regulator.[95]

'Advertisements' and 'investment advertisements'

10-21 The expression 'investment advertisement' is defined by the combination of s 57(2) and s 207(2) of the Financial Services Act 1986.

---

87 See s 47(4) and (5) FSA 1986, further.
88 Section 47(4)(a) FSA 1986.
89 Section 47(4)(b) FSA 1986.
90 Section 47(4)(c) FSA 1986.
91 Section 47(2) FSA 1986. See paras 10-46 to 10-53 later in this Chapter 10.
92 Section 47(5)(a) FSA 1986.
93 Section 47(5)(b) FSA 1986.
94 Section 57(1) FSA 1986. And see SIB Guidance Release No 3/89 (published in July 1989).
95 Which will usually be one of the self-regulating organisations (or 'SROs'). As for the advertising regime of the SFA, see SFA Rules 5-9 (in relation to the issue and approval of advertisements), 5-12 (in relation to the issue or approval of advertisements for an overseas person) and 5-15 (in relation to fair and clear communications).

In general terms, advertising is the action or practice of drawing public attention to something.[96] Under s 207(2), an 'advertisement' for these purposes is said to include 'every form' of advertising, whether in a publication or 'in any other manner' and references to the issue of an advertisement are to be construed accordingly. Section 207(2) also sets out some examples of possible 'advertisements' which include notices, circulars, catalogues and exhibitions of pictures or photographic or cinematographic films. Advertisements may also be by way of sound broadcasting or television. The essence of advertising is that it is 'a bringing into notice'[97] and an advertisement is the means by which something is made known; it is a statement calling attention to something.[98] It is probably the case that, for these purposes, an 'advertisement' needs to be directed at more than one person. It is, however, accepted that oral or verbal statements or communications[99] can amount to advertisements and, in practical terms, almost any promotional item is capable of amounting to an 'advertisement' for these purposes.

The expression 'investment advertisement' is defined by s 57(2) of the Financial Services Act 1986 and, essentially, there are three main elements. Investment advertisements are advertisements which either:

- invite persons to enter or offer to enter into an investment agreement; or

- invite persons to exercise any rights conferred by an investment to acquire, dispose of, underwrite or convert an investment; or

- which contain information calculated to lead directly or indirectly to persons doing so.[100]

'Investments'

The expression 'investment', which is used in the definition of 'investment advertisement', includes all the categories of 'investments' set out in Part I of Schedule 1 to the Financial Services Act 1986.

---

96 See *Collins Dictionary of the English Language* (1979). To 'publish' is generally regarded as to make known to some person other than the originator.

97 See the *Compact Oxford English Dictionary* (2nd edn, 1991).

98 *ibid.*

99 Such as a speech by a company chairman at an Annual General Meeting or the views expressed by persons participating in a television or radio interview.

100 Section 57(2) FSA 1986.

'Investment agreement'

10-25   An 'investment agreement' is defined as meaning 'any agreement the making or performance of which by either party' constitutes an investment activity[101] or would do so apart from the various exclusions set out in Parts III and IV of Schedule 1.[102] An investment agreement will include any agreement relating to the buying, selling, subscription for or underwriting of investments.[103]

'Calculated'

10-26   Advertisements containing information 'calculated' to lead directly or indirectly to persons entering into an investment agreement or exercising certain rights conferred by an investment may also amount to investment advertisements.[104] The expression 'calculated' has been taken by regulators[105] to mean 'likely'. That is to say, they have adopted a test of asking whether something is 'likely' rather than whether it is intended. Of course, whether or not information is likely to lead to persons buying or selling shares,[106] is a question of fact and degree. However, if it is correct to adopt the 'likely' test, the motives of the person issuing or causing the advertisement to be issued are not of primary relevance and it would not be a defence for him to show that it was never his intention that the advertisement should have the effect of inducing persons, for instance, to buy or sell investments. The question would be whether it contained information 'likely' to have that effect. If it did, the advertisement would be an investment advertisement.

An 'idiot' test

10-27   Before and, indeed, just after s 57 of the Financial Services Act 1986 became operative,[107] it was felt that almost any informational material relating to a company could constitute an investment advertisement. In practice, this produced some strange results and led many in the City to

---

101 One of the activities set out in Part II of Schedule 1 to the FSA 1986.

102 Section 44(9) FSA 1986.

103 These matters amount to 'Dealing in investments', an investment activity set out in para 12 of Schedule 1 FSA 1986.

104 Section 57(2) FSA 1986. And see Janet Dine, 'The scope of s 57 of the Financial Services Act 1986', 10(7) Co Law 145–148.

105 Including the Securities and Investments Board.

106 Thus, 'Dealing in investments'.

107 The FSA 1986 entered the statute book on 7 November 1986 although, generally speaking, its main provisions did not become operative until later. There were a number of commencement dates in relation to s 57 FSA 1986, further: 29 April 1988 but also 29 May 1988, 29 July 1988 and 6 May 1988 (see SI 1988/740).

adopt a more practical approach, namely an 'idiot' test particularly with regard to company awareness or informational material. In its usual form, this test was whether investors generally could be expected to buy or sell shares on the strength of the advertisement in question[108] or whether it was simply possible that some idiot might do so.[109] The fact that one or two persons out of thousands presented with particular information might be induced to buy or sell shares as a result should not, in itself, be sufficient to turn an advertisement into an investment advertisement. The adoption of such a test has tended to eliminate most purely informational or 'awareness' material concerning a company[110] even in the run-up to a flotation.[111] In that context, it is likely that investors make their investment decision on the basis of the listing particulars or prospectus which is produced and not on the basis of 'lesser' material. It is also thought unlikely that a document containing historical financial information, which had already been released to the market, would constitute an investment advertisement by reason only of that information.

'But who is the issuer?'

Where an advertisement may amount to an investment advertisement, **10-28** an underlying question is: who is or will be its issuer? This is important because s 57(1) of the Financial Services Act 1986 provides[112] that no person, other than an authorised person, shall issue or cause to be issued an investment advertisement in the United Kingdom unless its contents have been approved by an authorised person. But what is meant by the expressions 'issue' or 'cause to be issued'. There are various relevant dictionary definitions of 'issue' in this context. It is 'the act of sending or giving out something'.[113] It also means 'to "come out" or be sent forth officially or publicly; to be published or emitted'.[114] On this basis, it seems generally accepted that to 'issue', for these purposes, means to 'make public' or to 'make known'; in practical terms, to issue is to publish to an audience. In many cases, however, it will not be particularly clear who has issued a particular investment advertisement. If, for instance, a merchant bank drafts an information memorandum for a client and sends it to interested parties on behalf of that client, which of

---

108 In which event, it might well fall within s 57(2) FSA 1986.

109 In which event, s 57(2) FSA 1986 should probably not be in point.

110 Which is to say, material simply telling the public what a company does and how it does it.

111 Although a 'pathfinder prospectus' probably would be caught.

112 Subject to certain important practical exceptions. See para 10-40 below.

113 See *Collins Dictionary of the English Language* (1979).

114 See the *Compact Oxford English Dictionary* (2nd edn, 1991).

them has 'issued' the memorandum: the merchant bank or its client? At the moment, this question is largely one of fact and degree, to be decided on the basis of the particular circumstances of each case.[115] In practice, if there is any doubt, the contents of the investment advertisement in question should be approved by an authorised person.

Issue or cause to be issued 'in the United Kingdom'

10-29   A further question is whether an investment advertisement has actually been issued in the United Kingdom. The position is clear where the advertisement relates to the United Kingdom and its preparation and actual publication take place within the United Kingdom. However, the position is much more complex where these matters occur partly within and partly outside the United Kingdom, in various combinations.

10-30   Where an advertisement created and prepared within the United Kingdom is published only outside the United Kingdom, commonsense might suggest that the advertisement was not thereby issued in the United Kingdom. However, if its publication was controlled from within the United Kingdom, it is arguable that the advertisement was caused to be issued in the United Kingdom and many take the view that an 'advertisement' is 'issued', or at least is 'caused to be issued', where the person 'putting out' the advertisement is present. Thus, a mail shot is issued where it is posted and a television or radio advertisement is issued where it is transmitted from. Accordingly, persons acting in the United Kingdom but directing their advertisements to a foreign audience may nevertheless be 'issuing' advertisements in the United Kingdom.

10-31   Where an advertisement prepared and created outside the United Kingdom is published in the United Kingdom, it is clear that it is capable of coming within the scope of s 57 of the Financial Services Act 1986. This was confirmed by the case of *SIB v Pantell SA and Another* (1990)[116] in which the defendants sent 'circular' advertisements from outside the United Kingdom to persons within the United Kingdom. The question before the court mainly concerned the right of action of the plaintiff to apply for injunctive relief restraining the defendants from dealing with their assets in the United Kingdom pending final determination of the matter. The injunction was granted as there was a strongly arguable case that the activities of the defendants amounted to the carrying on of investment business in the United Kingdom in breach of s 3 of the

---

115 In the 'information memorandum' scenario, relevant factors will include the nature of the instructions given by the client to its merchant bank. Also, whether the document specifies the basis on which it was prepared and is now being issued.

116 [1990] 1 Ch 426, HC.

Financial Services Act 1986. However, Sir Nicolas Browne-Wilkinson V-C felt an alternative and possibly clearer approach would have involved consideration of whether there had been breaches of s 57 which related specifically to advertisements.[117] In any such case involving potential wrongdoing by non-United Kingdom persons, there are likely to be formidable problems of enforcement.

If an advertisement is published outside the United Kingdom but is made available to persons within the United Kingdom, there are certain circumstances in which it will be treated as having been issued in the United Kingdom.[118] In particular, an advertisement or other information issued outside the United Kingdom will be treated as having been issued in the United Kingdom if it is directed to persons in the United Kingdom or is made available to them otherwise than in a newspaper, journal, magazine or other periodical publication published and circulating principally outside the United Kingdom or in a sound or television broadcast transmitted principally for reception outside the United Kingdom.[119] Advertisements published outside the United Kingdom can therefore fall within the ambit of s 57 in two instances:

10-32

- *First*, where the advertisement is 'directed to' persons in the United Kingdom. Whether this has occurred will depend on the circumstances of the case, the contents of the particular advertisement and, perhaps also, who a reasonable man would consider to be the intended targets of that advertisement. In essence, was the advertisement directed at persons in the United Kingdom? It seems clear that this requires more specific targeting than where an advertisement is simply 'made available to' such persons and also that the subject-matter of the promotion must be obtainable by persons in the United Kingdom. This seems likely to require some actual intention to reach the United Kingdom market by those behind the advertisement although the message or the investment opportunity probably need not be exclusively directed to persons in the United Kingdom. For example, an advertisement of an investment opportunity which can be taken up by persons within the European Union might be regarded as having been directed to persons in the United Kingdom. A disclaimer on an advertisement to the effect that the investment opportunity featured was not intended to be available to persons in the United Kingdom would be a helpful indicator as to whether or not the advertisement was 'directed to' persons in the United Kingdom. The advertisement might, however,

---

117 See [1990] 1 Ch 426 at 433.
118 See s 207(3) FSA 1986, generally.
119 Section 207(3) FSA 1986.

still be caught.

- This is because, *secondly*, an advertisement or other information issued outside the United Kingdom will be treated as if issued in the United Kingdom where it has been 'made available' to persons in the United Kingdom otherwise than in a periodical publication which is published outside the United Kingdom and which circulates principally outside the United Kingdom or in a broadcast transmitted principally for reception outside the United Kingdom. Thus, advertisements in foreign newspapers *prima facie* are not deemed to be issued in the United Kingdom, provided the newspapers are published and circulated principally outside the United Kingdom even if a small part of their circulation is in the United Kingdom.[120]

10-33   Putting to one side whether or not one of the exceptions to s 57 would be applicable, if a prospectus offering shares in a foreign company is published outside the United Kingdom but is distributed to certain United Kingdom clients by a United Kingdom merchant bank, then it will be deemed to have been issued in the United Kingdom. It will have been made available to persons in the United Kingdom.[121] The question then arises as to whether or not it was issued by the merchant bank concerned. If the bank simply distributed a few copies of a document prepared by someone else, commonsense would suggest that the document was not issued by that bank. Accordingly, in these circumstances, as the document was not issued by the bank and as its contents are to be made public in the United Kingdom, those contents would need to be approved by that bank in its capacity as an authorised person.[122]

Sanctions for breach of section 57

10-34   There are *criminal sanctions* for breach of s 57 of the Financial Services Act 1986. It is a criminal offence punishable on conviction on indictment by imprisonment for a term not exceeding two years or by a fine or by both.[123] On summary conviction, the penalties are imprisonment for a term not exceeding six months or a fine or both.[124] There is, however, a limited defence. In the interests of newspaper editors and the like, a person in the ordinary course of non-investment business who issues an

---

120 Unless they are 'directed to' persons in the United Kingdom. See s 207(3) FSA 1986.
121 See s 207(3) FSA 1986.
122 Or it would seem that there will be a breach of s 57(1) FSA 1986.
123 Section 57(3)(a) FSA 1986.
124 Section 57(3)(b) FSA 1986. But the fine cannot exceed the 'statutory maximum'.

advertisement to the order of another person will not in certain circumstances be guilty of an offence. He will however need to prove that he believed on reasonable grounds that such issue involved no breach of s 57.[125]

Civil sanctions may also be applicable in that investment agreements **10-35** or obligations resulting from the defaulting investment advertisement may not be enforceable by the issuer of the advertisement,[126] at the discretion of the court,[127] and the other party may be entitled to recover any money paid or property transferred and also to be compensated for any loss sustained by him as a result of having parted with such money or property.[128] The court may however allow the investment agreement or obligation in question to be enforced or the money paid or property transferred under it to be retained if the court is satisfied:

- that the person against whom enforcement is sought or who is seeking to recover the relevant money or property was not influenced (or not influenced to any material extent) by the advertisement in making his decision to enter into the agreement or as to the exercise of the rights in question;[129] or

- that the advertisement was not misleading and fairly stated any risks involved.[130]

Approval by an authorised person

There is no breach of s 57 of the Financial Services Act 1986 if an **10-36** investment advertisement is issued or if its contents have been approved for issue by an authorised person. In issuing or approving an investment advertisement, there will be a number of regulatory requirements applicable to the authorised person in question. It should however be noted that s 57 does not set out the steps which must be followed nor the standards which must be applied by that authorised person.

Authorisation can, of course, be obtained in various ways[131] and **10-37** authorised persons are required to conduct their investment business in accordance with the rules and regulations promulgated by the body which authorises or regulates them. The rationale for the requirement that investment advertisements must either be issued or approved by an

---

125 See s 57(4) FSA 1986, further.
126 Or the person who caused it to be issued.
127 See s 57(8) FSA 1986.
128 See ss 57(5), (6) and (7) FSA 1986, further.
129 Section 57(8)(a) FSA 1986.
130 See s 57(8)(b) FSA 1986, further.
131 See Chapter 2 above, further.

authorised person is that, in issuing or approving, the authorised person in question will be subject to an advertising regime devised by his regulator and designed to protect the investing public.

10-38   Most persons involved professionally in the securities industry will be authorised, or employed by a person authorised, by a self-regulating organisation:[132] the Securities and Futures Authority.[133] In relation to advertising and marketing, there are specific provisions in Rule 5-9 of the SFA Rules governing the issue and approval of advertisements.[134]

10-39   Rule 5-9(1) of the SFA Rules sets out the basic standards which must be applied by an SFA member firm in issuing or in approving an investment advertisement. Where an SFA member issues or approves an investment advertisement, it must apply appropriate expertise[135] and be able to show that it believes on reasonable grounds that the advertisement is fair and not misleading.[136] Notwithstanding these requirements, it has not always been common practice for SFA members to conduct a formal verification process before approving the contents of an investment advertisement. They should, however, take all reasonable steps to ensure that the information contained in the relevant advertisement is fair and not misleading, that the advertisement contains no material errors and omits no material facts and that all expressions of opinion contained therein are made on reasonable grounds. The advantage of formal verification is that the notes used can prove the extent of the verification process. As a minimum, the following procedures should be carried out to enable the issuer or approver involved to show, if necessary, that it had reasonable grounds for considering an advertisement to be fair and not misleading:

- Those officers or employees taking part in the verification process should make detailed file notes of all meetings and conversations.

- All documents produced to verify statements in an investment advertisement should be carefully stored, together with a note of their source.

---

132 See Chapter 2 above, further.

133 The successor SRO to TSA and the AFBD.

134 Which may have to contain certain specified matters (see SFA Rules 5-9(7) and (8)) and also certain risk warnings (see SFA Rule 5-9(9)). See also SFA Rule 5-1(4) Rules as to the application of these provisions.

135 In issuing or approving an investment advertisement, an SFA member is required to apply appropriate expertise. It is therefore important that persons with sufficient experience are involved in the preparation and approval process. A firm should make a careful record of the persons so involved and should also note the expertise upon which it has relied.

136 See SFA Rule 5-9(1), further. See also SFA Rule 7-23(4) which provides that, where a firm is required by a rule to take reasonable steps or similar measures, the onus will be on the SFA member firm to show that it has taken those steps or measures. To prove that it has taken reasonable steps, a firm will therefore need to obtain some evidence to show what steps were taken (as to obtaining and verifying the accuracy of the material) and what other factors were taken into account in preparing or approving the advertisement.

- Before an investment advertisement is issued, the authorised person involved should obtain a certified copy of board minutes which show that the directors of the client, having given due consideration to the matter, believed the advertisement to be fair and not misleading, to contain no material errors and to omit no material facts and that all expressions of opinion contained therein were made on reasonable grounds.

'Exceptions' from section 57

There are certain scenarios in which it is provided that s 57 of the Financial Services Act 1986 will not be applicable to investment advertisements issued or caused to be issued in accordance with their terms. That is to say, the investment advertisements will not need to be issued or caused to be issued or have their contents approved for issue by an authorised person. These 'exceptions' from the restrictions on advertising, most of which are detailed and thus beyond the scope of this Chapter, are set out in s 58 of the Financial Services Act 1986 and also in subordinate legislation[137] made pursuant to s 58 of that Act.[138]

---

137 Up to 19 June 1995, there were five relevant statutory instruments. They were the Financial Services Act 1986 (Investment Advertisements) (Exemptions) Order 1988 (SI 1988/316); the Financial Services Act 1986 (Investment Advertisements) (Exemptions) (No 2) Order 1988 (SI 1988/716); the Financial Services Act 1986 (Investment Advertisements) (Exemptions) Order 1990 (SI 1990/27); the Financial Services Act 1986 (Investment Advertisements) (Exemptions) Order 1992 (SI 1992/274); and the Financial Services Act 1986 (Investment Advertisements) (Exemptions) (No 2) Order 1992 (SI 1992/813). With effect from 19 June 1995, those five instruments were consolidated and replaced by the Financial Services Act 1986 (Investment Advertisements) (Exemptions) Order 1995 (SI 1995/1266) and the Financial Services Act 1986 (Investment Advertisements) (Exemptions) (No 2) Order 1995 (SI 1995/1536). See paras 2-40 to 2-71 in Chapter 2 above, particularly para 2-48, further. See also the Investment Services Regulations 1995 (SI 1995/3275). See, finally, the Financial Services Act 1986 (Investment Advertisements) (Exceptions) Order 1996 (SI 1996/1586) which revoked and recreated SI 1995/1266 with some amendments.

138 See ss 58(3)–(5) FSA 1986.

MARKET MANIPULATION

The basic offence

10-41   As discussed earlier,[139] s 47 of the Financial Services Act 1986 sets out two categories of offence. Section 47(2)[140] concerns market manipulation. That is to say, it relates to conduct creating a false or misleading impression as to the market in or the price or value of investments. It should be noted that the 'section 47' offences are not mutually exclusive; a misleading statement about securities falling within s 47(1) could also create a false or misleading impression as to their value, thus falling within s 47(2) as well.[141]

The penalties

10-42   Breach of s 47(2) will amount to a criminal offence. A person found guilty of such an offence can be liable, on conviction on indictment, to imprisonment for a term not exceeding seven years or to a fine or to both.[142] On summary conviction, the maximum penalties are imprisonment for a term not exceeding six months or a fine or both.[143] No civil sanction of contract unenforceability is expressly provided for under s 47;[144] nor is a civil claim available to a private investor who might have suffered loss by virtue of s 62 of the Financial Services Act 1986.[145] However, the fitness and properness of an authorised person, found guilty of an offence under s 47, to continue to engage in investment business would clearly be in question and would presumably be reviewed by the relevant regulator. It should also be noted that, under s 61 of the Financial Services Act 1986,[146] an

---

139   In paras 10-16 to 10-19, above. As noted there, s 47(1) FSA 1986 (which seems derived from s 13 Prevention of Fraud (Investments) Act 1958), covers misleading statements, promises or forecasts which can amount to the first of the s 47 offences.

140   Which had no predecessor in the Prevention of Fraud (Investments) Act 1958 but see, for instance, s 70 Securities Industry Act 1970 (NSW). For a comparative treatment, see How Chih Lee, 'Market manipulation in the United States of America and in the United Kingdom' (parts 1 and 2) (1993) 14(5) Co Law 84–89 and 14(7) at 123–29.

141   See s 47 FSA 1986, generally. See also Alan Au, 'Stock market manipulation after the Financial Services Act 1986' (1989)4 (2) JIBL 53–64. And see 'SIB looks to the SEC', *The Times* (Pennington column), 8 March 1994.

142   Section 47(6)(a) FSA 1986.

143   Section 47(6)(b) FSA 1986.

144   Compare ss 3 and 5 FSA 1986.

145   Section 62(1) FSA 1986 and see the Financial Services Act 1986 (Restriction of Right of Action) Regulations 1991 (SI 1991/489).

146   Which relates to injunctions and restitution orders.

application could be made to the court[147] to prevent, or for a restitution order relating to profits accruing from, a breach of s 47.[148]

Market manipulation

The context in which the separate offence of 'market manipulation' may be committed is where a person does any act or engages in any course of conduct which creates a false or misleading impression as to the market in, the price or the value of any investments. The offence will be committed if the person does so for the purpose of creating that false or misleading impression and of thereby inducing another person to acquire, dispose of, subscribe for or underwrite the investments in question or to refrain from doing so or to exercise or refrain from exercising any rights conferred by those investments.[149]

10-43

A defence

There is a defence,[150] if the person in question can prove that he reasonably believed that his act or conduct would not create a false or misleading impression as to the market in, the price or the value of any investments.[151] This will depend on the circumstances and the defence may not necessarily be applicable simply because a particular course of conduct flows or results from an accepted or established market practice. It may not be sufficient for this defence to say, effectively, that 'everyone else does it and has done for years'.

10-44

---

147 In practice, by the Securities and Investments Board. See s 114(4) FSA 1986 and also arts 3 and 4 of and paras 7–9 of Schedule 1 and para 2 of Schedule 2 to the Financial Services Act 1986 (Delegation) Order 1987 (SI 1987/942). See also art 3(1) of the Financial Services Act 1986 (Delegation) Order 1991 (SI 1991/200).

148 See s 61 FSA 1986, further.

149 See s 47(2) FSA 1986. In the general context of securities law, see also 'Market Manipulation and Insider Dealing: Implications for Underwriters and Issuers', produced by City solicitors Slaughter & May, (1989) 3 (10) *Corporate Briefing* 248–250. For comment on the Sumitomo copper 'affair', which may yet be shown to have involved market manipulation or other 'market' offences, see 'Copper meltdown' by Garth Alexander and John Woples, *The Sunday Times*, 16 June 1996. Also, 'Terror of copper trader' by Garth Alexander, *The Sunday Times*, 30 June 1996. Criminal investigations are presently underway both in the UK and the USA. See also 'Up to a point, Lord Copper', *The Times* (Pennington column), 19 June 1996.

150 In proceedings brought against any person for a breach of s 47(2) FSA 1986.

151 Section 47(3) FSA 1986.

Territorial limits

10-45   There are some territorial limits as to the scope of this offence. It will only apply where the act in question is done or the course of conduct is engaged in in the United Kingdom[152] or the false or misleading impression is created in the United Kingdom.[153]

CONSPIRACY TO DEFRAUD

Offences of dishonesty

10-46   In very general terms, there are two basic types of offence which involve dishonesty: those which involve the invasion and appropriation of an interest of some sort[154] and those which simply involve dishonest behaviour of some sort whether or not it produces a desired result.[155] Conspiracy falls into the second category.

Conspiracy, statutory conspiracy and conspiracy to defraud

10-47   One of the inchoate offences,[156] 'conspiracy' has been defined as an agreement of two or more to do an unlawful act or a lawful act by unlawful means.[157] The *actus reus* of a conspiracy must therefore involve an agreement of some sort, between the parties, to commit an offence, and the agreement needs to be made apparent by words or actions. As an agreement must be present,[158] the *mens rea* of a conspiracy may be

---

152 Section 47(5)(a) FSA 1986.

153 Section 47(5)(b) FSA 1986.

154 Such as theft, which involves a dishonest appropriation of property belonging to another coupled with the intention of permanently depriving that other of the property in question. 'Thief' and 'steal' are construed accordingly: see s 1(1) Theft Act 1968.

155 Such as a conspiracy to defraud, the concoction by a person of a fraudulent undertaking in collaboration with another. Following the acquittals of Kevin and Ian Maxwell in January 1996, much doubt was expressed over the appropriateness of charging these offences in the context of complicated commercial arrangements. See, for instance, 'In the dock', the leading article in *The Times*, 20 January 1996. Many have suggested that civil proceedings would be more appropriate and perhaps easier for the 'prosecuting' authorities to bring to a successful conclusion. The image and reputation of the Serious Fraud Office has been much maligned notwithstanding internal reorganisation. See 'Dented image brought to book' by Jon Ashworth and Robert Miller, *The Times*, 9 April 1996. Its future may depend on the outcome of further high profile cases. Kevin Maxwell faced further charges resulting from the collapse of the 'Maxwell' empire. See *R v Lord Chancellor, ex p Maxwell*, Times Law Report, 27 June 1996, QBD. Those further charges were halted by the court in September 1996 with formal acquittals being entered and further criticism of the SFO resulting. See 'Serious farce', *The Times*, 20 September 1996.

156 Along with incitement and attempt.

157 *Per* Lord Denman in *Jones* (1832) 4 B & Ad 345 at 349.

158 See, for instance, *Walker* [1962] CLR 458.

difficult to isolate as an agreement will inevitably result from some sort of mental operation to reach it. A shared intention as to the end result will be sufficient although recklessness may be enough.[159]

The Criminal Law Act 1977[160] created an offence of 'statutory conspiracy', effectively limiting conspiracy to agreements for the commission of crime. Generally speaking, it provided[161] that a statutory conspiracy would be committed by two or more persons agreeing to a course of action which, if carried out, would involve the commission of a substantive offence by one or more of them.[162] The legislative intention seems to have been to abolish the offence of conspiracy at common law[163] with the exception of conspiracy to defraud which was specifically preserved and is not limited to agreements for the commission of crime.[164] Conspiracy to defraud remains a common law offence and, effectively, is an open-ended form of conspiracy. An agreement to commit an offence which involves fraud[165] will be a conspiracy to defraud.[166] In many ways, it is a safety-net offence for criminal prosecutors where a substantive offence of dishonesty is not, or not obviously, involved. However, conspiracy to defraud may be charged in circumstances where the agreed course of conduct would have involved a substantive offence.[167] The prosecution is not obliged to bring a charge of statutory conspiracy. The conspiracy may be prosecuted at common law or under the relevant statute.

10-48

---

159 See *Churchill v Walton* [1967] 2 AC 224; also *Allsop* (1977) 64 Cr App R 29.

160 1977 c 45 (hereafter 'CLA 1977').

161 In s 1 CLA 1977.

162 See ss 1(1), (2) and 5(1) CLA 1977. The substantive offence might, for instance, be theft.

163 Which was the effect of s 5(1) CLA 1977.

164 See s 5(2) CLA 1977. Conspiracy to defraud was, however, to be reviewed by the Law Commission to see what changes might need to be made, to avoid loopholes, if it was abolished. See Law Commission Working Paper No 56, *Conspiracy to Defraud* (1974) and *Conspiracy and Criminal Law Reform*, Law Com No 76 (1976) at paras 1.14 to 1.16. The Law Commission has subsequently recommended that conspiracy to defraud be preserved as an offence for a further period whilst a general review of offences of dishonesty is carried out: see *Conspiracy to Defraud*, Law Com No 228 (1994).

165 Such as theft, but there need not be a substantive offence.

166 See *Scott v Metropolitan Police Commissioner* [1974] 3 All ER 1032; also [1975] AC 819.

167 Where the agreement in question was made on or after 20 July 1987. See s 12 Criminal Justice Act 1987 which reversed the decision of the House of Lords in *R v Ayres* [1984] AC 447. As explained in *R v Cooke* [1986] AC 909. In relation to statutory conspiracy and conspiracy to defraud, see also RD Taylor, 'Distinctive Conspiracies' (1987) 103 LQR 14–19.

The ambit of 'fraud' in conspiracy to defraud

10-49   There is a wide ambit to the offence of conspiracy to defraud. Normally, in general terms, fraud is taken to mean a false pretence or other deception operating on the mind of a victim. But where conspiracy to defraud is in point, 'fraud' can also cover a surreptitious taking of property without deception.[168] There may be insufficient deception to amount to a substantive offence, yet the persons involved may still be guilty of conspiracy to defraud. A useful statement of the basis and ambit of conspiracy to defraud was made[169] in *Scott v Metropolitan Police Commissioner*,[170] where it was said that:

> ... it is clearly the law that an agreement by two or more by dishonesty to deprive a person of something which is his or to which he is or would be or might be entitled and an agreement by two or more by dishonesty to injure some proprietary right of his, suffices to constitute the offence of conspiracy to defraud.[171]

The object of the conspiracy

10-50   The potential width of this offence can be seen from the fact that the relevant agreement need not be to commit a substantive offence such as theft. For instance, in one case, the defendants used the facilities of their employer to dye items to profit themselves and not their employer. They were convicted of conspiracy to defraud their employer of the profit even though the employer had no proprietary interest in the profit capable of being 'stolen'.[172] The agreement may instead be to cause another person to act contrary to his public duty, for instance by granting an official licence of some sort.[173]

Relevance in securities law

10-51   Where a conspiracy is simply to obtain property dishonestly and that object is achieved, it is perhaps more usual for any subsequent criminal charge to be that of theft or perhaps that of obtaining property by deception. A charge of conspiracy to defraud will be relevant where there

---

168 *Per* Viscount Dilhorne in *Scott* [1975] AC 819 at 837–838.

169 Again by Viscount Dilhorne.

170 [1975] AC 819.

171 [1974] 3 All ER 1032 at 1039.

172 See *Button* (1848) 11 QB 929.

173 See *Welham v Director of Public Prosecutions* [1960] 1 All ER 805. See also, *Board of Trade v Owen* [1957] 1 All ER 411, which concerned an export licence.

has been a conspiracy dishonestly to obtain a pecuniary advantage other than property. An example would involve the making of a dishonest profit from the property of another by two or more wrongdoers. This is what happened in the case of *Scott v Metropolitan Police Commissioner*[174] which involved a large-scale conspiracy to persuade cinema employees to hand over films that were being shown. The films were copied in breach of copyright and then returned whilst the pirated copies were distributed commercially. It was held by the House of Lords that a charge of conspiracy to defraud the owners of the copyrights would lie. The scheme was fraudulent because its purpose was to make a profit from the unauthorised use of the property, when the exploitation of this use was part of the property right. A further example, concerning company directors, may be found in the case of *Sinclair*.[175] In that case, the directors passed over all of the assets of their company without taking any security. In the circumstances, they were found to be guilty of a conspiracy to defraud the company, its shareholders and its creditors. The directors agreed dishonestly to take a risk with the assets of the company by using them in a manner which was known not to be in the best interests of the company and to be prejudicial to its minority shareholders.

10-52

In very general terms, a charge of conspiracy to defraud has frequently been attractive to prosecutors because of its potential width, particularly in complicated swindles where commission of the relevant offence may only have been part of the scam. Essentially, it has been used to supplement the provisions governing the substantive offences of dishonesty. In simpler cases, where the relevant agreement involves a substantive offence, they would normally bring a charge of statutory conspiracy. In practice, it is perhaps unusual for an indictment to contain a conspiracy charge in relation to an offence together with a further charge for that offence.[176]

Penalties for conspiracy

10-53

If a person is found guilty of conspiracy to defraud, which remains a common law offence, he may be sentenced to imprisonment for a

---

174 [1975] AC 819; [1974] 3 All ER 1032. For these purposes, the important case of *Ghosh* [1982] QB 1053 is relevant to the question of whether there has been 'dishonesty'. Essentially, the question seems to be one of fact as to whether (i) what was done was dishonest according to the ordinary standards of reasonable and honest people and (ii) the defendant must have realised that what he was doing was dishonest according to those standards. See also *Wai Yu-tsang v R* [1992] 1 AC 269.

175 [1968] 3 All ER 241.

176 See *R v Jones* (1974) 59 Cr App R 120, CA, in relation to the joinder of charges. Essentially, a conspiracy charge combined with a charge for the relevant substantive offence may only be acceptable in certain circumstances if it can also be justified by the prosecution. See *R v Landy* [1981] 1 WLR 355 as to the particulars of the offence required to be set out by the Crown and *R v Hancock, R v Warner* and *R v Michael* [1996] Times Law Report, 11 July 1996, CA, further.

maximum of 10 years and/or a fine. As for statutory conspiracy, a person found guilty may be fined and/or sent to prison for a term not exceeding the maximum for which he could be imprisoned for committing the offence to which the conspiracy relates.[177]

THEFT

The basic definition

10-54   It must be appreciated that it is not possible to do more than merely outline the relevant law relating to theft in the paragraphs which follow. There is, however, a basic definition of the offence. A person is guilty of theft if he dishonestly appropriates property belonging to another with the intention of permanently depriving that other of it and the expressions 'thief' and 'steal' are to be construed on that basis.[178] It is also immaterial whether such an appropriation is made with a view to gain or for the personal benefit of the thief.[179] In the context of financial services and securities law, there have been a number of examples of persons working in the securities industry where theft has been an issue; for instance, financial advisers who have or are alleged to have stolen money from their customers.[180]

---

177 See s 12 Criminal Justice Act 1987 (hereafter 'CJA 1987') and also s 3 CLA 1977.

178 Section 1(1) Theft Act 1968 (hereafter 'TA 1968').

179 Section 1(2) TA 1968.

180 An example from the corporate world where theft was charged concerned Ernest Saunders, the former Guinness chief, who was convicted of false accounting and theft and sentenced to imprisonment for five years although released after serving about one-third of that term. The European Commission on Human Rights, however, subsequently ruled that he had been denied a fair trial as the methods used to secure evidence from him were oppressive and he was in effect forced to incriminate himself as a result of an investigation by the Department of Trade and Industry into the takeover bid for Distillers by Guinness in 1985. See various reports, including *The Times* , 19 September 1994. His convictions, and those of his fellow defendants, were reviewed. See Note 155 to Chapter 8, above, further. In contrast, George Walker, the former chairman and chief executive of Brent Walker, was acquitted of theft and false accounting charges after a trial lasting almost five months. His acquittal led to further criticism of the Serious Fraud Office. False accounting is an offence by virtue of s 17 Theft Act 1968 and can, on conviction on indictment, lead to imprisonment for a term not exceeding seven years. It is committed where a person dishonestly, with a view to gain for himself or another or with intent to cause loss to another, destroys, defaces, conceals or falsifies any account or any record or document made or required for any accounting purpose. It may also be committed where such a person, in furnishing information for any purpose, produces or makes use of any account which to his knowledge is or may be misleading, false or deceptive in a material particular. See s 17 TA 1968, further.

The penalty for theft

On conviction on indictment, a person found guilty of theft may be sent to prison for a term not exceeding seven years.[181] Theft may however be tried summarily or on indictment.

10-55

The *actus reus* of theft

In essence, the potential ambit of this offence is wide: there needs to be an appropriation of property belonging to another. Various factual matters must therefore be satisfied.

10-56

There must, for instance, be 'property' involved which is capable of being 'appropriated'. 'Property' is defined as including money and all other property, real or personal, including things in action and other intangible property.[182] With certain exceptions,[183] all 'property' may be stolen.

10-57

The 'property' involved must 'belong to another'. For these purposes, property is regarded as belonging to any person having possession or control of it or having any proprietary right or interest.[184] Where, for instance, a person receives property from another and is under an obligation[185] to that other to retain and deal with that property or its proceeds in a particular way, the property or proceeds are regarded as belonging to the other person.[186]

10-58

A thief must also 'appropriate' the property and any assumption by a person of the rights of an owner amounts to an appropriation.[187] This

10-59

---

181 Section 7 TA 1968; see, also, s 26(1) CJA 1991. The maximum was initially 10 years.

182 Section 4(1) TA 1968. For instance, see *R v Preddy* [1995] CLR 564, CA in relation to the electronic transfer of money. But see also *R v Preddy, R v Slade* and *R v Dhillon* [1996] *The Times* Law Report, 11 July, HL.

183 See ss 4(2)–(4) TA 1968 which relate to land, wild mushrooms (etc) and wild creatures.

184 Section 5(1) TA 1968. See s 5(2) in relation to trust property and s 5(4) in relation to property received by mistake. For an illustration of the equitable interests capable of being 'stolen', see *Clowes (No 2)* [1994] 2 All ER 316, CA and also comment by Jonathan Fisher in (1994) 5 JIBL 212. In that case, it was held that where a trustee mixes trust money with his own, the beneficiaries are entitled to a first charge on the mixed fund.

185 Perhaps as an agent, which would be the position of a broker acting for a customer. Compare *Hall* [1973] QB 126 (which related to a travel agent) and *Hallam and Blackburn* [1995] Crim LR 323 (which concerned payments to investment advisers for investment).

186 Section 5(3) TA 1968.

187 Section 3(1) TA 1968. See, by way of background material, the Criminal Law Revision Committee, Eighth Report (1966), *Theft and Related Offences*, para 34. And then consider *Lawrence v Metropolitan Police Commissioner* [1972] AC 626, *Morris* [1984] AC 320 and then *Gomez* [1993] AC 442. For comment, see [1993] Crim LR at 305. See also *Gallasso* [1993] Crim LR 459.

includes any later assumption of a right to property[188] where a person has come by it without stealing it.[189] Generally speaking, an 'appropriation' was usually thought to be something done in relation to property by a non-owner that only the owner could lawfully do or authorise, such as taking, destroying or offering it for sale.

The *mens rea* for theft

10-60   Generally speaking, an appropriation of property belonging to another will only amount to theft if it is done dishonestly and the thief also intends to deprive that other permanently of his property.[190]

10-61   The intention to deprive another permanently of his property is an essential constituent element of the *mens rea* of theft. There need be no permanent deprivation in fact, but the intention must be there. It is also provided that a person appropriating property belonging to another without meaning the other permanently to lose the thing itself will nevertheless be regarded as having the intention of permanently depriving the other of it if his intention is to treat the thing as his own to dispose of regardless of the rights of the other.[191] A lending or borrowing of such property may be sufficient to be so regarded if, but only if, it is for a period and in circumstances making it equivalent to an outright taking or disposal.[192]

10-62   The appropriation in question must also be 'dishonest' and this will need to be established by the prosecution. Essentially, the defendant must know that he is appropriating property belonging to someone else or be reckless in doing so. The Theft Act 1968 did not attempt a complete definition of 'dishonesty'. Instead, it provides certain circumstances in which an appropriation of property belonging to another will not be regarded as dishonest.[193] These scenarios are where the person in question appropriates that property in the belief: (1) that he has the legal

---

188 By keeping it or dealing with it as owner.

189 Whether innocently or not. Section 3(1) TA 1968. For an elegant critique of what seems to be the present position, see *The Theft Acts* by Edward Griew (7th edn, 1995) at paras 2-60 to 2-96.

190 See s 1(1) TA 1968.

191 See s 6(1) TA 1968. For some background material on this provision, see JR Spencer in [1977] Crim LR at 653. For some criticism, see *The Theft Acts* by Edward Griew, *op cit*, paras 2-102 *et seq*. For some judicial comment, see *Lloyd* [1985] QB 829 at 836, CA, which concerned the 'borrowing' of films for the production of pirated copies. This was held not to be theft.

192 Section 6(1) TA 1968.

193 See s 2(1) TA 1968.

right to do so, on behalf of himself or a third party;[194] (2) that the other person would consent if he knew of the appropriation and its circumstances;[195] or, (3) unless the property came to him as trustee or personal representative, that the person to whom the property belongs cannot be discovered by taking reasonable steps.[196] Essentially, these are circumstances in which most people would not regard an appropriation of property as being 'dishonest'. As for other scenarios, the question of 'dishonesty' is one of fact and not of law. In reaching an answer, the court will have to consider whether what was done was dishonest according to the ordinary standards of reasonable and honest people.[197]

Dishonesty and the intention to repay money

The Theft Act 1968 provides that an appropriation by a person of property belonging to another may be dishonest notwithstanding that the person is willing to pay for the property.[198] Also, it is immaterial whether an appropriation is made with a view to gain or for the benefit of the thief himself.[199] However, if a person who is in control of a fund wrongfully appropriates money, intending to repay it and being certain that he will be able to repay it so as to cause no loss or inconvenience to the owner, a jury may find that he has not been dishonest. There may be other cases, where money has been taken with the intention of repaying it, in which a defendant may be found not to have been dishonest. An important case was that of *Feely*[200] who was the manager of a betting shop who took £30 from the till to lend to his father. The Court of Appeal held that whether or not he had been dishonest was a question of fact for the jury to decide and, in doing so, jurors should apply '... the current standards of ordinary decent people ...'.[201] 'Dishonesty' was an ordinary word which should be left to a jury to interpret.

10-63

---

194 Section 2(1)(a) TA 1968.

195 Section 2(1)(b) TA 1968. Which means all the relevant circumstances. See *Lawrence* [1971] 1 QB 373 at 377.

196 Section 2(1)(c) TA 1968. Consider the position of a person finding lost property.

197 Also, were the facts as the defendant believed them to be? There is a succinct and characteristic proposition formulated by Glanville Williams in his *Textbook of Criminal Law* (Stevens & Sons) at p 661, but based on s 2(1) TA 1968 and on the decision of the Court of Appeal in *Feely* [1973] 1 All ER 341, CA. But see now *Ghosh* [1982] QB 1053.

198 Section 2(2) TA 1968.

199 Section 1(2) TA 1968.

200 [1973] 1 All ER 341, CA.

201 [1973] 1 All ER 341 at 345, CA. The leading case on 'dishonesty' is that of *Ghosh* [1982] QB 1053 and see para 10-62 above, but it can be seen that the factual questions for the court are, to some extent, derived from *Feely*. For some comment, see DW Elliott in [1976] Crim LR at 707.

OBTAINING PROPERTY BY DECEPTION

The basic offence

10-64 The offence of obtaining property by deception replaced the former offence of obtaining property by false pretenses. It is now the case that a person who by any deception dishonestly obtains property belonging to another, with the intention of permanently depriving the other of it, will on conviction on indictment be liable to imprisonment for a term not exceeding 10 years.[202] For these purposes, a person is regarded as 'obtaining' property if he obtains ownership, possession or control of it. 'Obtain', for these purposes, also includes obtaining for another or

10-65 enabling another to obtain or to retain.[203]

The basic requirements of this offence are therefore that there must be a deception which may be deliberate or reckless as to a matter of fact or law, however effected. The defendant must obtain property which belongs to another. The obtaining must be by virtue of the deception, it must be dishonest and it must be underpinned by an intention to deprive the owner permanently.

The deception

10-66

To most people, a 'deception' is usually defined as 'the act of deceiving or the state of being deceived' and to 'deceive' is 'to mislead by misrepresentation or lies'.[204] For the purposes of this offence, 'deception' is said to mean any deception whether deliberate or reckless by words or conduct as to fact or as to law, including a deception as to the present intentions of the person using the deception or any other person.[205] Such a deception will usually be as to fact and may be regarded as words or conduct producing a mistaken belief, such as where a customer orders a meal in a restaurant and the waiter takes his order and serves him food believing he will pay. Such a customer is representing by implication that he will pay the bill before leaving the restaurant and that representation continues until the bill is paid.[206] In very general terms,

---

202 See s 15(1) TA 1968.   203   Section 15(2) TA 1968.

204 See *Collins Dictionary of the English Language* (1979). The *Compact Oxford English Dictionary* (2nd edn, 1991) defines 'deception' as 'that which deceives; a piece of trickery; a cheat, sham'.

205 Section 15(4) TA 1968.

206 See *Director of Public Prosecutions v Ray* [1974] AC 370, HL. However, in that case, there was no offence of obtaining property by deception under s 15 TA 1968 because the intention of the defendant not to pay was only formed after the meal had been eaten. Such a defendant would now be charged with 'making off without payment'. See s 3 TA 1978.

'deception' is perhaps similar to the concept of 'deceit' in the law of tort and that of 'fraud' in the law of contract.

For the commission of this offence, the representation in question must be false. If it happens to be true, there will have been no deception. Any such deception may however be deliberate or made recklessly.[207] The deceiver may either have intended or have been reckless as to the deceit. In cases of false representation, which are thought to be the most common form of deception, the deceiver must either have known that his representation was untrue or have made the representation without knowing whether or not it was true. To be 'reckless' generally requires more than mere negligence.

10-67

The obtaining of the property

The aim of this offence is to punish deceptions made to obtain property.[208] It does not penalise deceptions which do not result in some obtaining of property by the defendant or another. For these purposes, a person is treated as 'obtaining' property if he obtains ownership, possession or control of it. 'Obtain' includes obtaining for another or enabling another to obtain or to retain.[209]

10-68

The obtaining must be caused by the deception. A defendant will not be guilty of this offence unless there is a causal connection between the deception and the obtaining. The deception must therefore have an effect on the mind of the victim, inducing him to act in reliance on the deception. Essentially, would the victim have done what he did had he known he was being deceived?[210] If the property in question is owned by a company, this offence can still be committed if the deception is aimed at a director or some other manager employed by the company. If a director of a company simply misappropriates property belonging to his employer, he may be guilty of this offence if he has deceived another officer of the company.[211]

10-69

---

207 See s 15(4) TA 1968. In this context, 'recklessness' is not thought to be a commonly occurring issue. See *Feeny* (1991) 94 Cr App R 1 at 6 and *The Theft Acts* by Edward Griew, *op cit*, pp 170–171.

208 See s 4(1) TA 1968, but note s 34(1) TA 1968. This offence may be committed with regard to any kind of property which is capable of transfer from one to another. In this regard, see *R v Preddy, R v Slade* and *R v Dhillon* [1996] Times Law Report, 11 July, HL, in relation to the making of payments between two bank accounts. It was held that no identifiable property passed from payer to payee whether payments were made telegraphically, electronically or by cheque.

209 See s 15(2) TA 1968.

210 See *Lambie* (1980) 71 Cr App R 350 and [1982] AC 449 and also *Metropolitan Police Commissioner v Charles* [1977] AC 177. As to causation, see *King and Stockwell* [1987] QB 547.

211 And see s 18 TA 1968.

10-70   It is also the case that the deception must come before any obtaining of the property in question. In one case, the defendant ordered petrol and, on being asked by the pump attendant whether it was to be charged to his firm, said that it should be so charged. At that stage, he represented that the car was being used for business purposes. It was held on appeal that the defendant was not guilty of this offence on the basis of that representation as he had already obtained the petrol.[212] The representation did not precede the obtaining.

The dishonesty

10-71   The *mens rea* for this offence requires a deception which was deliberate or reckless. The property in question must have been obtained dishonestly and this must also have been accompanied by an intention to deprive the owner permanently. For these purposes, s 6 of the Theft Act 1968 applies in relation to any such intention with the necessary adaptation of the reference to appropriating.[213] It will be for juries to decide questions of dishonesty employing the standards of ordinary people[214] and it is the 'obtaining' of property that must have been dishonest. It should be noted that the issues of 'dishonesty' and of 'deception', in a case where the defendant is charged with this offence of obtaining property by deception, must each be looked at in its own right. For a conviction, there must be findings of dishonesty as to the obtaining and intention or recklessness as to the deception.[215]

---

212 See *Collis-Smith* [1971] Crim LR 716, CA.

213 Section 15(3) TA 1968. And see *The Theft Acts* by Edward Griew, *op cit*, pp 172–174.

214 Essentially, on the basis adopted from *Ghosh* [1982] QB 1053. For a conviction, what the defendant did must have been dishonest according to the ordinary standards of reasonable and honest people and he must have realised it was dishonest according to those standards.

215 See *Feeny* (1991) 94 Cr App R 1 at 6.

APPENDICES

RELEVANT STATUTORY MATERIALS

APPENDIX A

CRIMINAL JUSTICE ACT 1993 (1993 c 36)

PART V
INSIDER DEALING

The offence of insider dealing

52. The offence

(1) An individual who has information as an insider is guilty of insider dealing if, in the circumstances mentioned in subsection (3), he deals in securities that are price-affected securities in relation to the information.

(2) An individual who has information as an insider is also guilty of insider dealing if –

    (a) he encourages another person to deal in securities that are (whether or not that other knows it) price-affected securities in relation to the information, knowing or having reasonable cause to believe that the dealing would take place in the circumstances mentioned in subsection (3); or

    (b) he discloses the information, otherwise than in the proper performance of the functions of his employment, office or profession, to another person.

(3) The circumstances referred to above are that the acquisition or disposal in question occurs on a regulated market, or that the person dealing relies on a professional intermediary or is himself acting as a professional intermediary.

(4) This section has effect subject to section 53.

53. Defences

(1) An individual is not guilty of insider dealing by virtue of dealing in securities if he shows –

    (a) that he did not at the time expect the dealing to result in a profit attributable to the fact that the information in question was price-sensitive information in relation to the securities, or

    (b) that at the time he believed on reasonable grounds that the information had been disclosed widely enough to ensure that none of those taking part in the dealing would be prejudiced by not having the information, or

(c) that he would have done what he did even if he had not had the information.

(2) An individual is not guilty of insider dealing by virtue of encouraging another person to deal in securities if he shows –

    (a) that he did not at the time expect the dealing to result in a profit attributable to the fact that the information in question was price-sensitive information in relation to the securities, or

    (b) that at the time he believed on reasonable grounds that the information had been or would be disclosed widely enough to ensure that none of those taking part in the dealing would be prejudiced by not having the information, or

    (c) that he would have done what he did even if he had not had the information.

(3) An individual is not guilty of insider dealing by virtue of a disclosure of information if he shows –

    (a) that he did not at the time expect any person, because of the disclosure, to deal in securities in the circumstances mentioned in subsection (3) of section 52; or

    (b) that, although he had such an expectation at the time, he did not expect the dealing to result in a profit attributable to the fact that the information was price-sensitive information in relation to the securities.

(4) Schedule 1 (special defences) shall have effect.

(5) The Treasury may by order amend Schedule 1.

(6) In this section references to a profit include references to the avoidance of a loss.

Interpretation

54. Securities to which Part V applies

(1) This Part applies to any security which –

    (a) falls within any paragraph of Schedule 2; and

    (b) satisfies any conditions applying to it under an order made by the Treasury for the purposes of this subsection;

and in the provisions of this Part (other than that Schedule) any reference to a security is a reference to a security to which this Part applies.

(2) The Treasury may by order amend Schedule 2.

55. 'Dealing' in securities

(1) For the purposes of this Part, a person deals in securities if –
- (a) he acquires or disposes of the securities (whether as principal or agent); or
- (b) he procures, directly or indirectly, an acquisition or disposal of the securities by any other person.

(2) For the purposes of this Part, 'acquire', in relation to a security, includes –
- (a) agreeing to acquire the security; and
- (b) entering into a contract which creates the security.

(3) For the purposes of this Part, 'dispose', in relation to a security, includes –
- (a) agreeing to dispose of the security; and
- (b) bringing to an end a contract which created the security.

(4) For the purposes of subsection (1), a person procures an acquisition or disposal of a security if the security is acquired or disposed of by a person who is –
- (a) his agent,
- (b) his nominee; or
- (c) a person who is acting at his direction, in relation to the acquisition or disposal.

(5) Subsection (4) is not exhaustive as to the circumstances in which one person may be regarded as procuring an acquisition or disposal of securities by another.

56. 'Inside information'

(1) For the purposes of this section and section 57, 'inside information' means information which –
- (a) relates to particular securities or to a particular issuer of securities or to particular issuers of securities and not to securities generally or to issuers of securities generally;
- (b) is specific or precise;
- (c) has not been made public; and
- (d) if it were made public would be likely to have a significant effect on the price of any securities.

(2) For the purposes of this Part, securities are 'price-affected securities' in relation to inside information, and inside information is 'price-sensitive information' in relation to securities, if and only if the information would, if made public, be likely to have a significant effect on the price of the securities.

(3) For the purposes of this section 'price' includes value.

57. 'Insiders'

(1) For the purposes of this Part, a person has information as an insider if and only if –

    (a) it is, and he knows that it is, inside information, and

    (b) he has it, and knows that he has it, from an inside source.

(2) For the purposes of subsection (1), a person has information from an inside source if and only if –

    (a) he has it through –

        (i) being a director, employee or shareholder of an issuer of securities; or

        (ii) having access to the information by virtue of his employment, office or profession; or

    (b) the direct or indirect source of his information is a person within paragraph (a).

58. Information 'made public'

(1) For the purposes of section 56, 'made public', in relation to information, shall be construed in accordance with the following provisions of this section; but those provisions are not exhaustive as to the meaning of that expression.

(2) Information is made public if –

    (a) it is published in accordance with the rules of a regulated market for the purpose of informing investors and their professional advisers;

    (b) it is contained in records which by virtue of any enactment are open to inspection by the public;

    (c) it can be readily acquired by those likely to deal in any securities –

        (i) to which the information relates, or

        (ii) of an issuer to which the information relates; or

    (d) it is derived from information which has been made public.

(3) Information may be treated as made public even though –

    (a) it can be acquired only by persons exercising diligence or expertise;

    (b) it is communicated to a section of the public and not to the public at large;

    (c) it can be acquired only by observation;

    (d) it is communicated only on payment of a fee; or

    (e) it is published only outside the United Kingdom.

59. 'Professional intermediary'

(1) For the purposes of this Part, a 'professional intermediary' is a person –

    (a) who carries on a business consisting of an activity mentioned in subsection (2) and who holds himself out to the public or any section of the public (including a section of the public constituted by persons such as himself) as willing to engage in any such business; or

    (b) who is employed by a person falling within paragraph (a) to carry out any such activity.

(2) The activities referred to in subsection (1) are –

    (a) acquiring or disposing of securities (whether as principal or agent); or

    (b) acting as an intermediary between persons taking part in any dealing in securities.

(3) A person is not to be treated as carrying on a business consisting of an activity mentioned in subsection (2) –

    (a) if the activity in question is merely incidental to some other activity not falling within subsection (2); or

    (b) merely because he occasionally conducts one of those activities.

(4) For the purposes of section 52, a person dealing in securities relies on a professional intermediary if and only if a person who is acting as a professional intermediary carries out an activity mentioned in subsection (2) in relation to that dealing.

60. Other interpretation provisions

(1) For the purposes of this Part, 'regulated market' means any market, however operated, which, by an order made by the Treasury, is identified (whether by name or by reference to criteria prescribed by the order) as a regulated market for the purposes of this Part.

(2) For the purposes of this Part an 'issuer', in relation to any securities, means any company, public sector body or individual by which or by whom the securities have been or are to be issued.

(3) For the purposes of this Part –

    (a) 'company' means any body (whether or not incorporated and wherever incorporated or constituted) which is not a public sector body; and

    (b) 'public sector body' means –

        (i) the government of the United Kingdom, of Northern Ireland or of any country or territory outside the United Kingdom;

        (ii) a local authority in the United Kingdom or elsewhere;

(iii) any international organisation the members of which include the United Kingdom or another member state;

(iv) the Bank of England; or

(v) the central bank of any sovereign State.

(4) For the purposes of this Part, information shall be treated as relating to an issuer of securities which is a company not only where it is about the company but also where it may affect the company's business prospects.

Miscellaneous

61. Penalties and prosecution

(1) An individual guilty of insider dealing shall be liable –

(a) on summary conviction, to a fine not exceeding the statutory maximum or imprisonment for a term not exceeding six months or to both; or

(b) on conviction on indictment, to a fine or imprisonment for a term not exceeding seven years or to both.

(2) Proceedings for offences under this Part shall not be instituted in England and Wales except by or with the consent of –

(a) the Secretary of State; or

(b) the Director of Public Prosecutions.

(3) In relation to proceedings in Northern Ireland for offences under this Part, subsection (2) shall have effect as if the reference to the Director of Public Prosecutions were a reference to the Director of Public Prosecutions for Northern Ireland.

62. Territorial scope of offence of insider dealing

(1) An individual is not guilty of an offence falling within subsection (1) of section 52 unless –

(a) he was within the United Kingdom at the time when he is alleged to have done any act constituting or forming part of the alleged dealing;

(b) the regulated market on which the dealing is alleged to have occurred is one which, by an order made by the Treasury, is identified (whether by name or by reference to criteria prescribed by the order) as being, for the purposes of this Part, regulated in the United Kingdom; or

(c) the professional intermediary was within the United Kingdom at the time when he is alleged to have done anything by means of which the offence is alleged to have been committed.

(2) An individual is not guilty of an offence falling within subsection (2) of section 52 unless –

(a) he was within the United Kingdom at the time when he is alleged to have disclosed the information or encouraged the dealing; or

(b) the alleged recipient of the information or encouragement was within the United Kingdom at the time when he is alleged to have received the information or encouragement.

63. Limits on section 52

(1) Section 52 does not apply to anything done by an individual acting on behalf of a public sector body in pursuit of monetary policies or policies with respect to exchange rates or the management of public debt or foreign exchange reserves.

(2) No contract shall be void or unenforceable by reason only of s 52.

64. Orders

(1) Any power under this Part to make an order shall be exercisable by statutory instrument.

(2) No order shall be made under this Part unless a draft of it has been laid before and approved by a resolution of each House of Parliament.

(3) An order under this Part –

(a) may make different provision for different cases; and

(b) may contain such incidental, supplemental and transitional provisions as the Treasury consider expedient.

PART VII
SUPPLEMENTARY

78. Commencement etc

(1) Sections 70 and 71 shall come into force at the end of the period of two months beginning with the day on which this Act is passed.

(2) Sections 68, 69, 75, 76 and 79(1) to (12), paragraph 2 of Schedule 5 and, in so far as relating to the Criminal Procedure (Scotland) Act 1975 and the Prisoners and Criminal Proceedings (Scotland) Act 1993, Schedule 6, shall come into force on the passing of this Act.

(3) The other provisions of this Act shall come into force on such day as may be appointed by the Secretary of State by an order made by statutory instrument.

(4) Different days may be appointed under subsection (3) for different provisions and different purposes.

(5) Nothing in any provision in Part I applies to any act, omission or other event occurring before the coming into force of that provision.

(6) Where a person is charged with a relevant offence which was committed before the coming into force of a provision of Part II, Part III, or (as the case may be) Part IV, that provision shall not affect the question whether or not that person is guilty of the offence or the powers of the court in the event of his being convicted of that offence.

(7) Section 4A(3) and (4) of the Drug Trafficking Offences Act 1986 (inserted by section 14) shall not apply to any proceedings –

    (a) for an offence committed before the commencement of section 14; or

    (b) for one or more offences, any one of which was so committed.

(8) Section 52B(3) and (4) of the Northern Ireland (Emergency Provisions) Act 1991 (inserted by section 42) shall not apply to any proceedings –

    (a) for an offence committed before the commencement of section 42; or

    (b) for one or more offences, any one of which was so committed.

(9) In subsection (6) 'relevant offence' means an offence in relation to which provision is made by Part II, Part III or Part IV, other than an offence created by that Part.

(10) An order under subsection (3) may contain such transitional provisions and savings as the Secretary of State considers appropriate.

(11) For the purposes of section 27 of the Prevention of Terrorism (Temporary Provisions) Act 1989 (temporary provisions), any amendment made in that Act by a provision of Part IV of, or paragraph 15 of Schedule 5 to, this Act shall be treated, as from the time when that provision comes into force, as having been continued in force by the order under subsection (6) of that section which has effect at that time.

(12) For the purposes of section 69 of the Northern Ireland (Emergency Provisions) Act 1991 (temporary provisions), any amendment made in that Act by a provision of Part IV of, or paragraph 17(1), (2), (5), (6) and (7) of Schedule 5 to, this Act (other than sections 43 and 45) shall be treated, as from the time when that provision comes into force, as having been continued in force by the order under section 69(3) of the Act of 1991 which has effect at that time.

79. Short title, extent etc

(1) This Act may be cited as the Criminal Justice Act 1993.

(2) The following provisions of this Act extend to the United Kingdom –

Part V;

sections 21(1) and (3)(h), 23, 24, 45 to 51, 70 to 72, 77, 78 and this section;

Schedules 1 and 2; and paragraphs 4, 5 and 6 of Schedule 4.

(3) The following provisions of this Act extend only to Great Britain – sections 13(9) to (11), 21(3)(e), 24(2), (3) and (7) to (10), 29 to 32, 34(1), 35, 67(1) and 73; and paragraph 3 of Schedule 4.

(4) The following provisions of this Act extend only to Scotland – sections 17, 19, 20(2), 21(3)(c) and (d)22(2), 24(12) to (15), 26(2), 33, 68, 69, 75 and 76; and paragraph 2 of Schedule 4.

(5) Sections 21(3)(f) and 34(2) extend to Scotland and Northern Ireland only.

(6) Sections 36 to 44 extend only to Northern Ireland.

(7) Section 72 also extends to the Channel Islands and the Isle of Man.

(8) The provisions of Schedules 5 and 6 have the same extent as the provisions on which they operate.

(9) Otherwise, this Act extends to England and Wales only.

(10) Her Majesty may by Order in Council direct that such provisions of this Act as may be specified in the Order shall extend, with such exceptions and modifications as appear to Her Majesty to be appropriate, to any colony.

(11) Subject to any Order made after the passing of this Act by virtue of subsection (1)(a) of section 3 of the Northern Ireland Constitution Act 1973, the regulation of insider dealing shall not be a transferred matter for the purposes of that Act but shall for the purposes of subsection (2) of that section be treated as specified in Schedule 3 to that Act.

(12) An Order in Council under paragraph 1(1)(b)of Schedule 1 to the Northern Ireland Act 1974 (legislation for Northern Ireland in the interim period) which contains a statement that it is made only for purposes corresponding to purposes of any of sections 16, 18 and 29 to

(a) shall not be subject to paragraph 1(4) and (5) of that Schedule (affirmative resolution of both Houses of Parliament); but

(b) shall be subject to annulment in pursuance of a resolution of either House of Parliament.

(13) Schedule 5 (consequential amendments) shall have effect.

(14) The repeals and revocations set out in Schedule 6 (which include the repeal of two enactments which are spent) shall have effect.

SCHEDULE I

SPECIAL DEFENCES

Market makers

1. (1) An individual is not guilty of insider dealing by virtue of dealing in securities or encouraging another person to deal if he shows that he acted in good faith in the course of –

   (a) his business as a market maker; or

   (b) his employment in the business of a market maker.

(2) A market maker is a person who –

   (a) holds himself out at all normal times in compliance with the rules of a regulated market or an approved organisation as willing to acquire or dispose of securities; and

   (b) is recognised as doing so under those rules.

(3) In this paragraph 'approved organisation' means an international securities self-regulating organisation approved under paragraph 25B of Schedule I to the Financial Services Act 1986.

Market information

2. (1) An individual is not guilty of insider dealing by virtue of dealing in securities or encouraging another person to deal if he shows that –

   (a) the information which he had as an insider was market information; and

   (b) it was reasonable for an individual in his position to have acted as he did despite having that information as an insider at the time.

(2) In determining whether it is reasonable for an individual to do any act despite having market information at the time, there shall, in particular, be taken into account –

   (a) the content of the information;

   (b) the circumstances in which he first had the information and in what capacity; and

   (c) the capacity in which he now acts.

3. An individual is not guilty of insider dealing by virtue of dealing in securities or encouraging another person to deal if he shows –

(a) that he acted –

    (i) in connection with an acquisition or disposal which was under consideration or the subject of negotiation, or in the course of a series of such acquisitions or disposals; and

    (ii) with a view to facilitating the accomplishment of the acquisition or disposal or the series of acquisitions or disposals; and

(b) that the information which he had as an insider was market information arising directly out of his involvement in the acquisition or disposal or series of acquisitions or disposals

4. For the purposes of paragraphs 2 and 3 market information is information consisting of one or more of the following facts –

    (a) that securities of a particular kind have been or are to be acquired or disposed of, or that their acquisition or disposal is under consideration or the subject of negotiation;

    (b) that securities of a particular kind have not been or are not to be acquired or disposed of;

    (c) the number of securities acquired or disposed of or to be acquired or disposed of or whose acquisition or disposal is under consideration or the subject of negotiation;

    (d) the price (or range of prices) at which securities have been or are to be acquired or disposed of or the price (or range of prices) at which securities whose acquisition or disposal is under consideration or the subject of negotiation may be acquired or disposed of;

    (e) the identity of the persons involved or likely to be involved in any capacity in an acquisition or disposal.

Price stabilisation

5. (1) An individual is not guilty of insider dealing by virtue of dealing in securities or encouraging another person to deal if he shows that he acted in conformity with the price stabilisation rules.

(2) In this paragraph 'the price stabilisation rules' means rules which –

    (a) are made under section 48 of the Financial Services Act 1986 (conduct of business rules); and

    (b) make provision of a description mentioned in paragraph (i) of subsection (2) of that section (price stabilisation rules).

SCHEDULE 2

SECURITIES

Shares

1. Shares and stock in the share capital of a company ('shares').

Debt securities

2. Any instrument creating or acknowledging indebtedness which is issued by a company or public sector body, including, in particular, debentures, debenture stock, loan stock, bonds and certificates of deposit ('debt securities').

Warrants

3. Any right (whether conferred by warrant or otherwise) to subscribe for shares or debt securities ('warrants').

Depositary receipts

4. (1) The rights under any depositary receipt.
   (2) For the purposes of sub-paragraph (I) a 'depositary receipt' means a certificate or other record (whether or not in the form of a document –

   (a) which is issued by or on behalf of a person who holds any relevant securities of a particular issuer; and

   (b) which acknowledges that another person is entitled to rights in relation to the relevant securities or relevant securities of the same kind.

   (3) In sub-paragraph (2) 'relevant securities' means shares, debt securities and warrants.

Options

5. Any option to acquire or dispose of any security falling within any other paragraph of this Schedule.

Futures

6. (1) Rights under a contract for the acquisition or disposal of relevant securities under which delivery is to be made at a future date and at a price agreed when the contract is made.

(2) In sub-paragraph (1) –

    (a) the references to a future date and to a price agreed when the contract is made include references to a date and a price determined in accordance with terms of the contract; and

    (b) 'relevant securities' means any security falling within any other paragraph of this Schedule.

Contracts for differences

7. (1) Rights under a contract which does not provide for the delivery of securities but whose purpose or pretended purpose is to secure a profit or avoid a loss by reference to fluctuations in—

    (a) a share index or other similar factor connected with relevant securities;

    (b) the price of particular relevant securities; or

    (c) the interest rate offered on money placed on deposit.

(2) In sub-paragraph (I) 'relevant securities' means any security falling within any other paragraph of this Schedule.

SCHEDULE 6

REPEALS AND REVOCATIONS

PART I
REPEALS

Chapter	Short title	Extent of repeal
1975 c 21	The Criminal Procedure (Scotland) Act 1975	In section 442B, the words 'against sentence alone'.
1980 c 43	The Magistrates' Courts Act 1980	In section 12(1)(a) the words 'and section 18 of the Criminal Justice Act 1991 (unit fines)'.
1985 c 8	The Company Securities (Insider Dealing) Act 1986	The whole Act.
1986 c 32	The Drug Trafficking Offences Act 1986	In section 1, in subsection (5)(b)(iii), the words from 'section 39' to 'bankruptcy orders)' and subsection (8). In section 5(3), the words 'sections 3 and 4 of'. In section 26A(3), the words from 'or by' to the end. In section 27(5), the words 'or, as the case may be, the sheriff'. In section 38(2), the entries relating to a confiscation order and a defendant.
1986 c 60	The Financial Services Act 1986	Sections 173 to 176. In section 189(1)(b), the words '(including insider dealing)'. In Schedule 16, paragraphs 28 and 43.

Chapter	Short title	Extent of repeal
1987 c 22	The Banking Act 1987	In section 84(1), in the Table, in the entry beginning 'An inspector appointed under Part XV of the Companies (Northern Ireland) Order' in the left-hand column the words 'or under Article 16A of the Company Securities (Insider Dealing) (Northern Ireland) Order 1986' and in the right hand column the words 'or that Article'.
1987 c 38	The Criminal Justice Act 1987	In section 3(i), the words 'or any corresponding enactment having effect in Northern Ireland'.
1988 c 33	The Criminal Justice Act 1988	Section 48. Section 98.
1989 c 4	The Prevention of Terrorism (Temporary Provisions) Act 1989	In section 9(1), the word 'or' immediately before paragraph (b).
1989 c 40	The Companies Act 1989	Section 209.
1990 c 5	The Criminal Justice (International Co-operation) Act 1990	Section 14(3) and (5).
1991 c 24	The Northern Ireland (Emergency Provisions) Act 1991	In section 48(3), the words 'during the period of postponement'. In section 50(2), the word 'or' immediately before paragraph (c). Section 51(3). Section 67(6).
1991 c 53	The Criminal Justice Act 1991	Section 17(3)(e). Section 19. Section 20(5). Section 22. Section 28(3). In section 30(1), the words 'or the Lord Chancellor'. In Schedule 4, Part V. In Schedule 11, paragraph 24.
1993 c 9	The Prisoners and Criminal Proceedings (Scotland) Act 1993	In section 10(1), the words '(whether before or after the commencement of this section)'.

PART II
REVOCATIONS

Number	Title	Extent of revocation
SI 1986/1034 (NI 8)	The Company Securities (Insider Dealing) (Northern Ireland) Order 1986	The whole Order.
SI 1989/2404 (NI 18)	The Companies (Northern Ireland) Order 1989	In Article 2(2), the definition of 'the Insider Dealing Order'. In Article 11(1), the words 'or Article 16A of the Insider Dealing Order'. Articles 27 to 34. Article 35(2) and (3).
SI 1989/2405 (NI 19)	The Insolvency (Northern Ireland) Order 1989	Article 104A(1)(b).
SI 1990/1504(NI 10)	The Companies (No 2) 1990	In Article 2(2), the definition (Northern Ireland) Order of 'the Insider Dealing Order'. Articles 21 to 23.
SI 1992/3218	The Banking Coordination (Second Council Directive) Regulations 1992	In Schedule 8, paragraphs 8(3), 9(2) and 10(3). In Schedule 10, paragraphs 17 and 25.

APPENDIX B

INSIDER DEALING
(SECURITIES AND REGULATED MARKETS)
ORDER 1994 (SI 1994/187)

Whereas a draft of this Order has been approved by a resolution of each House of Parliament pursuant to section 64(2) of the Criminal Justice Act 1993(a);

Now, therefore, the Treasury, in exercise of the powers conferred on them by sections 54(1), 60(1), 62(1) and 64(3) of that Act and of all other powers enabling them in that behalf, hereby make the following Order:

Title, commencement and interpretation

1. This Order may be cited as the Insider Dealing (Securities and Regulated Markets) Order 1994 and shall come into force on the twenty eighth day after the day on which it is made.

2. In this Order a 'State within the European Economic Area' means a State which is a member of the European Communities and the Republics of Austria, Finland and Iceland, the Kingdoms of Norway and Sweden and the Principality of Liechtenstein.

Securities

3. Articles 4 to 8 set out conditions for the purposes of section 54(1) of the Criminal Justice Act 1993 (securities to which Part V of the Act of 1993 applies).

4. The following condition applies in relation to any security which falls within any paragraph of Schedule 2 to the Act of 1993, that is, that it is officially listed in a State within the European Economic Area or that it is admitted to dealing on, or has its price quoted on or under the rules of, a regulated market.

5. The following alternative condition applies in relation to a warrant, that is, that the right under it is a right to subscribe for any share or debt security of the same class as a share or debt security which satisfies the condition in article 4.

6. The following alternative condition applies in relation to a depositary receipt, that is, that the rights under it are in respect of any share or debt security which satisfies the condition in article 4.

7. The following alternative conditions apply in relation to an option or a future, that is, that the option or rights under the future are in respect of –

    (a) any share or debt security which satisfies the condition in article 4, or

    (b) any depositary receipt which satisfies the condition in article 4 or article 6.

8. The following alternative condition applies in relation to a contract for difference that is, that the purpose or pretended purpose of the contract is to secure a profit or avoid a loss by reference to fluctuations in –

    (a) the price of any shares or debt securities which satisfy the condition in article 4, or

    (b) an index of the price of such shares or debt securities.

Regulated markets

9. The following markets are regulated markets for the purposes of Part V of the Act of 1993 –

    any market which is established under the rules of an investment exchange specified in the Schedule to this Order

United Kingdom regulated markets

10. The regulated markets which are regulated in the United Kingdom for the purposes of Part V of the Act of 1993 are any market which is established under the rules of –

    (a) the International Stock Exchange of the United Kingdom and the Republic Ireland Limited, other than the market which operates in the Republic of Ireland known as the Irish Unit of the International Stock Exchange of the United Kingdom and the Republic of Ireland Limited;

    (b) LIFFE Administration & Management; and

    (c) OMLX, the London Securities and Derivatives Exchange Limited.

Tim Wood
Irvine Patnick.

1st February 1994.

Two of the Lords Commissioners
of Her Majesty's Treasury.

SCHEDULE

REGULATED MARKETS

Any market which is established under the rules of one of the following investment exchanges:

Amsterdam Stock Exchange.

Antwerp Stock Exchange.

Athens Stock Exchange.

Barcelona Stock Exchange.

Bavarian Stock Exchange.

Berlin Stock Exchange.

Bilbao Stock Exchange.

Bologna Stock Exchange.

Bordeaux Stock Exchange.

Bremen Stock Exchange.

Brussels Stock Exchange.

Copenhagen Stock Exchange.

Dusseldorf Stock Exchange.

Florence Stock Exchange.

Frankfurt Stock Exchange.

Genoa Stock Exchange.

Ghent Stock Exchange.

Hamburg Stock Exchange.

Hanover Stock Exchange.

Helsinki Stock Exchange.

The International Stock Exchange of the United Kingdom and the Republic of Ireland Limited

Liege Stock Exchange.

Lille Stock Exchange.

Lisbon Stock Exchange.

LIFFE Administration & Management.

Luxembourg Stock Exchange.

Lyon Stock Exchange.

Madrid Stock Exchange.

Marseille Stock Exchange.

Milan Stock Exchange.

Nancy Stock Exchange.

Nantes Stock Exchange.

Naples Stock Exchange.

The exchange known as NASDAQ.

OMLX, the London Securities and Derivatives Exchange Limited.

Oporto Stock Exchange.

Oslo Stock Exchange.

Palermo Stock Exchange.
Paris Stock Exchange.
Rome Stock Exchange.
Securities Exchange of Iceland.
Stockholm Stock Exchange.
Stuttgart Stock Exchange.
Trieste Stock Exchange.
Tunn Stock Exchange.
Valencia Stock Exchange.
Venice Stock Exchange.
Vienna Stock Exchange.

APPENDIX C

INSIDER DEALING
(SECURITIES AND REGULATED MARKETS)
(AMENDMENT)
ORDER 1996 (SI 1996/1561)

Whereas a draft of this Order has been approved by a resolution of each House of Parliament pursuant to section 64(2) of the Criminal Justice Act 1993[a];

Now, therefore, the Treasury, in exercise of the powers conferred on them by sections 60(1), 62(1) and 64(3) of that Act and of all other powers enabling them in that behalf, hereby make the following Order:–

1. This Order may be cited as the Insider Dealing (Securities and Regulated Markets) (Amendment) Order 1996 and shall come into force on 1st July 1996.

2. In this Order, 'the 1994 Order' shall mean the Insider Dealing (Securities and Regulated Markets) Order 1994[b].

3. (1) For paragraph (a) of article 10 of the 1994 Order (United Kingdom regulated markets) there shall be substituted the following paragraph: '(a) the London Stock Exchange Limited';

(2) In paragraph (b) of that article, there shall be omitted the word 'and', and after paragraph (c) there shall be inserted: 'and (d) Tradepoint Financial Networks plc.'

4. In the Schedule to the 1994 Order (regulated markets)
- (a) the following shall be omitted:
  'Bordeaux Stock Exchange.'
  'Ghent Stock Exchange.'
  'Liege Stock Exchange.'
  'Lille Stock Exchange.'
  'Marseille Stock Exchange.'
  'Nancy Stock Exchange.'
  'Nantes Stock Exchange.'

- (b) for the words 'the International Stock Exchange of the United Kingdom and the Republic of Ireland Limited' there shall be substituted: 'Iceland Stock Exchange. The Irish Stock Exchange Limited';

- (c) after 'LIFFE Administration & Management' there shall be inserted 'The London Stock Exchange Ltd';

(a) 1993 c 36.

(b) SI 1994/187.

(d) after 'Stuttgart Stock Echange', there shall be inserted 'Tradepoint Financial Networks plc.';

(e) after 'The exchange known as NASDAQ', there shall be inserted 'The exchange known as the Nouveau Marché .'.

Simon Burns
Michael Bates
Two of the Lords Commissioners
of Her Majesty's Treasury.

14th June 1996.

INDEX